JAN -- 2015

Estes Valley
Library

# ROCKY MOUNTAIN LIFE,

OR,

## STARTLING SCENES

AND

## PERILOUS ADVENTURES

IN THE

# FAR WEST,

DURING AN EXPEDITION OF THREE YEARS.

BY RUFUS B. SAGE.

BOSTON:
WENTWORTH & COMPANY,
86 WASHINGTON STREET.

Entered, according to Act of Congress, in the year 1857, by
WENTWORTH & COMPANY,
In the Clerk's Office of the District Court of the District of Massachusetts.

This scarce antiquarian book is included in our special *Legacy Reprint Series*. In the interest of creating a more extensive selection of rare historical book reprints, we have chosen to reproduce this title even though it may possibly have occasional imperfections such as missing and blurred pages, missing text, poor pictures, markings, dark backgrounds and other reproduction issues beyond our control. Because this work is culturally important, we have made it available as a part of our commitment to protecting, preserving and promoting the world's literature. Thank you for your understanding.

# PREFACE.

THE following work was written immediately after the author had returned from the perilous and eventful expedition which is here narrated. The intense interest which every citizen of the Union feels in relation to that vast region of our country lying between the Mississippi and the Pacific Ocean, will, it is believed, render the publication of a volume like this of more than usual importance at the present time. The lofty cliffs of the Rocky Mountains are soon to echo to the tread of advancing civilization, as symbolized in the Pacific railway, which will, in a few years, speed the iron horse and his living freight from Boston to San Francisco, forming a bond of social and commercial intercourse across the continent.

Attack on a Herd of Buffaloes.—Page 52.

# CONTENTS.

### CHAPTER I.

Objects of a proposed excursion. Primary plans and movements. A Digression. Rendezvous for Oregon emigrants and Santa Fe traders. Sensations on a first visit to the border Prairies. Frontier Indians.     29

### CHAPTER II.

Preparations for leaving. Scenes at Camp. Things as they appeared. Simplicity of mountaineers. Sleep in the open air. Character, habits, and costume of mountaineers. Heterogeneous ingredients of Company. The commandant. En route. Comical exhibition and adventure with a Spanish company. Grouse. Elm Grove. A storm. Santa Fe traders. Indian battle.     34

### CHAPTER III.

The Pottowatomies. Crossing the Wakarousha. Adventure at the Springs. The Caw chief. Kansas river and Indians. Pleading for whiskey. Hickory timber. Prairie tea. Scenes at the N. Fork of Blue. Wild honey. Return party. Mountaineers in California. Adventure with a buffalo. Indian atrocities. Liquor and the Fur Trade. Strict guard. High prices.     45

### CHAPTER IV.

Country from the frontiers to Big Blue; its geological character, &c. Novel cure for fever and ague. Indian trails. Game. Large rabbits. Antelope, and their peculiarities. Beaver cuttings. Big Blue and its vicinity. Dangerous country. Pawnee bravery. Night-alarm, (Prairies on fire.) Platte river. Predominant characteristics of the Grand Prairies, and theory explanative of of their phenomenon. Something to laugh at. "Big Jim" and the antelope.     54

### CHAPTER V.

Deserted camp. Big Jim's third attempt as a hunter. Buffalo and other particulars. Big Jim lying guard. Butchering. Strange selections. Extraordinary eating, and excellence of buffalo meat. Brady's Island. The murderer's fate. Substitute for wood. A storm. Game in camp. Strange infatuation. Tenacity of buffalo to life, and how to hunt them. Cross S. Fork of Platte. Big Jim's fourth adventure.     63

## CHAPTER VI.

Ash creek. Pawnee and Sioux battle-ground. Bread-root. The Eagle's Nest. Mad wolf. Number and variety of prairie wolves,—their sagacity. Mad bull. Making and curing meat. Big Jim still unfortunate. Johnson's creek. McFarlan's Castle. Deceptiveness of distances. Express from the Fort. Brave Bear. Bull Tail. Talk with the Indians. Speech of Marto-cog-erahne. Reply. Tahtungah-sana's address. 75

## CHAPTER VII.

The Chimney. A bet. Spur of the Rocky Mountains. Scott's Bluff. Romantic scenery. Mimic city. A pyramid. A monument. An elevated garden. Mountain sheep. An Eden. Death in camp. The wanderer's grave. Horse creek and gold. Goche's hole. Arrival at Fort Platte. Remarks by the way. Prairie travel. Locality and description of the Fort. Indian lodges. Migratory habits of mountain and prairie tribes. Scenes at Fort. Drunken Indians. Tragical event. Indian funeral. Speech of Etespa-huska on the death of his father. 90

## CHAPTER VIII.

Coast clear, and Trade opened. More visitors. Smoking out the natives. Incident illustrative of Indian character. Expeditions for trade. Black Hills. Rawhide. An Indian and a buffalo chase. Deep snow, extreme cold, and painful journey. L'eau-qui-court. Remarks. Lost. White river; its valley, fruits, and game. Building site. The Devil's Tea-pot. Troubles with Indians. Theft and its punishment. Indian soldiers. Christmas extras. Outrageous conduct. Rascality of traders. "That Old Serpent." Indian superstition, religious tenets and practices. Notions upon general morality. 103

## CHAPTER IX.

Dangers connected with the liquor trade. Difficulty with Bull Eagle. Scenes of bloodshed and horror. Cheating in the fur trade. How the red man becomes tutored in vice. A chief's daughter offered in exchange for liquor. Indian mode of courtship and marriage. Squaws an article of traffic. Divorce. Plurality of wives. 116

## CHAPTER X.

Tahtunga-egoniska. High gaming. Weur-sena Warkpollo, a strange story. The Death Song, a tale of love. Medicine-men. Extraordinary performance of Tahtunga-mobellu. Wonderful feats of jugglery. 125

## CHAPTER XI.

Food for horses. Squaws and their performances. Dogs and dog-meat. Return to Fort. Starvation. Travel by guess. Death from drinking. Medicine-making. A Burial. Little Lodge and the French trader. A speech in council. Journey to White river. High winds and snow. Intense sufferings and painful results. 135

## CHAPTER XII.

Another drunken spree. Horses devoured by wolves. An upset. A blowing up. Daring feat of wolves. A girl offered for liquor. Winter on the Platte. Boat building. Hunting expedition. Journey up the Platte. Island camp. Narrow escape. Snow storm. Warm Spring. Pass of the Platte into the prairies. A valley. Bitter Cottonwood. Indian forts. Wild fruit. Root-digging. Cherry tea and its uses. Geology of the country. Soils, grasses, herbs, plants, and purity of atmosphere. Horse-shoe creek. A panther. Prairie dogs and their peculiarities. 143

## CHAPTER XIII.

The Creek valley. The Platte as a mountain stream. Cañon. Romantic prospect. Comical bear story. Perilous encounter with a wounded bull. Geological remarks. Division of party. Safety of spring travel. La Bonte's creek. Remarks by the way. Service-berry. Deer Creek. General observations. Moccasin making. Box elder. Bear killed. Excellence of its flesh. Different kinds of bears in Oregon and the mountains. The grizzly bear, his nature and habits. 150

## CHAPTER XIV.

Desperate encounter with a grizzly bear, and extraordinary instance of suffering. Close contest. A comical incident. Cross Platte. Cañon camp. Sage trees. Mountain sheep, and all about them. Independence Rock; why so called, and description of it. Devil's Gate. Landscape scenery. 159

## CHAPTER XV.

Return route. Oregon trail from Independence Rock through the South Pass. Cross the Sweet Water and Platte. Mountain Fowl. Journey up Medicine Bow. Dangerous country. A fight with the Sioux. The "Carcague." A surprise. Visit to the Crow village. Number and character of the Crow nation. Selling a prisoner for tobacco. Description of Laramie Plains. 165

## CHAPTER XVI.

Sibille's-hole. Novel bitters. Chugwater. Gold. Curiosity. Affairs at the Fort. Amusements. Gambling among squaws, and games played. Squaw dresses, and riding fashion. Items of interest to the curious, proving the intercourse of the ancient Romans with the people of this continent. 173

## CHAPTER XVII.

Singular exhibition of natural affection. Embark for the States. Scarcity of provisions and consequent hardship and suffering. Extraordinary daring of wolves. Difficulties of navigation. Novel diet. Fishing. A fish story, and another to match it. A bull story. Hard aground and dismal situation. Extreme exposure. Cold, hungry, and wet. Again afloat. Re-supply of provisions. Camp on fire. A picture of Platte navigation. Country north of river. Adventure with a bull. Indian benevolence. Summary of hardships and deprivations. Abandon voyage. 185

## CHAPTER XVIII.

Hunting excursion. Thirst more painful than hunger. Geological observations. Mournful casualty. Sad scene of sepulture. Melancholy night. Voyage in an empty boat. Ruins of a Pawnee village at Cedar Bluff. Plover creek. Cache Grove. Thousand Islands. Abandon boat. Exploring company. A horrible situation. Agony to torment. Pawnee village. Exemplary benevolence of an Indian chief. Miserable fourth of July. Four days' starvation. Arrival at Council Bluff. Proceed to Independence. 193

## CHAPTER XIX.

The country between the Pawnee village and Bellevieu, and from that to Fort Leavenworth. Leave Independence for the Mountains. Meet Pawnees. Indian hospitality. Journey up the South Fork Platte. Fort Grove. Beaver creek. Bijou. Chabonard's camp. Country described. Medicine Lodge. The Chyennes; their character and history. Arrive at Fort Lancaster. Different localities in its neighborhood. Fatal Duel. Ruins. 200

## CHAPTER XX.

Old acquaintances. Indian murders. Mode of travelling in a dangerous country Mexican traders. Summary way of teaching manners. Fort Lancaster and surrounding country. Resume journey. Cherry creek and connecting observations. Sketch of the Arapahos, their country, character, &c. Camp of free traders. Blackfoot camp. Daugherty's creek. Observations relative to the Divide. Mexican cupidity. Strange visitors. The lone travellers. Arrive at the Arkansas. General remarks. Curious specimens of cacti. Fontaine qui Bouit, or Natural Soda fountain. Indian superstition. Enchanting scenery. Extraordinary wall of sandstone. 210

## CHAPTER XXI.

Vicinity of the Arkansas. Settlement. The Pueblo. Rio San Carlos, its valleys and scenery. Shooting by moonlight. Taos. Review of the country travelled over. Taos; its vicinity, scenery, and mines. Ranchos and Rancheros. Mexican houses; their domestic economy, and filth. Abject poverty and deplorable condition of the lower classes of Mexicans, with a general review of their character, and some of the causes contributing to their present degradation. The Pueblo Indians and their strange notions. Ancient temple. Character of the Pueblos. Journey to the Uintah river, and observations by the way. Taos Utahs, Pa-utahs, Uintah and Lake Utahs. The

Diggers; misery of their situation, strange mode of lying, with a sketch of their character. The Navijos; their civilization, hostility to Spaniards, ludicrous barbarity, bravery, &c., with a sketch of their country, and why they are less favorable to the whites than formerly. 221

## CHAPTER XXII.

Uintah trade. Snake Indians; their country and character. Description of Upper California. The Eastern Section. Great Salt Lake and circumjacent country. Desert. Digger country, and regions south. Fertility of soil. Prevailing rock and minerals. Abundance of wild fruit, grain, and game. Valley of the Colorado. Magnificent scenery. Valleys of the Uintah and other rivers. Vicinity of the Gila. Face of the country, soil &c. Sweet spots. Mildness of climate, and its healthiness. The natives. Sparsity of inhabitants. No government. All about the Colorado and Gila rivers. Abundance of fish. Trade in pearl oyster shells. Practicable routes from the United States. 232

## CHAPTER XXIII.

Minerals. Western California. The Sacramento and contiguous regions. Principal rivers. Fish. Commercial advantages. Bay of San Francisco. Other Bays and Harbors. Description of the country; territory northwest of the Sacramento; Tlamath Mountains; California range and its vicinity; southern parts; timber, river-bottoms; Valleys of Sacramento, del Plumas, and Tulare; their extent, fertility, timber, and fruit; wild grain and clover, spontaneous; wonderful fecundity of soil, and its products; the productions, climate, rains, and dews; geological and mineralogical character; face of the country; its water; its healthiness; pasture; superabundance of cattle, horses, and sheep, their prices, &c.; beasts of prey; the inhabitants, who; Indians, their character and condition; Capital of the Province, with other towns; advantages of San Francisco; inland settlements; foreigners and Mexicans; Government; its full military strength. Remarks. 239

## CHAPTER XXIV.

Visitors at Uintah. Adventures of a trapping party. The Munchies, or white Indians; some account of them. Amusements at rendezvous. Mysterious city, and attempts at its exploration,—speculation relative to its inhabitants. Leave for Fort Hall. Camp at Bear river. Boundary between the U. States and Mexico. Green valleys, &c. Country en route. Brown's-hole. Geological observations. Soda, beer, and Steamboat springs; their peculiarities. Minerals. Valley of Bear river; its fertility, timber, and abundance of wild fruit. Buffalo berries. Superior advantages of this section. Mineral tar. 250

## CHAPTER XXV.

Fort Hall; its history, and locality. Information relative to Oregon. Boundaries and extent of the territory. Its rivers and lakes, with a concise description of them severally. Abundance and variety of fish and water-fowl. Harbors and islands. Oregon as a whole; its mountains and geographical divisions. Eastern Divison; its wild scenery, valleys, soil, and timber; volcanic ravages; country between Clarke's river and the Columbia. North of the Columbia; its general character. Middle Division; its valleys, prairies, highlands, and forests. Western Division; a beautiful country; extensive valleys of extraordinary fertility; productive plains; abundance of timber, its astonishing size and variety. A brief summary of facts. 258

## CHAPTER XXVI.

Climate of Oregon; its variableness; its rains; a southern climate in a northern latitude. Productiveness; grain, fruits, and flowers, wild and cultivated. Geological characteristics. Soils and prevailing rock. Minerals, &c. Variety of game. Wolves. Horses, and other domestic animals. Population, white and native; Indian tribes, their character and condition. Missionary stations, and their improvements. Present trade of Oregon. Posts of the Hudson Bay Company. Settlements. Oregon City, its situation and advantages; about Linnton; about Wallammette valley, Fualitine plains and Umpqua river; Vancouvre, and its superior advantages. Kindness of Hudson Bay Company to settlers. 269

## CHAPTER XVII.

The manufacturing facilities of Oregon. Commercial and agricultural advantages reviewed. Rail Road to the Pacific. Route, mode of travelling, and requisite equipment for emigrants. Importance of Oregon to the United States. Incident in the early history of Fort Hall. Why the Blackfeet are hostile, and bright spots in their character. Mild weather. Leave for the Platte. Journey to the Yampah, and sketch of the intermediate country. New Park. Head of Grand river. The landscape. Different routes to Fort Lancaster. Old Park. 277

## CHAPTER XXVIII.

From Grand river to Bayou Salâde. Observations by the way. Description of the Bayou. Voracity of magpies. Journey to Cherry creek. Country en route. Crystal creek. Abundance of game. Antelope hunting. Remarkable sagacity of wolves. Snow storms and amusement. Ravens. Move camp. Comfortable winter quarters. Animal food conducive to general health and longevity. A laughable instance of sound sleeping. Astonishing wolfine rapacity. Beaver lodges and all about beaver. Hunting excursion. Vasques' creek, its valleys, table lands, mountains, and prairies. Camp. Left alone. Sensations, and care to avoid danger. A nocturnal visitor. Thrilling adventure and narrow escape. A lofty specimen of "gettin down stairs." Geological statistics. 287

## CHAPTER XXIX.

Return to the Fort. Texan recruiting officer. New plans. Volunteer. The Chance Shot, or Special Providence. Texan camp. Country contiguous to the Arkansas, from Fontaine qui Bouit to the Rio de las Animas. Things at rendezvous. A glance at the company. Disposal of force. March up the de las Animas. The country; Timpa valley, and its adjoining hills, to the de las Animas. The latter stream; its cañon, valley and enchanting scenery. Tedious egress. Unparalleled suffering from hunger, toil, and cold. Wolf flesh and buffalo hide. Painful consequences of eating cacti. A feast of mule meat after seven days' starvation. Camp at the Taos trail. The adjacent country. Strict guard. A chase. The meet reward for treason. 300

## CHAPTER XXX.

March down the Cimarone. Junction of the two divisions. Country between the de las Animas and the Cimarone. Perilous descent. Cañon of the Cimarone. Soil and prevailing rock. A fort. Grandeur and sublimity of scenery. Beauty of rocks. Cimarone of the pain. Fruits and game. Widespread desolation. A dreary country. Summer on the Desert. Remarks. Encounter with Indians. Nature's nobleman. Wild horses and different modes of catching them. Failure of expected reinforcements. March into the enemy's country. Ancient engravings upon a rock. Boy in the wolf's den. A man lost. Forced march. Torment of thirst. Remarks. The lost found. Expulsion for cowardice,—its effect. 309

## CHAPTER XXXI.

Mexican camp. Pursuit. Advance upon Mora. Enemy discovered. Country between the Rio de las Animas and Mora; its picturesque beauty. Admirable point of observation. Fortified position. Battle of the pass; order of attack, passage of the river, storming the enemy's camp, and number of killed, wounded and prisoners. Council of war. Prisoners released. Message to Amijo. Return march. Mexican army. Attacked, and results of action. Mexican bravery. Retreat. Cross the Table Mountain. New species of wild onions. March down the de las Animas. Discouragements accumulate. Disband. Sketch of factions. Texan prisoners. Arrival of reinforcements. Battle of the Arroyo: killed, wounded, and prisoners. Retreat of Amijo. " Stampede." Frightful encounter with the Cumanches and Kuyawas. Discharge of troops. Affair with Capt. Cook. Surrender to U. S. Dragoons, and failure of expedition. Return to Texas. Journey to the Platte. Country between the Arkansas and Beaver creek. Feasting at camp. Crows' eggs. Lateness of season. Snow-storm in June. An Indian fort. Serio-comico adventure with a wolf. Indians. Song of the night-bird. 318

## CHAPTER XXXII.

**Lost.** Night on the Prairie. Head of the Kansas river. Minerals. Country. Gold. Wonderful incident relative to a wounded bull. Indians. Join the Arapahos. Moving village. Country between Beaver creek and the Platte. Cañon. Reach Fort Lancaster. Fortune bettered. News from the States. Murder. Extraordinary instances of human tenacity to life. Arrival of Indians. Theft. Chyenne outrage. Return of Oregon emigrants. "Old Bob," and his adventures. A "Protracted Meeting," or Indian Medicine-making. Indian oath. Jaunt to the mountains. Mountain scenery. Camp on Thompson's creek. Wild fruits. Concentration of valleys. Romantic view. A gem in the mountains. Grand river pass. Salt lakes. Astonishing scope of vision. The black-tailed deer. Peculiarity in horses. Remarkable natural fortification. Return. Travelling by guess.   331

## CHAPTER XXXIII.

**Newspapers.** False reports. Singular grasses. Sale of skins at Fort Lancaster. An excursion. An incident. Camp. Huge horns. Leopard. Panther. Slaughter of eagles. Dressing skins. The hunter's camp. Vasques' creek. The weather. Return of comrades to Fort. Sweets of solitude. Exposure in a snow-storm. The cañon of S. Fork Platte. A ridge. A valley. Beautiful locality. Choice site for a settlement. Flowers in February. A hunting incident. Fate of the premature flowers. Adventure with a sheep. Discovered by Indians. A pleasant meeting. Camp at Crystal creek. Thoughts of home. Resolve on going. Commence journey. The caravan. "Big Timber." Country to the "Crossing." Big Salt Bottom. Flowers. A stranger of other lands. Difficulty with Indians. "Friday." Tedious travelling. No timber. Detention. Country. Pawnee Fork. Mountain and Spanish companies. Spy Buck, the Shawnee war-chief. Pawnee Fork.—Cure for a rattlesnake's bite. Further detention. Sketch of adjacent country. Pawnee Rocks. En route with Friday. Musquetoes. Observations. Friday as a hunter.   346

## CHAPTER XXXIV.

**The** Arapaho American, a sketch of real life. Tenets of the mountain Indians in reference to a future state of rewards and punishments. The "water bull." Country between Cow creek and Council Grove. Inviting locality for settlement. Sudden rise of water. Separate routes. Dangerous travelling. Osage village. Osages, and all about them. Arrival at Van Buren, Arkansas. Concluding remarks.   357

View on Missouri River opposite Fort Leavenworth.

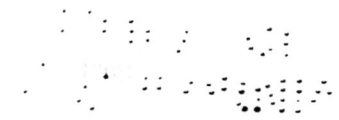

# ROCKY MOUNTAIN LIFE.

### CHAPTER I

Objects of a proposed excursion.—Primary plans and movements.—A digression—Rendezvous for Oregon emigrants and Santa Fe traders.—Sensations on a first visit to the border Prairies.—Frontier Indians.

My purpose in visiting the Rocky Mountains, and countries adjacent, having hitherto proved a fruitful source of inquiry to the many persons I meet, when aware of my having devoted three years to travel in those remote regions, and I am so plied with almost numberless other questions, I know of no better way to dispose of them satisfactorily, than by doing what I had thought of at the outset, to wit: writing a book.

But, says one, more books have been already written upon subjects of a kindred nature, than will ever find readers. True, indeed; yet I must venture one more; and this much I promise at the start: it shall be different, in most respects, from all that have preceded it; and if I fail to produce an agreeable variety of adventures, interwoven with a large fund of valuable information, then I shall not have accomplished my purpose.

Yet, 'why did I go?—what was my object?' Let me explain: Dame Nature bestowed upon me lavishly that innate curiosity, and fondness for things strange and new, of which every one is more or less possessed. Phrenologists would declare my organ of Inquisitiveness to be largely developed; and, certain it is, I have a great liking to tread upon unfrequented ground, and mingle among scenes at once novel and romantic. Love of adventure, then, was the great prompter, while an enfeebled state of health sensibly admonished me to seek in other parts that invigorating air and climate denied by the diseased atmosphere of a populous country. I also wished to acquaint myself with the geography of those comparatively unexplored regions,—their geological character, curiosities, resources, and natural advantages, together with their real condition, present inhabitants, inducements to emigrants, and most favorable localities for settlements, to enable me to speak from personal knowledge upon subjects so interesting to the public mind, at the present time, as are the above. Here, then, were objects every way worthy of attention, and vested with an importance that would render my excursion not a mere idle jaunt for the gratification of selfish curiosity. This much by way of prelude,—now to the task in hand.

While yet undecided as to the most advisable mode of prosecuting my intended enterprise, on learning that a party of adventurers were rendezvoused at Westport, Mo., preparatory to their long and arduous journey to the new-formed settlements of the Columbia river, I hastened to that place, where I arrived in the month of May, 1841, with the design of becoming one of their number. In this, however, I was doomed to disappointment by being too late. A few weeks subsequent marked the return of several fur companies, from their annual excursions to the Indian tribes inhabiting the regions adjacent to the head-waters of the Platte and Arkansas rivers, whose outward trips are performed in the fall months. Impatient at delay and despairing of a more eligible opportunity, for at least some time to come, I made prompt arrangements with one of them, to accompany it, *en route*, as far as the Rocky Mountains, intending to proceed thereafter as circumstances or inclination might suggest. This plan of travelling was adhered to, notwithstanding the detention of some three months, which retarded its prosecution.

I would here beg indulgence of the reader to a seeming digression. The peculiar locality of the places to whose vicinity he is now introduced, owing to the deep interest cherished in the public mind relative to the Oregon country, will doubtless call for more than a mere passing notice: I allude to the towns of Independence and Westport. Situated as they are, at the utmost verge of civilization, and upon the direct route to Oregon and regions adjacent, they must retain and command, as the great starting points for emigrants and traders, that importance already assumed by general consent. Their facilities of access from all parts of the Union, both by land and water, are nowhere exceeded. The proud Missouri rolls its turbid waves within six miles of either place, opening the highway of steam communication, while numberless prime roads that converge from every direction, point to them as their common focus. Thus, the staid New Englander may exchange his native hills for the frontier prairies in the short interval of two weeks; and in half that time the citizen of the sunny South may reach the appointed rendezvous; and, nearer by, the hardy emigrant may commence his long overland journey, from his own door, fully supplied with all the necessaries for its successful termination.

Independence is the seat of justice for Jackson county, Mo., about four hundred miles west by north of St. Louis, and contains a population of nearly two thousand. Westport is a small town in the same county, near the mouth of the Kansas river,—three miles from the Indian territory, and thirty below the U. S. Dragoon station at Fort Leavenworth. The regular routes to Santa Fe and Oregon date their commencement at these places. The country in this vicinity is beginning to be generally settled by thrifty farmers, from whom all the articles necessary for travellers and traders, may be procured upon reasonable terms.

Starting from either of the above points, a short ride bears the adventurer across the state line, and affords him the opportunity of taking his initiatory lessons amid the realities of prairie life. Here, most of the trading and emigrant companies remain encamped for several weeks, to recruit

KING OF THE SHAWNEES. — *Page* 33.

their animals and complete the needful arrangements, prior to undertaking the toilsome and dangerous journey before them.

The scenery of this neighborhood is truly delightful. It seems indeed like one Nature's favored spots, where Flora presides in all her regal splendor, and with the fragrance of wild flowers, perfumes the breath of spring and lades the summer breeze with willing incense;—now, sporting beside her fountains and revelling in her dales,—then, smiling from her hill-tops, or luxurating beneath her groves.

I shall never forget the pleasing sensations produced by my first visit to the border-prairies. It was in the month of June, soon after my arrival at Westport. The day was clear and beautiful. A gentle shower the preceding night had purified the atmosphere, and the laughing flowerets, newly invigorated from the nectarine draught, seemed to vie with each other in the exhalation of their sweetest odors. The blushing strawberry, scarce yet divested of its rich burden of fruit, kissed my every step. The buttercup, tulip, pink, violet, and daisy, with a variety of other beauties, unknown to the choicest collections of civilized life, on every side captivated the eye and delighted the fancy.

The ground was clothed with luxuriant herbage. The grass, where left uncropped by grazing herds of cattle and horses, had attained a surprising growth. The landscape brought within the scope of vision a most magnificent prospect. The groves, clad in their gayest foliage and nodding to the wind, ever and anon, crowned the gentle acclivities or reared their heads from the valleys, as if planted by the hand of art to point the wayfarer to Elysian retreats. The gushing fountains, softly breathing their untaught melody, before and on either hand, at short intervals, greeted the ear and tempted the taste. The lark, linnet, and martin, uniting with other feathered songsters, poured forth heir sweetest strains in one grand concert, and made the air vocal with their warblings; and the brown-plumed grouse, witless of the approach of man, till dangerously near, would here and there emerge wellnigh from under foot, and whiz through the air with almost lightning speed, leaving me half frightened at her unlooked for presence and sudden exit. Hither and yon, truant bands of horses and cattle, from the less inviting pastures of the settlements, were seen in the distance, cropping the choice herbage before them, or gambolling in all the pride of native freedom.

Amid such scenes I delight to wander, and often, at this late day, will my thoughts return, unbidden, to converse with them anew. There is a charm in the loneliness—an enchantment in the solitude—a witching variety in the sameness, that must ever impress the traveller, when, for the first time, he enters within the confines of the great western prairies.

One thing further and I will have done with this digression. Connected with the foregoing, it may not be deemed amiss to say something in relation to the Indian tribes inhabiting the territory adjacent to this common camping-place. The nearest native settlement is some twelve miles distant, and belongs to the Shawnees. This nation numbers in all fourteen or fifteen hundred men, women and children. Their immediate neighbors are the Delawares and Wyandotts,—the former claiming a population of eleven hundred, and the latter, three or four hundred. Many connected with these tribes outstrip the nearer whites, in point of civilization and refinement,—excelling them both in honesty and morality, and all that elevates and ennobles the human character. Their wild habits have become in a great measure subdued by the restraining influences of christianity, and they themselves transformed into industrious cultivators of the soil,—occupying neat mansions with smiling fields around them.

Nor are they altogether neglectful of the means of education. The mission schools are generally well attended by ready pupils, in no respect less backward than the more favored ones of other lands. It is not rare even, considering the smallness of their number, to meet among them with persons of liberal education and accomplishments. Their mode of dress assimilates that of the whites, though, as yet, fashion has made comparatively but small inroads. The unsophisticated eye would find prolific source for amusement in the uncouth appearance of their females on public occasions. Perchance a gay Indian maiden comes flaunting past, with a huge fur-hat awkwardly placed upon her head,—embanded by broad strips of figured tin, instead of ribbons,—and ears distended with large flattened rings of silver, reaching to her shoulders; and here another, solely habited in a long wollen under-dress, obtrudes to view, and skips along in all the pride and pomposity of a regular city belle! Such are sights by no means uncommon.

These tribes have a regular civil government of their own, and all laws instituted for the general welfare are duly respected. They are, also, becoming more temperate in their habits, fully convinced that ardent spirits have hitherto proved the greatest enemy to the red man. The churches of various christain denominations, established among them, are in a flourishing condition, and include with their members many whose lives of examplary piety adorn their professions.

Taken as a whole, the several Indian tribes, occupying this beautiful and fertile section of country, are living witnesses to the softening and benign influences of enlightened christian effort, and furnish indubitable evidence of the susceptibility of the Aborigine for civilization and improvement.

## CHAPTER II.

Preparations for leaving.—Scenes at Camp.—Things as they appeared.—Simplicity of mountaineers.—Sleep in the open air.—Character, habits, and costume of mountaineers.—Heterogeneous ingredients of Company.—The commandant.—En route.—Comical exhibition and adventure with a Spanish company.—Grouse.—Elm Grove.—A storm.—Santa Fe traders.—Indian battle.

AFTER many vexatious delays and disappointments, the time was at length fixed for our departure, and leaving Independance on the 2d of September, I proceeded to join the encampment without the state line. It was nearly night before I reached my destination, and the camp-fires were already

SHAWNEE MAIDEN.—Page 34.

lighted, in front of which the officiating cook was busily engaged in preparing the evening repast. To the windward were the dusky forms of ten or fifteen men,—some standing, others sitting *a la Turk*, and others half-reclining or quietly extended at full length upon the ground,—watching the operative of the culinary department with great seeming interest.

Enchairing myself upon a small log, I began to survey the surrounding objects. In the back ground stood four large Connestoga waggons, with ample canvass tops, and one dearborn, all tastefully drawn up in crescent form. To the right a small pyramid-shaped tent, with its snow-white covering, disclosed itself to the eye, and presented an air of comfort. To the left the caravan animals, securely picketed, at regular distances of some fifteen yards apart, occupied an area of several acres. Close at hand a crystal streamlet traced its course, murmuring adown the valley; and still beyond, a lovely grove waved its branches in the breeze, and contributed its willing mite to enliven and beautify the scene. The camp-fires in front, formed a kind of gateway to a small enclosure, shut in as above described. Here were congregated the company, or at least, that portion of it yet arrived. Some had already spread their easily adjusted couches upon the ground, in readiness for the coming night, and seemed only awaiting supper to forget their cares and troubles in the sweet embrace of sleep.

Every thing presented such an air of primitive simplicity not altogether estranged to comfort, I began to think it nowise marvellous that this mode of life should afford such strong attractions to those inured to it.

Supper disposed of, the area within camp soon became tenanted by the devotees of slumber,—some snoring away most melodiously, and others conversing in an animated tone, now jovial, now grave, and at intervals, causing the night-air to resound with merry peals of laughter. At length the sleep-god began to assert his wonted supremacy, and silence in some measure reigned throughout camp.

The bed of a mountaineer is an article neither complex in its nature nor difficult in its adjustment. A single buffalo robe folded double and spread upon the ground, with a rock, or knoll, or some like substitute for a pillow, furnishes the sole base-work upon which the sleeper reclines, and, enveloped in an additional blanket or robe, contentedly enjoys his rest. Wishing to initiate myself to the new mode of life before me, I was not slow to imitate the example of the promiscuous throng, and the lapse of a few moments found me in a fair way to pass quite pleasantly my first night's repose in the open air.

With the first gray of morning I arose refreshed and invigorated, nor even suffered the slightest ill effect from my unusual exposure to a humid and unwholesome night-air. The whole camp, soon after, began to disclose a scene of cheerfulness and animation. The cattle and horses, unloosed from their fastenings, and accompanied by keepers, were again permitted to roam at large, and in a short time were most industriously engaged in administering to the calls of appetite.

After breakfast I improved the opportunity to look about and scan more closely the appearance of my *compagnons de voyage*. This opened to view a new field for the study of men and manners.

A mountain company generally comprises some quaint specimens of human nature, and, perhaps, few more so than the one to which I here introduce the reader. To particularize would exceed my limits, nor could I do full justice to the subject in hand by dealing in generalities;—however, I yield to the latter. There are many crude originals mixed with the prime ingredients of these companies. A genuine mountaineer is a problem hard to solve. He seems a kind of *sui genus*, an oddity, both in dress, language, and appearance, from the rest of mankind. Associated with nature in her most simple forms by habit and manner of life, he gradually learns to despise the restraints of civilization, and assimilates himself to the rude and unpolished character of the scenes with which he is most conversant. Frank and open in his manners and generous in his disposition, he is, at the same time, cautious and reserved. In his frankness he will allow no one to acquire an undue advantage of him, though in his generosity, he will oftentimes expend the last cent to assist a fellow in need. Implacable in his hatred, he is also steadfast in his friendship, and knows no sacrifice too great for the benefit of those he esteems. Free as the pure air he breathes, and proudly conscious of his own independence, he will neither tyrannize over others, nor submit to be trampled upon,—and is always prepared to meet the perils he may chance to encounter, with an undaunted front. Inured to hardship and deprivation, his wants are few, and he is the last to repine at the misfortunes which so often befall him. Patience becomes as it were interwoven with his very nature, and he submits to the greatest disasters without a murmur. His powers of endurance, from frequent exercise, attain a strength and capacity almost incredible,—such as are altogether unknown to the more delicately nurtured. His is a trade, to become master of which requires a long and faithful apprenticeship. Of this none seems more conscious than himself, and woe to the "*greenhorn*" who too prematurely assumes to be "journeyman." His ideas, his arguments, his illustrations, all partake of the unpolished simplicity of his associations; though abounding often in the most vivid imagery, pointed inferences, and luminous expositions, they need a key to make them intelligible to the novice.

His dress and appearance are equally singular. His skin, from constant exposure, assumes a hue almost as dark as that of the Aborigine, and his features and physical structure attain a rough and hardy cast. His hair, through inattention, becomes long, coarse, and bushy, and loosely dangles upon his shoulders. His head is surmounted by a low crowned wool-hat, or a rude substitute of his own manufacture. His clothes are of buckskin, gaily fringed at the seams with strings of the same material, cut and made in a fashion peculiar to himself and associates. The deer and buffalo furnish him the required covering for his feet, which he fabricates at the impulse of want. His waist is encircled with a belt of leather, holding encased his butcher-knife and pistols—while from his neck is suspended a bullet-pouch securely fastened to the belt in front, and beneath the right arm hangs a powder-horn transversely from his shoulder, behind which, upon the strap attached to it, are affixed his bullet-mould, ball-screw, wiper, awl, &c. With a gun-stick made of some hard wood, and a good rifle placed in his hands, carrying from thirty to thirty-five balls to the pound, the reader will have before him a correct likeness of a genuine mountaineer, when fully equipped.

This costume prevails not only in the mountains proper, but also in the less settled portions of Oregon and California. The mountaineer is his own manufacturer, tailor, shoemaker, and butcher; and, fully accoutred and supplied with ammunition in a good game country, he can always feed and clothe himself, and enjoy all the comforts his situation affords. No wonder, then, his proud spirit, expanding with the intuitive knowledge of noble independence, becomes devotedly attached to those regions and habits that permit him to stalk forth, a sovereign amid nature's lovliest works.

Our company, however, were not all mountaineers; some were only "entered apprentices," and others mere "*greenhorns*"—taking every thing into consideration, perhaps, it was quite as agreeably composed as circumstances would well admit of. In glancing over the crowd, I remarked several countenances sinister and malign, but consented to suspend judgment till the character of each should be proven by his conduct. Hence, in the succeeding pages, I shall only speak of characters as I have occasion to speak of men. As a whole, the party before me presented a choice collection of local varieties,—here was the native of France, of Canada, of England, of Hudson Bay, of Connecticut, of Pennsylvania, of New York, of Kentucky, of Illinois, of Missouri, and of the Rocky Mountains, all congregated to act in unison for a specified purpose. It might well require the pencil of Hogarth to picture such a motley group.

Our company had not as yet attained its full numercial strength; a small division of it was some distance in advance, another behind, and at least two days would be necessary to complete the arrangements prior to leaving. The idea of spending two days in camp, notwithstanding the beauty of its location, was by no means agreeable; but as the case was beyond remedy, I quietly submitted, and managed to while away the tedious interval as best I could.

A brief acquaintance with our commandant, found him a man of small stature and gentlemanly deportment, though savoring somewhat of arrogance and self-sufficiency,—faults, by the way, not uncommon in little men. He had been engaged in the Indian trade for several years past, and had seen many "ups and downs" in former life. Graduating from West Point in his younger days, he soon after received the commission of Lieutenant of Dragoons, in the U. S. Army, and served in that capacity for some six or eight years, on the frontier and at Forts Gibson and Leavenworth. Possessed of the confidence of his men, his subsequent resignation was the occasion of much regret with those he had been accustomed to command. The private soldier loved him for his generous frankness and readiness to overlook minor offences, even upon the first show of penitence.

Such unbounded popularity at length excited the jealousy of his brother officers, and gave birth to a combination against him, which nothing could appease short of his removal from the army. Aware of his ardent temperament and strong party notions as a politician, and equally violent upon the opposite side, they managed to inveigle him into a discussion of the measures and plans of the then administration of national affairs. Arguing in the excitement of feeling, he made use of an unguarded expression, denouncing the Chief Magistrate. This was immediately noted down, and charges were promptly preferred against him, for "*abuse of a superior officer!*" The whole affair was then referred to a Court Martial, composed exclusively of political opponents. The evidence was so strong he had little to expect from their hands, and consequently threw up his commission, to avert the disgrace of being *cashiered*, since which he has been engaged in his present business.

He appeared to be a man of general information, and well versed in science and literature. Indeed, I felt highly gratified in making an acquaintance so far congenial to my own taste.

An accession of two waggons and four men having completed our number, the morning of September 4th was ushered in with the din of preparations for an immediate start. The lading of the waggons was then severally overhauled and more compactly adjusted, and our arms were deposited with other freight until such time as circumstances should call for them. All was hurry and confusion, and ofttimes the sharp tone of angry dispute arose above the jargon of the tumultuous throng.

At length the word was given to advance, and in an instant the whole caravan was in motion; those disconnected with the waggons, mounted upon horseback, led the van, followed by the teams and their attendants in Indian file, as the loose cattle and horses brought up the rear. The scene to me portrayed a novelty quite amusing. I began to think a more comical-looking set could scarcely be found any where; but the events of the day soon convinced me of my mistake.

Travelling leisurely along for some six or eight miles, strange objects were seen in the distance, which, on nearer approach, proved a company of Mexican traders, on their way to Independence for an equipment of goods. As they filed past us, I had full scope for the exercise of my risibilities.

If a mountaineer and a mountain company are laughable objects, a Mexican and a Mexican company are triply so. The first thing that excites attention upon meeting one of this mongrel race, is his ludicrous apology for pantaloons. This is generally made of deer or buffalo skin, similar to our present fashion, except the legs, which are left unsewed from the thigh downwards; a loose pair of cotton drawers, cut and made in like manner, and worn beneath, imparts to his every movements a most grotesque appearance, leaving at each step of the wearer his denuded leg, with that of his pantaloons on one side, and drawers on the other, fluttering in the breeze! The next thing that meets the gaze, is his black, slouching, broad-brimmed hat, (*sombrero*,) though little darker than the features it obscures, and far less so than the coarse, jet-colored hair that protrudes from beneath it, and falls confusedly upon his shoulders. Next, if the weather tolerates the habit, a coarse parti-colored blanket (*charape*) envelopes the body, from his shoulders downwards, fixed to its place by an aperture in the centre through which the head is thrust, and securely girted at pleasure by a waist-band of leather. His arms, if arms he has, consist of a rude bow and arrows slung to his back, or an old fusee, not unfrequently without flint, lock, or ammunition; but doubly armed, and proudly, too, is he who can carry a good rifle with powder and lead—even if he *be* ignorant of their use.

Thus appearing, these creatures, some mounted upon mules, with heavy spurs attached to their heels, (bearing gaffs an inch and a half in length, jingling in response to the rolling motions of the wearer,) ensconced in bungling Spanish saddles, (finished with such ample leather skirts as almost hid the diminutive animal that bore them, and large wooden stirrups, some three

WAGON TRAIN.—*Page* 40.

inches broad,) were riding at their ease; while others, half naked, were trudging along on foot, driving their teams, or following the erratic mules of the caravan, to heap upon them the ready maledictions of their prolific vocabulary. Passing on, we were accosted:

"Como lo pasa, cabelleros?"

The salutation was returned by a simple nod.

"Habla la lengua Espanola, senors?"

A shake of the head was the only response.

"Es esta el camino de Independenca?"

No reply.

"Carraho! Que quantos jornadas tenemos en la camino de Independenca?"

Still no one answered.

"Scha! Maldijo tualmas! Los Americanos esta dijabelo!"

By this time the crowd had passed and left us no longer annoyed by its presence. The conclusion irresistibly forced itself upon my mind, "if these are true specimens of Mexicans, it is no wonder they incite both the pity and contempt of the rest of the world." Subsequent intercourse with them, however, has served to convince me that first impressions, in this case, instead of exceeding the reality, fell far short of the true mark!

Continuing our course, we saw large numbers of prairie-hens, and succeeded in killing several. These birds assimilate the English grouse in appearance, and are of a dusky-brown color,—with short tails, and narrow-peaked wings,—and little less in size than the domestic fowl. Their flesh is tender and of superior flavor. When alarmed, they start with a cackling noise, and whiz through the air not unlike the partridge. They are very numerous on the frontier prairies, and extend to the Rocky Mountains, Oregon, California and New Mexico.

About sundown we reached a small creek known as Elm Grove, and encamped for the night, with every indication of an approaching storm. Strict orders were accordingly given for securing the animals, and the process of "picketing" was speedily under way. This consisted in driving small stakes ("pickets") firmly into the ground, at proper distances apart, to which the animals were severally tied by strong cords,—a plan that should find nightly practice among all travellers of the grand prairies, to prevent those losses which, despite the utmost precaution, will not unfrequently occur.

Timber proved quite scarce in this vicinity, and it was with great difficulty we procured sufficient for cooking purposes. The men now began to prepare for the coming storm. Some disposed of themselves in, and others under, the waggons, making barricades to the windward; others erected shantees, by means of slender sticks, planted in parallel rows five or six feet apart, and interwoven at the tops, so as to form an arch of suitable height, over which was spread a roofage of robes or blankets,—while others, snugly ensconced beneath the ready pitched tent, bade defiance to wind and weather.

Being one of those selecting a place under the waggons, I retired at an early hour to snooze away the night; and despite the anticipations of an unpleasant time, I soon lost myself in a sweet slumber, utterly unconscious of every thing around me. In thoughts I wandered back to the home of my childhood, to converse with friends whose names and features fond memory has chained to my heart, while imagination roamed with delight amid those scenes endeared to me by earliest and most cherished recollections. But all the sweet pencillings of fancy were at once spoiled by the uncivil intrusion of a full torrent of water, that came pouring from the hill-side and forced its impetuous way into the valley below,—deluging me from head to foot in its descent. My condition, as the reader may well suppose, was far from being enviable. However, resolved to make the best of a bad thing, after wringing the water from my drenched bedding, I selected another spot and again adjusted myself to pass the dreary interval till morning; this I succeeded in doing,—how or in what manner, it is unnecessary to say. Sleep was utterly out of the question, and I am quite sure I never hailed the welcome morn with greater delight than on this occasion.

Others of the company fared almost as bad as myself, and there was scarcely a dry bed in camp. But the little concern evinced by the mountaineers for their mishap, surprised me most. They crawled from their beds, reeking with wet, as good humoredly as though their nocturnal bath had in no wise disturbed their equanimity, or impaired their comfort.

The morning proved so disagreeable two of our party, who were accompanying us for the purpose of adventure, concluding this a kind of adventure they were unwilling to meet, wisely resolved to take the back track, and accordingly left for home. Towards night the rain ceased, and, the clouds having dispersed, we were again *en route*. Travelling on till late, we encamped in the open prairie, and early the next morning resumed our course. Having reached a small creek, about 10 o'clock, we halted for breakfast, where another Santa Fe company came up. This proved a party of Americans, with some six or eight waggons and a large number of horses and mules, on their homeward journey. They had also in their possession an elk nearly full grown, two black-tailed deer,* an antelope and a white-tailed fawn.

Through them we received intelligence of a battle recently fought between the Pawnee and Arapaho Indians, at the lower Cimarone Springs, south of the Arkansas. The former had been defeated with great slaughter,—losing their horses and seventy-two of their bravest warriors, to increase the trophies and enliven the scalp-dances of their enemies. This action occurred directly upon the Santa Fe trail, and the dead yet bestrewed the prairie, as our informants passed, half devoured by wolves, and filling the air with noisome stench as they wasted beneath the influence of a scorching sun.

An approving murmur ran through the crowd while listening to the recital, and all united to denounce the Pawnees as a dangerous and villanous set, and wished for their utter extermination.

---

* The black-tailed deer are larger than the common deer, and are found only in the snow-mountains. For a description of them the reader is referred to subsequent pages.

## CHAPTER III.

The Pottowatomies.—Crossing the Wakarousha.—Adventure at the Springs.—The Caw chief.—Kansas river and Indians.—Pleading for whiskey.—Hickory timber.—Prairie tea.—Scenes at the N. Fork of Blue.—Wild honey.—Return party.—Mountaineers in California.—Adventure with a buffalo.—Indian atrocities.—Liquor and the Fur Trade.—Strict guard.—High prices.

CONTINUING our course, we bore to the right, and struck the northern or Platte trail, and, after travelling eight or ten miles, made camp upon a small creek skirted with heavy timber, called Black Jack. An early start the next morning brought us to the Wakarousha, a considerable tributary of the Kansas, where a junction was formed with our advance party. The territory lying upon this stream as far south as Council Grove, (a noted place on the Mexican trail, 144 miles west from Independence,) belongs to the Pottowatomies. These Indians are very wealthy and are partially civilized,—the most of them being tillers of the ground. Their dwellings are of very simple construction,—large strips of bark firmly tied to a frame-work of poles with small apertures to admit light, furnishing the exterior, while the interior is finished by the suspension of two or three blankets between the apartments, as partitions, and erecting a few scaffolds for bedsteads. The fire-place in warm weather is out of doors, but in the winter it occupies the centre of the building, from which the smoke—unaided by jamb or chimney—is left to find its way through an opening in the roof. Some, however, are beginning to improve in their style of architecture, and now and then we find a tolerably spacious and comfortable house among them.

The Catholics have several missionaries with this tribe, and are using great exertions, if not to ameliorate their condition, at least, to proselyte them to their own peculiar faith. The missionaries of other christian denominations are also devoting themselves for their benefit, and not unfrequently with gratifying success.

The remainder of the day was occupied in crossing the creek—a task by no means easy,—its banks being so precipitous we were compelled to lower our waggons by means of ropes. In so doing it required the utmost caution to prevent them from oversetting or becoming broken in the abrupt descent.

The night following was passed upon the opposite bank. After travelling some twelve miles the next day, we encamped a short distance to the right of the trail, at a place known as the Springs. Scarcely had we halted when two footmen appeared from an opposite direction—one of them leading a horse—whom a nearer advance proved to be a white man and an Indian. The former was immediately recognized by our *engages* as an old acquaintance, by the name of Brown, who had been their recent *compagnon de voyage* from the mountains. His story was soon told. A few days subsequent to his arrival in the States, a difficulty had occurred between him and another person, who received a severe wound from a knife by the hand of Brown during the affray, when the latter was necessitated to consult his own safety by a hurried flight. He accordingly bade farewell both to enemies and law, and left for the Indian country—travelling most of the way by night. Two weeks afterwards he arrived in the Kansas nation, and remained with the Indian now accompanying him, to await our return.

Having listened to his story, I began to survey his strange companion. He was a village chief of the Kansas (Caw) tribe, and the first of his race I had ever seen so nearly dressed in his native costume. In person he was tall and stout-built,—with broad shoulders and chest, brawny arms and legs, and features evincing the uncontaminated blood of the Aborigine. His hair was closely shaved to the scalp, with the exception of a narrow tuft centrewise from forehead to crown, so trimmed it stood on end like the bristles of a warring hog; then his whole head and face were so lavishly bedaubed with vermilion, our experienced city belles would doubtless have considered it an unpardonable waste of that *useful material!*

A string of bears'-claws, tastefully arranged, encircled his neck, while ample folds of brass wire above the wrists and elbows furnished his armillary, and from his ears hung rude ornaments,—some of silver, others of brass or iron—cruelly distending the flexible members that bore them. A dirty white blanket drawn closely around the shoulders enveloped the body, which, with a breech-cloth and leggins, formed his sole covering. A bow and arrows, slung to his back by a strap passing over the left shoulder and under the right arm, were his only weapons. A belt, begirting the waist, sustained his tobacco-pouch and butcher-knife, and completed his attire and armament.

Thus habited appeared before us the Caw chief, holding in one hand the lead-rope of his horse, and in the other the wing of a wild turkey, with a a long-stemmed pipe, carved from a hard red stone, handsomely wrought and finely polished. Taken altogether, he presented an amusing spectacle—a real curiosity.

Having shaken hands with the company and turned his horse to graze, in a few moments his pipe was subjected to its destined use, and, as the inhaled fumes merrily curved from his mouth and nostrils, he ever and anon presented it for the indulgence of the bystanders. His knowledge of English was limited to the simple monosyllable "good," which he took occasion to pronounce at intervals as he thought proper.

*Sept. 8th.* Continuing on, we encamped towards night at a small creek within six miles of the crossing of the Kansas river. Here a bevy of our chief's villagers, rigged in their rude fashion, came flocking up, apparently to gratify their curiosity in gazing at us, but really in expectation of some trifling presents, or in quest of a favorable opportunity for indulging their inate propensities for theft. However, they found little encouragement, as the vigilance of our guards more than equalled the cunning of our visitors. During their stay we were frequently solicited for donations of tobacco and ammunition, (as they expressed it,) in payment for passing through their country. This was individually demanded with all the assurance of government revenue officers, or the keepers of regular toll-bridges, strongly reminding one of the petty nations upon the borders of Canaan

THE CAW CHIEF. — *Page 46.*

that required tribute of the Israelites passing through them to possess the land of their forefathers.

*Sept. 9th.* Early in the forenoon we came to the Kansas, and were employed till nearly night in effecting a ford. This proved rather difficult, as the water was deep and the bottom sandy;—the course, bearing directly across, till near midway of the river, follows the current for six or eight hundred yards, and then turns abruptly to the opposite shore. The Kansas, at the crossing, was not far from six hundred yards wide, with steep banks of clay and sand. The fording accomplished, we travelled some six miles, and encamped for the night. Our visitors yet honored us with their presence; some, under pretence of trading horses; others, of bartering for tobacco, whiskey, coffee, and ammunition; but most of them for the real purpose of begging and stealing.

The Caw Indians are a branch of the Osage tribe—speaking the same language, and identified by the same manners and customs. They number a population of sixteen hundred, and claim all the territory west of the Delaware, Shawnee, and Pottowatomie line, to the head waters of the Kansas. Their main village is on the left bank of the river, a few miles above the crossing. Their houses are built Pawnee fashion, being coniform and covered with a thick coat of dirt, presenting a hole at the apex to emit the smoke, and another at the side to serve the double purpose of a door and window. The whole building describes a complete circle, in whose centre is placed the hearth-fire, and at the circumference the couches of its inmates. Its floor is the bare ground, and its ceiling the grass, brush, and poles which uphold the superincumbent earth forming the roof and sides.

The Caws are generally a lazy and slovenly people, raising but little corn, and scarcely any vegetables. For a living they depend mostly upon the chase. Their regular hunts are in the summer, fall, and winter, at which time they all leave for the buffalo range, and return laden with a full supply of choice provisions. The robes and skins thus obtained, furnish their clothing and articles for traffic.

As yet, civilization has made but small advances among them. Some, however, are tolerably well educated, and a Protestant mission established with them, is beginning its slow but successful operations for their good,— while two or three families of half-breeds, near by, occupy neat houses, and have splendid farms and improvements, thus affording a wholesome contrast to the poverty and misery of their rude neighbors.

The distance from Independence to this place, by the mountain trail, is some eighty miles, over a beautiful and fertile country, which I shall hereafter take occasion to notice more fully. Before leaving, we were further increased by the accession of two Canadian *voyageurs*—French of course. Our force now numbered some twenty-four—one sufficiently formidable for all the dangers of the route.

*Sept. 10th.* Resuming our way, we proceeded till late at night, still attended by our Indian friends; (not the originals, but a "few more of the same sort," who *kindly* supplied their places,—seeking to levy fresh drafts upon patience and generosity.) These were more importunate for liquor than any preceding them—though, in fact, the whole nation is nowise remiss in their devotion to King Alcohol. One fellow, in particular, exhausted all his

5

ingenuity to obtain the wherewith to "*wet his whistle*." He was a shrivel-faced old man, and occasioned much sport, from his supplications in broken English, which ran pretty much as follows:

"Big man, me. Chief,—Black Warrior. Me, American soldier! Love Americans, heap. Big man, me! Love whiskey, heap. White man good. Whiskey good. Love whiskey, me,—drink heap whiskey. No give me whiskey drink? Me, Chief. Me, American. Me, Black Warrior. Heap big man, me! Love Americans. Take him hand, shake. White man good. Whiskey good. Me love whiskey! Love him heap! No give Black Warrior whiskey? No?—one leetle drink? Whiskey good. Me love him. Make Black Warrior strong. Big man, me,—Chief. American soldier. Me love American. Shake him hand. Fight him, bad Indian, no love white man. Kill him. White man good. Me love white man. Whiskey good. Me love whiskey. No give Black Warrior whiskey,—one leetle drink? Me, Chief. Big man, me." Etc.

In this strain the old fellow continued so long as he found listeners, but without success, although, as I afterwards learned, two waggons were freighted with the noxious article; none of it was suffered to find its way down the throats of our thirsty guests.

Pursuing a westerly course, nearly parallel with the Kansas, for three successive days, we passed the 14th encamped at Big Vermilion, for the purpose of procuring a quantity of hickory for gun-sticks and bow-timber. Hickory is unknown to the Rocky Mountains, and this being the last place on the route affording it, each of our company took care to provide himself with an extra gun-stick. Small pieces, suitable for bows, find market among the mountain Indians, ranging at the price of a robe each, while gun-sticks command one dollar apiece, from the hunters and trappers.

We were also careful to provide an extra quantity of ox-bows, axle-trees, &c., as a resource in case of accidents or breakage. These are articles with which every caravan should be furnished on a journey across the grand prairies.

In this vicinity a species of shrub, which I had before noticed in various places, (designated as "red-root" by our voyageurs,) became quite abundant. The red-root is highly esteemed as a substitute for *tea*, and my own experience attests its superiority of flavor to any article of that kind imported from China. In appearance it is very similar to the tea of commerce, and it affords at all times a most excellent beverage. It is found only upon the prairies between the frontiers and Big Blue, and in some portions of the Rocky Mountains.

Leaving Big Vermilion, we travelled rapidly the two days subsequent, and arrived at the North Fork of Blue,—a large and deep stream, tributary to the Kansas. We were here detained till the 24th—the creek being impassable on account of high water.

However, the beauty of the place and variety of its landscape scenery, served in a great measure to alleviate the weariness of delay. The country was most agreeably interspersed with hills, uplands, and dales—amply watered and variegated with woods and prairies, attired in all the gaudy loveliness of wild-flowers. The busy bee, afraid of the cruel persecutions of man, had here sought a secure retreat to pursue, unmolested, her melliferous employ, and fill the dark chambers of her oaken palaces year by year with honeyed stores. The air was almost vocal with the music of her wings, and the flowerets were enlivened by the gentle touches of her embrace. The odor of honey filled the breeze, which, wafting the mingled melody of birds and insects with the incense of flowers, o'er the smiling prairie till lost in space, seemed more like the breath of Eden than the exhalations of earth.

As might be supposed, we were not slow in levying upon the delicious stores, which the industrious insects, claiming this as their dominion, had laid away for themselves. During our stay no less than four bee-trees were levelled, and every pan, kettle, pail, keg, or empty dish in the whole camp was filled to overflowing, and every stomach to repletion, with honey of almost crystalline transparency. The great abundance of deer, turkey, and other game in the vicinity, also contributed their share of amusement, and enlivened the interval of detention.

At length, by a partial subsidence of the water, we were enabled to effect a crossing and renew our journey. Pursuing a course W. N. W., on the 27th we met a small party of whites on their return from the mountains, and, yielding to the temptation presented by a luxuriant and well-wooded valley, with a pretty streamlet, the two parties made common camp. Our new acquaintances were taking a large drove of horses, and several domesticated buffalo, with them to the States. Their horses had been mostly obtained from Upper California, the year previous, by a band of mountaineers, under the lead of one Thompson. This band, numbering twenty-two in all, had made a descent upon the Mexican *ranchos* and captured between two and three thousand head of horses and mules. A corps of some sixty Mexican cavalry pursued and attacked them, but were defeated and pursued in turn, with the loss of several mules and their entire camp equipage: after which the adventurers were permitted to regain their mountain homes, without further molestation; but, in passing the cheerless desert, between the Sierra Nevada and Colorado, the heat, dust, and thirst were so intolerably oppressive, that full one half of their animals died. The remainder, however, were brought to rendezvous, and variously disposed of, to suit the wants and wishes of their captors.

The buffalo, in possession of our wayfaring friends, had been caught while calves, and reared by domestic cows. They appeared as tame and easily managed as other cattle. One of them, a two-year-old heifer, was rather vicious in its habits, having been spoiled, while a calf, by the too great familiarity of its keeper. After listening to a full exposition of its bad qualities, our commandant offered to bet he could handle, or even ride, the unruly beast at pleasure.

"Can you?" said the owner. "Do it, and my best horse is yours!"

"I take all such offers!" returned the commandant. "A horse could not be easier earned!" he continued, stepping towards the ill-tutored animal. "Come, boss!—Poor boss!—bossy, bossy!" addressing the buffalo, which commenced advancing,—at first slowly, then, with a sudden bound, ran full tilt against the admirer, leaving him prostrate upon the ground, as it turned away, dancing and throwing its heels exultingly at the exploit.

"Bless my stars!" he exclaimed, on recovering himself; "I'd no idea 'twould serve me so!"

"Ha, ha, ha!" retorted the owner. "You seem to pick upon a strange place for a snooze! What in the world were you doing before that skittish beast?"

The roar of laughter which followed, told how well the joke was relished by the crowd.

Reports from the mountains brought intelligence of recent difficulties between the whites and Sioux,—the latter having murdered several trappers. A battle had also been fought in the Snake country, in which the Sioux were defeated with a loss of twenty killed and wounded,—the whites suffered in the loss of their leader (Frapp) and four others. Another affair had come off, at Fort Platte, between two factions of that tribe, while on a drunken spree, resulting in the death of Schena-Chischille, their chief, and several of his party.

The most acceptable item of intelligence was the probability of our reaching the buffalo range in ten days, at least, where we should find vast quantities of those animals. This led our voyageurs to expatiate anew upon the choice varieties of the feast of good things we might expect on that occasion.

Bidding adieu to our transient camp-mates, we were soon again *en route*. The day following, being unfit for travel, was devoted to overhauling and re-adjusting the freight of the waggons. Here, for the first time, I ascertained the fact, that a portion of the above consisted of no less than *twenty-four barrels of alcohol*, designed for the Indian trade!

This announcement may occasion surprise to many, when aware that the laws of Congress prohibit, under severe penalties, the introduction of liquor among the Indians, as an article of traffic,—subjecting the offender to a heavy fine and confiscation of effects. Trading companies, however, find ways and means to smuggle it through, by the waggon-load, under the very noses of government officers, stationed along the frontiers to enforce the observance of laws.

I am irresistibly led to the conclusion, that these gentry are wilfully negligent of their duty; and, no doubt, there are often *weighty inducements* presented to them to shut their eyes, close their ears, and avert their faces, to let the guilty pass unmolested. It seems almost impossible that a blind man, retaining the senses of smell, taste and hearing, could remain ignorant of a thing so palpably plain. The alcohol is put into waggons, at Westport or Independence, *in open day-light*, and taken into the territory, *in open day light*, where it remains a week or more awaiting the arrival of its owners. Two Government agents reside at Westport, while six or eight companies of Dragoons are stationed at Fort Leavenworth, ostensibly for the purpose of protecting the Indians and suppressing this infamous traffic,—and yet it suffers no diminution from *their vigilance!* What *faithful* public officers! How prompt in the discharge of their *whole duty!*

These gentlemen cannot plead ignorance as an excuse. They well know that alcohol is one of the principal articles in Indian trade—this fact is notorious—no one pretends to deny it; not even the *traders themselves*— and yet, because no one takes the trouble to produce a specimen of the *kind* of freight taken, more or less, by all mountain companies, and FORCE them to *see, taste, touch,* and *smell,* they affect ignorance! It is thus the

## HIGH PRICES. 53

benevolent designs of our Government are consummated by these pensioners upon the public treasury!

Had they the will so to do, it would be no difficult matter to put a stop to all such exportations. The departure of any one of these companies for the mountains, is a thing too difficult to be effected unknown and stealthily. It becomes public talk for days and even weeks previous. Scarcely anything would be easier than for those whose business it is, to keep on the look out, and enforce the law to its full extent upon each offender. A few examples of this kind would interpose an insuperable barrier to the further prosecution of an illicit traffic in the manner it is at present carried on. A few faithful public officers, and attentive to their duty, regardless of fear or *favor*, would soon accomplish an object so desirable.

In subsequent pages of this work I shall have occasion to notice a few of the many evils resulting from this criminal neglect,—but at present forbear further remarks.

Our arms were now put in order for immediate use,—each individual apportioning to himself a good supply of ammunition, to be ready at all times in case of attack. Guards were ordered to be constantly on the alert. The company was divided into two parties,—one for day and the other for night guard, and these again were subdivided for alternate relieves,—thus, one of each subdivision serving a day and a night, and the reserve the day and night succeeding. The day-guard consisted of only two persons, upon duty every other day, but the night-guard numbered ten,—two being on duty for two hours were then relieved by the two next in succession, and they by the next, and so on.

Strict orders were also given to prevent any from leaving camp, or parting from the caravan while travelling. In fact, every thing began to assume a warlike aspect, as if we were really in danger and apprehensive of an immediate rencounter.

Several boxes of clothing, &c., were also opened for such as wished to purchase. But every article disposed of was sold at an enormous rate: tobacco bringing from one to three dollars per lb., according to quality; butcher-knives, from one dollar to one fifty each; hose, one dollar per pair; shirts, from three to five dollars each, according to quality; blankets, from twelve to sixteen dollars; coats, from fifteen to forty dollars; coarse shoes, four dollars per pair; six-penny calicoes, fifty cts. per yd.; beads, one dollar per bunch, etc. These were of an indifferent quality, and afforded the vender some three or four hundred per cent. advance upon purchase-price. In fact, with regard to prices, conscience had nothing to do with the matter.

5*

## CHAPTER IV.

Country from the frontiers to Big Blue, its geological character, &c.—Novel cure for fever and ague.—Indian trails.—Game.—Sage rabbits.—Antelope, and their peculiarities.—Beaver cuttings.—Big Blue and its vicinity.—Dangerous country.—Pawnee bravery.—Night-alarm, (Prairies on fire.)—Platte river.—Predominant characteristics of the Grand Prairies, and theory explanatory of their phenomenon.—Something to laugh at.—" Big Jim," and the antelope.

*Sept. 26th.* WE are now camped upon a small creek, nearly destitute of timber, within two miles of Big Blue, or the N. W. branch of the Kansas river. The geography of this part of the country is incorrectly described upon all the published maps I have yet seen. The Republican Fork, which is the principal branch of the Kansas, is uniformly represented as the most northwesterly branch of that river, forming a junction with it at or below the usual crossing. This is not the case.

The two forks of Blue, from the northwest, united, form a large and important stream, which, according to my impression, discharges its waters into the Kansas itself, and not into the Republican. Of this, however, I am not quite positive. But be that as it may, admitting the Republican to be the main stream, Big Blue must be, as a matter of course, the most northwesterly branch of the Kansas river.

Proceeding up the Blue, the geological character of the country undergoes an entire and radical change, and the traveller is introduced to a different order of things from that previously observed.

Perhaps, therefore, it is not out of place to present a general review of the territory thus far.

The interval from the frontier of Missouri to Big Blue, a distance upwards of two hundred miles, affords great uniformity in all its more prominent characteristics. It generally comprises beautifully undulating prairies, of a moist argillaceous soil, rich in sedimentary deposites and vegetable matter. It is somewhat rocky in places, but well watered by the almost innumerable streams that find their way into the Kansas, Platte and Arkansas rivers. The creeks, with but few exceptions, are heavily timbered with oak, hickory, walnut, maple, cottonwood, and other varieties found in more eastern forests. The hills too, in some parts, are more than usually abundant in springs, and covered with stately groves, as tastefully arranged as if planted by the hand of man, while luxuriant grass and fragrant flowers usurp the place of underbrush. The prairies, hemmed in on every side by the woodlands skirting the water-courses, present to the eye proud oceans of flowery verdure, tossing their wavelets to the breeze and perfuming the air with the breath of spring.

The streams are clear, with rocky or pebbly bottoms and high, steep banks—abounding in choice specimens of the finny tribes and varieties of the testaceous order, of the *genus muscula.* The valley of the Kansas is wide and of a deep brown vegetable mould, susceptible of a high state of cultivation. The whole country is well adapted to the double purpose of agriculture and the growth of stock.

The prevailing rock is sandstone of various shades and compactness, with siliceous and fossiliferous limestone. These specifications are generally exhibited in a detached and fragmentary form, but rarely in strata as disclosed upon the surface.

Taken as a whole, the territory holds out many inducements to emigrants, and, whenever brought into market, will no doubt become speedily and thickly populated.*

*Sept. 30th.* We are again under headway. A French engagé, who had been suffering for several days past from a severe attack of the fever and ague, experienced a sudden and novel cure. Unable to travel, quarters were prepared for him in one of the whiskey waggons, where he was comfortably disposed of as we continued our course. In passing a rough place the waggon overset, when out came the invalid head foremost, and *out came the whiskey barrels* showering full upon him! The suddenness of the fall, with the surprise and excitement of the occasion,—one, or both, or all, or some other cause unknown, effected a complete cure,—for certain it is, he did not suffer another attack of the fever and ague during the whole journey, and the next day was able to discharge his duties as well as ever.

On striking the Big Blue, the mountain road bears a north-northwest course to the head of that stream, and from thence over an interval of highlands to the Platte river. The distance travelled up the Blue requires some eight days, for heavy waggons. Continuing our way, about noon we passed several Indian trails, in addition to one ten or twelve or fifteen miles back. These consist of a number of well-beaten, parrallel foot-paths, bearing a northwest and southwest direction. They are formed by the passing and repassing of the Otoes, Iowas, and Foxes, to and from their hunting grounds, towards the head-waters of the Kansas.

On the 3d of October we reached the antelope range, and saw four or five of these animals scouring the boundless expanse, or ascending some favorable eminence to gaze upon us. Slight signs of buffalo also appeared, and everything seemed to indicate the approach to a game country.

Parting a short distance from the trail, a large sage rabbit bounded up before me,—the first of his species I ever saw. This animal is nearly three times the size of the common rabbit, and of a white color, slightly tinged with grey. It derives its name from being found principally in countries abounding with *absinthe* or wild sage. In the regions adjacent to the mountains, these animals occur more frequently,—and even among the mountains, where their tails and ears are tipped with jetty black. Their fur is soft and fine,—equalling if not surpassing that of the Russia rabbit. Their flesh is also of a superior flavor, as I have had opportunities of testing.

Towards night, three antelope appearing near the trail, our hunter made

* By a recent treaty with the Kansas Indians, our government has become possessed of nearly the whole of this beautiful section.

an unsuccessful attempt to approach them, which afforded me a first inkling of the nature and character of these animals.

The antelope of the grand prairie differs but little in size and shape from the common sheep, and is coated with long, brittle hair,—of a ruddy brown color, except at the tail and head, where it is short and white. The female is hornless, except an occasional blunt corneous excrescence, some two or three inches long, protruding from the head. The male, however, is equipped with hook-shaped antlers, ebony colored, and six or eight inches in length, which he sheds annually in the months of November and December.

This is the fleetest inhabitant of the prairie. No horse can compete with it in speed. Quick of sight, keen of scent, and acute of ear, it seems ever on the alert at the approach of real or supposed danger,—now swiftly advancing towards the object of its alarm or curiosity,—then circling before you with the fleetness of the storm-wind, to mount some eminence far away beyond reach, and gaze in security. Then, again, ere you have time to catch breath for admiration, it repeats its semi-gyration from an opposite direction, still nearer and swifter, till past,—as if indeed borne on the wings of lightning—and yet again surveys you in the distance. Now, running from point, to point it examines you upon all sides, as it cautiously passes round,—then, snuffing the breeze, it again calls to aid its fleetness of limb, and with the velocity of thought is lost to view in the vast expanse.

Possessed of an inordinate share of inquisitiveness, it not unfrequently falls a victim to its own curiosity. The hunter, turbaned with a red handkerchief and half concealed behind some object, first raising, then depressing his head, then withdrawing it entirely from view, then again disclosing it to the curious animal, is almost certain to allure his game within gunshot.

I have seen numbers killed in this manner. In the spring season they appear more sensitive than at any other time, and are easily lured to their fate.

With the exhibition of this strange propensity, I have time and again been minded of its more fully developed moral prototype in man. How frequently do we see persons around us who indulge their appetites and passions, as often for mere curiosity as fancied pleasure,—venturing nearer and still nearer towards the objects that command their attention and lure them into the vortex of ruin, till, with sure and deadly aim, the shafts of the tempter pierce the waning vitals of morality, and plunge the victims headlong into a yawning abyss, where they are lost to themselves, to society, and to the world—lost forever!

Here, then, is furnished for us a moral:—Beware how you indulge a vain curiosity that lures to evil;—never parley with temptation.

These animals are found from the Big Blue to the mountains—in Oregon, California, Santa Fe, and N. W. Texas. Their flesh is tender and sweet,—quite equal to venison, though seldom fat, owing, as is supposed, to their almost incessant mobility.

Near our night-camp I noticed fresh beaver "cuttings," some of which consisted of trees, six inches in diameter, levelled by these sagacious animals.

The vicinity disclosed frequent boulders of red and dark ferruginous sandstone, with a soil somewhat arenose, reclining upon a changeable deposite of sand and gravel, succeeded by a substratum of parti-colored and friable sandstone. The valley of the Blue is bordered by hills of graceful slope, both green and beautiful.

I here remarked for the first time the appearance of *cacti*, which herefrom becomes quite common, and proves the pest of many places adjacent to the mountains.

The Blue is a deep, narrow stream, with a swift current, over a bed of gravel and pebbles, and is fringed by groves of oak, cotton-wood, and willow. Its valley is between one and two miles in width, with a superfice of variable fertility, but generally consisting of good arable land.

This section of country is considered very dangerous in the summer and fall months, on account of the strolling bands of Pawnees which infest it. The *voyageur* holds the latter in great dread, unless he chances to be accompanied by a sufficient force to bid defiance to their approach. A party, numerically weak and indifferently armed, meets with rough treatment at their hands while on the open prairies. Persons and property are rarely respected, and the unfortunate traveller is not only plundered, but often whipt or murdered without mercy.

This, however, may not be said of all—it is only the young warriors, when beyond the restraint of their chiefs and seniors, who perpetrate such outrages; though, to their praise be it said, instances of this kind are quite seldom, at present, compared with former years.

The courage of these Indians is held in little repute by mountaineers; and, that this opinion is not unfounded, the following incident will prove. It was related to me by an actor in the scene:

A small party of whites on their cruise down the Platte with a cargo of furs, "lay by" to make meat, near the forks of that stream. Buffalo being at some distance from camp, our adventurers were compelled to perform the duties of pack-horses in conveying the proceeds of their hunting excursions. One day, four of them left for this object, and having proceeded some six or eight miles, a war-party of Pawnees suddenly emerged from behind an eminence, directly fronting them. Alarmed at the unwelcome apparition, and imagining the whole country to be alive with Indians, they immediately ran, and were pursued towards camp. One of the number, a big, lazy fellow, and rather "green" withal, soon became tired, and sung out to his companions:

"Don't let's run so fast. Blast me, if I can keep up!"

"Come on,—come on!" cried they. "A *thousand* 'shaved heads' are upon us, half frozen for hair!"

"Pooh! I'll bet five dollars there aint thirty!"

"Done! But, who'll count the bloody varmints?"

"Why, I'll do it, just for my own satisfaction." So saying, he wheeled and advanced towards the Pawnees, as his wondering companions halted a little distance off, to learn the result of his fool-daring.

Surprised at this strange movement, the enemy also came to a stand, affording a fine opportunity to ascertain their number, which only amounted to *nineteen!*

"I've won!" exclaimed our hero. "Let's charge, and give 'em the ver devil!"

The word went for command, and the four hunters dashed boldly towards the terrified savages, who in turn *fled*, with greater velocity than they had called into exercise at any time during their advance,—illustrating the truth of the saying, "tyrants are always cowards." Legs proved quite convenient articles for the Pawnee *braves!* They were out of sight in a few minutes, and were very careful not to stop until they had left their pursuers far in the rear.

A Pawnee with a defenceless enemy in his power, like some examples among the whites, is unrivalled in courage and daring; but where there is resistance offered, and fighting to be done, he, as well as the Irishman's chickens, "comes up *missing!*" He is always bravest when farthest from danger.

We were careful to observe the strictest vigilance at night, to prevent the loss of horses from lurking bands of Indians. The animals of the caravan were uniformly picketed in compact order, and sentinels, posted at suitable distances, continued to pace their rounds, from dark till daylight; while each of the company slept by his arms, in readiness at any moment to repel an attack.

Having travelled for seven successive days, we made camp late in the afternoon at the head of the right fork of Blue.

During the day we had noticed a dense smoke some distance in the rear, but, with the wind in an opposite direction, no uneasiness was felt on that account. The sentries were soon at their posts, and everything was snugly disposed of for the night. Those not on duty improved the opportunity to gain respite from the fatigues of the day, and, in a brief interval, were snoring away at an admirable rate.

The polar-star by its "pointers" had just told the hour of midnight, when these hurried words rang through the camp:

"Lave, ho! Lave!* Prairies on fire! Quick—catch up! catch up!"

This startling announcement instantly brought every man to his feet;—and such a scene as now met the eye! How awful, and how grand! The wind, now changed and freshened, to the right and rear, was tossing the flames towards us, rapidly—lighting the heavens with their lurid glare, and transforming the darkness of night into a more than noon-day splendor!

Here was, indeed, an *"ocean of flame!"* far as the eye could reach—dancing with fiery wavelets in the wind, or rolling its burning surges, in mad fury, eager to lick up every vestige of vegetation or semblance of combustible that appeared in its way!—now shooting its glowing missiles far, far ahead, like meteors athwart the sky, or towering aloft from the weeds and tall grass, describing most hideous and fantastic forms, that, moving with the wind, more resembled a cotillion of demons among their native flames than aught terrestial!—then driving whole sheets of the raging element into the withered herbage in front, like the advance scouts

* "Lave" appears to be a corruption of the Spanish word levar, to get up, or arouse, as from sleep. It is in common use among mountaineers.

of an invading army, swept onward its desolating course, leaving in its track naught save a blackened waste of smoking ruins!

Altogether, it was a sublime spectacle, a stupendous scene, grand and imposing beyond description, and terrible in its beauty! Commingled with sensations of wonder and admiration, it tended to impress the beholder with feelings of painful melancholy. The broad expanse, but a few moments since arrayed in all the mourning grandeur of fading autumn, was now a naked desert, and every vestige of loveliness in an instant snatched from view!

How sudden, how awful, how marked the change! and yet, how magnificent in its career, though doleful its sequel!

We were speedily under way, with as much earnestness of advance as that of righteous Lot, in his escape from burning Sodom.* For a while the pursuing enemy kept even pace, and threatened to overtake us, till, headed by the strong wind, which meanwhile had changed its course, it began to slacken its speed and abate its greediness.

About sunrise we crossed the regular Pawnee trails, (leading to and from their hunting grounds, which bore the appearance of being much frequented,) and at 10 o'clock, A. M., reached the Platte river, having travelled a distance of thirty miles without halting.

The mountain road strikes the above stream at lat. 40° 41' 06" north, long. 99° 17' 47" west from Greenwich, some twenty miles below the head of Grand Island. This island is densely wooded and broad, and extends for fifty or sixty miles in length. The river banks are very sparsely timbered, a deficiency we had occasion to remark during the remainder of our journey.

The valley of the Platte at this place is six or seven miles wide, and the river itself between one and two miles from bank to bank. Its waters are very shallow, and are scattered over their broad bed in almost innumerable channels, nearly obscured by the naked sand-bars that bechequer its entire course through the grand prairie. Its peculiarity in this respect gave birth to the name of *Platte*, (shallow,) which it received from the French, and *Chartre*, (surface,) from the Mexicans,—the Indians, according to Washington Irving, calling it *Nebraska*,† a term synonymous with that of the French and Americans,—however, I am ignorant in reference to the latter.

---

* The great peril of our situation, and the pressing necessity of a hurried flight, may be readily inferred from the fact, that one waggon was freighted with a large quantity of gunpowder. None of us were quite so brave or present-minded as several Mexicans, in the employ of Messrs. Bent & St. Vrain, on an occasion somewhat similar. While journeying across the grand prairies, the powder-waggon accidentally caught fire, which was noticed immediately by the Mexican attendants, who hurriedly clasped it upon all sides, to prevent the vehicle from being blown to pieces, while one of them proceeded deliberately to extinguish the flames! Neither could we stand comparison with a lieutenant of the Mexican army, at Santa Fe, who, on opening a keg of powder, made use of a RED-HOT IRON in lieu of an auger, for that purpose. It is needless to say, a tremendous explosion followed. Several of the bystanders were killed, but the lieutenant miraculously escaped. He soon after received a Captain's commission from the Commander-in-chief, in consideration of his indomitable COURAGE!

† The Sioux have bestowed the appellation of Duck river upon the North Fork of Platte.

The bottom upon the south bank is between three and four miles broad, and of a light, deep, and rich soil, occasionally sandy, but covered with thick and lusty vegetation. Back from the valley, ranges of broken sand-hills mark the transition to the high arid prairies in the rear, where vegetation becomes more dwarfish and stinted in its growth, and is intermingled with frequent *cacti*.

These immense plains are generally clad with a short, curly grass, (the buffalo grass,) very fine and nutritious, and well adapted to the sustenance of the countless herds of buffalo and other wild animals that feed upon it. Their soil is generally of a thin vegetable mould, upon a substratum of indurated sand and gravel.

In many places it is quite sterile, producing little other than sand-burrs and a specimen of thin, coarse grass, that sadly fail to conceal its forbidding surface; in others, it is but little better than a desert waste of sand-hills, or white sun-baked clay, so hard and impervious that neither herb nor grass can take root to grow upon it; and in others, it presents a light superfice, both rich and productive, beclad with all that can beautify and adorn a wilderness of verdure.

The springs and streams of water are "few and far between,"—an evil, however, slightly atoned for by the occasional pools formed in favoring depressions during the rainy season, which are retained in their places by the extreme hardness of the soil. Were it not for these it would be almost impossible, in many directions, to travel the vast prairies lying between the Arkansas and Missouri, from long. 22° 30′ west from Washington to the Rocky Mountains. That this section of country should ever become inhabited by civilized man, to any extent, except in the vicinity of large water-courses, is an idea too preposterous to be entertained for a single moment.

As the reader is now inducted to the grand prairie as it is, it may not be amiss to say something relative to this phenomenon, before dismissing the subject in hand.

The *steppes* of Asia, the *pampas* of South America, and the *prairies* of the great West, so far as my information extends, are possessed of one general and uniform character. There is something deeply mysterious associated with them, that puzzles the philosopher and cosmogonist to explain. Why is it neither timber nor shrubs, as a general thing, are found within their confines? Why have not the same causes operated here which produced the stately forests of other regions?

The above questions are often asked, and as often answered; but never satisfactorily.

Some respond by a reference to their frequent burnings,—others to some chemical defect in their soil,—others, to the disgeniality of their climate,—others, to their infecund aridity,—and yet, others, to the supposition that some operation of nature or art has effected the destruction of quondam forests, and reduced them to their present condition.

Each of these answers, though, doubtless, partially true in many respects, fails to solve the problem before us.

Here we have, in many places, almost measureless extents of fertile soil, moist and abundantly watered, by rains, springs, and ever-flowing streams, with all the desiderata for the producing of trees,—and what withholds them? Other sections of country, under less favorable circumstances, are not wanting in this respect.

Why is it? Timber of every kind adapted to the zone and climate will grow as thriftily when planted here, as elsewhere. The frontier forests of our Western States have been observed for years past to make slow but constant encroachment upon contiguous prairies, from all sides, where, as yet, they have a foothold;—and why? Partly, because their enlargement is not circumvented by those annual burnings that formerly devoured every tender shoot daring to raise its head above ground; and, partly, through the operation of other causes, sure and gradual in their effect, which have planted the groves of other lands and taught their branches to wave in the breeze. Doubtless the same causes would produce the same results, all over these vast regions, as elsewhere.

But, why have they not?—why are the prairies timberless? Simply, because a sufficiency of time has not yet elapsed for the operation of these causes,—timber has hitherto had no possible chance for generation. The phenomenon, if rightly viewed, will thus explain itself. Geology points to the time when these vast solitudes were the bed of old Ocean and the home of waves,—but, gradually emerging or suddenly elevated from the watery abyss, they now present some of the more recent formations of dry land.

Herbage and grass, being more easily propagated than trees,—sown as are their seeds by the birds and scattered by the winds of heaven,—in a brief interval, beswathed the new-born earth with smiling green. Thus clothed with verdancy, they soon became the favorite pastures of the countless herds that thronged them. With game, appeared the red man to hunt it, and with him the yearly conflagrations that now repel the intruding woodlands and confirm the unbroken sway of solitude amid her far extending domains.

Here, then, we have spread before us the prairies as we find them,—the problem of their existence needs no further solution.

*Oct. 12th.* Still continuing up the Platte by its south bank, we made camp at night near the head of Grand Island. During our progress we saw large quantities of wild geese and cranes in the river bottoms, that presented tempting marks for our *voyageurs*. One of the latter,—a tall, raw-boned, half-crazed, and self-confident Missouri "Ned,"—good natured and inane,—sporting the familiar *soubriquet* of "Big Jim,"—wishing to prove the truth of the Dogberry axiom, that "some things may be done as well others," started to approach a large flock of sand-hill cranes, parading half obscured in a plat of grass near the road side.

The wary birds, however, caught glimpse of the approaching Nimrod and flew. Still our hero advanced, crawling upon all-fours, to within sixty or seventy yards of their recent position, when, raising up, he espyed an object which his excited imagination portrayed a crane, and promptly yielded to it the contents of his rifle.

Of course the obstinate creature remained in *statu quo.*

Re-loading with all possible speed, he again fired! But the second shot proved futile as the first.

Determined the next should count whether or no, he advanced still nearer, and had raised for his third discharge, before the naked truth burst upon his astonished vision,—he had been shooting at a bunch of dead grass! Shouldering his rifle he now rejoined the caravan, and was received by the wags who had witnessed his exploit, as follows:

"Ho, Jim! I say, Jim! Did you kill it?"

"Hang me, but it stood fire well,—didn't it?"

"Reckon you wanted a bigger charge."

"Strange you couldn't knock it cold at that distance!"

"May be your gun's out of order?"

"Yes. I'll bet a stewed crane of it. Have you noticed the "*sights*" lately?"

"Why, Jim. Really you've had *bad luck!* What, within sixty yards and not kill? I can beat that, all day!"

"Ha, ha, Jim! Shoot him grass!"

This rally was received, by our hero, in good part, who joined in the sport with as much *gusto* as though some one else were the victim.

The day, however, was not permitted to pass without another display of the prowess of "Big Jim."

A doe antelope, attracted by the strange appearance of the moving caravan, and impelled by its innate curiosity, had ventured to a tempting proximity. Mounted upon a fleet horse and supposing he could easily ride down the antelope, our hero started in pursuit.

Intently surveying the passing scene, the agile animal permitted him to advance within a few yards of her before she took the alarm. Now was a novel race. Away went antelope and away went Jim, in full chase. The former was soon far ahead, and stopped to gaze upon her pursuer.

Supposing she had become tired and was about to yield, our hero came dashing on, impetuously, under whip and spur, fully intent upon her capture. But, again, away went antelope, and away went Jim, whose steed, ambitious as its rider, and proud in its own fleetness, strained every nerve for the crisis. Even the antelope seemed to have found a champion to contest her unrivalled and universally acknowledged superiority. With distended mouth and protruding tongue, panting in the excitement of fear, and foaming in the vehemency of effort, she gained but slowly upon the bounding charger, as both swept over the prairie almost with speed of the storm-wind!

Now, again, she stops to gaze upon her pursuer. By this time all began to feel an interest in the result of the strange race. The word resounded:

"Go it, Jim! you'll beat the beater, yet!"

Once more, the antelope shoots from before both horse and rider, like the swift-winged arrow twanged from a giant's bow!

A broad ravine intercepting her course was cleared at a bound, and left the flying animal far upon the other side. At a bound the steed also cleared the barrier, but, in striking upon the opposite bank, it plunged headlong upon the yielding ground, tossing its rider far away in advance, all safely sprawling in a sand heap.

The luckless wight, on recovering, found his noble beast so sprained by the fall it could scarcely stand, and its every nerve vibrating with frightful tremors. Of course here was the *finale* of the race, as both now returned to the caravan,—the recent rider, on foot, leading his jaded steed,—

the ridden slowly limping behind,—presenting a marked contrast between the opening and closing scene.

The ill-fated horse was too much disabled for further service during the journey.

As our hero joined the company, the joke-loving wags again broke loose:

"Well, Jim. I say,—ahem! did you catch the tarnal critter?"

"Pooh! Why didn't you hold on, and not let her slide through your fingers in that way!"

"Why, man! You wasn't spry enough, when you jumped off your horse, or you might have caught her—just as easy!"

"I'd like to know what you was diving arter in that sand-bauk!—the antelope wasn't there!"

"Oh, Jim! Shoot him grass, kill horse. Me look next time he run antelope."

The passive recipient of these sallies had little peace from henceforth, and soon began to wish he had never seen an antelope or heard of a crane.

## CHAPTER V.

Deserted camp.—Big Jim's third attempt as a hunter.—Buffalo and other particulars.—Big Jim lying guard.—Butchering.—Strange selections.—Extraordinary eating, and excellence of buffalo meat.—Brady's Island.—The murderer's fate.—Substitute for wood.—A storm.—Game in camp.—Strange infatuation.—Tenacity of buffalo to life, and how to hunt them.—Cross S. Fork of Platte.—Big Jim's fourth adventure.

NEAR camp was the site recently occupied by the Pawnee village, whose occupants had evidently deserted it with the utmost precipitancy, leaving lodge-skins, mortars, bowls, pans, and a variety of other articles strown confusedly upon all sides. They had doubtless become alarmed at the approach of some real or supposed enemy, and consulted their own safety in flight.

Having started early the next day, our hunter soon brought in two fine antelope, the sight of which again raised the ambition of Big Jim, who would fain do deeds of equal wonder; and he accordingly strolled off into the hills with that intent. After shooting at several of the wary animals without success, he began to get tired of the sport, and concluding the "poverty-stricken" creatures not worth the powder and lead, set his face for the caravan.

Plodding leisurely along, he espied a prairie snake, and, o'erjoyed at the thought of counting a "*coup*," gathered his rifle by the small, and brought it down with such force, he not only killed the snake, but broke his gun-stock short off at the breech. With the pieces, one in each hand, he made his appearance before his comrades, who hailed him:

"Hallo, Jim. What's that you've killed?"

"Gun broke. Why, you must have overloaded it!"

"When'll you go hunting again?—'case I want to go too!"

"Poor Jim! Shoot grass, kill horse, break gun! Wat in de wor. does him mean!"

"Never mind, Jim. Don't be skeered at these fellows. It takes you to play the devil and *break* things!"

Towards night, several buffalo bulls having made their appearance, our hunter, mounting a horse, started for the chase, and in a brief interval, returned laden with a supply of meat. Camp had already been struck, and preparations for the new item of fare were under speedy headway.

The beef proved miserably poor; but when cooked, indifferent as it was, I imagined it the best I had ever tasted. So keen was my relish, it seemed impossible to get enough. Each of us devoured an enormous quantity for supper,—and not content with that, several forsook their beds during the night to renew the feast,—as though they had been actually starving for a month.

The greediness of the " greenhorns," was the prolific source of amusement to our *voyageurs*, who made the night-air resound with laughter at the avidity with which the unsophisticated ones " walked into the affections of the old bull," as they expressed it. " Keep on your belts till we get among cows," said they, "then let out a notch or two, and take a full meal."

It was equally amusing to me, and rather disgusting withal, to see the " old birds," as they called themselves, dispose of the only liver brought in camp. Instead of boiling, frying, or roasting it, they laid hold of it raw, and, sopping it mouthful by mouthful in *gall*, swallowed it with surprising *gusto*.

This strange proceeding was at first altogether incomprehensible, but, ere the reader shall have followed me through all my adventures in the wilds of the great West, he will find me to have obtained a full knowledge of its several merits.

The beef of the male buffalo at this season of the year, is poorer than at any other. From April till the first of June, it attains its prime, in point of excellence. In July and August, these animals prosecute their knight-errantic campaign, and, between running, fighting and gallantry, find little time to graze, finally emerging from the contested field, with hides well gored, and scarcely flesh enough upon their bones to make a decent shadow.

It is nowise marvellous, then, that our lavish appropriation of bullmeat at this time, when it is unprecedentedly tough, strong-tasted, and poor, should excite the mirth of our better-informed beholders.

The night was a cold one, and claimed for it Big Jim as second guard. When called for "relieve," with a borrowed gun, he commenced. his rounds,—but the cold soon drove him to the camp-fire.

Here, weariness and the somnific effects of a generous heat, speedily found him stretched at full length towards the fire, snoring away at a sound rate, the subject of their combined influence

The guard time had already expired, and his partner on duty, perceiving the pleasant situation of the indomitable Jim, called the next "relieve," and retired.

These paced their rounds, and the fourth guard succeeded, but still our hero occupied the same place in which he had *lain* his "tour." The sentinels were about to take their posts, as a loud sharp voice resounded through camp.

"Quit, there! What d'ye mean?"

Hastening to the spot from which the cry proceeded, who should be seen but Big Jim, in great agony, rubbing his foot with most pitiable grimace:

His slumbers had been disturbed by a falling log, of the camp-fire, which had planted its glowing weight full against one of his feet,—becrisping the sole of his shoe and severely scorching its tenant, before awakening him. Dreaming some one had hold of his foot, and started by a sudden acuteness of pain, he exclaimed as above quoted.

The sentinels laughed at his mishap, and turning to pace their rounds, drawled out:

"*What d'ye mean?* Sure enough, what d'ye mean! Shoot grass, kill horse, break gun, *lay guard*, burn shoe, and scorch foot;—all in two days and two nights! Poor devil,—why ye no born wid better luck!"

With the morning, the subject of his recent adventures called forth fresh scintillations of waggish wit,—while the unrivalled capacity of our hero, as a gormandizer, gave cue to the cuts that followed:

"Well, my head for a foot-ball, if that aint the greatest idea yet. What!—*roast foot, basted with leather,*—and his own at that! Such a meal none but Jim would ever have thought of!"

"Why, man! What put you in the notion of that dish?"

"Strange, indeed, if you can't find the wherewith to stuff your devil, without cooking your feet! Souse, to be sure! Here, you can take my hat!"

The luckless wight had now enough to engage his attention during the remainder of the journey, and began to wish he had never seen a mountain company, or left his sweet home in Missouri to cross the great prairies with such a crowd,—but all to no purpose; he was too late to retrace his steps alone.

*Oct. 13th.* Starting at early day, we travelled till about 11 o'clock, A. M., and halted for breakfast. The teams were scarcely turned to graze, when a dense band of buffalo cows made their appearance, from the back prairie, wending their way towards the river.

Expectation was on tip-toe, and all appetites doubly sharpened for an anticipated feast, as our hunter and his assistant started to intercept the witless animals at the river bank.

The two placed themselves in a chosen position and awaited the heavily moving throng, which soon advanced to within shooting distance. The sharp crack of a rifle now stopped their headway, and caused them to recoil a few paces, leaving one of their number struggling in death. Another discharge followed, and the affrighted herd were seen flying from their concealed enemy, with all the energy that innate dread of danger and death lent to their ready feet,—but not until another victim had dank the sod with the unsought libation of its heart's blood.

It pained me, as I came up, to witness the noble beasts as they lay extended upon the gore-dyed ground. But the present was no time for regret; we were to feed upon their carcasses.

The process of butchering was a new developement of that most useful science. The carcase was first turned upon the belly, and braced to a position by its distended legs. The operator then commenced his labors by gathering the long hair of the "*boss*," and severing a piece obliquely at the junction of the neck and shoulders,—then parting the hide from neck to rump, a few passes of his ready knife laid bare the sides,—next paring away the loose skin and preparing a hold, with one hand he pulled the shoulder towards him and with the other severed it from the body;—cutting aslant the uprights of the *spina dorsi* and "hump ribs," along the lateral to the curve, and parting the "fleece" from the tough flesh at that point he deposited it upon a clean grass-spot.

The same process being described upon the opposite side, the carcase was then slightly inclined, and, by aid of the leg-bone bisected at the knee-joint, the "hump-ribs" were parted from the vertebræ; after which, passing his knife aside the ninth rib and around the ends at the midriff, he laid hold of the dissevered side, and, with two or three well directed jerks, removed it to be laid upon his choicely assorted pile; a few other brief minutiæ then completed the task.

Meanwhile, divers of the company had joined the butcher, and, while some were greedily feeding upon liver and gall, others helped themselves to marrow-bones, "*boudins*," and *intestinum medulæ*, (choice selections with mountaineers,) and others, laden with rich spoils, hastened their return to commence the more agreeable task of cooking and eating.

The remaining animal was butchered in a trice, and select portions of each were then placed upon a pack-horse and conveyed to the waggons.

The assortment was, indeed, a splendid one. The "dépouille" (fleece-fat) was full two inches thick upon the animal's back, and the other dainties were enough to charm the eyes and excite the voracity of an epicure.

The camp-fires soon presented a busy and amusing spectacle. Each one was ornamented with delicious roasts, *en appolas*, on sticks planted aslope around it, attentively watched by the longing *voyageurs*, who awaited the slow process of cooking. Some were seen with thin slices from the larder, barely heated through by the agency of a few coals, retreating from the admiring throng to enjoy *solo* their half-cooked morsels,—others, paring off bit by bit from the fresh-turned hissing roasts, while their opposite received the finishing operation of the fire,—and others, tossing their everted *boudins* into the flames, and in a few seconds withdrawing for the repast, each seizing his ample share, bemouthed the end in quick succession to sever the chosen esculent, which, while yielding to the eager teeth, coursed miniature rivulets of oily exuberance from the extremities of the active orifice, bedaubing both face and chin, and leaving its delighted eater in all the *glories of grease!*

Every man had now become his own cook, and, not to be backward, I closed in with the overture.

Seizing a frying-pan replete with tempting levies from the "fleece," I

BUFFALO HUNT.—Page 64.

twice subjected it to its duty, and as often its delicious contents found ample store-house; and even yet my longing appetite seemed loth to cry "hold, enough!"

The agreeable odor exhaled from the drippings of the frying flesh, contained in the pan, invited the taste,—a temptation claiming me for its subject. Catching up the vessel, a testing sip made way for the whole of its contents, at a single draught,—full six gills! Strange as it may seem, I did not experience the least unpleasant feeling as the result of my extraordinary potation.

The stomach never rebels against buffalo-fat. Persons, subsisting entirely upon the flesh of these animals, prefer an assortment of at least one third solid dépouille.

The *voyageur* is never more satisfied than when he has a good supply of buffalo-beef at his command. It is then his greasy visage bespeaks content, and his jocund voice and merry laugh evince the deep-felt pleasure and gratification that reign within.

Talk not to him of the delicacies of civilized life,—of pies, puddings, soups, fricasees, roast-beef, pound-cake, and desert,—he cares for none of these things, and will laugh at your *verdancy!*

He knows his own preference, and will tell you your boasted excellencies are not to be compared with it. If you object to the sameness of his simple fare, he will recount the several varieties of its parts, and descant upon each of their peculiar merits. He will illustrate the numerous and dissimilar modes of so preparing them, that they cannot fail to excite by their presence and appease by their taste the appetite of the most fastidious. And then, in point of *health,* there is nothing equal to buffalo-meat. It, alone, will cure dyspepsy, prevent consumption, amend a broken constitution, put flesh upon the bones of a *skeleton,* and *restore a dead man again to life!*—if you will give credence to one half of the manifold virtues he carefully names in your hearing.

*Oct. 14th.* We were early *en route,* and made some twenty miles. Our hunter, during the day, rejoined the caravan, laden with the best portions of three other fat cows, to add to the fund of life and good humor enjoyed by each.

Late in the afternoon, we made camp opposite a heavily wooded island, called Brady's Island, in memory of a man, so named, who was murdered upon it by his companion some eight years ago.

The two were connected with a boat, laden with furs, on its passage to the States. They had frequently quarrelled, and were generally upon otherwise bad terms. On the day of the fatal occurrence, they were left alone in camp by the rest of the boat's crew, who went in quest of buffalo. At their return, Brady was found lying in his blood,—killed, as his companion affirmed, by the accidental discharge of his own rifle.

The tale was received quite doubtingly, and its listeners were only deterred from the execution of summary vengeance upon the murderer by thought of the bare possibility of its truth.

The body of the unfortunate man was buried near the spot,—but being subsequently disinterred by the wolves, his bones were left to bleach and moulder in the sun and rains of heaven. Some of them were lying scattered near by, upon our arrival, which were collected by the sympathizing *voyageurs*, who bestowed upon them those rites of sepulture they had been so long and cruelly denied.

The reader will naturally enquire, what became of the supposed murderer? His was a fearful retribution,—a mournful tale of suffering, worse than death, till death itself in pity came to his relief.

Soon after the melancholy incident previously related, the shallowness of the Platte river compelled the company to abandon their boat, and make the best of their way to the States on foot,—a distance of two hundred and fifty miles to the nearest inhabitants, either Indian or white.

Their provisions running short, and no game at hand, a separation was had about midway of their journey, and each one hurried to its termination as rapidly as possible. The murderer, being but an indifferent walker, was soon left far in the rear.

His comrades, on their arrival at the Pawnee village, sent two Indians to bring him in, and continued their course to Council Bluffs.

Nothing further was known of the subject of our sketch, till some eight or nine days subsequent, when a small party of engagés in the employ of the American Fur Company, on passing the Pawnee village, were met by the head-chief, who requested them to visit a white man lying sick at his lodge.

They went. He was the murderer, at the point of death. His story was briefly told.

The night succeeding the departure of his companions, in an attempt to light a fire with his pistol, to disperse by its smoke the myriads of musquetoes that swarmed around and nearly devoured him, an unknown charge it contained was lodged in his thigh-bone—severing it to a thousand pieces. In this condition he lay helpless. To walk was impossible;—he could scarcely move, far less dress his wounds in a proper manner. He managed, however, to affix a piece of red flannel to an upright stick, to tell the transient traveller the site of his supposed last resting place, then, crawling with difficulty to the river-side, he remained six days and nights—tormented by musquitoes, reduced by pain, and wasted by continued hunger, till scarcely the wreck of manhood was left him.

It was then he longed for death to terminate his agony. Still he could not endure the thoughts of dying.

Early in the morning of the seventh day, his ear caught the indistinct murmur of sounds. Were they human voices?—No, he must be dreaming. He hears them again. It is no dream;—they are human voices! They approach. Is it to his assistance?

O'erjoyed he beholds two Pawnees bending over him, with compassion pictured expressively upon their countenances. They gave him meat,—they dressed his wounds, and did everything in their power to alleviate his misery.

Oh, say not there is no pity in the bosom of the red man!

Having constructed a rude litter of poles, and using their own robes for his bed, they carefully conveyed him upon their shoulders to the place he yet occupied.

But the care of sympathizing attendants failed to atone for previous neg lect. Mortification had already taken place, and death claimed him for a victim. He expired in the presence of those whom the good chief had called to his bed-side;—but, before his tongue refused to speak, he confessed the *murder of Brady*, and owned the justice of his punishment in all the untold miseries he had been compelled to endure.

"Vengeance is *mine*, and I will REPAY IT, saith the Lord!"

On resuming our journey the road gradually bore towards the hills upon the left, (which presented an outline of conical eminences, rising, as the traveller advances, to an elevation of four or five hundred feet,) and finally crossed them at the point of an angle formed near the confluence of the two great forks of the Platte, upon the east side; from thence, descending to the opposite bottom, we reached a timberless spring and made camp soon after nightfall.

The lack of wood at this place was readily met by the great abundance of *bois de vache*, (buffalo-chips,) the common substitute of the prairies; and, in a brief interval, the camp-fires were merrily blazing, with all the appliances of cookery about them.

Early the next morning, our hunter rejoined the caravan, bringing with him the spoils of two more cows. He had passed the night upon the prairie alone, without coat or blanket, or anything to screen him from the bleak autumn winds, that swept over the naked plains, dancing their dirges to the dying year.

The sky gave evidence of an approaching storm, and we hastily started in quest of some more sheltered spot in which to weather it. A few miles brought us to the river, and, availing ourselves of a small supply of drift wood, we made halt.

The combustibles the vicinity afforded were soon collected, and the camp-fires imparted their generous warmth despite the falling rain. Nor were they permitted to remain long unembellished by the numerous kettles, frying-pans, and roasting-sticks at command.

I here enjoyed full test of some of the many varieties of mountain fare hitherto so freely enlarged upon by our *voyageurs*,—which, as they now asserted, would make a man "shed rain like an otter, and stand cold like a polar bear!"—quaintly adding, "if he could always *live* upon such 'didins,' he need *never die!*"

I must in justice confess that the real merits of our present "bill of fare," by far exceeded my previous expectations.

The rain continued till near night; but little did we care. The choicest the prairie afforded, was now before us, and, rain or shine, we were contented. Sound in health and buoyant in spirits, we fully enjoyed ourselves, despite the frowning elements.

A little before sundown, the rain subsided into a thick fog, and an old bull, in the consequent obscurity, straggled close upon camp.

The abrupt passage of a rifle-ball through his lights, was his first *feeling* sense of the presence of danger. The affrighted customer then retreated a few steps, and, falling, surrendered himself to the resistless power of cold lead.

A large band of cows also made their appearance, in the same manner, and our hunter struck out to waylay them.

Permitting the unwitting animals to advance within good shooting distance, a discharge from his rifle brought down one of their number. The band then recoiled slightly; but, snuffing the odor of blood, they returned immediately to their prostrate companion.

This was enough,—a charm now riveted them to the spot,—a strange infatuation had seized upon them. They began by spurning the ground with their feet,—then, bellowing, gored the fallen beast, as if forcing her to rise,—then, rolling upon the grass, in demonstrative sympathy,—and, now that she had ceased to struggle and lay yet quivering in death, they licked her bleeding wounds and seemed to exercise a kind of mournful rivalry in the bestowment of their testimonials of affection.

She is encircled by her companions. An effort to approach from without is resisted by those within. A fight ensues, and all becomes confusion. Each turns against her neighbor, and continues the strife till the space around the carcase is again vacated; whereupon a general rush once more centers to the spot, and all unite to react the former scene.

In this manner they persisted in their frenzied devotion to the fallen one, as if determined to restore her to life and action, or perish by her side.

Meanwhile the hunter's rifle had been busily employed. But they heeded it not. Four more of their number lay gasping in death upon the ensanguined ground; and still they seemed no more disposed to leave the scene of slaughter than at first. Sixteen successive shots were fired, each bearing blood, wounds and death, and yet the spell was no nearer broken.

It was a spectacle vested with melancholy animation. The pawing, goring, bellowing, licking of wounds, and struggles of rival affection, remained the same, with no visible abatement of their vehemency.

The sun had set, and the sable hue of twilight empalled the blood-dank slaughter-ground. The death-dealing rifle had ceased its sharp crack, and the gore-scenting wolves, half starved and eager for their supposed prey, came flocking upon every side, mingling their wobegone howlings with the piteous moans of the spell-bound herd, and the loud whistlings of the prairie winds,—and yet, they lingered.

At last the impatient hunter advanced. More affrighted at the presence of man than the companionship of death, they now gave way, and reluctantly left the field to him, who had so unfeelingly occasioned their burthen of mourning and woe;—still, ever and anon stopping to gaze, as if longing to return and die with those they loved!

All hands were now summoned to aid at the work of butchery; but the fast-enshrouding darkness soon drove us back to camp, leaving the task not half completed.

Our withdrawal from the premises was the signal for possession by the eager wolves, whose ceaseless yelpings the livelong night, made the gloomy interval doubly dismal. By morning, nothing but bones and thick pieces of skin marked the scene of their recent revellings!

Thus early, I had learned, that to approach buffalo with success, the hunter should carefully maintain the leeward, such being their remarkable sensitiveness, they will sooner flee from the smell than the sight of a man. Their sense of smell, with the wind, in fact, far exceeds their scope of vision. It is so extremely acute, that even the fresh footsteps of a man. crossing their path, are to them a sure cause of alarm and flight.

Of all the diversities of game indigenous to the mountains and prairies of the great West, with the exception, perhaps, of the grizzly bear, no animal is more tenacious of life than the buffalo. To shoot it in the head, is an inane effort. No rifle can project a ball with sufficient force to perforate the thick hair and hide to its brain, through the double scull-bone that protects it. A paunch shot is equally vain. The only sure points for the marksman are, the heart, lights, kidneys, or vertebræ; and even then the unyielding victim not unfrequently escapes.

Buffalo, wounded in the skirts of the lights, have been known to live for several days afterwards. I have witnessed their escape, even after the reception of fifteen bullet-wounds, and most of them at such points as would have proved fatal to almost any other animal.

In the summer of '43, I myself killed one of them, that had been shot through the pussy surface at the *butt of the heart*, apparently four or five days previous, which doubtless would have recovered had it remained unmolested.

A gun, suitable for killing this kind of game, should never carry to exceed forty bal's to the pound—a lesser bore would be almost entirely useless. The distance generally required for a shot, the smallness of the ball, its liability to variation from the wind, with its failure to "hold up" and retain its force, contribute to render the use of such a piece little else than idle waste of ammunition.

*Oct. 17th.* The sun arose bright and clear, and with its first appearance the caravan was in motion. Proceeding up the South Fork some ten miles we halted for breakfast, and made arrangements for fording the stream.

Near us lay the carcase of one of the cows wounded on the previous evening, and as yet scarcely dead. She had travelled thus far after being shot in the lights.

Our crossing was effected with little difficulty, but occupied till late in the afternoon. The river was full a mile wide and very shallow, with a soft sandy bed, requiring the strength of all the united teams to each waggon. The day proved cold, and the water was like an application of ice to the naked skin. Our teamsters, who were compelled to cross and recross, some dozen times, felt in not the best humor, and were better pleased than any one else at the termination of their unpleasant task.

Having safely gained the opposite bank, we travelled up the river five or six miles, and halted for the night.

During our course the bottoms upon either side presented one dense, interminable band of buffalo, far as the eye could reach. The whole prairie pictured a living mass, moved by impulsive dread, as the breeze heralded our approach, and the countless multitude made way before and on either hand.

Ever and anon, an old bull would linger, as if to intimidate, and not unfrequently venture within gun-shot. One fellow, in particular, passed sidelong, for a mile or more, stopping at intervals to gaze upon us, shaking his shaggy head in defiance, as much as to say, "you dare not come near!"

Big Jim saw this, and his pride was wounded. The bull, in his opinion, had challenged the whole party, and there was no one stout-hearted enough to accept it.

Here was a chance for a full display of his bravery and skill. Ever since we had reached the buffalo range, his proud spirit had yearned to become the death of some one of these terrible monsters, that he might relate the deed of perilous exploit to wondering posterity, and incite the rising generation to emulate his noble achievement.

But, alas, for the fadeless laurels he might otherwise have won, in an evil hour his rifle had been sacrificed for the extermination of a huge, venomous serpent. He did the deed at one fell blow;—brave, but unfortunate! Yet he had one consolation amid his troubles,—no victory is ever gained without some loss to the conquerors.

Still, he needed his gun, for without it how was he to avenge the foul insult the savage beast of the prairie was even now hurling in the very face of the shrinking crowd? Something must be done.

With these cogitations, an idea struck him,—he could borrow a rifle; so, advancing to a comrade, he exclaimed:

"Do lend me your rifle, one minute!"

"Yes, Jim," was the ready reply. "But see you don't break it over the first paltry little snake you come across!"

"That's a lie. 'Twas a big rattle-snake I broke mine over. 'Twasn't a paltry little snake!"

Thus, vindicating his assaulted reputation, he took the gun and hastened to prostrate the impudent barbarian inviting attack.

Jim looked at the bull, and the bull looked at Jim,—shaking his head, and throwing the loose sand from beneath him high into the air with his feet, and goring the ground with his horns of burnished ebony. If the creature had looked terrible before, he now looked fourfold more so, in Jim's estimation.

Thinking caution the parent of safety, our hero was unwilling to venture further, and so, prostrating himself at full length behind a clustre of *absinthe*, (sage,) he planted his battery, having his high-crowned hat for a rest, and blazed away at the bull's head.

The hardened wretch stood the shot without flinching. Looking for a moment at the spot from whence the strange salute had proceeded, and again shaking his head and snorting with scorn, he wheeled and slowly trotted off.

Eager to get a second trial to finish the work so nobly begun, our hero commenced pursuit. Seeing him advancing, the bull thought it time to show his heels, and in a few minutes was lost in the distance.

The courageous Nimrod now, for the first time, bethought him of his hat, which, in the ardor of his bold charge, he had left at the spot chosen as his stand to hurl death and destruction to the naughty bull. He hastened to regain it—but no hat could be found;—the winds had borne it far away over the prairie, to be worne out in search of a wearer, and the unlucky *bravo*, hatless, rejoined the caravan.

Here the truth at once flashed upon the minds of the waggish clique, that had hitherto proved his sore annoyance, and they began anew:

"Now that beats me, clear out! How came you to give the bull your hat and leave yourself bare-headed? That's another wrinkle!"

"It's no such thing," said Jim. "The wind took it away;—and it's none of your business neither. *I paid for it!*"

"True. But what did the wind want with your hat? Sure, if it needed a foot-ball, to toss over the prairies, it would have taken your head, the *lightest* of the two!"

"You're a fool!" retorted Jim, indignantly.

"There, now. That's the time you cotcht it, my boy. Why, fellow, Mr. Jeems took off his hat, out of pure *politeness,*—to win the good opinion of the bull. He were right. Didn't you see how the gentleman-cow *bowed* and *scraped* in turn. Why, *he throw'd the dirt clean over his back*, not to be outdone in good breeding! Ah, but the pesky wind! While Mr. Jeems were showing his brotten up, what had it to do, but to snatch his hat and *run off with it!* Mr. Jeems are no fool! and the feller what says he am,—(I want you all to understand me; Mr. Jeems have been most shamefully abused and misused, and I can whip the chaps what's done it—provided they'll let me;—I say, then, I want you all to understand me!) Mr. Jeems *are* no fool, and the man what says he am—is,—(I can't think of words bad enough,)—is—is, as *near the mark* as though he'd drove *centre!*"

"Aye. Jim's right. You are all a pack of dough-heads to make fun of him in the way you do. Suppose you'd be struck *comical!* Then what'd ye think of yourselves!"

"Poor Jim. Shoot grass, kill horse, break gun, burn shoe, scorch foot, and go bare-headed! Wat him mean?"

"I say, Jim. When 're going a hunting again?—'case I want to go 'long too!"

## CHAPTER VI.

Ash Creek.—Pawnee and Sioux battle-ground.—Bread-root.—The Eagle's Nest.—Mad wolf.—Number and variety of prairie wolves,—their sagacity.—Mad bull.—Making and curing meat.—Big Jim still unfortunate.—Johnson's creek.—McFarlan's Castle.—Deceptiveness of distances.—Express from the Fort.—Brave Bear.—Bull Tail.—Talk with the Indians.—Speech of Marto-cogershne.—Reply.—Tahtungah-sana's address.

*Oct 18th.* BEARING to the right, over a high undulating prairie, we struck the North Fork of the Platte, after a drive of about twelve miles, and continuing up its left bank a short distance, camped for the night at the mouth of Ash Creek.

The stream at this place is a broad bed of sand, entirely dry, except in the spring months. Higher up, however, it affords a generous supply of pure running water, sustained by the numerous feeders that force their way into it, from the high grounds dividing the two rivers.

The valley is of variable width, and well timbered with beautiful ash groves, from which the creek derives its name. Here are also found several varieties of wild fruit indigenous to the mountains. As a whole, it presents to the eye a pretty flower-garden, walled in by huge piles of argillaceous rock, and watered by murmuring streamlets whose banks are ornamented with shade trees and shubbery.

Near camp had been the scene of a fierce and bloody battle between the Pawnees and Sioux, in the winter of 1835. The affray commenced early in the morning, and continued till near night. A trader, who was present with the Sioux, on the occasion, describes it as having been remarkably close. Every inch of ground was disputed—now the Pawnees advancing upon the retreating Sioux; and now the Sioux, while the Pawnees gave way; but, returning to the charge with redoubled fury, the former once more recoiled. The arrows flew in full showers,—the bullets whistled the death-song of many a warrior,—the yells of combating savages filled the air, and drowned the lesser din of arms.

At length arrows and balls were exhausted upon both sides,—but still the battle raged fiercer than before.

War-club, tomahawk and butcher-knife were bandied with terrific force, as the hostile parties engaged hand to hand, and the clash of resounding blows, commingling with the clamor of unearthly voices which rent the very heavens, seemed more to prefigure the contest of fiends than aught else.

Finally the Pawnees abandoned the field to their victorious enemies, leaving sixty of their warriors upon the ensanguined battle-ground. But the Sioux had paid dearly for their advantage;—forty-five of their bravest men lay mingled with the slain. The defeated party were pursued only a short distance, and then permitted to return without further molestation to their village, at the Forks of the Platte.

This disaster so completely disheartened the Pawness, they immediately abandoned their station and moved down the river some four hundred miles,—nor have they again ventured so high up, unless in strong war-parties.

About the same time the village on Republican fork of Kansas was also abandoned, and its inhabitants united with the Loups.

The evidences of this cruel death-harvest were yet scattered over the prairie, whose bones and sculls looked sad, indeed. One of the latter was noticed, near camp, with a huge wasp's nest occupying the vacuum once filled by the subtle organs of intellect. Strange tenant, truly, of a human scull,—but, perhaps, not an unfit antitype of the fierce passions that whilom claimed it as their dwelling place.

A specimen of the bread-root, (*psoralea esculenta*,) was procured from the creek-bank by one of the *voyageurs*. This is very common in the vicinity of the mountains, and attains a size from twenty to thirty inches in circumference. It is taprooted, and generally prefers the rich sandy soil of bottoms and ravines,—not unfrequently penetrating to the depth of five or six feet. In shape, it is much like the common beet. Its exterior is covered with a thick ligument of tough fibres, curiously interwoven, enveloping a white pulpy substance, which is very sweet and pleasantly tasted.

The day following we proceeded some twenty miles, and camped at a place called the Eagle's Nest.

THE WAR EAGLE. — *Page* 79.

A few scattering trees at the right of the bottom, here mark the transition to the high prairie. One of these was the war-eagle's eyry, upon which she rears her annual brood, and teaches it to soar far away, or levy tribute from the surrounding wilderness.

The proud bird of Jove was yet sailing aloft, in silent majesty, almost lost to vision in the long space of intervening blue that told the grandeur of her flight; and, tinged with the purple and gold of the setting sun, she seemed looking down with a jealous eye upon the unwonted invaders of he earthly home. A few light clouds, garnished with day's departing glory danced athwart the western sky, as the full moon arose, hastening to re-enter her nightly pathway, and course amid the array of glittering worlds, and smile upon the wide realms of Solitude;—while countless herds of grazing buffalo covered the prairies on either side of the broad and silent river; and naught met the listening ear, save the dolesome hooting of the midnight owl, as she resumed her nocturnal ditty, to enhance the deep melancholy of loneliness; or the shrill whistlings of the prairie-winds, as they sported in mirth and chanted their requiems to the dying year; or the terrific bellowings of the hoarse-toned bison, the softening cadence of whose voices sounded trebly mournful as it swept far along and became lost in the distance; or yet, the dismal howlings of the half-starved wolves, that gathered by scores upon every hill-top and renewed, in more piteous accents, their ceaseless concert;—all these united to invest the scene, so magnificent in itself, with a savage wildness, at once incitive of terror and admiration.

In our progress during the day I remarked, at frequent intervals, bare places coated with saline efflorescences, and occasional plats of fine bluish grass, (herba salée,)—appearances quite common from this onward.

Our night slumbers were disturbed by the quick discharge of firearms, which instantly brought every man to his feet, rifle in hand. The cause of this alarm was the appearance of a mad wolf among the caravan animals, and several shots were fired before the guard could despatch him. He proved one of the largest of his species, and looked fearful as his blood-red eyeballs and foaming mouth were exposed by the camp-fire.

In the morning it was ascertained he had bitten nine head of horses and cattle.

The buffalo range affords every variety of wolves, common to the mountains and regions still further west. Of these there are five distinct classifications, viz: The big white, or buffalo wolf; the shaggy brown; the black; the gray, or prairie wolf; and the cayeute, (wa-chunka-monet,) or medicine-wolf of the Indians.

The white and brown wolves are the most numerous, and follow the buffalo in bands of hundreds, subsisting upon the carcases of such as die of themselves or are slaughtered as their necessities demand.

These wolves behave with great sagacity in their predatory operations, and appear to exercise a perfect understanding and concert of action with each other on such occasions. First, stationing themselves by files at given distances along the course their intended victim is expected to run, two or more of them enter the herd of unconscious buffalo, and, singling out the fattest one, drive it to the track at which their companions await to take part in the grand race. This done, the victim is made to run the gauntlet between two rows of wolves. As it advances, others join their fresh numbers to the chase, till at length, tired down and exhausted in strength, the ill-fated animal falls ready prey to their greediness. The poor creature is first hamstrung to prevent its escape, and then literally devoured alive!

The black wolf is seldom met with in these parts. It nearly equals the white and brown in size, and is fully as large as the common cur-dog.

The prairie wolf is not more than half the size of the above mentioned, and much less ferocious. Its color is of a dark gray, and its fur quite soft and fine.

The cayeute or medicine-wolf compares with the common feist, and is of a grayish color, much like that of the wild rabbit of the States. Its fur is fine and thick, and might be turned to good account for the manufacture of caps, muffs, &c.

The Indians cherish many superstitious notions in regard to this animal, and hold it in great veneration. They consider it as the messenger employed by the Great Spirit, on special occasions, to herald the approach of events interesting to the welfare of his red children, and for that reason they are never known to harm or molest it.

Just at daylight, a large band of buffalo crossed the river nearly opposite to camp. It was headed by an old bull, that led the way, grunting and bellowing as he advanced, as if in mock personation of the bugieman of a corps of cavalry. Some three or four hundred cows and calves followed, side by side, with marked and regular tread, like platoons of infantry marching in set step to music, presenting a truly comical exhibition.

A *voyageur* seized his rifle and saluted with its contents the music-master and captain-general of the advancing army, as he was about to ascend the river bank. In an instant the whole detachment to "right about face," and retreat precipitately to the rearward shore, with no other music than the clatter of hoofs and the splashing of water, or order than the confused rivalry for speedy escape from the unexpected presence of danger.

*Oct. 20th.* Resuming our course, during the forenoon, the strange deportment of a buffalo bull near the trail arrested attention.

He was running in a circle, at the height of his speed, and narrowing its sphere at each gyration. Several of us rode out to him,—but he still, continued, (with frothing mouth and protruding tongue, swollen to the utmost distention of his jaws, rolling eye-balls, like globes of clotted gore; and bellowing for pain,) following the fast-decreasing limits of his strange course, regardless of our presence.

He soon commenced whirling round and round, with faltering, half stumbling steps, and finally fell prostrate before us, apparently in the last paroxysm of mortal agony. In vain he struggled to rise, while his tongue lied from between his jaws, chafed in fruitless effort to close them, and his head, keeping time with the convulsive throes of his fast-waning strength, tore up the prairie-sod and lashed the ground in the mad fury of effort.

The spectacle was one of the most striking exhibitions of excruciating pain I ever witnessed. Even the rough mountaineers were excited to pity, and gladly alleviated his miseries by hastening his end. A friendly bullet put a period to his sufferings, and placed him far beyond the reach of summer's heat and winter's cold, mad wolves and all the inexpressible horrors of hydrophobia.

At our noon encampment we commenced the process of "making meat," preparatory to passing a long distance devoid of game; and, as the reader may be anxious to know what kind of an operation this is, I will explain. It consists simply in cutting into thin slices the boneless parts of buffalo, or other meat, and drying them in the wind or sun. Meat thus cured may be preserved for years without salt. Ropes of raw hide were stretched around the waggons, upon which the results of our labor were left to the finishing effects of the wind and sun as we proceeded,—thus making an important saving in the item of time.

It is astonishing how long a time fresh meat may be kept without injury, upon the grand prairies, in dry weather, when it receives the free access of air. Some of that killed on our first arrival among buffalo was yet hanging to the waggons, as sweet and sound as ever. I have known it to be preserved, in this way, for ten or twelve days in the heart of summer. Meat, packed in snow, while in a frozen state, may be retained fresh for months without injury. I have known an instance of its being thus kept from January till June. The air is so pure and dry, it requires but little effort to preserve meat, for any requisite length of time, almost at any season of the year.

Our hunter, having proceeded in advance of the waggons during the afternoon, was overtaken about sundown at a place selected for night-camp, which he had ornamented with the carcases of three cows,—and there again, was soon witnessed another display of rare feasting, such as mountaineers alone know how to appreciate and enjoy.

The night proved cold and uncomfortable, and the bright-glowing camp fires presented most captivating inducements to the shivering sentinels, as they paced their dreary rounds, to step within its cheering influence. Big Jim, who was on the third "relieve," thought it too bad he should be compelled to suffer so much from cold, while a nice warm fire was permitted to waste its kind heat upon the bleak air of night, without so much as one to enjoy its beneficence.

No, it would not do. "Why mayn't I just as well stand guard at the fire, as elsewhere? I can, I'm sure. I'll *stand* this time, and not *lay* as I did before, and then there'll be no danger of falling asleep and burning one's self; nor'll they have the chance to twit me about lying guard and burning shins. I'll head 'em this time, and they wont know the difference."

So saying, he approached the fire, and, giving it a kick, extended his hands towards its blaze,—ever and anon rubbing them together and then again spreading them to receive its pleasing warmth; then turning his back to partake alike of its comforting influences and obviate the jealousy that might otherwise be engendered between front and rear.

Now, he stands attent,—he hears something move. He stretches himself to his full height, on tip-toe, and gazes in the black envelope of surrounding night, made doubly obscure in contrast with the refulgence of the camp-fire.

"How dark it has grown!" said Jim. "What can it be? Wonder if it's Indians. Pooh! it's nothing but the wind. Bless me, I can't see the use of a poor devil's standing guard on such a dark night as this! (stepping backward still nearer the fire,) he can't see nothing, if he does. Feugh,—what is it smells so? (turning round.) Good gracious, how hot my back is!"

The mystery of Jim's present predicament is easily explained. The skirts of his jeans coat, having come in contact with the wind-tossed flames, caught fire, and were burned to the shoulders before he was aware of the accident. The garment was rendered entirely useless, and even his pantaloons were burnt to his skin, in several places.

Jim began to think it as bad to *stand* as to *lay* guard, and concluded that, of the two, fire was more dangerous than Indians;—for, one thing was certain, the Indians had never yet injured him, but he could not say as much of *fire!*

In the morning, as may be supposed, our hero's last mishap was the prolific subject of comment, and the wags were promptly on the alert to amuse themselves still further at his expense:

"Say, would you believe it!—That's the way Jim's hit upon to *shine* in this crowd,—he burns up his old coat to make a *light!*"

"Ah, ha! So he means to shine by the light of his old clothes, and come it over us in an underhand manner! Jim, that 'll never do;—I tell you, once for all."

"Wonder if he wont burn up himself next?"

"He? No. He's too *green* and *sappy* to burn himself, and so he takes his old clothes!"

"Poor Jim. Shoot grass, kill horse, break gun, burn shoe, scorch foot, lose hat, stick coat in him fire! Poor fellow. No can do without Jim, no how."

The third day succeeding the last mentioned adventure, we passed a stream, called by the traders Johnson's creek, in memory of a man by that name who was murdered in its vicinity, several years since, by the Indians.

He was a missionary, and on his way to Oregon, with a party headed by one John Gray. As they were about to raise camp, one morning, a band of Yanktau-Sioux came charging over the hills, and preparations were made to resist them. Such a course Mr. Johnson felt scrupulous of acceding to, and stoutly protested against it,—affirming it to be wrong.

As the savages approached, the ill-fated man stepped forward to meet them unarmed, despite the remonstrances of his comrades,—imagining the Indians would not kill him, as he was a missionary and had came to do them good.

They, however, proved regardless of him or his intended good, and he fell the victim of his own foolish credulity. Three Indians fell in the conflict that ensued, and he and they filled the same grave.

*Oct. 24th.* About noon we crossed Gonneville's creek, a large easterly affluent of the Platte. This stream also derives its name from a trapper, killed near it in an Indian fight, some eight years since.

Upon the south bank of Gonneville's creek, ten or twelve miles from the river, is a singular natural formation, known as the Court House, or McFarlan's Castle, on account of its fancied resemblance to such a structure. It rises in an abrupt quadrangular form, to a height of three or four hundred feet, and covers an area of two hundred yards in length by one hundred and fifty broad. Occupying a perfectly level site in an open prairie, it stands as the proud palace of Solitude, amid her boundless domains.

Its position commands a view of the country for forty miles around, and meets the eye of the traveller for several successive days, in journeying up the Platte. We have been in sight of it for three days, and even now seem no nearer than at first, notwithstanding our course, meanwhile, has borne not far from a direct line towards it.

Here, for the first time, I remarked the deceptiveness of distances, on the high prairies and in regions adjacent to the mountains. Sometimes an object will appear as if within a mile, at most, which cannot be reached short of fifteen or twenty miles; then, again, objects will seem to be much further off than they really are.

I attribute this, in part, to three several causes:—First, the variable state of the atmosphere, in regard to density. Second, the absence or plenitude of humid exhalations and effluviæ in the air of different regions. Third, the peculiar locality of some places in regard to the reception of the sun's rays.

In passing from Gonneville's creek to Fort Platte, we encountered no more buffalo,—these animals having been driven back into the high prairies by bands of strolling Indians.

If the prospect had hitherto been lonesome, it now seemed threefold lonely. The hard-beaten footpaths that had furrowed the bottoms and plains, in all directions, ever since our first entrance to the buffalo range, were still seen; but, unhonored by the presence and unmarked by the footprints of their whilom travellers, they looked like the once oft-trodden streets of some deserted city.

Late in the afternoon we were joined by two engagés from Fort Platte, whose object it was to hasten our advance. Soon after, we entered upon a stretch of burnt prairie, and were compelled to travel till daylight the next morning, before a sufficiency of grass could be found for a camping place.

*Oct. 25th.* Resuming our course about midday, we had proceeded only a few miles, when a mounted Indian appeared upon the opposite bank of the river, and accosted us:

"Chay, cullo!—Hanno chaum-pa-monet ha Mena-huska tour?" (Tell me, friend!—Are those the Long-knife's[*] waggons?)

---

[*] This term seems to call for a word of explanation. Our company was designated by the Indians as the Long-knife, or American company,—a term by which all

On being answered in the affirmative, he commenced crossing to join us.

Plunging into the river with his horse, he had proceeded about midway of the stream, when the panting beast suddenly sank into the quicksand, throwing its rider head foremost into the water. At length, having effected a ford, he hurried up to us, profusely dripping with wet as evidence of the thoroughness of his recent drenching.

First shaking hands with the company, he began to inquire about liquor, affirming the waggons contained that article, and adding, it was "right the Long-knife should bring the fire-water to *give* to the red man," as did the Bad-medicine,—but it was wrong to sell it. For his part he would not buy the fire-water. He would buy blankets, knives, beads, and ammunition,—not the fire-water; but the Long-knife should give it to him.

The personage thus introduced was one of the chiefs of the Brulé-Sioux, and sported the name of Marto-cogershne, or Brave Bear. He was a turbulent fellow, that proved the pest of his village traders. Slim and spare-made in person, he was somewhat pale and sickly looking, and seemed about thirty years of age. His arms were a short fusee, with a bow and arrows slung to his shoulders, and a butcher-knife affixed to his belt. His hair was long, parted in front, and turned backwards; that upon the occiput, being bound in a cluster with panther's skin, hung in a plated cue and almost trailed the ground, while a lone eagle's plume completed his head-dress. A robe enveloped his body, which, with moccasins, leggins, and breech-cloth, constituted his full costume,—a description of dress responding to that almost universally common among mountain tribes.

We were soon joined by others of his people, who eagerly enquired respecting the amount of liquor brought with us.

Among these were several individuals recognized by our *voyageurs* as old acquaintances; particularly one, an old chief called Bull Tail, (Tah-tunga-sana,) who was distinguished in attire from all his fellows by the addition of a hair-seal cap and a frock-coat, which he had received as presents from the whites.

One of our party gave a favorable account of the old fellow, and related a story much to his credit.

The narrator, during the previous winter, while searching for stray horses among the hills, had become so bewildered he was unable to find his way back to camp. He thus wandered for four successive days, unarmed, without food, and with but a single robe for covering. His destiny would, doubtless, have been to perish, had not the kind hearted Tah-tunga-sana discovered him, and, pitying his forlorn condition, taken him to the village, upon his own horse, some twenty miles off, going himself on foot the entire distance. Here, the lost one was treated to the best the lodge of his deliverer afforded, and, when sufficiently recovered, he was escorted to the nearest station of the whites.

I turned for another look at the worthy chieftain, who now rode up and greeted his protegé with much cordiality.

Americans are known among them. The American Fur Company, employing almost exclusively Frenchmen, or individuals speaking the French language, receives the appellation of Wah-ceicha, or the Bad-medicine company,—a phrase universally applied to the French among the mountain tribes.

CHIEF OF THE BRULÉ SIOUX. — *Page* 84.

He appeared to be about eighty years of age, and was gray-headed, spare-visaged, and much wrinkled. His coat, buttoned close around him, served for a robe, while his matted ear-locks disclosed upon the one side a raven's and upon the other a hawk's feather, for ornaments. His face, like those of his companions, was liberally bedaubed with vermilion, and each cheek embellished with alternate spots of white and black, by way of variety. His only weapons were a bow, arrows, and a tomahawk-pipe.

As a whole, he presented rather a shabby and ludicrous appearance, that, were it not for the recollection of his worthy conduct, would have excited, in the mind of the beholder, far more of contempt than interest.

A Sioux squaw, the wife of a French engagé, accompanying us on her return from the States, now received the marked attention of our visitors. It is rare that an Indian will shake hands with a woman; but now, they might break through the restraints of custom; this was a special case; she had visited the white man's lodge, and could tell them many interesting things,—she was something more than a common squaw,—they might shake hands with her. She was accordingly greeted in a most flattering manner, and found tedious employment in answering the numerous questions with which she was plied.

Continuing for a few miles further, we made camp just at nightfall, and were promptly joined by a new recruit of inquisitive visitors, from an adjoining village.

The whole throng of Indians now numbered some thirty, and demanded a "talk" with the Long-knife. Upon this a circle was formed, with the whites upon one side and Indians upon the other, when Marto-cogershne opened the harangue in behalf of his people.

He commenced in a low, distinct tone of voice. His robe, dawn loosely around him, was held to its place by the left hand, exposing his right arm and shoulder. As he proceeded he became more animated, and seemed to enter into the full spirit of his discourse. The modulations of his voice, its deep intonations and expressive cadences, coupled with a corresponding appropriateness of every look and gesture, presented one of the most perfect specimens of delivery I ever witnessed.

His speech, as imperfectly translated upon the occasion, ran as follows:

"Long-knife: We are glad to see you—we are glad to see your people, and shake you all by the hand, that we may smoke together and be friends.

"Long-knife: We are glad the Great Spirit has put it into your heart to return with the road-travellers, (waggons,) and the white buffalo, (oxen,) and the medicine-dogs, (horses,) bearing fire-water, (whiskey,) blankets, and many other good things, ere yet the chill winds and snows have compelled His children to light the lodge-fires of winter. The Long-knife brings choice things to the red man, and it is good that we trade. (Applause.)

"The Great Spirit is good to His children. To us He has given the buffalo, the elk, the deer, and the antelope, that we may be fed and clothed, and furnished with lodges to shelter us from the storms and cold. To us He has given the mountains and prairies, for hunting grounds. For us He has taught the streams to flow, and planted trees upon their banks, to give us food and drink, that we may meet around our lodge-fires with comfort and rejoice in His goodness, even while he spreads his white robe upon the hills, and lays the couch of winter upon the plains.

"All these—all this country—*everything* that the Long-knife beholds are ours. The Yellow-hair* said truly,—all, all belong to us;—we have them —the Great Spirit has given them to us,—they are ours! (Great applause.)

"Long-knife: You have come to trade with us:—it is good. Your people are wise, and make many things;—you bring them to us, and we take them; but we give you robes and horses in their stead;—we pay you for them all. Yet, the Long-knife pays not for all he takes from us.

"Do I say the Long-knife steals? No. The Long-knife will not steal. He says, none but *bad men* steal, and the Long-knife is not bad. *But yet he takes our property without paying for it!* He kills our game, he eats our meat, he burns our wood, he drinks our water, and he travels our country,— and *what* does *he* give the red man in exchange for all this? (Unbounded applause.)

"Long-knife and friend: My people are generous,—they are brave,— they are all soldiers. The Long-knife bears the fire-water in his road-travellers, (waggons;)—we have heard of it and are glad.

"My people would drink of the fire-water that their strong hearts may become stronger. It is good that they should drink it,—it is good that the Long-knife should give it to them; that we be twice glad to see him, and bless him in our hearts while we drink around our lodge-fires. (Applause.)

"Long-knife: Would you be our friend? Then give us the fire-water. My people are generous, but they are brave. The Long-knife has *taken our property*, let him refuse not the fire-water, lest they be angry and rise like the mountain bear, nerved for conflict. Then will they take it of themselves and avenge the wrongs of the red man!" (Great applause.)

Upon this, the Brave Bear resumed his seat, and the commandant began his reply, which was rendered into the Sioux language, by their interpreter. The purport of it was:

"It is true, the Great Spirit is good to His children. He made all things of which the Brave Bear speaks, and He has given them to his children. The white and the red man are alike his children; the buffalo, the elk, the deer, and the antelope, with the wood, the water, and the whole country around, equally belong to both.

"I and many people have come as friends, to trade with you. We have smoked with you before. The Long-knife takes nothing from you he pays not for. He buys the things he bears to you in a far distant country, and throws for them the white-iron.† He brings them to you and swaps them for robes and horses.

"He takes nothing without paying for it, unless it be that which the Great Spirit has given equally to his children,—the white and the red man.

---

* This is the name applied, by the Indians, to Gen. Clarke, one of the leaders of the first party of whites that ever crossed the mountains. An allusion is here had to an expression made use of in his talk to the Sioux on that occasion.

† Silver. This phrase is the Sioux mode of expressing the act of paying money for any article.

"Would the Brave Bear and his people be friends to us? We are friendly—we are generous. We will give tobacco to the Brave Bear, that he and his people may smoke and be our friends. But the Long-knife will not here give him the fire-water. Let him come to the Long-knife's lodge, then shall he have of it a little, that he may bless the Long-knife in his heart. The Brave Bear can have none now.

"The Brave Bear says, his people are generous, but they are brave,—they are all soldiers. Be it so. My people are generous,—*they* are brave—*they* are all soldiers! Does the Brave Bear wish for fight? My people are ready to either smoke or fight! The Brave Bear says, unless I give him the fire-water for his people, *they* will nerve their arms for conflict, and take it! Will they? Let them try! The Long-knife says, *let them try!*"

The conclusion of this reply was received with a bad grace by those to whom it was addressed, and created great excitement among them. Several left for the village, obviously for the purpose of arming and returning with increased numbers to the meditated attack.

Meanwhile our arms were put in a proper condition for resistance, and all needful arrangements made to give the assailants a warm reception should they commence upon us. This done, our commandant brought a few plugs of tobacco, and, laying them before the Brave Bear, said:

"It is good that the Brave Bear and his people should smoke. Here is tobacco,—let him take it to his warriors that we and they be friends;—or would he rather fight?"

Bull Tail, (Tah-tunga-sana,) who had had hitherto remained silent, now arose and addressed his companions:

"Tah-tunga-sana is grieved at the words of the Brave Bear. Would my brothers fight the Long-knife, and rob him of what he has brought to us, that they may become fools by drinking the fire-water?

"Who shall then bring us medicine-irons (guns) to kill our meat; or knives to butcher it; or blankets and beads for our squaws; or the red-earth (vermilion) to paint our faces when we arm for war? And, who shall bring us all the other things so needful for us?

"The Long-knife will not do it. You rob him. No one will bring them to us. We shall be without them! We shall be poor indeed!

"Brothers: Why would you drink the fire-water, and become fools? Would it not be better that the Long-knife no more bring it to us? We give for it our robes and our horses;—it does us no good. It makes us poor. We fight our own brothers, and kill those we love, because the fire-water is in us and makes our hearts bad! The fire-water is the red man's *enemy!*

"Brothers: Tah-tunga-sana is old;—will you listen to him. He has been always the friend of the pale-face. When first the Yellow-hair (Gen. Clarke) came to the red man's lodge, Tah-tunga-sana took him by the hand. He will always take the pale-face by the hand. He loves the pale-face. The pale-face is his brother,—he is *our* brother!—He brings us many good things.

"Brothers: The Long-knife has spoken well. It is good that we smoke, —that we, and the Long-knife, and his people may be friends. Let us accept his present, and go to our lodges, and there tell to our children how kind the Long-knife is to the red man."

The speech was received in silence,—no one expressing either approbation or dissent, as the old man resumed his seat. The Brave Bear hung his head sullenly, but said nothing.

The talk had evidently come to a close. At last, Bull Tail arose, and, shaking hands with the commandant and each of the company, took the tobacco and left for the village. The others soon after, one by one, followed his example, and we were finally rid of their unwelcome presence;—not, however, until they had stolen an axe and several other articles, despite the strictness of our vigilance.

## CHAPTER VII.

The Chimney.—A bet.—Spur of the Rocky Mountains.—Scott's Bluff.—Romantic scenery.—Mimic city.—A pyramid.—A monument.—An elevated garden.—Mountain sheep.—An Eden.—Death in camp.—The wanderer's grave.—Horse Creek and gold.—Goche's hole.—Arrival at Fort Platte.—Remarks by the way.—Prairie travel.—Locality and description of the Fort.—Indian lodges.—Migratory habits of mountain and prairie tribes.—Scenes at Fort.—Drunken Indians.—Tragical event.—Indian funeral.—Speech of Etsepa-huska on the death of his father.

*Oct. 26th.* RAISING camp at daylight we resumed our way, and soon afterwards arrived opposite the "Chimney," an extraordinary natural curiosity that had continued in view and excited our admiration for some four days past.

This singular formation surmounts a conical eminence which rises, isolated and lonely, in the open prairie, reaching a height of three hundred feet. It is composed of terrene limestone and marl, quadrangularly shaped, like the spire of some church, six feet by ten at its base, with an altitude of more than two hundred feet,—making, together with the mound, an elevation of five hundred feet.* A grand and imposing spectacle, truly;—a wonderful display of the eccentricity of Nature!

How came such an immense pile so singularly situated? What causes united their aid to throw up this lone column, so majestic in its solitude, to overlook the vast and unbroken plains that surround it?

The "Chimney" is situated about three miles to the left of the mountain trail, though it seems no more than eight hundred yards distant. Upon this question our party entertained no small diversity of opinion. Some of the less knowing were confident it could not exceed a half mile; and one fellow offered to bet five dollars he could run to it in fifteen minutes.

*Formerly the "Chimney" was much higher than at present, and could be distinctly seen in a clear day as far as Ash creek. The wind and the rain are continually reducing it; and it is said to be full fifty feet less than it was nine years ago. Calculating from this datum, what must have been its altitude no longer remote than a couple of centuries!

The banter was promptly accepted, and the "greenhorn," doffing his coat and hat, started in full expectation of winning the wager. But, instead of fifteen, it took him forty-five minutes to reach the spot!

The day after passing the "Chimney," we entered a broad defile of lofty ridges, and made camp. This locality is known as Scott's Bluff, which is, properly speaking, a wing of the Rocky Mountains.

From Ash creek to this place, an almost precipitous wall of arenaceous rock, limestone, and marl, shuts the high prairie from the river bottoms. As the traveller proceeds, this wall or ledge gradually increases in height, and recedes from the river, sometimes to a distance of thirty or forty miles, till it unites in a chain of hills, many of which are covered with sturdy pines, and others are mere heaps of naked sand or indurated earth. The ridge then continues its course until it at length becomes united with the lateral chain of the Rocky Mountains, which bounds the "Plains of Laramie" upon the southeast.

At Scott's Bluff these hills crowd themselves abruptly towards the Platte, where they present a most romantic and picturesque scenery.

Our camp was in a rich opening, or valley, two miles wide, and walled in upon the right and left by perpendicular masses of earth and rock, that tower to a height of from three to eight hundred feet. In reaching it, the trail bore leftward from the river, about seven miles, through a level prairie, by which we were inducted to the valley, without any perceptible variation of its general surface.

Near the entrance, upon our left, the spectacle was grand and imposing beyond description. It seemed as if Nature, in mere sportiveness, had thought to excel the noblest works of art, and rear up a mimic city as the grand metropolis of her empire.

There stood the representations of palaces, with their domes and balustrades; churches, with their spires and cupolas; and streets, with their gigantic dwellings, stores, work-shops, and ware-houses. And there, also, were parks, pleasure-grounds, and public squares, all so admirably defined by the agency of the winds and rains of ages, that the traveller might readily imagine himself to have arrived within the precincts of the deserted city of some peopleless country, whose splendor and magnificence once more than vied with the far-famed Palmyra of the desert, even in its best days.

To the right arose a pile of sand-rock and marl in pyramidal form, three hundred feet high, that occupied its prairie site detached from hill or other eminence.

Near this stood a more singular natural formation than any previously noticed. It described a complete circle, of one thousand feet in circumference, and attained an altitude of not far from four hundred feet. Its sides were of great regularity, and represented masses of solid masonwork, rising abruptly till within sixty or seventy feet of the summit, where they accline in a blunt, cone-like manner, reducing the periphery to one third that of its base. At this point is reposed a semi-spherical form, regularly jutting with a gradual swell upon all sides—then tapering to an oval shape till near the apex, at which the whole mass is surmounted by a rude imitation of sculptured flame, pointing upwards to the sun, as if this strange monument of nature had been erected in honor of the great source of light and heat!

Still further to the right, upon the river bank, is another immense pile, exceeding either of the before described in altitude. It is an oblong square, and presents erect lateral walls upon three sides, leaving upon the fourth a gradual acclivity which faces the river. Its summit expands into a beautiful terrace containing an area of several acres, which at the proper season is adorned with herbs, flowers, shrubbery, and grass, like a pleasure garden upon some house-top, and commands a view of the whole country, lending enchantment to the neighboring scenes. Its base is about one mile long by twelve hundred yards wide, and points endwise from the river towards the valley.

Then comes the continuous wall which bounds the locality upon the right. This likewise presents a level summit, varying from fifteen yards to a half mile in breadth, for a distance of ten miles, when, slowly sinking in its course, it finally becomes lost in the prairie.

Covered with grass and shrubs, it is the favorite home of the mountain sheep, where she breeds and rears her young, secure in her inaccessible fastnesses; and ofttimes from its precipitous edge, at elevations of six or eight hundred feet above the adjacent prairie, will her head and mammoth horns be seen, peering in wonder upon the rare traveller, as he passes adown the valley.

The interval between the two mural ridges is of uniform width for about ten miles, and is watered by a beautiful stream nearly the whole distance, when it inducts the traveller to the open prairie,—leaving the immense wall which bounded it upon the leftward, at his entrance, transformed to high conical hills, covered with pines, and almost lost to view in the growing space; while that upon his right, diminishing in size, gradually disappears and unites with the far-spreading plain.

Most of the varieties of wild fruits indigenous to the mountains are found in this vicinity, and also numerous bands of buffalo, elk, deer, sheep, and antelope, with the grizzly bear.

In the summer months the prospect is most delightful, and affords to the admiring beholder an Eden of fruits and flowers. No higher encomium could be passed upon it than by employing the homely phrase of one of our *voyageurs*. In speaking of the varied enchantments of its scenery at that season, he said: "I could die here, then,—certain of being not far from heaven!"

Before leaving this romantic spot, feelings of gloom and melancholy usurped those of pleasing admiration, by the death of one of our number.

The deceased was on his way to the mountains for the recovery of his health, with a frame fearfully reduced by the ravages of that fell destroyer, consumption. For several days past he had declined rapidly, owing to the weather and the unavoidable exposure incident to our mode of travelling. To-day the cold was more than usually severe, and an uncomfortable rain and sleet commenced soon after camping. In an attempt to pass from the waggons to the fire, he staggered and fell;—before any one of us could arrive to his assistance, he had breathed his last.

We buried him upon the bank of the stream that wends its course through the valley. Darkness, with its sable pall, had enveloped the scene as we covered him from view, and left the winds and the wolves to howl his requiem, until the voice of spring shall bid the wild-flowers grow and bloom upon his grave.

This lovely valley had before this witnessed the death-scene of one who left his bones to bleach within its limits. His name was Scott, from whom the neighboring eminences derive their present appellation.

Attracted by the enchanting beauty of the place and the great abundance of game the vicinity afforded, he wandered hither alone and made it his temporary residence. While thus enjoying the varied sweets of solitude, he became the prey of sickness and gasped his life away;—and none were there to watch over him, but the sun by day and the stars by night; or fan his fevered brow, save the kindly breezes; or bemoan his hapless fate, other than the gurgling stream that sighed its passing sympathy beside the couch of death!

There is a mournful interest and a touching melancholy associated with this simple story, that must thrill with emotion the finer feelings of our nature. The incident, which had so recently transpired, contributed to enhance these gloomy sensations to an extent I never before experienced. I felt—I cannot tell how. I felt like giving vent to my feelings in verse.— Yet, I cannot write poetry. I made the attempt, however, and here is the result before the reader:

### THE WANDERER'S GRAVE.

Away from friends, away from home,
  And all the heart holds dear,
A weary wand'rer laid him down,—
  Nor kindly aid was near.—

And sickness prey'd upon his frame
  And told its tale of woe,
While sorrow mark'd his pallid cheeks
  And sank his spirit low.

Nor waiting friends stood round his couch
  A healing to impart,—
Nor human voice spoke sympathy,
  To sooth his aching heart.

The stars of night his watchers were,—
  His fan the rude winds' breath,
And while they sigh'd their hollow moans,
  He closed his eyes in death.

Upon the prairie's vast expanse
  This weary wand'rer lay;
And far from friends, and far from home,
  He breath'd his life away!

A lovely valley marks the spot
  That claims his lowly bed;
But o'er the wand'rer's hapless fate
  No friendly tear was shed.

No willing grave received the corse
  Of this poor lonely one;—
His bones, alas, were left to bleach
  And moulder 'neath the sun!

The night-wolf howl'd his requiem,—
  The rude winds danced his dirge;
And e'er anon, in mournful chime,
  Sigh'd forth the mellow surge!

The Spring shall teach the rising grass
  To twine for him a tomb;
And, o'er the spot where he doth lie,
  Shall bid the wild flowers bloom.

But, far from friends, and far from home,
  Ah, dismal thought, to die!
Oh, let me 'mid my friends expire,
  And with my fathers lie.

*Oct. 27th.* The day being clear and pleasant, we travelled rapidly, and in the course of the afternoon reached Horse creek. This stream is a large affluent of the Platte, heading in the Black Hills, and, tracing its way in a northeasterly direction, through a timberless country, (in many places mere barren wastes,) makes its debouchment nearly fifteen miles above Scott's Bluff.

The region adjacent to its head is represented as being rich in minerals, among which is gold; and from my limited information respecting its geological character, I am inclined to accredit the rumor. The story runs thus:

Six or eight years since, Du Shay, an old French hunter, while ranging in the parts above alluded to, on crossing one of the two principal forks that unite to form the main stream, observed a singular looking something in the creek bed, which he picked up. It was apparently a fragment of rock, very heavy, and contained numerous yellow specks.

Having deposited it in his bullet-pouch for preservation, subsequently, in approaching a band of buffalo, its weight became so annoying he thoughtlessly threw it away. The year following he visited Santa Fe, at which place his pouch was accidentally emptied, and, among its contents, several bright particles, that had become parted from the rock, attracted the attention of the Mexicans. These were carefully gathered up, and, upon due examination, proved to be virgin gold.

The old man, on his return, searched diligently for the spot that afforded the treasure he had so foolishly thrown away,—but (not being intellectually one of the brightest gems of nature's casket, and feeble and childish withal) he was unable to find it, or even to decide upon which of the two streams it belonged.

Upon one of the affluents of Horse creek, thirty or forty miles south of the Platte, is a beautiful valley, shut in by two ridges of precipitous hills, known as Goche's hole.

This locality, in wildness and picturesque beauty, claims affinity to the neigborhood of Scott's Bluff. Its area is broad and of several miles extent, —inacessible except at two or three points. The surrounding hills are generally composed of marl and earthy limestone. Towering in vertical walls to the height of many hundred feet, they present the appearance of a strongly fortified place. The soil is remarkably rich, well watered, and timbered,—strikingly contrasting with the nude sterility and desolation of the circumjacent country.

A heavy fall of snow during the night prevented our leaving camp until the fourth day subsequent, when were again *en route*. Having passed the night of Nov. 1st at Morain's Point, the next day we arrived at Fort Platte. This latter place is situated a short distance above the mouth of Larramie river, and is our point of present destination.

From Horse creek to the Larramie river, the bottoms, in many places, afforded dense groves of heavy timber—the more agreeable as we had been so long accustomed to open and woodless prairies.

The geological character of the country is nearly the same with that previously described—though possessed of greater humidity of soil. The formations, noticed in the vicinity of Scott's Bluff and Goche's hole, have merged into strata of limestone of various shades and compactness, with occasional layers of primitive sandstone.

The prairies were beautifully undulating, and covered with lusty growths of dried vegetation. The hills, now and then, were ornamented with a few scattering pines and cedars, which stood like lonely sentinels to watch the progress of changing seasons.

As some of my readers may entertain the design of visiting these remote regions, or passing beyond them to the more distant shores of the Pacific, it may not be deemed a digression for me to present a few hints as to the most advisable mode of travelling upon this long and wearisome journey.

A caravan of waggons should make only two camps per day. Travellers should adopt the rule to start at daylight and continue until ten o'clock, A. M.,—then, having halted some six hours, (if it be summer, if spring or fall, four only,) again resume their way till after sundown.

Fifteen miles, upon an average, are as far as an ox team should travel per day,—mules or horses might keep on for twenty miles.

Caravans ought always to lay by in rainy weather, as the wet and irritation consequent upon draught, gall the neck and shoulders of their animals and soon render them unfit for service;—every precaution should be taken to preserve their strength and soundness, as upon them rests the sole dependence of a travelling company.

A mounted party ought, as a general thing, to observe the same rules, and not think of averaging over twenty-five miles per day. They might travel later; but in such cases, they should always proportionally lengthen their noon halt.

In the above manner the entire journey from Indpendence to the Pacific may be performed without injury to animals, or the expenses attendant upon a relay.

Fort Platte, being next to Fort Hall, the most important point on the route to Oregon, calls for a brief description. This post occupies the left bank of the North Fork of Platte river, three-fourths of a mile above the mouth of Larramie, in lat. 42° 12' 10'' north, long. 105° 20' 13'' west from Greenwich,* and stands upon the direct waggon road to Oregon, *via* South Pass.

It is situated in the immediate vicinity of the Oglallia and Brulé divisions of the Sioux nation, and but little remote from the Chyennes and Arapaho tribes. Its structure is a fair specimen of most of the establishments employed in the Indian trade. Its walls are "adobies," (sun-baked brick,) four feet thick, by twenty high—enclosing an area of two hundred and fifty feet in length, by two hundred broad. At the northwest and southwest corners are bastions which command its approaches in all directions.

Within the walls are some twelve buildings in all, consisting as follows: Office, store, warehouse, meat-house, smith's shop, carpenter's shop, kitchen, and five dwellings,—so arranged as to form a yard and *corel*, sufficiently large for the accommodation and security of more than two hundred head of animals. The number of men usually employed about the establishment is some thirty, whose chief duty it is to promote the interests of the trade, and otherwise act as circumstances require.

The Fort is located in a level plain, fertile and interesting, bounded upon all sides by hills, many of which present to view the nodding forms of pines and cedars, that bescatter their surface,—while the river bottoms, at various points, are thickly studded with proud growths of cottonwood, ash, willow, and box-elder, thus affording its needful supplies of timber and fuel.

One mile south of it, upon the Larramie, is Fort John, a station of the American Fur Company. Between these two posts a strong opposition is maintained in regard to the business of the country, little to the credit of either.

At the time of our arrival at the Fort, two villages of Indians were encamped near by. Their lodges, being the first I ever saw, proved objects of great interest to me.

The lodge of a mountain Indian consists of a frame work of light poles, some twenty-five feet long, bound together at the small ends, and raised by planting the opposite extremities aslope, at given distances apart, so as to describe a circle, at the base, converging to a triangular apex, for roof and sides;—over this is spread a covering of buffalo robes, so nicely dressed and seamed, it readily sheds rain and excludes the fierce winds to which the country is subject. A small aperture at the top, affords passage for the

---

* Obs. Lt. Fremont, in 1842.

smoke emitted from the fire occupyng the centre ground work. The entrance is at the side, where a large piece of undressed buffalo skin (hung from the top and so placed as to be opened or closed, at pleasure, upon the ingress or egress of the inmate) furnishes the simple substitute for a door.

These lodges (some of them containing quantities of roofage to the amount of ten or fifteen buffalo skins) are large and commodious; and, even comfortable, in the severest weather; the heat from the centre fire, being refracted on striking the sloping sides, communicates an agreeable warmth to every part.

An Indian lodge, in the summer, is admirably adapted to the pleasure of its occupants,—by raising the lower extremeties of the envelope and securing them at a proper elevation, a free passage of air is obtained, which greatly contributes to increase the merits of the delightful shade afforded by the superstructure.

A lodge of the largest size may easily be made to accommodate fifteen persons. The interior is arranged by placing the fixtures for sleeping at the circumference of the circle, which afford seats to the inmates, and thus a sufficient space is left vacant between them and the centre fire.

This kind of dwelling is the one almost universally adopted by the mountain and prairie Indians, and is, perhaps, better suited to their condition and mode of life than any other that could be devised.

Dependent solely upon the chase for a subsistence, the various Indian tribes inhabiting the mountains and countries adjacent can occupy no fixed residences. Contrary to the habits of more eastern nations, among whom agriculture commands attention to a greater or less extent, they are continually necessitated to rove from place to place in pursuit of game.

Give to one of them a bow, arrows, knife, lodge, and running horse, and he is rich, happy and contented. When the erratic propensities of the buffalo (upon which is his almost exclusive dependence) compel him to change his location, he has only to pull down his lodge, saddle his horse, and away.

So accustomed are they to this incessant rambling, they regard it more as a pleasure than an inconvenience. I have frequently seen hundreds of families moving together,—presenting to the unsophisticated beholder a novel and amusing spectacle,—with their horses, mules, dogs, men, squaws, children, and all the paraphernalia of savage domestic economy, and the rude accoutrements of peace and war, commingled indiscriminately.

The Sioux tribe, to whose country we have now introduced the reader, is, perhaps, the largest Indian nation upon the continent of North America, with the exception of the ancient Mexicans, if indeed they may be called Indians. This tribe occupies a territory extending from the St. Peters, of the Mississippi, to the Missouri, and from thence to the forks of the Platte, and up that river to its head-waters. They are supposed to number not far from eighty thousand men, women, and children, and are divided into many fractional parts, each bearing its own name, yet speaking the same language and claiming a common nationality.

Of these divisions are the Bruléς, Oglallas, Yanktaus, Piankshaws,

Minecosias, Blackfeet, Broken-arrows, and Assenaboins, with many others whose names have escaped my recollection. The only perceptible difference in language, is, in the pronuciation of words like the following, *meallo, appello* and *Lacota,*—those upon the Mississippi, and some in the vicinity of the Missouri, pronouncing them *meaddo, appeddo,* and *Dacota.*

The members of this nation, so far as my observation extends, are a cowardly, treacherous, thieving set, taken as a body—and are well deserving the appellation of mean and contemptible; though there are some honorable exceptions to the remark.

Any effort to civilize them must necessarily prove tedious, if not altogether impracticable, while they adhere to their present roving habits;—though three several missionary stations have been recently established among them, with slight success; viz: at St. Peters, Lac qui Parle, and Traverse des Sioux. But the Indians of those sections, being under the more direct influence of the U. S. Government, have begun to abandon their former wandering habits, and betake themselves to agricultural pursuits.

The term Sioux, as applied to this nation, is of Franco-Canadian origin—being a corruption of the word *sued,* and means *drunk* or *drunken,*—in allusion to their excessive fondness for liquor and predilection to inebriacy. The name by which they call themselves, and are known among other tribes, is *Lacota,* or *Cut-throats,*—for such is the literal meaning of the term; and rarely, indeed, were ever a pack of scoundrels more justly entitled to the appellation.

The night of our arrival at Fort Platte was the signal for a grand jollification to all hands, (with two or three exceptions,) who soon got most *gloriously drunk,* and such an illustration of the beauties of harmony as was then perpetrated, would have rivalled Bedlam itself, or even the famous council chamber beyond the Styx.

Yelling, screeching, firing, shouting, fighting, swearing, drinking, and such like *interesting* performances, were kept up without intermission,—and woe to the poor fellow who looked for repose that night,—he might as well have thought of sleeping with a thousand cannon bellowing at his ears.

The scene was prolonged till near sundown the next day, and several made their egress from this beastly carousal, minus shirts and coats,—with swollen eyes, bloody noses, and empty pockets,—the latter circumstance will be easily understood upon the mere mention of the fact, that liquor, in this country, is sold for four dollars per pint.

The day following was ushered in by the enactment of another scene of comico-tragical character.

The Indians encamped in the vicinity, being extremely solicitous to imitate the example of their "illustrious predecessors," soon as the first tints of morning began to paint the east, commenced their demands for fire-water; and, ere the sun had told an hour of his course, they were pretty well advanced in the state of "how came ye so," and seemed to exercise their musical powers in wonderful rivalry with their white brethren.

Men, women, and children were seen running from lodge to lodge with

INDIAN FUNERAL. — *Page* 101.

vessels of liquor, inviting their friends and relatives to drink; while whooping, singing, drunkenness, and trading for fresh supplies to administer to the demands of intoxication, had evidently become the order of the day. Soon, individuals were noticed passing from one to another, with mouths full of the coveted fire-water, drawing the lips of favored friends in close contact, as if to kiss, and ejecting the contents of their own into the eager mouths of others,—thus affording the delighted recipients tests of their fervent esteem in the heat and strength of the strange draught.

At this stage of the game the American Fur Company, as is charged, commenced dealing out to them, gratuitously, strong drugged liquor, for the double purpose of preventing a sale of the article by its competitor in in trade, and of creating sickness, or inciting contention among the Indians, while under the influence of sudden intoxication,—hoping thereby to induce the latter to charge its ill effects upon an opposite source, and thus, by destroying the credit of its rival, monopolize for itself the whole trade.

It is hard to predict, with certainty, what would have been the result of this reckless policy, had it been continued through the day. Already its effects became apparent, and small knots of drunken Indians were seen in various directions, quarrelling, preparing to fight, or fighting,—while others lay stretched upon the ground in helpless impotency, or staggered from place to place with all the revolting attendencies of intoxication.

The *dram-a*, however, was here brought to a temporary close by an incident which made a strange contrast in its immediate results.

One of the head chiefs of the Brulé village, in riding at full speed from Fort John to Fort Platte, being a little too drunk to navigate, plunged headlong from his horse and *broke his neck* when within a few rods of his destination. Then was a touching display of confusion and excitement. Men and squaws commenced bawling like children;—the whites were bad, very bad, said they, in their grief, to give Susu-ceicha the fire-water that caused his death. But the height of their censure was directed against the American Fur Company, as its liquor had done the deed.

The body of the deceased chief was brought to the Fort, by his relatives, with a request that the whites should assist at its burial; but they were in a sorry plight for such a service. There, however, were found sufficiently sober for the task, and accordingly commenced operations.

A scaffold was soon erected for the reception of the body, which, in the mean time, had been fitted for its last airy tenement. This duty was performed by the relatives of the deceased in the following manner: it was first washed, then arrayed in the habiliments last worn by Susuceicha during life, and sewed in several envelopes of lodge-skin, with the bow, arrows, and pipe once claiming him as their owner. This done, all things were ready for the proposed burial.

The corpse was then borne to its final resting place, followed by a throng of relatives and friends. While moving onward with the dead, the train of mourners filled the air with their lamentations and rehearsals of the virtues and meritorious deeds of their late chief.

Arrived at the scaffold, the corpse was carefully reposed upon it facing the east, while beneath its head was placed a small sack of meat, tobacco and vermilion, with a comb, looking-glass, and knife, and at its feet, a small banner that had been carried in the procession. A covering of scarlet cloth was then spread over it, and the body firmly lashed to its place by long strips of raw hide. This done, the horse of the chieftain was produced as a sacrifice for the benefit of his master in his long journey to the celestial hunting ground.

The above mode of sepulture is that commonly practised by the mountain tribes. It is seldom indeed they ever dispose of their dead in any other way than by placing them either upon scaffolds, branches of trees, or in some elevated position, not unfrequently covered by lodges, where they are left to moulder and waste in the winds and rain, till the bones falling one by one upon the prairie, are gathered up by surviving friends, and finally entombed in mother earth.

The corpse of the ill-fated man being thus securely fixed in the airy couch assigned it, to await the speedy process of dissolution, and mingle with its kindred earth, that its bones might find their proper places beneath the prairie sod, the village once acknowledging him as its head now met round the scaffold, men, women, children, and little ones, to bewail the sad fate that had bereaved them of their loved chieftain.

First, encircling it at a respectful distance, were seated the old men, next the young men and warriors, and next the squaws and children. Etespa-huska, (Long Bow,) eldest son of the deceased, thereupon commenced speaking, while the weeping throng ceased its tumult to listen to his words:

"Oh, Susu-ceicha! thy son bemourns thee, even as was wont the fledgelings of the war-eagle to cry for the one that nourished them, ere yet thy swift arrow had laid him in dust. Sorrow fills the heart of Etespa-huska; sadness crushes it to the ground and sinks it beneath the sod upon which he treads.

"Thou hast gone, oh Susu-ceicha! Death hath conquered thee, whom none but death could conquer; and who shall now teach thy son to be brave as thou was brave; to be good as thou wast good; to fight the foe of thy people and acquaint thy chosen ones with the war-song of triumph! to deck his lodge with the scalps of the slain, and bid the feet of the young move swiftly in the dance? And who shall teach Etespa-huska to follow the chase and plunge his arrows into the yielding sides of the tired bull? Who shall teach him to call for his prey from the deer, the elk, and the antelope, as thou hast done, or win honors from the slaughtered bear?

"None. Etespa-huska has no teacher. He is alone. Susu-ceicha is dead!

"But thou wilt soon gain the happy country. Thy journey is short. There wilt thou bestride the fleet horses that never tire, and roam amid the fruits and flowers, the sweet waters and pleasure-groves of that lovely clime; for thou art worthy.

"And, oh, Wakantunga! (Great Spirit,) do thou pity Etespa-huska. Do thou teach him to be brave and good like his father, for who is there to pity or teach him now he is left alone!"

Then, turning to the audience he continued:

"Brothers: Strong was the arm of Susu-ceicha, and fleet was the arrow shot from his bow. Thirty and five of the enemy hath he slain in battle, whose waving locks were the trophies that ofttimes measured the quick step of the scalp-dance. Fourscore and ten were the medicine-dogs he brought from the land of the foeman, that their shrill neighings might greet the ears, and their strong backs carry the people he loved; for brave was the heart of Susu-ceicha!

"What warrior ever came to his lodge and went hungry, or naked, or needy away? What widow or orphan of his people blessed not their chief, when he returned from the chase and apportioned to them their wonted dues from the choice spoils of the buffalo? for generous was the soul of Susu-ceicha.

"Brothers: Susu-ceicha is dead. No more shall his voice be heard in your councils, or his courage lead you to victory, or his generosity rejoice the hearts of the needy, the widow, and the orphan. Etespahuska laments a father and a teacher. The Burnt-thighs* a mighty chieftain; and the nation its bravest warrior! We all mourn him; sorrow fills the hearts, and tears wash the cheeks of his people. It is good that we bemourn him, and mingle with the winds the voices of our lamentation, for who shall now stand in the place of Susu-ceicha.

"Brothers: Let us stamp his memory upon our hearts and imitate his virtues, that our acts may rear to him a living monument, which may endure till time itself shall die!"

No sooner had the orator ceased, than a tremendous howl of grief burst from the whole assemblage, men, women, and children, which was renewed in quick succession for several hours, when finally the bewailing multitude retired to their lodges.

## CHAPTER VIII.

Coast clear, and Trade opened.—More visitors.—Smoking out the natives.—Incident illustrative of Indian character.—Expeditions for trade.—Black Hills.—Rawhide.—An Indian and a buffalo chase.—Deep snow, extreme cold, and painful journey.—L'eau-qui-court.—Remarks.—Lost.—White river; its valley, fruits, and game.—Building site.—The Devil's Tea-pot.—Troubles with Indians.—Theft and its punishment.—Indian soldiers.—Christmas extras.—Outrageous conduct.—Rascality of traders.—"That Old Serpent."—Indian superstition, religious tenets and practices.—Notions upon general morality.

THE events of the day had for the present put an effectual stop to dissipation among the Indians, and not long afterwards they began to pull down their lodges and remove to the neghborhood of buffalo, for the purpose of selecting winter-quarters.

The disgusting scenes connected with our arrival at the Fort had pretty much ceased on the evening of the second day, and everything, with a few exceptions, began to assume its wonted aspect.

* This is the interpretation of the Indian name which the French have supplied by the word Brulé.

The winter trade was now considered fully opened. Parties were sent with goods from the Fort to different villages, for the purpose of barter, and affairs began to show a business-like appearance.

Some two weeks subsequently, a band of Brulés arrived in the vicinity. They had come for a drunken spree, and soon opened a brisk trade in liquor.

Our visitors crowded the Fort houses in quest of articles of plunder, and became an incessant source of annoyance to the engagés. One room, in particular, was thronged almost to the exclusion of its regular occupants. The latter, losing all patience, at length hit upon a plan to rid themselves of the intruders.

After closely covering the chimney funnel, by aid of some half rotten chips a smoke was raised; the doors and windows being closed to prevent its egress. In an instant the apartment became filled to suffocation,—quite too much so for the endurance of the wondering savages, who gladly withdrew to gain the pure air of the exterior. On being told it was the Long-knife's medicine,* they replied:

"Ugh! Wakea sutiello ha Mena-huska tour!" (Ugh! The Long-knife's medicine is *strong!*)

During their stay at the Fort, an incident occurred which will serve to illustrate a singular trait in the character of these Indians.

A brave, named Bello-tunga, (Big Eagle,) received a blow over the head from a half crazed drunken trader, which came very near terminating in serious consequences. What would have been the result, it is hard to tell, had not the whites promptly interfered, and, with much effort, succeeded in pacifying the enraged savage by presenting him a horse.

At first he would admit of no compromise short of the offender's blood—he had been struck by the pale-face, and blood must atone for the aggression,—unless that should wipe out the disgrace, he could never again lift up his head among his people,—they would call him a coward, and say the white man struck Bello-tunga and he dared not to resent it.

The services of his father, hereupon, were secured in behalf of the offending party, which, after great ado, finally effected an adjustment of the difficulty.

An Indian considers it the greatest indignity to receive a blow from any one, even from his own brother;—and, unless the affair is settled by the bestowment of a *trespass offering* on the part of the aggressor, he is almost sure to seek revenge, either through blood or the destruction of property. This is a more especial characteristic of the Sioux than of any other nation. In fact, the Snakes, Crows, Arapahos, Chyennes, and most other tribes are far less nice in its observance,—though all regard the like an insult that justly calls for revenge.

Soon after, an expedition was detached to Fort Lancaster, on the South Fork Platte, and another to White river, an affluent of the Missouri, some

---

* This word, in Indian signification, means any person or thing possessed of extraordinary or supernatural powers, as well as any act for conciliating the favor and obtaining the assistance of the Great Spirit. That medicine is the strongest which is the most efficient for its intended purposes.

eighty miles northwest of the main trading post. The latter party included myself with its number.

Our purpose was to build houses in the vicinity of White river, and thus secure the trade of several villages of Brulés that had selected their winter quarters in the neighborhood, and were anxiously awaiting our arrival.

On the last of November we were under way with two carts freighted with goods and liquor, accompanied by only six whites, one negro, and an Indian.

Crossing the Platte opposite the Fort, we continued our course, west by north, over a broken and tumulous prairie, occasionally diversified by thick clusters of pines and furrowed by deep ravines, and abounding in diminutive valleys, whose tall, withered grass gave evidence of the rich soil producing it. To our left the high, frowning summits of the Black Hills began to show themselves in the long distance, like dark clouds, and planted their dense pine forests upon the broken ridges whose irregular courses invaded the cheerless prairie far eastward.

A ride of twenty miles brought us to Rawhide, where we passed the following night and day.

This creek traces its course over a broad sandy bed, through a wide valley of rich clayey loam, slightly timbered and luxuriant in grasses. Towards its head, it is shut in upon both sides by high pine hills; but, in passing on, these mural confines are exchanged for the prairies, and the creek finally debouches into the Platte.

An abundance of prelée and rushes afforded fine pasturage to our animals, and a kindly grove of dry cottonwood gave us requisite fuel for camp-fire.

Before leaving, we were joined by another Indian mounted upon a dark bay horse, the noblest animal of its kind I remember to have seen among the mountain tribes. It had been stolen from the Snakes during the past summer, as its present owner informed us, and he seemed not a little proud of the admiration we bestowed upon it.

The new comer proved Arketcheta-waka, (Medicine Soldier,) a brother of Bello-tunga, the brave referred to on a former occasion. Seating himself by the fire, he looked dejected and melancholy, and his face bore indubitable evidence of a personal encounter with some one.

On enquiring the cause of this, we learned that he had left his father's lodge by reason of a quarrel he had had with his eldest brother,—the latter having struck him with a fire-brand and burnt his body in several places during a drunken spree,—he was now on his way to White river, there to await the suitable time for revenge, when he should kill his brother.

We told him this would not be right;—it was liquor that had done him the wrong, and not his brother;—liquor was bad!

He seemed to acknowledge the truth of our suggestions, and asked "why the pale-faces brought the fire-water to do the red man so much harm?" Our trader replied, "The whites want robes, and can get them for liquor when nothing else will do it."

The answer evidently perplexed him, while he sat gazing silently into the fire, with his arms akimbo upon his knees, and palms supporting his chin, as if striving to work out to his own satisfaction this strange problem in morality.

The third day we resumed our course, and, after a drive of six or eight miles, came upon a large band of buffalo. Here, at our request, the Medicine Soldier doffed his robe, slung his arrow-case over his naked shoulders, mounted his horse bow in hand, and started for the chase.

At first he rode slowly, as if reserving the speed of his charger till the proper time. The buffalo permitted him to approach within a few hundred yards before they commenced flight. Then was a magnificent spectacle.

The affrighted beasts flew over the ground with all the speed that extreme terror lent to their straightened nerves, and plied their nimble feet with a velocity almost incredible—but they were no match for the noble steed the Indian bestrode. He was among them in a trice, and horse, Indian, and buffalo were lost in identity, as they swept over a snow-clad prairie, in one thick, black mass, like the career of a fierce tornado, tossing the loose drifts upwards in small particles, that, in their descent, pictured white clouds falling to the earth, ever and anon enshrouding the whole band from view.

Now their course is turned and makes directly towards us. They pass, all foaming with sweat—with lolling tongues and panting breath—but they still seem loath to abate from the energy of their wild terror.

Soon the Indian and his gallant steed part from them. He has selected the choicest of the band and pursues her singly. Side by side both cow and horse keep even pace, while the ready archer pours in his arrows,—some of them, forcing their entire way through the bleeding beast, fall loosely to the ground upon the opposite side.

At length, spent by the toilsome flight, exhausted by loss of blood, and pierced through her vitals by the practised marksman that follows her, she halts for fight.

Now, she plunges with mad fury at the horse,—the well-trained steed clears the force of her charge at a bound. Again, she halts,—the blood spouts from her nostrils and mouth—she staggers. Again, she musters her expiring energies for one more desperate onset at her enemy, as if determined, if die she must, not to die unavenged. Her charge proves futile as the former. A death-sickness comes over her. Her life is fast ebbing from within her. She reels,—she totters—she falls,—and breathes her life away upon the blood-dyed snow.

A few moments' delay put us in possession of an ample supply of fresh meat,—the Indian reserving the robe only as his share. The cow proved a most excellent selection, and did honor to the judgment of the hunter.

As we travelled on, the snow, which scarcely an hour since had first attracted our attention, became deeper and deeper, and our progress more tedious and difficult.

From bare ground and comparatively moderate climate, we were fully inducted to the region of snow, ice, and winter. The prairie was high and undulating. To our left an immense wall of secondary rock surmounted a ridge of naked hills, that described in its course the curve of a rainbow, enclosing upon three sides a large valley facing the east,—thence, stretching westward and raising higher and higher, hastened to mingle its heads among the cloud-capped summits and snows of the neighboring mountains.

From a light coating of loose snow our course soon became obstructed

CHASING A BUFFALO.— *Page 108.*

by still deepening layers, covered with a thick crust, scarcely strong enough to bear our weight, but quite sufficient to wrench and jar us at every step, and make our advance threefold tiresome.

The cold was so intense, we were forced to walk to keep from freezing. Our difficulties thickened the farther we progressed. Night closed in upon us, and we could no longer distinguish our course. Yet we kept on, in hopes of reaching some creek or spring where we might await the coming day.

Slowly, onward,—plunge, plunge, at every step;—now prostrate at full length upon the hard crust, and then again staggering in resistless mimicry of drunken men.

The chill winds sweeping over the dreary expanse pierced us through at each whiff, and seemed to penetrate every nerve, and joint, and muscle, as if to transform our hearts' blood into icicles. But still it was plunge, plunge along; onward, plunge, fall; but yet onward! There is no stopping place here,—'tis push on or die!

Thus, travelling for three or four hours, not knowing whither, we came finally to the leeward of a high hill. The agreeable change produced by the absence of wind, called forth a hearty response. "Camp, ho," was echoed upon all sides. But here was no water for ourselves or our animals. We must yet go on. Still we lingered—loath to leave the favored spot. The Indian, who had been absent for a brief space, now came up, shouting:

"Mine, washtasta!" (Water, very good!)
"Tarkoo mine?" asked the trader. (What water?)
"Mine-loosa. Tunga warkpollo." (Running-water. A large creek.)

It proved L'eau-qui-court, the stream upon which we had intended to pass the night.

Pushing on, a few moments brought us to its banks, in a deep valley covered with snow. A fire was then promptly built from a small quantity of wood we had the precaution to take with us from Rawhide, and all hands were soon as comfortably conditioned as circumstances would admit.

A hearty supper served to appease the appetites so keenly sharpened by a toilsome journey of thirty miles, occupying from sunrise till ten o'clock at night. This over, each one cleared for himself a place upon the frozen ground, and, spreading down his bed, quickly forgot his cares and sufferings in the welcome embrace of sleep.

L'eau-qui-court, or Running-water, heads in a small lake under the base of the first range of Black Hills, and, following an easternly course, empties into the Missouri, about one hundred and fifty or two hundred miles above Council Bluff. It derives its name from the rapidity of its current, which rolls over a pebbly bed with great velocity.

At this place it is narrow and deep, with steep banks, and not a stick of timber is to be found on it, above or below, for twenty miles. At the lake where it heads, there is an abundance of timber; large groves of cottonwood are also found at some distance below our present camp.

The intermediate country, from Rawhide, is a cold and cheerless expanse almost at all seasons of the year. From the commencement of fall to the very close of spring, it is subject to frost and snow;—for what cause, it is hard to conjecture. Its surface, though quite elevated, is not sufficiently so to make such marked difference in climate between it and adjoining sections.

The next day proved cloudy; we, however, resumed our course which led over a rough, tumulous country, covered with snow and darkened by occasional clusters of pines.

Early in the morning our Indians left us and took a nearer route to the village. Soon after we became bewildered in the obscurity of the atmosphere, and travelled till night unconscious whether right or wrong. Finally, coming to a deep ravine that obstructed further progress, we turned to a neighboring grove of pines, at the point of an eminence, and made camp. It was a bleak airy place, but by aid of a huge fire of dry pine we were quite comfortable, despite a heavy fall of snow during the night.

With the morning our perplexities were renewed. Directly in front lay a broad and impassable ravine, beyond which a high mountain range arose to view. Should we go up or down? After much debate we decided upon the latter, and, bearing northward during the day, struck the head of a stream which subsequently proved White river.

This stream traces its way through a broad valley, enclosed upon either side by high pine hills. Its banks are studded with thick groves of cottonwood, elm, ash, box-elder, and willow,—with nearly all the varieties of fruit-bearing shrubs and trees indigenous to the mountains. In the item of plums and cherries, it gave evidence of exuberant fecundity. The bushes, in many instances, yet bore the dried relics of their burthen, as if to tempt the beholder's taste,—while the tall grass and rosebuds,* every where attested the summer-verdure and beauty of the valley in which they grew.

The snow that had hitherto impeded our progress, now gradually became less as we advanced down the valley, and soon gave place to bare ground. Game appeared in great numbers, attracted from the adjoining hills to pass the winter in this inviting locality.

A journey of two days brought us to the site selected for houses, and, consequently to a halt, for the present.

The place was surrounded by wild and romantic scenery. Directly in front, upon the opposite side of the creek, arose a perpendicular wall of marl and half formed sandstone, towering, stratum above stratum, to a height of three or four hundred feet, and overlooking the valley above and below,—while further on, a steep hill-side, covered with tall, straight, and almost branchless pines, burst upon the view.

Rearward a gradual acclivity led to a high plateau, some two miles broad, coated with long, tall grass, when a ridge of abrupt pine hills introduced the more distant mountains, with their rugged sides and frowning summits,—and, higher up, an immense pile of earthy limestone, sur-

---

*Rosebuds are found in great quantities in many places, throughout the mountains, during the winter, and attain a large size. They are highly esteemed by many as an article of food, and have not unfrequently been the means of preserving life in cases of extreme hunger and lack of other eatables.

mounting a wing of hills as it approached the river, presented a medley of curious and fantastic shapes,—objects alike of amusement and wonder.

One of the latter, denominated the "Devil's Tea-pot," exhibited externally an almost perfect facsimile of that kind of vessel. It was of gigantic proportions,—being one hundred feet high, and, occupying a conspicuous position, may be seen for a distance of many miles.

The Indians from a near village, immediately upon our arrival, came flocking around for the threefold purpose of begging, trading and stealing; and, from this forward, we rarely experienced an interval free from their anoyance.

Prompt arrangements were here commenced for building a store room and trading house;—but meanwhile, we were forced to keep strict guard both night and day.

Two braves were secured to "act soldier," and assist in keeping the thieving propensities of their people in check. Yet, notwithstanding the united vigilance of all hands, the latter would frequently perpetrate their petit larcenies under our very eyes, without being detected in the act,—so adroit were they at the business. An instance of this kind happening to myself is perhaps worth relating.

Previously to the erection of houses, we were necessitated to sleep in the open air. Wearied by the lateness of the hour, one night I spread down my couch by the camp-fire, with the intention of retiring. The weather being very cold, I had scarcely turned to warm myself, when a backward glance revealed the sudden disappearance of my sleeping appendages—robes blankets and all!

Informing the trader of my mishap, and catching a glimpse of the thief as he dodged past a knot of Indians at the further extremity of the camp, gun in hand, I started after the nimble lark; but the thick bushes and darkness soon shut him from view and left me in fruitless pursuit.

At length, relinquishing the hope of ever regaining the stolen articles, and vexed at the impious savage, who, instead of obeying the Scripture injunction of "take up *thy* bed and *walk*," had snatched MY bed and RUN! I returned to camp. Here I was shown a robe, by the trader, that had been brought in scarcely a minute before and offered in barter for liquor;—it was one of the two I had lost.

The bearer was now promptly charged as being accessory to the theft. This he stoutly denied, alleging that the robe had been given him by another Indian for the purpose he had offered it.

Upon this the affair was referred to our soldiers, who, after much parleying and no little threatening, succeeded in causing him to return the missing articles. The fellow then demanded of me a cup of liquor as pay for bringing them back. Mustering to my aid a few words of Sioux, I replied: "Mea warche yau wechacha ceicha, opata-ne ha warktash-ne coga!—I neither like bad men, nor will I pay for doing bad."

Marto-nazher, (Standing Bear,) one of our soldiers, on hearing my answer, arose and addressed the crowd in an earnest and impressive manner. He was grieved on account of the many depredations continually committed by his people upon the property of the whites. It is wrong—very wrong, said he, to conduct in this manner;—if such wickedness is allowed, the whites will abandon the country. Whites do not steal from us.—Something must be done—an example must be had—the perpetrators of these outrages must be punished.

"You, Schena-sarpah," he continued, throwing his piercing glance full upon the chop-fallen culprit, who hung his head for shame at being caught in a manner so little to his credit, "Aye, you Scena-sarpah do carry a bow and arrows; you call yourself a brave; and yet you steal from our friends, the pale-faces!

"Do brave men steal from their friends? No! Schena-sarpah should alone steal from his enemies, if he be a brave man and a soldier.

"Who are they that steal from their friends? Squaws and children, as Schena-sarpah well knows. Then he is no better than they! Why should he carry a bow? Why go to war, or follow the chase? Squaws and children do neither. None but brave men go to war—none but they should follow the chase.

"Schena-sarpa needs no bow. Let him go to his lodge. There let him make robes and moccasins for braves, and take care of children with squaws,—for such should be his occupation, and only such should be his companions!"

So saying, he approached the unresisting thief, and, taking from him his bow, arrows, and panther-skin quiver, resumed his seat. Then, breaking the arrows and shooting them away, one by one, among the trees, he snapped the bow across his knee and threw it into the fire. The bright flame from the burning bow had barely died away, when the quiver was consigned to the same fate. As the last fragments of the effeminate's weapons mouldered to ashes, a smile of satisfaction played upon the countenance of the Standing Bear, at the thought of having avenged the wrongs of the white man.

And, truly, this was an infliction of summary punishment. The amount of property destroyed exceeded the value of a horse, and, in the estimation of an Indian, constitutes a man's chief wealth. The offender was thus not only left disarmed by the operation, but made poor, and reduced to a level with the squaws and children to whom he was set apart. He bemoaned his loss most piteously, and started for his lodge, bellowing like a motherless calf.

Another instance of theft occurred soon after, almost as remarkable. A robe was stolen from off one of our party, while he was asleep, and bartered for whiskey, without his knowing it!

Our Indian soldiers were of great service in conducting the trade. If any difficulty occurred, they were always at hand to assist in its adjustment, and preserve order and quiet so far as lay in their power. If any visitor became troublesome, they at once ordered him to his lodge, and enforced their commands in case of resistance.

Every trader is necessitated to employ one or more braves to assist him in his business at the villages. An Indian considers it a great honor thus to receive the confidence of a white man and "act soldier" for him, as he denominates it. Some of them have not unfrequently gone so far as to kill those of their people who proved guilty of misusing the traders by whom they were employed.

They exercise a kind of supervisory office in the management of affairs which could not well be dipensed with,—and very often have the lives of traders been preserved by the judgment and discretion of these men.

*Dec. 25th.* Christmas finds us in our new residence, which, with the exception of a chimney, is now completed.

This great annual festival is observed with all the exhilarating hilarity and good cheer that circumstances will allow. Several little extras for the occasion have been procured from the Indians, which prove quite wholesome and pleasant-tasted. One of these, called *washena,* consists of dried meat pulverized and mixed with marrow; another is a preparation of cherries, preserved when first picked by pounding and sun-drying them, (they are served by mixing them with *bouillie,* or the liquor of fresh-boiled meat, thus giving to it an agreeable winish taste;) a third is marrow-fat, an article in many respects superior to butter; and, lastly, we obtained a kind of flour made from the *pomme blanc,* (white apple,) answering very well as a substitute for that of grain.

The above assortment, with a small supply of sugar and coffee, as well as several other dainties variously prepared, affords an excellent dinner,—and, though different in kind, by no means inferior in quality to the generality of dinners for which the day is noted in more civilized communities.

The day following our turbulent neighbors were augmented in number by the accession of another village of Brulés, and Marto-cogershne, of whom I have spoken upon a former occasion, became with his family our constant annoyance.

Visiting us at one time, squaws and all—as was his daily custom—to beg liquor, (which, some way or other, he always obtained,) the brother of our tormentor demanded a quantity of that article to take with him to his lodge. This, after many sharp words, was offered; but, having no vessel for its conveyance, he extended his demands to a kettle,—which, of course, was refused; whereupon he threatened vengeance unless both were forthcoming upon the *mococo,*\* (prairie,) and required still farther the gift of a pair of moccasins.

Our trader replied, "The liquor is for you, and here are the moccasins, (pulling off his own and passing them to him,) but the kettle you cannot have."

The affair thus ended for the present, and the modest beggar retired to his lodge. The next morning, however, two of our horses were found pierced with arrows, and so badly, that they died soon after.

At another time, Marto-cogershne became so enraged at being refused a whole keg of liquor "on the prairie," he rushed upon the trader with his butcher-knife to kill him. What would have been the result, it is hard to tell, had I not stayed the descending weapon by seizing the fellow's arm. Here our soldiers interfered and put him out of the house,—closing the door upon him. The exasperated savage then commenced shooting upon us through the door;—two Indian boys passing in the interval also furnish-

\* This expression implies the bestowment of anything as a free gift. It is also used to denote a random way of speaking with regard to truth.

ed marks for his gun, and not long subsequently a mule and an ox belonging to us fell to appease his insulted dignity.

However, the *chef d'ouvre* of his rascality was exhibited in stealing our whole *cavallard*,* consisting of ten head of horses and mules, which he drove into the mountains. We were compelled to give a quantity of liquor and ammunition, two blankets, and several other articles before we could secure their return.

From the movement of things, he was evidently instigated by the American Fur Company traders to do us all the mischief in his power. Certain it is, he was their regular "soldier," and received from them numerous presents in consideration of his good conduct.

The employees of this company are frequently guilty of such disgraceful conduct. In connection with this conclusion I might cite instance upon instance, and string out a volume of proof, were it necessary.

Soon after Christmas we commenced erecting our chimney. The materials for it were procured from an adjoining bank. While engaged in quarrying them, the operator came to a crevice filled with a strange fleshy substance, coiled together like the folds of a huge rope. "Hallo!" cried he, with astonishment, "here's the Devil, himself!"

The extraordinary announcement brought all hands to the spot to get a peep at "Old Nick," and the Indians, also, witnessing the unusual commotion, came hurrying up to learn its cause.

The result proved, that, if not the Devil, it was his great prototype,—it was that "Old Serpent," with all his progeny.

By means of a stick, *thirty-six large snakes* were exposed to view,— some of them six feet in length. They were in a torpid state, the result of the severe cold of winter.

Having drawn them out, one by one, it was proposed to treat them to a warm bath. Accordingly, after placing them in a hole for the purpose, a keetle of scalding water was thrown upon them. The vivifying effects of this unwonted application restored them to a sudden animation, when, wriggling and twisting for a few moments in all the contortions of agony, they at last tacitly curled up and expired.

The Indians were much shocked on seeing this, and expressed their astonishment at our reckless presumption by their deeply accented "tula," —turning away from the spot with evident emotions of terror.

On inquiring the cause, I learned in answer, that the various Indian tribes in the vicinity of the mountains are accustomed to regard the snake with a kind of superstitious veneration, and consider the act of killing it a sure harbinger of calamity. In the observance of this singular notion, they are scrupulously exact;—but, in despite of repeated inquiries, I have been unable to obtain the reasons upon which the whim is based.

These tribes cherish many religious tenets, rites, and customs,—some general and others peculiar only to individuals.

* This is a mountain phrase of Spanish origin, (cavellardo,) and means a band of horses or mules.

An Indian will never pronounce the name of the Big Medicine, or Great Spirit, other than in a reverential manner, nor upon trival occasions.

This being is considered the Great Superintendent of all things, whose power sustains the universe,—causing day and night with the varying seasons,—making the grass to grow, the water to run, and the rains to fall, for the good of man and beast.

Some imagine He lives in the sun; others, in the air; others, in the ground; and others in the immensity of His works.

The animal or thing possessed of wonderful or extraordinary powers, such as their ignorance ascribes to be the attributes of the Supreme Being, they look upon as endowed with a greater or less share of His presence, and venerate it accordingly. Thus, the sun, fire, lightning, thunder, fountains of peculiar medicinal qualities, extraordinary localities, and various other things are alike objects of religious regard.

Although their theological sentiments are generally the same, the manner of showing their respect for this Overruling Providence differs with different tribes, families, and even persons. For instance,—some tribes shave their heads in token of their submission to Him. Others mark themselves for His own by some peculiar manner of cutting their ears for the reception of ornaments;—while others burn their thighs, tattoo their breasts, scar their arms, or flatten the heads of infants, for a like purpose.

The instrument, with which such ceremonies are performed, is invariably thrown away. In case of cutting the ears of an infant, the gift bestowed upon the operator is regarded as indicative of its success during life;—parents have been known to give as high as ten horses on like occasions.

Some make indelible marks of a blue color upon their chins and foreheads,—or the figures of lizards, snakes, arrows, or other objects upon their arms.

Some show their reverence in the peculiar manner of receiving the pipe and passing it to another;—others by certain ceremonies before smoking,—thus, pointing the pipe-stem to the zenith, then towards the ground, then horizontally upon either side, as if saying, "Oh thou, whose habitation is immensity, accept this as the willing tribute of homage from thy child."

They will never allow a bone of any kind to be broken within their lodges, and express great consternation and alarm at such an occurrence. Some will not permit a stick of wood to be struck with a knife or other edged tool while burning, and others exhibit their devotion by some peculiarity in the structure of their lodges, or the mode of placing their medicine-bags, the length and shape of their arrows, their fashion of hair-dressing, and various minutiæ of like character.

Others again will never eat unless they bestow the first mouthful as an offering to the prairie,—believing that, as the prairie affords water, grass, and game, for the good of the red man, it is the fullest embodiment of the Essence of Good; therefore, in the observance of this practice, they not only acknowledge their faith in the existence of the Great Spirit, but set apart the first of their substance as test of their piety.

Their ideas of the existence of a principle, or being, who is the author and prompter of evil, are crude and indefinite.

They are ready to acknowledge its reality, but seem to consider its person more manifest in man himself than any other creature or thing. Their enemies they esteem as the more special incarnation of this principle, and next to them they regard a worthless, mean, and cowardly individual of their own people. They also look upon creatures of an injurious and hurtful nature, as the greater or less impersonation of evil.

Their notions of right and wrong are equally simple.

It is right to be brave, to do good to friends, to relieve the needy, to feed the hungry, and to worship the Great Spirit,—these are acts of general morality. There are various other duties taught by their code relative to intercourse with each other,—to children and parents, husbands and wives, deference to age, chastity etc., the performance of which is essential to virtue.

The line of demarkation between virtue and vice is yet more simple and comprehensive ;—every thing derelict of right is wrong.

I shall recur to several points, connected with the foregoing subjects, in another place.

## CHAPTER IX.

Dangers connected with the liquor trade.—Difficulty with Bull Eagle.—Scenes of bloodshed and horror.—Cheating in the fur trade.—How the red man becomes tutored in vice.—A chief's daughter offered in exchange for liquor.—Indian mode of courtship and marriage.—Squaws an article of traffic.—Divorce.—Plurality of wives.

THE difficulty and danger, not to say crime and bloodshed, connected with the illicit trade in alcohol, as conducted among our western Indians, is great and imminent. To illustrate this point, I need only to place before the reader a summary of facts which occurred, many of them under my own observation, during the winter of 1842.

Soon after our arrival at White river a man was sent to a neighboring village with a keg of diluted alcohol, for the purpose of barter. The Indians, feeling more disposed to drink than pay for it, demanded the keg as a gift "on the prairie." This was refused. They threatened—a fight ensued, (the soldiers and trader defending the keg and the Indians trying to take it.) Weapons were used, and the result was, both soldiers and trader were beaten off,—the latter, after being dragged through the lodge-fire three or four times, narrowly escaped with his life.

A party of Indians under the excitement of strong drink, attacked and took a trading house of the American Fur Company, near by,—robbing it of both liquor and goods.

Two parties in the Fur Company's employ, from different posts, met at a neighboring village,—one having goods and the other alcohol. The Indians, as usual, got drunk, and commenced a fight among themselves ;—because the goods-trader happened to be in the lodge of one of the weaker party, they attacked him. He was compelled to flee, and barely escaped with his life through the friendly interference of the squaws. His goods

BULL EAGLE DRINKING THE FIRE-WATER. — *Page* 119.

were all stolen;—while one of the Indians who defended him was brutally murdered, and several others wounded.

Not long afterwards, our trader was shot at, three or four times, while engaged in this dangerous traffic, and one of his soldiers severely wounded.

About the same time, the trader of another company received a deep stab, while dealing out the vile trash, and would have been killed but for the energetic efforts of his soldiers.

Previously to the above, the Indians seized upon a trader and compelled him to stand over a hot fire until he was nearly roasted alive,—meanwhile, helping themselves to his stock in hand.

Soon after, two warriors came to trade for a blanket at our post,—one of whom was drunk. While being waited upon, the latter drew his knife and was in the very act of stabbing the unsuspecting clerk, as I caught his wrist and arrested the blow.

At another time, as our trader was standing surrounded by us all, he was shot at by a drunken Indian, who, by the merest accident, missed his object.

Again, one night a party of drunken Indians undertook to fire the house in order to consume us alive, but were providentially prevented, owing to its being constructed of green pine logs.

The most dangerous time I experienced during the winter was near the close of it. An Indian employed as our soldier, became crazed upon the drugged liquor of the American Fur Company, and made his appearance before us in a high state of excitement. This fellow had been denominated by his people the Bull Eagle, (Tahtunga-mobellu,) and was a chief,—highly esteemed as a medicine-man, and regarded as the greatest brave in the Sioux nation. He was a tall, well-made, noble-looking person—and,—such eyes! I never saw the like planted beneath the brows of any other mortal. They glared like lightning, and, as they fell upon the individual to whom directed, seemed to penetrate the very soul and read the embryo thoughts of his heart.

Through the misrepresentations of those in the interest of the Fur Company, he fancied himself misused by our trader, and came determined on revenge. Arms in hand and stripped for the contest, accompanied by his wife and two or three friends, he confronted us,—his strange appearance told for what. In the fury of passion his every look gave evidence of the raging demon within.

Here, lest he should be misunderstood, he premised by a full statement of his grievances. They were many, but the chief of them was, that our trader had employed another to "act soldier" in his stead, while he was too drunk to perform the duties of that appointment. "I have been dressed* as a soldier," said he, " to be laughed at, and now Peazeezee† must die !"

The room was full of Indians, and one of them, an old man, exclaimed: " When Peazeezee dies, let me go under,‡—I must live no longer!"

* Previously, he had been presented with a citizen's dress to secure him for the company's interest.
† Yellow-hair. The Indian name for our trader.
‡ This term implies death, or the act of dying.

"Is this your love for the pale-face?" returned the infuriated chieftain. "Then die you first!"

Upon this, seizing the defenceless old man, he drew his knife and made a heart-thrust. The intended victim, however, grasped the descending blade in his bare hand and arrested its course—but his fingers were nearly severed in so doing. Here the wife of Bull Eagle rushed up to her husband and seized him by both arms, while others interfered, and the scene of conflict was removed from the apartment to the space in front.

Now was a general fight. The women and children, crying for terror, ran about in the utmost confusion and dismay,—while raving combatants yelled and whooped, as knives, clubs, and tomahawks were busily dealing wounds and scattering blood.

Soon after, the parties retired to their village, and the melée ended with only six wounded.

In a brief interval the Bull Eagle again returned, accompanied by his wife,—the latter earnestly endeavoring to dissuade him from his purpose.

A shot was his first salute, on entering the door, which a timely thrust from the squaw averted from its object. The kind-hearted creature then grasped the bow. Relinquishing it in her hands, the madman made a pass at the trader with his tomahawk,—this blow was dodged, and the heroine, rushing between the two, prevented its repetition. Dropping his tomahawk, he then fell upon the object of his hatred, butcher-knife in hand.

But here he found himself in the firm grasp of several friendly Indians, by whom he was borne from the room.

This state of affairs was the signal for another engagement between Bull Eagle, at the head of his partizans, and the friends of the whites,—more desperate and bloody than the former. With great difficulty we retained our arms from the forcible grasp of the contending factions. This, to us, was a moment fraught with extreme peril—not knowing friend from foe, and instantly apprehensive of the knives and arrows of the avengeful throng. It was, indeed, a moment when the agony of suspense quivered with thrilling intensity upon every nerve, and vibrated in every sinew. To fight, would have been a relief. But, whom should we fight? It might have been our best friends—for who could discriminate? The death of one connected with either party, at our hands, would have proved the signal for our instant slaughter. Both would have united to exterminate us,—and, beset as we were, upon all sides, prudence dictated a strict nutrality. Sometimes fifteen or twenty would be struggling for our arms at once,—a strong temptation, as the reader may rest assured, for us to use them in self-defence.

Meanwhile the conflict continued with unabated fury. Several attempts were made upon the life of Bull Eagle, but without success. Two were killed and others wounded, when a final stop was put to the further effusion of blood by the withdrawal of the chieftan to his lodge.

In about an hour subsequent, he returned for the second time,—but reason had now resumed her sway, and he came to apologize for his bad conduct. Calling our trader his "very good, his best friend," he cried for grief that he had attempted to kill him. He averred that liquor had made him a *fool*, and said he should never cease to regret the great wickedness he had thought of doing to his "best friend." Ever after this affair, he remained our steadfast friend, and presented our trader with six superfine robes, in evidence of the sincerity of his repentance.

The foregoing results of this infamous traffic, are only a few of the many instances of like nature I might cite, in proof of its imminent danger to those engaged in its prosecution;—but this is not the darkest part of the picture. There are yet scenes in reserve, more bloody and dreadful than those above recited, though not, perhaps, quite as perilous to the whites themselves. They all occurred in the winter of 1842, during the brief period of two months, and resulted immediately from the sale of liquor.

I shall not enter into details, but content myself by laying before the reader a mere synopsis of facts.

In November, the American Fur Company, from Fort John, sent a quantity of their drugged liquor to an Indian village, on Chugwater, as a gift, for the purpose of preventing the sale of that article by their competitors in trade. The consequence was, the poor creatures all got drunk, and a fight ensued, which ended in the death of two head chiefs, Bull Bear and Yellow Lodge, and six of their friends,—besides the wounding of fourteen others, who took part in the affray.

Soon after, an affair occurred from the same cause, resulting in the death of three.

About the same time, another of like nature took place in the Chyenne village, and three more were killed.

Several were also killed, in the interval, in the vicinity of the Chyenne and Missouri rivers, by their friends and companions, while under the maddening influence of intoxicating drink,—the precise number is not known.

The very last trade at the close of the season, produced its usual deeds of bloodshed and murder. Two Indians were killed, and the person who sold to them the vile article narrowly escaped with his life.

I might go on still further with the sickening sketch; but, as enough has already been said to shock the sensibilities of the reader, in endeavoring to afford him some idea of the enormities and untold horrors connected with this criminal traffic, I must forbear.

The liquor used in this business, is generally third or fourth proof whiskey, which, after being diluted by a mixture of three parts water, is sold to the Indians at the exorbitant rate of three cups per robe,—the cups usually holding about three gills each.

But, notwithstanding the above unconscionable price, a large share of the profits result from the ingenious roguery of those conducting the trade.

Sometimes the measuring-cup is not more than half full;—then, again the act of measuring is little other than mere feint, (the purchaser receiving not one fourth the quantity paid for.)

When he becomes so intoxicated as to be unable to distinguish the difference between water and liquor, (a thing not rare,) the former is passed off upon him as the genuine article.

Another mode of cheating is, by holding the cup in such a manner that the two front fingers occupy a place upon the inside, and thus save to the trader nearly a gill at each filling.

Some have two cups, (one of the usual size, and the other less,) which are so exchanged as to induce the purchaser to believe he is obtaining a third more than he actually receives; and others, yet more cunning, fill the measure half full of tallow and deal out the liquor from off it,—the witless dupe, not thinking to examine the bottom, supposes he receives the requisite quantity.

No wonder the Indian, with such examples before him, learns to hate the white man, and despise and abhor his boasted civilization. No wonder he looks with an eye of suspicion, alike upon his religion and his learning, and revolts at the thought of either, as the ingenious devices of scientific roguery. He is taught all the white man's vices before he learns any of his virtues. The emissaries of Satan, by their untiring efforts, effectually stop his ears, blind his eyes, and harden his heart, ere yet the heralds of the Gospel set foot upon his soil, to tell him of the blessings of Christianity, and the way to happiness and to heaven.

If the Indian is bad, it is because the white man has made him so. Uncontaminated by intercourse with the offscourings of civilization, who come to cheat and despoil him of his property, and deprive him of his comforts, you find him quite a different being. You find him brave, generous, and hospitable, as well as possessed of many exemplary moral qualities. If he is a savage, he might, in many respects, prove a safe and worthy teacher to those who pride themselves upon a more enlightened education.

He has a heart instinctive of more genuine good feeling than his white neighbor—a soul of more firm integrity—a spirit of more unyielding independence. Place the white man in his condition, divested of all the restraints of law, and unacquainted with the learning and arts of civilized life—surrounded by all the associations of the savage state—and the Indian, by comparison, will then exhibit, in a more striking light, that innate superiority he in reality possesses.

No: The Indian should not be despised. He holds weighty claims upon our pity, our compassion, and our respect,—but never should he be despised.

Old Bull Tail, of whom I had occasion to speak in a former chapter having forgotten the wholesome sentiments he advanced at the time referred to, took it into his head to have a spree. But, as he was not possessed of the means to obtain the wherewith, he adopted a somewhat novel substitute.

He had an only daughter,—and she was handsome—the pride of her family and the boast of her village. She was lovely, and all the high qualities of a princess were exhibited in her deportment. But, Bull Tail must drink; why not give his daughter to the Yellow-hair and receive from him a keg of liquor as a marriage present?

This thought was acted out, and one morning the old chief came to us, followed by his daughter, who, aware of her father's designs, gave vent to her grief in a flood of tears.

As he entered the door, our trader addressed him:

*Trader.* Bull Tail is welcome to the lodge of the Long-knife;—but, why is his daughter, the pride of his heart, bathed in tears? It pains me that one so beautiful should weep.

## INDIAN MODE OF COURTSHIP.

*Bull Tail.* Chintzille is a foolish girl. Her father loves her, and therefore she cries.

*Trader.* The contrary should prove a greater cause for grief!

*Bull Tail.* The Yellow-hair speaks well, and truth only falls from his lips.

*Trader.* How, then, can she sorrow? Bid her speak and tell me, that I may whisper in her ear words of comfort.

*Bull Tail.* Nay, pale-face; but I will tell thee. Bull Tail loves his daughter much—very much; he loves the Yellow-hair much!—he loves them both, very much. The Great Spirit has put the thought into his mind that both might be alike his children; then would his heart leap for joy at the twice-spoken name of father!

*Trader.* What do I hear? I know not the meaning of thy words.

*Bull Tail.* Sure, pale-face, thou art slow to understand! Bull Tail would give his daughter to the Yellow-hair,—for who like him is so worthy to take her to his lodge? Bull Tail has for a long time called the paleface his brother, and now he would claim the Yellow-hair as his son. Loves he not Chintzille?

*Trader.* Were I to deny my joy at the words of Bull Tail, my tongue would lie! The Yellow-hair has no wife, and who, like the lovely Chintzille, is so worthy that he should take her to his bosom? How could he ever show his gratitude to her noble father!

*Bull Tail.* The gift is free, and Bull Tail will be honored in its acceptance,—his friends will all be glad with him. But, that they may bless the Yellow-hair, let him fill up the hollow-wood* with fire-water, and Bull Tail will take it to his lodge;—then the maiden shall be thine.

*Trader.* But, Chintzille grieves,—she loves not the Yellow-hair!

*Bull Tail.* Chintzille is foolish. Let the Yellow-hair measure the fire-water and she shall be thine!

*Trader.* Nay, but the Yellow-hair may not do this. Chintzille should never be the wife of him she loves not!

The old man continued to plead for some time, in order to bring to a successful issue the negotiation by which he hoped to "wet his whistle" and gain a son-in-law,—but all to no purpose. Our trader could not be persuaded to form an alliance so entangling upon any such terms, and the chieftain left with all the lineaments of disappointment and chagrin depicted upon his countenance.

The mode of marriage prevalent among the mountain and prairie tribes would seem rather strange and somewhat unfair to the better informed of civilized communities.

The lady has little to say or do in the business. When an Indian takes it into his head to get married and meets with the squaw suiting his fancy, he wastes no time in useless courtship, but hastens to her father and demands of him to know how much he loves his daughter and what gift of horses will make his heart rejoice in a son-in-law?

The father, after consulting with his daughter and her mother, states the

* Keg.

terms. If these prove agreeable to the suitor, he immediately accepts them, and the twain "become one flesh" without further ceremony.

In case the woman has no father, her eldest brother fills his place,—and if she have neither father nor brother, her next nearest relative assumes the responsibility of bestowing her in marriage.

If she be the eldest daughter, and has unmarried sisters, the bridegroom becomes equally entitled to them, and is looked upon as their common husband.

The first year succeeding this new relation, the bride's family consider all the horses and other valuables of the new-made husband as their own; the second year he is permitted to retain his personal property for the use of himself and wife;—but the third year he enjoys an equal right with his relatives to everything in their possession.

The decision of parents in the bestowment of a daughter in marriage is generally controlled by the largeness of the amount offered; thus showing that civilized life is not the only condition in which individuals are sometimes governed by sordid motives in pronouncing upon questions of such vital importance to the welfare of others.

The female is the only party upon whom the marriage contract is considered binding.

The man may sunder it at any time suiting his convenience or caprice. He has the power, even, to dispose of his wife to another, or, at a mere word, to absolve himself from all obligation to her. In case of the latter, the discarded one returns to her father's lodge,—ready again to test the realities of this uncertain relationship, whenever an opportunity presents itself meeting with the approval of those who assume to make barter of her affections and person.

A woman, to be happy in this state of society, should never indulge in that fancied passion, pictured in such glowing colors by crack-brained poets and novel-writers, called *love;*—or, if she has the assurance to do otherwise, it should be of that more versatile and accommodating order, so often exhibited in more refined circles, which may be reclaimed and transferred as interest or circumstances suggest. Her affections are not at her own disposal, and, to render life tolerable, she must learn to love *only as* she is loved, and to love herself above all others.

Next to horses, women constitute an Indian's chief wealth. This circumstance not unfrequently results in one individual appropriating to himself six or eight.

The squaw is compelled to dress robes and skins, make moccasins, cure and take care of meat, attend to the horses, procure fire-wood, and perform sundry other little drudgeries that an Indian will not do. Through her he becomes possessed of the means of procuring from the whites such articles as his necessities or fancy may require. A plurality of wives with him, therefore, is more a matter of economy than otherwise.

## CHAPTER X.

Tahtunga-goniska.—High gaming.—Weur-sena Warkpollo, a strange story.—The Death Song, a tale of love.—Medicine-men.—Extraordinary performance of Tahtunga-mobellu.—Wonderful feats of jugglery.

AMONG our daily visitors was Tahtunga-egoniska, a head chief of the Brulé village.

Years had bleached his locks with their taming frosts and taught him self-government. Well disposed as a man, he never became a participant in those disgusting scenes of intoxication that almost continually transpired around us. He was a mere looker on—a moralizer; and, as he witnessed the blameworthy conduct of his people, an ill-suppressed sigh was frequently audible, and the inward workings of regret were plainly defined upon his countenance. Melancholy too had left her traces upon him, and, as he sat day by day in gloomy silence, he seemed the very impersonation of grief.

Whenever the throng dispersed for a few moments, he would improve the opportunity for conversation with us; for in the benevolence of his heart he loved the whites, and was greatly pained at the injuries and injustice it was so often their lot to endure.

But he had a story of his own to tell; it was a tale of affliction—a stab at the best feelings of a father's heart! And, by whom? By the very whites he loved! Aye, by the very men whose business it was to degrade his people and ruin them by the contaminating effects of an unhallowed intercourse!

Six months had scarcely yet passed since the old chief had been called to mourn his youthful hope, and the pride and joy of his declining years—his first-born son! And that son had fallen by the hand of the white man!

Still, the sorrow-stricken father harbored no thought of revenge; he sought nothing for himself save the locks of that son, that he might hang them within his lodge, and gaze upon them and weep!

His simple tale was so touching in its nature it served to enlist the deep sympathies of our hearts. We began to regard him with much deference, and felt quite at home in his company. He would frequently entertain us with his anecdotes as occasions suggested, and at such times he invariably proved both agreeable and communicative.

The history of his own life, too, was far from uninteresting. He was the only one of the Brulé chiefs, then living, who had signed the first treaty with the whites, since which he had ever observed its stipulations with scrupulous exactness, and still carefully retained a silver medal bestowed upon him by the Government agent at that time.

Some of his stories were garbed with a strange romance, and though they may appear foreign to truth in many respects, I cannot resist the temptation of presenting a few of them to the reader.

One day, several Indians had betted largely upon a "game of hand;"* this called forth from the old man the following story:

"When a young man I delighted in war, and seldom did a party of our people visit the enemy that included me not with its number. These scars tell where I stood when arrows flew thick—hastening to spill the blood of the brave.

"Rarely did we return empty-handed from the foeman's land—without horses to ride or scalps to dance. Yet, at times we came back like fools, and were ashamed to appear at the soldiers' feasts.

"One of these times I well recollect, and I will tell of it to my white children, that they also may remember it.

"We were proceeding against the Crows, and, like experienced warriors, had sent our spy in advance to look for the enemy. Hurrying on, in momentary expectation of a conflict, the stout hearts of our braves were appalled by his return without robe or arms, and scalpless—and with a face suffused in blood.

"This was his story: The enemy, aware of our approach, were awaiting us in great numbers. Encountering their scouts, he had been robbed and scalped, and left for dead. In this situation he lay till darkness shut down upon the mountain and the night-breeze gave him strength to meet us and advise our speedy return.

"Believing the strange tale, we hastened to revisit our lodges, and be laughed at.

"Three moons sped, and we again penetrated the land of the foemen. The scalpless warrior, far in advance of the main party, once more discharged the duties of a spy.

"This time a whoop of triumph announced the result of his mission, as he made his appearance with the scalps of two, waving from his spear.

"He tarried not to relate his adventure, but urged us instantly onward. Following him, we were led to the enemy;—we fought and were victorious.

"Among the slain was one whose scalp was wanting. Who has done this? asked the wondering braves. But none answered. Our spy, smiling, at length broke silence:

"'Behind yon hill,' said he, 'a fountain chants melody fit for warriors' ears,—let's to it, that we may drink.'

"Following his direction, he led to a silvery spring overhung by crags and shaded by cottonwoods.

"'Drink, warriors,' he exclaimed; when, withdrawing abruptly, he soon returned, and with the arms and robe which were his own in other days.

"Warriors,' resumed the spy: 'you wondered at my mishap, and lamented my hard lot when last we visited the Crowman's country;—you wondered at the condition of one among the recent slain, and asked for a reason;—and, doubtless, you wonder still more that I now stand before

---

* This is a common game with the mountain Indians. It is commenced by one of the players who encloses a gravel-stone or a bullet in the curve of his two hands by placing the palms together, then, after sundry tosts and evolutions, suddenly parting them. If the opposing party is shrewd enough to guess in which hand the stone is retained, he wins; if not not, he loses. Large amounts are often wagered upon the result of this play.

you bearing the store of which I was deprived!—and fain you would know in what manner I obtained the hair of two.

"'Three times has the night-queen turned her full face to smile upon the prowess of Lacota arms, since at this very spot I met an enemy. We rushed towards each other for the attack. 'Twas then he cried:

"'Are we not both braves? why should we fight? When our people meet in the fray, then may we join arms,—till then, a truce.'

"'To this I replied,

"'Says Crowman peace?—then, be there peace.'

"'Thus said, we shook hands and sat down by the fountain.

"'Willing to amuse the foe, I gathered a pebble and proposed a game of hand. The challenge was accepted, and we played,—first, arrow against arrow, then bow against bow, robe against robe, and scalp against scalp.

"'I was unsuccessful and lost all,—arrow, bow, robe, and scalp. I gave up all, but with the extorted promise that we should here meet again for another trial of skill.

"'True to the word, we did meet again. We played, and this time, the Good Spirit showed me kindness.

"'Winning back arrows, bow and robe, I staked them all against the lost scalp. The game was a close one; but again the Good Spirit favored me, and I won.

"'Crowman,' said I, 'scalp against scalp.'

"'The banter was accepted, and the play continued. He lost, and I, with my winnings, arose to leave.

"'Warrior,' exclaimed the luckless player, 'meet me in the fight, that we may try the game of arms.'

"'Thy words please me,' I answered. 'Will the Crowman name the place?'

"'A valley lies beyond this hill,—there my people await their enemies, and there let me hope to see you with them.'

"'To that place I led you. We fought and conquered. My opponent at play was among the slain. Need I tell you who took his scalp?'"

The old man seemed to take pleasure in acquainting us with the manners and customs of his people, and was ever ready to assign a reason for any of them, whenever such existed. He repeated to us the names of all the streams, mountains, and prominent localities of the country, and explained the causes of their several christenings.

Some thirty miles to the westward of us, flowed a large creek, called by the Indians, "Weur-sena Warkpollo," or Old Woman's creek. This stream is an affluent of the Chyenne river, and takes its rise at the base of a mountain bearing the same name.

The mountain is an object of great veneration with the Sioux, who rarely enter into its neighborhood without bestowing upon it a present of meat. The old man entertained us with the following explanation of a custom so singular:

"My grandfather told me a tale he had received from the old men before him, and it is a strange one.

"Many ages past bring us back to the time when the Lacotas lived in a country far above the sun of winter.*

* The north.

"Here, then, the Shoshone reared his white lodge, and scoured the prairies in pursuit of game; while, as yet, the whole country abounded with lakes and ponds of water, and only the highlands and mountains were left for the buffalo and deer.

"But years passed on,—the mountains and highlands continued to prey upon the waters, and the creeks and rivers gradually reduced the limits of their possessions.

"Years again fled. The Shoshones, attracted by some better region, far away, or driven from their homes by the hostile encroachments of other tribes, gave place to the Scarred-arms.*

"In the course of generations, the Lacotas and the Scarred-arms warred with each other; they fought with varied success for many years.

"Once a party of the Lacotas penenetrated into the heart of the enemy's country; on their return, they fell into an ambuscade, and only six of them were left to tell the fate of their companions.

"Hotly pursued by the Scarred-arms, they sought refuge in a mountain. There an obscure passage led to a recess in the mountain's side, which they entered, and were pleased to find within it a gravelly floor, and a pure fountain of sweet water.

"Tempted by the conveniences and security of the place, they thought to remain for a few days that they might recover their strength. A small fire was built accordingly, and the six braves seated themselves around it, recounting to each other their perils and dangerous exploits, and planning some mode of extrication from their present difficulties.

"Thus busied, a rustling noise from a dark corner of the apartment startled them,—but still more were they aroused by the half-disclosed form of a person moving in the distance. Words gave place to silence, as the warriors, seizing their arms, awaited the feared assault. But the figure, on advancing nearer, proved that of a feeble old woman, who addressed the wondering group in their own language.

"'Children,' said she, 'you have been against the Scarred-arms,—you have fought them,—and of a strong party, you alone survive. I know it all.

"'You seek in my lodge a refuge from your pursuers,—and the sound of your voices with the heat of your council-fire has disturbed my rest and awoke me from a long, long trance.

"'Your looks enquire my story.

"'Many ages have gone, (for days, moons, seasons, and ages are painted before me as they pass,) since the Shoshones, who lived where now live the Scarred-arms, visited the lodges of the Lacotas, and bade the prairie drink the blood of slaughtered braves. I was their captive, and with the scalps of the slain I was taken from the graves of my people, many days travel.

"'The Shoshone brought me to this country, when yet the buffalo grazed upon the hills and mountains, only; for the valleys and plains were the home of waters.

"'Living with the Shoshone, I was not happy. I thought of my peo-

*Chyennes. The name owes its origin to the practice of scarring the left arm crosswise yet adhered to by the males of that nation.

ple, with all those dear to me, and prayed the Good Spirit that I might again behold them ere my passage to the death-land.

"'I fled, hoping to reach the home of my birth;—but age had enfeebled me, and being pursued, I sought refuge in this cave. Here, having passed a night and a day in earnest communion with the Big Medicine,—a strange feeling came upon me. I slumbered, in a dreamy state of consciousness, from then till now.

"'But your looks again ask, who are the Shoshones?—what became of them? And from whence were the Scarred-arms?'

"'The Lacotas will soon know the Shoshones, and bring from their lodges many scalps and medicine-dogs. Divided into two tribes, that nation long since sought home in other lands. One crossed the snow-hills towards the sun-setting;—the Lacotas shall visit them, and avenge the blood and wrongs of ages. The other journeyed far away towards the sun of winter, and now live to the leftward of the places where the Hispanola builds his earth-lodge.*

"'Then came the Scarred-arms from a far off country, a land of much snow and cold. Pleased with the thickly tenanted hunting grounds that here met them, they stopped for the chase, and, by a possession through successive generations, have learned to consider these grounds as their own. But they are not theirs.

"'The Great Spirit gives them to the Lacotas, and they shall inhabit the land of their daughter's captivity.

"'Why wait ye here? Go and avenge the blood of your comrades upon the Scarred-arms. They even now light their camp-fire by the stream at the mountain's base. Fear not,—their scalps are yours! Then return ye to my people, that ye may come and receive your inheritance.

"'Haste ye, that I may die. And, oh Warkantunga! inasmuch as thou hast answered the prayer of thine handmaid, and shown to me the faces of my people, take me from hence.'

"The awe-struck warriors withdrew. They found the enemy encamped at the foot of the mountain. They attacked him and were victorious;—thirty-five scalps were the trophies of their success.

"On reaching their homes the strange adventure excited the astonishment of the whole nation. The Scarred-arms were attacked by our warriors, thus nerved with the hope of triumph, and were eventually driven from the country now possessed by the Locotas as their own.

"The grateful braves soon sought out the mountain, to do reverence to the medicine-woman who had told them so many good things. A niche in the mountain-side, from whence issued a sparkling streamlet, told their place of refuge; but the cave and the woman alike had disappeared.

"Each successive season do our warriors visit the Shoshones for scalps and medicine-dogs,—and each of our braves, as he passes the Old Woman's

---

* It is a singular fact, that the Cumanches and Snakes, (Shoshones,) though living nearly a thousand miles distant from each other, with hostile tribes intervening, speak precisely the same language, and call themselves by the same general name. They have lost all tradition, however, of having formed one nation, in any previous age.

mountain, fails not to bestow upon it his tribute of veneration, or quench his thirst from the creek that bears her name."

A place on White river—where the stream pours its full force against the base of a lofty peak, and the powerful attrition of its waters has formed a rocky precipice of several hundred feet in height—is known as "The Death Song." The singularity of this name led me to enquire the reasons which prompted its bestowment. Ever ready to answer questions of this nature, the old chief related the following story:

"Once, on a time, the Oglallas and Burnt-thighs held their encampmen upon the river, opposite to the high point of which my son enquires. While there, a dog-soldier\* of the Burnt-thighs received the offer of six horses from an Oglalla brave, for his only daughter—a sweet flower—such an one as oft pierces the warrior's heart with her charms, when the arrows of enemies fall harmless at his feet. The offer was quickly accepted—for the dog-soldier was poor.

"When Chischille (for that was the name of the fair one) heard she was to become the wife of the Oglalla, she cried for grief,—and so obstinate was her resistance, the marriage was deferred for several days on that account.

"But, why did Chischille grieve? She had looked upon a handsome warrior of her own village, and she loved him. She forgot her duty, as a daughter, to love only at her father's bidding. Her heart had been playing truant and had lost itself in the labyrinths of girlish fancy. Bitter were the fruits of that presumption.

"Chischille, in the interval, contrived to meet the one of her choice, and the two fled towards a distant village, there to live in the undisturbed enjoyment of their youthful loves.

"But, alas, for them! They were pursued, and overtaken. The life of the young warrior atoned for his temerity,—while Chischille was cruelly beaten and brought back to her father's lodge.

"The Oglalla had already paid the purchase price, and, ere the morrow's sunset, was to receive his fair prize at the hand of the dog-soldier.

"Chischille, arising with the dawn, fresh-plaited her hair, and arraying herself in her proudest attire, left the lodge. No one thought strange at seeing her thus gaily dressed for her wedding day, and, as she tripped along, many a warrior's heart beat high and loud at the thought that a creature so lovely was to become the bride of another.

"Directing her course to the river, she crossed it and ascended the high peak upon the opposite side. There, seating herself upon the utmost verge of the precipice, she gazed calmly from its dizzy height.

"In her lofty station, with her raven locks streaming in the winds, and the matchless beauty of her person so enchantingly exposed to view, she seemed more like a being of the Spirit-Land than aught human. The sweetest prairie-flower was ne'er half so lovely.

"Her strange attitude arrested the eyes of all.

"'Why sits she there?—she will fall and be dashed to pieces!' was the general cry. 'But listen—she sings!'

---

\* This is the title of those selected to superintend the civil affairs of a village.

"'Why should I stay,—he is gone. Light of my eyes,—joy of my soul,—show me thy dwelling!—'Tis not here,—'tis far away in the Spirit Land. Thither he is gone. Why should I stay? Let me go!'

"'Hear you that?' said one. 'She sings her death song. She will throw herself from the cliff!'

"At this, a dozen warriors, headed by him who claimed her hand, started to rescue the sweet singer from intended self-destruction.

"Again she chants:

"'Spirit of Death, set me free! Dreary is earth. Joyless is time. Heart, thou art desolate! Wed thee another? Nay. Death is thy husband! Farewell, oh sun! Vain is your light. Farewell, oh earth! Vain are your plains, your flowers, your grassy dales, your purling streams, and shady groves! I loved you once,—but now no longer love! Tasteless are your sweets,—cheerless your pleasures! Thee I woo, kind Death! Wahuspa calls me hence. In life we were one. We'll bask together in the Spirit Land. Who shall sunder there? Short is my pass to thee. Wahuspa, I come!'

"Upon this she threw herself forward, as the warriors grasped at her; but, leaving her robe in their hands, she plunged headlong and was dashed to pieces among the rocks below!*

"E'er since, the young warrior sighs as he beholds this peak, and thinks of the maiden's death song."

Conversing upon the subject of medicine-men, he was asked, why those individuals are so highly esteemed by his people? To this he replied:

"These men are regarded as the peculiar favorites of the Great Spirit, to whom is imparted a more than ordinary share of His power and wisdom. We respect them, therefore, in proportion to the abilities they receive, even as we reverence the Great Spirit."

Here the question was proposed, how are their abilities above those of others?

"The Yellow-hair counts as his soldier Tahtunga-mobellu,—a man of strong medicine. To him the Great Spirit has imparted the power of healing, by imbibing, at pleasure, the diseases of the sick, and discharging them from his eyes and nose in the form of live snakes.†

"On a time, years past, our young men went to the Pawnees and came back crying; for sixteen slain of their number were left to grace an enemy's triumph.

"It was winter, and the moans of men and maidens mingled with the howling winds. Sorrow beclouded every brow, and brave looked upon brave as if to enquire, 'Who shall wipe out this disgrace?' Then it was a medicine-chief stood up, and his words were:

"'Be it for me to consult the Good Spirit.'

---

* A tale which went the rounds of the public prints, several years since, entitled the "Maiden's Leap," affords a seeming coincidence in the mode of suicide; but, by comparing the two, the reader will observe a broad dissimilarity of detail. In penning the above I was guided solely by the leading incidents as related in my hearing.

† Tahtunga-mobellu receives the averment of all his villagers in proof of this strange feat.

"So saying, he entered his lodge alone, nor suffered any to come near during the long fast that followed. Darkness had closed four times upon the prairie, and the sun again hastened to hide behind the mountain peaks, when, calling the young men to him, the medicine-man said:

"'Fetch me now meat and water, with a new robe, and bid my people come near, that they may know the words that I would speak.'

"The obedient braves made haste and did as bidden. Folding the robe, he sat upon it and partook of the refreshments placed before him. After eating he arose, and six large snakes, crawling from the robe one after another, sprang to his shoulder, and, whispering in his ear, vanished from sight. The last snake had just told his message when the chief began:

"'The Good Spirit wills it, that we remove from hence. Three moons being dead, let three hundred warriors return, and their hearts shall be made glad with medicine-dogs and the scalps of enemies.'

"The village left, and, at the time appointed, the warriors returned. They met the enemy,—fought, and were victorious. Sixty-three scalps and one hundred medicine-dogs were the fruits of their success."

Before dismissing the subject, many other particulars were cited in proof of the extraordinary abilities of different medicine-men, but the above being the most remarkable, I have thought proper to pass over the remainder in silence.

NOTE.—An account, still more wonderful than either of the foregoing, was subsequently narrated in my hearing, while among the Arapaho Indians; and, without vouching for the truth of all its particulars, I am unwilling to withhold it from the reader.

The performance alluded to is said to have occurred, some three years since, in the presence of the whole Arapaho village, incredible as it may seem. The actor was a Riccaree by nation, and is well known to the mountain traders.

In the centre of a large circle of men, women, and children, stood the subject of the appended sketch, stripped to the waist, as the gunner's mark. A shot perforated his body with a bullet, which entered at the chest and emerged from the opposite side. He instantly fell, and the blood flowing in streams dyed the grass where he lay, and everything seemed to prefigure the reality of death.

While in this condition, his wife approached and besprinkled his face with water; soon after which he arose, as from a slumber—the blood still pouring from him. Beplastering his wound with mud before and behind, the blood ceased to flow, when he commenced yawning and stretching; in a few minutes the plaster was removed by a pass of the hand, and neither blood, nor wound, nor the sign of a scratch or scar appeared! There stood the self-restored medicine-man, before the wondering throng, alive and well, and in all the pride of his strength!

He then brought his naked son into the ring, a lad of some eight years, and, standing at a distance of several yards, bow in hand, he pierced him through and through, from diaphragm to vertebræ, at three successive shots.

The boy fell dead, to every appearance, and the thick blood freely coursed from his wounds.

The performer then clasped the body in his arms and bore it around the ring for the inspection of all, three times in succession. Upon this he breathed into his mouth and nostrils, and, after suffusing his face with water and covering his wounds with a mud plaster, he commenced brief manipulations upon his stomach, which soon ended in a complete recovery, nor left a single trace of injury about him.

Both of these feats, if performed as said, can scarcely admit the possibility of trick or slight of hand, and must stand as the most astonishing instances of jugglery on record.

AN INDIAN CONJUROR. — Page 132.

## CHAPTER XI.

Food for horses.—Squaws and their performances.—Dogs and dog-meat.—Return to Fort.—Starvation.—Travel by guess.—Death from drinking.—Medicine-making.—A burial.—Little Lodge and the French trader.—A speech in council.—Journey to White river.—High winds and deep snow.—Intense sufferings and painful results.

A LARGE grove of cottonwood near us, day after day was graced by groups of village squaws, armed with axes, for the procurement of horse food.

The bark of this tree is eaten freely by both horses and mules, and answers well as a substitute for corn or oats. Animals will thrive upon it in a remarkable manner, and even in the summer months they prefer it to grass. The bark of red elm is also used for the same purpose.

The operations of the squaws at such times contributed greatly to our amusement. Climbing fearlessly to the topmost branch of the highest tree, they would there lop off the surrounding boughs, with as much apparent ease as though footed upon *terra firma*.

And then, the enormous loads they would carry, lashed together with cords and slung to their backs, were enough to make a giant stagger. Dogs, harnessed to travées, had their part to perform, and ofttimes were they a source of vexation to their mistresses.

A squaw, trudging along under a full donkey-load of cottonwood, and followed by a squad of half-naked children, presented a spectacle quite interesting; but this was rendered rather comical, withal, when two or three draught-dogs with their heavy-laden travées reluctantly brought up the rear—every now and then lying down for weariness, or squatting to loll and gaze at their companions.

Now, she coaxes and caresses to urge them forward—they still delay. Then she turns briskly towards them with a stick,—get out, dogs!—"Yierh! Warktashne ceicha," cries the squaw, accompanying her denunciation with blows, and away go the yelping troop as fast as legs can carry them.

Dogs are the necessary appendage of every Indian lodge, and generally form an equal portion of the village population. They present almost all the different varieties of the canine species, from the wolf to the spaniel, and from the spaniel to the hairless dog of Africa. The wolf, however, is predominant, and, taken together, they more assimilate a gang of wolves than anything else. Indeed, the different varieties of prairie wolves hold familiar intercourse with the village dogs, and associate with them on friendly terms.

The species used for draught, is a large, stout-built, wolfish-looking creature, of the Exquimaux breed. Trained to his duties in early life, he is generally both submissive and tractable. The drudgery of a squaw, which is at all times onerous, without his ready aid would prove past endurance.

But these dogs are also useful in another respect. Their flesh furnishes an article highly esteemed for food, and which almost invariably graces the soldiers' feast and every other scene of conviviality. However much the squamishness of the reader may revolt at the suggestion, justice impels me to say, the flesh of a fat Indian dog, suitably cooked, is not inferior to fresh pork; and, by placing side by side select parts of the two, it would be no easy task even for a good judge to tell the difference, by either looks or taste, unless he were previously informed.

Towards the last of January, buffalo having left the vicinity, the Indians, as a necessary consequence, were compelled to move. A great scarcity of provisions prevailed among them, and we ourselves were scarcely better off than they.

Our stock in hand was nearly exhausted, and an abandonment of the post became absolutely necessary,—a thing, however, which could not be performed without a fresh supply of horses and cattle from Fort Platte. For this purpose, I volunteered my services, and, accompanied by two engagés, was promptly under way.

A few hours' ride brought us to the head of White river, where, consuming at a meal our scanty eatables, from that onward we were left entirely destitute.

This was the first occasion subjecting me to the pains of hunger for so long a time. The second day I experienced the greatest annoyance, and then it was I felt some of the realities of starvation. The third day, however, I awoke in the morning scarcely thinking of breakfast. In fact, my appetite seemed quite passive, and the only sensation I felt was a kind of weakness and lassitude, evincing the lack of proper nourishment.

The morning was cloudy and threatening. Soon after leaving camp, snow began to fall, thick and fast. The day proved so dark, objects were indiscernible at the distance of a hundred yards in advance. Travelling, as we were, over a trackless prairie, with nothing to guide us but the wind and the position of the grass, it was by the merest accident we reached our destination a few minutes before nightfall.

Our sudden appearance was the occasion of general surprise to the Fort hands, and, after a brief explanation, we began to make amends for previous abstinence.

At first, a few mouthfuls sufficed,—but soon I again felt hungry and could be satisfied only with a double quantity,—in an equally short time my stomach demanded a still further supply, and, by the next day, hunger became so keen it seemed almost insatiable. An interval of three or four weeks was requisite before it assumed its wonted tone.

During our stay here, an Indian family, occupying one of the Fort rooms, indulged themselves in a drunken spree.

Having procured a quantity of the American Fur Company's liquor, the effects of their lavish potations soon became manifest to all within hearing distance. But the din of drunken revelry erelong assumed the wail of mourning and sorrow.

Hearing the strange commotion, I entered the room to ascertain the cause. There lay, helpless upon the floor, and apparently at the point of death, a squaw of some eighteen years;—she, in her eagerness, had swallowed nearly a pint of the vile stuff, undiluted, and now experienced its dreadful consequences.

But most conspicuous in the throng was a large, obese, cross-eyed Indian, earnestly engaged in his medicine-performances for her recovery.

A breech-cloth was his sole garb, as, with eyes half strained from their sockets and volving in a strange unearthly manner, he stood, first upon one foot and then upon the other, alternately—then, stamping the floor as if to crush it through, and meanwhile, grunting, screeching, and bellowing, and beating his breast or the wall with his clenched fists,—then, with inhaled breath, swelling like a puff-ball, he would bend over his patient and apply sugescents to her mouth, throat and breast.

This done, sundry ejections of saliva prepared his mouth for the reception of an ample draught of water, with which he bespatted her face and forehead.

But yet, all these extraordinary efforts failed to produce their designed effect. The poor squaw grew weaker, and her breathing became fainter and more difficult.

Some powerful restorative must be adopted, or she will soon be beyond the reach of medicine,—so thought the officiating doctor; or, at least, his succeeding antics indicated that such were the cogitations of his mind. Standing for a minute or two in the attitude of reflection, an idea stuck him. Ah, he has it now! This cannot fail.

Snatching a butcher-knife and hastening with it to the fire, he heats the point to redness upon the coals,—then balancing it between his teeth, at a toss he flings it vaulting above his head and backward upon the floor,—then, re-catching it, he goes through the performance a second and a third time.

Thus premised, he addresses himself with threefold energy to the grotesque and uncouth manœuvres before described. If he had stamped his feet, he now stamps them with a determination hitherto unknown;—if he had thumped his breast and beat the walls, he now thumps and beats as if each blow were intended to prostrate the object against which it was directed,—if he had grunted, screeched, and bellowed, he now grunts, screeches, bellows, and yells, till the very room quakes with the reverberations of domoniac noise;—if he had gagged, puffed, and swelled, he now gags, puffs, and swells, as if he would explode from the potency of his extraordinary inflations.

Then, with an air of confidence, he hies to his patient and commences a process of manipulation from her breast downwards, and reverse,—and then again he repeats his previous operations, with scrupulous exactness and unsparing effort, in all their varied minutiæ.

But, alas for the medicine-man!—the squaw died, despite the omnipotence of his skill!

Then was enacted another such a scene of piteous wailing, as Indians alone have in requisition, as vent for their grief.

After the usual preliminaries, the corpse of the deceased was placed upon a scaffold beside that of Susu-ceicha, the old chief of whom I have spoken in a former chapter. Each member of the bereaved family deposited a tuft of hair in the sack containing the meat and trinkets placed beneath her head. A smooth piece of cottonwood slab was then affixed to the scaffold, upon which were traced, in vermilion, certain quadrangular characters of unknown meaning,—answering well to the idea of an inscription of name and age.

A difficulty occurred about this time between a trader of the American Fur Company and an Oglalla chief, known as Little Lodge. The latter had become crazed by liquor, and, being rather turbulent, was put out of the Fort. But, effecting a re-entrance, he again proved equally annoying. The trader then commenced quarrelling with him, and undertook to seize his arms. This the Indian resisted, when the trader discharged a pistol at him, but missed his object. Here was a deadly affront, that blood alone could wipe away.

With great difficulty, the Indian was finally disarmed and bound. He was thus secured till the next day, when he was liberated;—still, however, he muttered threats of revenge.

Two or three weeks subsequently, Little Lodge was present at a soldiers' feast, and the question of war with the Americans was a prominent subject of consideration.

Several speeches were made, both for and against it; and, though the prevailing sentiment seemed to be of an adverse kind, it scarcely required a half dozen words to turn the scale upon either side.

Little Lodge arose to address the council, and the friends of the whites, knowing the vengeful spirit that yet rankled in his bosom at the remembrance of his recent injuries, began to fear for the continuance of peace.

Contrary to the universal expectation, he contended for its maintenance. "But," said he, "Little Lodge has grievances of his own, and they call for redress.

"There is one among the pale-faces whose blood must wash away the foul blot that rests upon the name of Little Lodge. I know him well. He is not a Long-knife. The Long-knives are all the friends of Little Lodge. Let the Lacota take them by the hand whenever he meets them upon the prairie. It is good that he do so. They are very many and exceedingly rich. Their country is a large one, and far away towards the sunrising. They, too, are strong for war. They have big hearts and strong, and they are very good to the red man. They bring to him many good things; why, then, should the Lacota hate the Long-knife?

"Do my brothers ask who it is of the pale-faces the Little Lodge would remove from the light of day? Know, then, he is not of the Long-knives, —he is of the Warceichas, (Frenchmen.) The Warceichas are not Long-knives!

"And, do my brothers ask, who are the Warceichas?

"Aye, who are they? Little Lodge cannot tell;—who of all the Lacotas can? Who ever heard of the country of these men? No one. They have no country,—they are no people. They are as the wandering dogs* that infest our hunting grounds and prey upon the game formed by the Good Spirit for the red man's sustenance. They steal into the land of

---

* Chunka-monet, or travelling dogs, is the name applied by these Indians to wolves.

the red man, and sneak around from place to place;—for they have no home; they have no country; they are no people!

"One of these it was who bade the medicine-iron speak its death-word to Little Lodge, and sought to spill the blood of a Lacota brave, after that he had made him a fool by means of his thickened* fire-water!

"Should Little Lodge fall by the hand of the Warceicha? He might fall by the hand of a Long-knife, and the nation would honor his memory, —but *never*, should the Warceicha bring him low!

"Then, is it not good that Little Lodge should be avenged upon this lost dog—this outcast of the world—that the whelps of a motherless breed may cease to insult and wrong the Lacotas? Which of all my brothers will say nay?"

The address was received in silence,—no one presuming to oppose an answer to its sentiments. Whether the speaker executed his threats of vengeance against the offending trader, I am yet unadvised.

Having remained two nights and a day at Fort Platte, we again started for White river, taking with us three yoke of oxen and several horses, one of which was laden with dried meat.

The snow greatly retarded our progress from the first, and so obscured the trail we were compelled to travel mostly by guess. The sun, too, was shut out by a tenebrous atmosphere, and we could judge of our proper course only by observing the movements of the clouds,† with the general range of the hills and ravines, or inclination of the grass.

The broad expanse of unbroken snow lying from Rawhide to L'eau-qui-court, brought a chill tremor with the thought of crossing it. Yet, go we must! It was no time to falter when the fate of others, perhaps, depended upon our prompt advance.

But the effort was no child's play. If we had experienced a tedious time during a former journey, what could we expect now? The whole interval of thirty miles was covered with snow, that grew deeper and deeper as we proceeded. Every hollow and ravine was filled, and the route otherwise seriously impeded by huge drifts and embankments.

We were frequently compelled to break foot-paths for our animals, and ever and anon pull them by main strength from the deep pitfalls into which they would plunge and become almost lost to view. In this manner our progress was slow,—the average depth through which we waded being but little less than two feet.

The rising of a fierce head wind, piercing as the blasts of Nova Zembla, drove the snow into our faces with mad fury and added immeasurably to our sufferings.

* Allusion is here made to the drugged liquor supposed to have been palmed upon him by the trader.

† The idea of directing our course by the movements of the clouds is doubtless a novel suggestion to most readers; but its philosophy will be readily comprehended by a bare mention of the fact, that the winds of these regions almost invariably blow from a west-southwest point; and, as they are usually high, it is no very extraordinary performance to calculate the bearing of north or south, even in the most obscure weather.

In this manner night shut down upon us, while yet far distant from any camping-place. And, such a night! Oh, storms and deadly winter, foul and fierce! how swept ye "through the darkened sky," and with your awful howlings rendered "the savage wilderness more wild!"

The creeping cold on every nerve played freely, in haste to sting our vitals, and lay us each

"——————— along the snows a stiffen'd corse,
Stretch'd out and bleaching in the northern blast!"

The impress of this event can never be effaced from my mind. It was midnight ere we arrived at the timberless L'eau-qui-court and struck camp. Our animals needed water, but we had neither axe or tomahawk to cut through the thick ice with which the creek was coated. As a remedy for this lack, all three of us advanced upon it, and, by our united efforts at jumping, caused a lengthy fissure with gentle escarpments towards each shore, that left midway an ample pool.

Having driven the cattle to this, in their clumsy movements upon the ice, two of them fell, and, sliding down the inclined plain, lay struggling in the freezing water, unable to rise. Our only resort was to drag them to the shore by main strength; for, left in their then condition, they must have frozen to death in a very short time.

Here commenced a series of pulling and wrenching, that, in our chilled and exhausted state, we were ill-prepared to endure.

For awhile our efforts proved vain. A backward-slide succeeded each headway-pull, and vexed us with useless toil. Thus we worried for nearly three hours in water knee-deep!

At length, having procured a rope and fastened one end to their horns and the other around a pointed rock upon the shore, and gathering the slack at each successive thrust, we finally succeeded in placing them both, one after the other, upon dry land.

But, now we were in a thrice sorry plight. Not a stick of wood could be raised, far or near, of which to build a fire, and *bois de vache*, the great substitute of the prairies, was too deeply covered with snow for procurement. Our clothes, wet to the waist, were frozen upon us, and the merciless wind, with stinging keenness, pierced us through at every breath, and stood us forth as living monuments of *ice!*

Could men of iron endure such incomprehensible hardships,—such inexpressible sufferings? Yet we survived them all!

Spreading a few robes upon the snow, we lay down for sleep, dinnerless and supperless. I was now seized with a chill, which lasted for two hours or more; and so violent were its actions I could scarcely keep the covering upon me.

My companions, however, though not similarly afflicted, were worse off than myself. One had his hands and ears frozen, and the other his hands and feet,—the painful consequences of which, as the frost began to yield to the influenco of generated warmth, were too apparent in their groans and writhings.

Morning at length came, and the sun arose bright and clear. The

HORSE ATTACKED BY WOLVES.— *Page* 143.

winds had ceased their ragings, and a clement atmosphere seemed pouring upon us the balm of sympathy for miseries so recently endured.

But their direful effects were not thus easily eradicated. The feet of one poor fellow were so badly frozen, it was three months before he entirely recovered; while another lost a portion of one of his ears. As for myself, a severe cold settled in my teeth, producing an intensely painful ache and swoollen face, that continued for eight or ten days.

It seems almost miraculous that we should have escaped so easily, and often, even after so long an interval, I shudder at the recollection of this anguishing scene.

Two days subsequently we reached our destination, and found all things pretty much *in statu quo.*

## CHAPTER XII.

Another drunken spree.—Horses devoured by wolves.—An upset.—A blowing up.—Daring feat of wolves.—A girl offered for liquor.—Winter on the Platte.—Boat building.—Hunting expedition.—Journey up the Platte.—Island camp.—Narrow escape.—Snow storm—Warm Spring.—Pass of the Platte into the prairies.—A valley.—Bitter Cottonwood.—Indian forts.—Wild fruit.—Root-digging.—Cherry tea and its uses.—Geology of the country.—Soils, grasses, herbs, plants, and purity of atmosphere.—Horse-shoe creek.—A panther.—Prairie dogs and their peculiarities.

Our intended evacuation of the post was posponed till the week following, and, meanwhile, the few customers, that still hung on, were careful to improve the passing opportunity of steeping their senses in liquor.

Another general drunken frolic was the consequence, ending as usual in a fight and still further attempts upon the life of our trader.

Soon after this, our catalogue of disasters was increased by the death of two horses, which fell a prey to wolves.

The case was an aggravated one, and provoking in the extreme. Both of them were "buffalo horses," and the fleetest and most valuable in our possession,—in fact, they were the only ones of which we ventured to boast. We had others of little worth, so poor and feeble they could oppose none resistance to magpies,* and much less to the rapacity of wolves.

But, no. These blood-thirsty depredators, desirous of a feast of fat things, were determined to have it, reckless of cost,—and, the encrimsoned tracks, coursing the snowy plain in every direction where passed the swift

---

* The magpie of the mountains is the torment of all sore-backed horses, particularly during the winter season. Despite opposition it will feed upon their skinless flesh, often to the very bones.

chargers in vain effort to escape, proved that they won their supper at an enormous expense of leg-wear.

*Feb. 4th.* All things being in readiness, we bade farewell to winter-quarters, and commenced our journey.

Crossing the river soon after, on ascending the opposite bank, a cart upset and deposited its contents in the water. The load, consisting of robes and powder, became thoroughly saturated, and we were employed a full hour in fishing it out. The stream being waist-deep and filled with floating ice, amid which we were forced to plunge, our task was far from a pleasant one.

The freight needed drying, and we were detained two days for that purpose. Meanwhile the drenched powder was subjected to the experiments of one of our engagés. Having spread it to dry, he was carelessly bending over it, when a spark from the camp-fire struck the ready ignitible; a sprightly flash, enveloping the luckless wight in a sheet or flame, told the instant result. Springing to his feet, he exclaimed:

" Bless my stars ! That's what I call regular *blowing up !*"

" Aye, aye, my lad," says one. " You was always a *bright* youth,—but never before did you appear half so *brilliant.* 'Tis a fact, or I'm a liar !"

Resuming our course, the second night following was passed at a pool of water between L'eau-qui-court and Rawhide. Here, having placed my shoes under my head for better security, I slept soundly till morning. Rising at an early hour, I turned for them, but one was missing, and, after searching far and near, it could not be found.

The mystery of its disappearance, however, was fully solved by the numerous wolf tracks that appeared on all sides;—some straggling marauder had stolen it during the night, and quietly deposited it in his empty stomach as the substitute for an early breakfast.

Our camp at Rawhide was beset with a throng of Indians from an adjoining village, who, as usual, were loudly clamorous and importunate for liquor. A beautiful young squaw was brought in, to exchange for that article. However, their solicitations were of no avail and their vitiated appetites went unappeased.

On the 12th of February we reached the Fort, and thus ended our disastrous and eventful expedition.

Winter in the neighborhood of the Platte had been remarkably mild, and at no time during the season had the snow remained upon the ground to exceed a day. Vegetation, even thus early, was beginning to put forth, and bring to view the beauty and loveliness of spring.

Preparations were already on foot for building a boat for the transportation of furs to the States by way of the river, and, at the solicitation of of the company's agent, I reluctantly consented to take charge of it during the voyage,—thus deferring, for the present, my design of visiting Oregon. The timber used in its construction was procured from the neighboring pine hills, and prepared by a laborious process of hand, with the aid of a pit-saw. The ribs and other timber were obtained from an ash grove, a few miles above the Fort, and three men were busily engaged in putting all things in readiness for the expected spring rise—an event which seldom occurs before the 15th of May.

The winter's trade having closed, an interval of nearly three months' leisure followed, which resulted in a hunting expedition that included myself with six others.

Anxious to explore the mountains, we set our faces westward; but, owing to the reported closeness of game *en route*, very little provisions were taken with other necessaries.

Keeping the river bottom by a rocky ridge for some ten miles, our course led through several beautiful groves and broad stretches of rich alluvial soil, that presented an encouraging prospect to agriculturists. After a few hours' ride we came to a point at which the stream sweeps round the ridge's base, causing a vertical wall of lias and sandstone nearly one hundred and fifty feet high.

Abandoning the river bottom at this place, we ascended to the high prairie on the left, where an interesting plateau greeted us, extending far away to the south and west, till it became lost in the neighboring mountains. Continuing on a short distance, we again struck the river, at a small opening between two hills, and made camp in a grove of willows.

Opposite this place is a large heavily wooded island, of a blueish loam, upon a subtratum of fossiliferous limestone.

Above and below are lofty walls of limestone and ferruginous rock, that, in many places, overhang the sweeping waters at their base, and form roofage beneath which swarms of prairie swallows are wont to raise their annual broods.

Consuming our scanty supply of provisions at a single meal, each soon disposed of himself for the night. A mild atmosphere invited to repose; and, enwrapped in a single robe, my troubles were speedily forgotten in a quiet slumber.

But during the succeeding interval, a change came over the spirit of my dream. I was suddenly aroused by the crash of a huge tree, that fell across my bed, and only a providential curve arching upwards, had saved me from instant death!

"Hurra, for me!" I exclaimed, as my startled campmates came clustering around,—" It's better to be born *lucky* than RICH!"

The wind was now blowing a perfect hurricane, and the trees tottered around us, threatening every moment to fall. In an hour or so, however, the gale abating, we again addressed ourselves to sleep.

Towards morning, feeling a disagreeable warmth and superincumbent pressure, I was induced to uncover, and, looking out, the cause was explained by the presence of a dense snow that covered the ground to the depth of several inches. The fallen snow was melting fast, and that yet descending soon merged into rain.

A pretty-looking set of fellows were we, in a comparatively short time! —blankets, robes, clothes, and every article about us were wet—soaking wet—and covered with mud. It required an effort of several hours to kindle a fire, so thoroughly saturated was everything with water;—this done, we all gathered around it, and—such a group!—Oh, the beauties of mud and water! A painter might describe it,—I cannot.

13

If the reader imagines we felt in a superlative good humor while standing there, breakfastless, shivering, and wet, he has conjured up a strange illusion.

It having ceased raining about mid-day, in the course of the afternoon we enjoyed a beautiful sunshine for a couple of hours, which enabled us to assume a better travelling plight; and, favored by a mild atmosphere and clear sky, on the following morning, we again resumed our course.

Striking upon an Indian trail, we bore leftward from the river, and, in a short ride, came to a sand creek shut in by precipitous embankments of limestone, through which our road led by a narrow defile. A transparent spring gushes from the right bank with considerable noise, furnishing a beautiful streamlet to its hitherto high bed, which is known as the "Warm Spring."

A short distance above the mouth of this creek, the Platte makes its final egress from the Black Hills through a tunnel-like pass, walled in upon either side by precipitous cliffs of red-sandstone and siliceous limestone, sometimes overhanging the stream at their base, and towering to a height of from three to five hundred feet. The high table lands constituting these immense walls, are surmounted with shrubs and occasional pines and cedars, that unite to present a wild romantic scenery.

Continuing on, and bearing still further leftward, we passed a beautiful valley, graced with several springs and a small grove of cottonwood, with cherry and plum bushes, near which rose a conical hill abundant in fossiliferous limestone of a snowy whiteness. A diminutive pond in the vicinity afforded several varieties of the testaceous order, both *bivalves* and *univalves*—a circumstance quite rare among mountain waters. The soil of this locality appeared to be a compound of clay, sand, and marl, and well adapted to agriculture.

Passing this, our course led over a gently undulating prairie, bounded on either side by pine hills. The soil was generally of a reddish, sandy loam, intermixed with clay; and, judging from the long dry grass of the preceding year, it was both rich and productive.

Towards night we arrived at a large creek, bearing the name of Bitter Cottonwood,—so called from the abundance of that species of poplar in its valley.

These trees generally grow very tall and straight with expansive tops, —averaging from twenty-five to one hundred and fifty feet in height.

The creek occupies a wide, sandy bed, over which the water is dispersed in several shallow streams. The valley is broad and of a jetty, vegetable mould, variegated, at intervals, with layers of gravel deposited by aqueous currents, and is bounded on both sides by abrupt acclivities leading to the beautiful plateaux and lofty pine hills so abundant in the neighborhood.

The remains of three or four Indian forts were situated adjoining the place selected for our encampment. These were built of logs, arranged in a circular form, and enclosing an area, sufficient for the acccmmodation of twenty or thirty warriors. The walls were generally about six feet high, with single entrances, and apertures in various places for the use of their defenders in case of attack.

All Indian forts, meeting my observation in subsequent travels, with one or two exceptions, were of the same general description. Some, however are almost entirely roofed in by an arched covering, presenting a coniform appearance. The only exception to this mode of fortification was of a quadrangular form, and in a solitary instance the materials were of rock. The latter structure I shall take occasion to describe in due course.

The valley gave abundant indication of wild fruit at the proper season,—such as plums, cherries, currants, goose and buffalo berries, (*shepherdia argentea*.) The signs of game were very plentiful, particularly elk;—after camp two or three of us sallied out with our rifles in quest of these wary animals, while others were busily employed in digging for roots to appease the gnawing of appetite, which began to make itself most sensibly felt by all.

About sundown both parties came in,—the hunters quite dispirited, not having seen any thing in the shape of elk or other game,—but the root diggers had been more lucky and brought with them a small supply of nutritious aliments, which were divided equally among the company,—and, through scarcely a half dozen mouthfuls were apportioned to each, they answered, to some extent, the designed object.

These roots consisted of two varieties, viz: *pomme blanc*, and *commote*.

The *pomme blanc*, or white apple, is a native of the prairies and mountains, oval shaped and about three and a half inches in circumference. It is encased in a thin fibrous tegument, which, when removed, exposes an interior of white pulpy substance, much like a turnip in taste. It generally grows at a depth of three or four inches, in the soil of hill-sides and plateaux, where is found a reddish clay loam abundant in fragmentary rocks and gravel. The stalk attains a height of about three inches, and in general description is quite like a well known article, common to the States, called "sheep-sorrel." At the proper season it bears a handsome white blossom, that would suffer no disparagement when placed in juxtaposition with many of the choicer specimens of our gardens.

The *commote*\* is a root much like the common radish in size and shape, while a brownish skin envelopes a substance of milky whiteness, soft and nutritious, and of an agreeable taste. It is found most abundant in river bottoms, and requires a rich alluvial soil, well mixed with sedimentary deposites and vegetable matter. It generally penetrates to a depth of about four inches. Its leaves resemble those of the carrot in shape and color, and seldom grow to exceed two inches from the ground, while a stalk equally unpretending, bears a blueish blossom, not without some just claim to beauty.

The *pomme blanc* and *commote* are equally good whether boiled or raw, and are uniformly harmless, even with those unaccustomed to their use as an article of food.

Making way with our scanty supply, a fire was struck and a kettle of tea prepared from wild cherry bark, which proved quite wholesome.

This, as I ascertained, is a drink quite common among mountaineers and Indians in the spring season, and is used for purifying the blood and reducing it to suitable consistency for the temperature of summer. As the successful performer of the task assigned, I most cordially attest to

---

\*I am ignorant of the meaning or derivation of this name.

its virtues, and recommend it as the most innocent and effective medicine, if medicine it may be called, that can be employed for a result so necessary to general health.

Early on the succeeding day we resumed our journey.

I now for the first time noticed a gradual change in the geological character of the country. The soil in many places appears to be sterile, and is generally of a red clayish nature, mixed with sand and fragmentary rock, and strongly impregnated with mineral salts, among which nitre forms a prominent component. Some spots, for a considerable extent, are entirely destitute of vegetation, and present a surface whitened by saline efflorescences, among which nitre and sulphate of soda form a predominant part.

The character of the various moulds (with the exception of the alluvion in the vicinity of the rivers and creeks) is almost entirely primitive, like numerous strata of rocks upon which they repose.

The grass, from the dry specimens of the previous summer's growth, appeared to be of a longer and a coarser kind, and more sparse and isolated. The short buffalo-grass of the grand prairie had almost entirely disappeared,—in some places a blueish salt grass (herba salée) showed itself in plats uncropped by game. *Artemisie*,\* or rather *greasewood* of the mountaineers, became quite abundant, as did *absinthe*, or wild sage, together with severals specimens of the *cacti* family, which are the common pest of the mountain prairies.

The purifying effects of saline exhalations, with the odor of the *greasewood* and *absinthe* of the prairies, plateaux and table lands, and the balsam and cedar of the adjacent mountains, afforded an atmosphere, even at this unfavorable season, as aromatic as the air of Eden and as wholesome as the deathless clime of Elysium.

Eastward lay a broad expanse of prairie, bounded only by the horizon, while westward and upon either hand, the high summits of the Black Hills, with their pines and snows, told our ingress to other and wilder scenes.

Our course for some twenty or twenty-five miles led through a broad valley, though occasionally winding among rugged hills of red-sandstone and primitive rock, with denuded sides and level summits, covered with shrubs and dwarfish pines.

Towards night, on reaching a small stream, called Horse-shoe creek, we struck camp. One of the party having killed a buck deer, we were promptly on hand, and not at all backward in obeying the calls of appetite, sharpened by a continuous abstinence of three days.

---

\* Lt. Fremont, in his report relative to the proceedings of the expedition of 1842, '3, and '4, has designated some three varieties of shrubs by the general term artemisie, among which are greasewood and prairie sage. Although the latter are of the same family, the difference in their appearance is so marked, I have thought it proper to observe a nominal distinction, and for that reason, they are called in subsequent pages by terms familiar to the mountaineers.

Deer-meat at this season of the year is very poor eating,—especially that of the buck,—it being both lean and tough; but, indifferent as it was, we were too hungry to be nice.

Previous to reaching camp I rode along the base of a small mountain, some distance to the right of the main party, in quest of game; there I caught glimpse of the first panther I had yet met with. Jumping from my horse, I thought to give him a passing shot,—but he, neither liking my looks nor the smell of gunpowder, made hasty retreat to his mountain home.

Passing leisurely on, my course led through a large village of prairie-dogs, which reminds me of having heretofore neglected a description of these singular animals.

I am at a loss to imagine what it is in the habits or looks of the prairie-dog that entitles him to that appellation.

In appearance and size he more approximates a large species of the *sciurus* family, commonly called the fox-squirrel, than anything I can name. His tail, however, is but an inch and a half long, while his ears and legs are also short;—as a whole, perhaps, he is a trifle larger and more corpulent than the fox-squirrel. His "bark" is precisely like the occasional chatterings of that animal, and his color is of a brownish red.

His habits are quite inoffensive and lead him to procure his food from roots and grass. Clumsy in his motions, he seldom ventures far from home—fearful of the numerous enemies that beset him on all sides, both from birds and beasts of prey.

These animals congregate together in large villages, and dig their burrows adjoining each other;—the dirt thrown from them often forming cone-like elevations three or four feet high, in whose tops are the entrances. The latter are nearly of a perpendicular descent for two feet, and then slope away to a great distance under ground.

These villagers locate without regard to the vicinity of water, and it is gravely doubted, by many persons, whether they make the same use of that fluid as other animals;—I have seen large settlements of them in high arid prairies, at a distance of fifteen or twenty miles from either stream or pool of water, and in regions subject to neither rain nor dews.

They are keen of sight and scent, and seemed governed by some code of federative regulations for mutual safety. Their guards are regularly posted at the suburbs of every village, whose duty it is to be continually on the alert and give timely warning of the approach of danger.

This the cautious sentinels discharge by standing erect at the slightest tainture of the air, or startling noise, or strange appearance; and, having ascertained by careful observations its nature and cause, they sound the sharp yelp and chatter of alarm, in a hurried manner,—then, betaking themselves to the watch-towers that protect the entrances to their burrows, from the verge of the steep parapets they again renew their warning notes, when the whilom busy populace, bescattered at brief distances for amusement or food, return with all possible despatch to their ready holes and disappear from view.

The faithful sentinels are last to retreat from their posts, and not unfrequently maintain their ground at the hazard of individual safety.

On the disappearance of the cause of alarm, they are the first to communicate the pleasing intelligence, and soon the reassured community again betake themselves to their business and sports.

The prairie-owl and rattlesnake maintain friendly relations with these inoffensive villagers, and not unfrequently the three heterogeneous associates occupy the same subterranean appartments;—a strange companionship of birds, beasts, and reptiles!

The prairie dog is extremely tenacious of life, and can seldom be killed with a rifle, unless by a brain-shot; and then, even, it is difficult to secure him, as his companions will immediately convey the carcase into their holes beyond reach.

The flesh of these animals is tender and quite palatable, and their oil superior in fineness, and absence from all grosser ingredients, to that of any other known animals; it is highly valued as a medicine in certain cases.

## CHAPTER XIII.

The Creek valley.—The Platte as a mountain stream.—Cañon.—Romantic prospect.—Comical bear story.—Perilous encounter with a wounded bull.—Geological remarks.—Division of party.—Safety of spring travel.—La Bonte's creek.—Remarks by the way.—Service-berry.—Deer Creek.—General observations.—Moccasin making.—Box-elder.—Bear killed.—Excellence of its flesh.—Different kinds of bears in Oregon and the mountains.—The grizzly bear, his nature and habits.

HORSE-SHOE creek is a stream of considerable size, that traces its way through a broad valley of rich alluvion, well timbered with cottonwood and box-elder, and affording all the usual varieties of mountain fruit. The grass of the preceding year's growth was quite rank and stout, giving evidence of a fertile soil.

Resuming our course, we again bore towards the river with the design of crossing, and, after a few hours' ride came to its banks, through a broad opening between two ridges of hills that communicated with it from the high prairies and table lands upon the left.

Here, however, fording was impracticable, the stream being too high and the current swift.

The Platte of the mountains retains scarcely one characteristic of the river with which the reader has hitherto become so familiarized. It is now confined to a bed of rock and gravel, not exceeding two hundred yards in width, and is of unwonted clearness and transparency. Its banks are steep, and the attrition of high waters discloses a deep vegetable mould in their vicinity, favorable to the growth of grain or other produce.

A small bottom of rich sandy loam upon the opposite side lay at the base of a high ridge of table lands, which presented its rugged sides of red-sandstone, almost vertical in their position, and ornamented with an occasional-stunted pine, or cedar, or shrub of the buffalo-berry, (*shepherdia argentea*,) while at their base reposed, in huge masses, a profuse medley of fallen fragments, strown around in all the wild confusion of savage scenery.

A few hundred yards to the left, the Platte forces its way through a barrier of table lands, forming one of those striking peculiarities incident to mountain streams, called a "cañon."*

Improving the opportunity afforded by a short stay, I ascended an eminence to enjoy a full vew of the grand spectacle. The mountain through which the river finds passage, at this place, is from five to eight hundred feet high, opposing perpendicular walls upon each side, that at many points overhang the narrow stream which sweeps with its foaming waters among the rocks below.

This cañon is nearly two miles in length. About midway of the distance the whole stream is precipitated in an unbroken volume from a ledge of rocks, causing a cataract of some twenty or twenty-five feet descent.

Standing upon the dizzy verge of this frightful chasm, and gazing adown its dark abyss, the aspect is one of terrific sublimity, and such an one as will cause the beholder to shrink back with instinctive dread!

These walls are principally of red-sandstone, and ferruginous rock, the precise character of which I was unable to determine. Upon the summit I noticed an abundance of silex, with some elegant specimens of crystalline quartz, that, reflecting the sun's rays, shone like gems in the crown of a mountain-god; a number of singular ligneous petrifactions also met my observation, principally consisting of pine and cedar.

The surrounding country brought within the scope of vision an interesting and romantic scene. The lofty table land in front (with diversified surfaces of granitic rock and vegetable earth, affording a scanty nourishment for herbage and foothold for dwarfish cedars and pines) spread far away to the snow-clad mountains of the north,—while rearward at its base lay the broad valley through which passes the Oregon trail, shut in upon two sides by rugged hills; and farther on arise the snowy sides of the Laramie chain, with their cloud-capped summits. To the left, peak towering above peak, in gradual succession, point to the ridge dividing the waters of the Atlantic and Pacific; and, to the right, the lessening eminences, *vallons*, and plateaux, guide the eye to where the boundless prairie revels in wild beauty and owns itself the realm of eternal Solitude!

How magnificent must be the scene when spring arrays the surrounding landscape in her own loveliness, and bedecks the wilderness with gaudy verdure!

Bearing again to the left, we continued our course by a winding buffalo-path which soon brought us to a broad valley bordering upon the Platte.

*The Spanish word "cañon" implies a narrow, tunnel-like passage between high and precipitous banks, formed by mountains or table lands. It is pronounced KANYON, and is a familiar term in the vocabulary of a mountaineer.

Riding on, we soon came to a large sand creek; and, observing several bulls in the vicinity, we accepted the advantage offered by a small grove of cottonwoods and willows, with a clear spring, and struck camp.

During the day, the oddity of an old Franco-Canadian, who accompanied us, afforded me considerable amusement. Observing that he had carried his gun uncharged for several days past, a circumstance so singular in this country led me to enquire the cause. The old fellow, with the most laughable *sang froid*, answered as follows:

"Me carry fusee load? No, no! monsieur. No good, carry fusee load sur le printems. Certes, much bear come out—him dangereux. Me live long en le montagnes; oui, no remarque—duo, tree, great many year! Sacre dem bear,—vat you call him en la Americàn?"

"Grizzly bear, I suppose you mean," said I.

"Oui, oui, monsieur; much grâces, monsieur! Oui, gizzle bear; me parler bon Americàn, que no remarque gizzle bear! éntonner! Sacre dem gizzle bear, him come out une day, kill me de près."

"Well," continued I; "what has that to do with carrying your gun unloaded?"

"Oui, oui; pardonner, monsieur. Me parler tel une bon Americàn! Me réciter, sacre dem bear,—vat you call him, monsieur? Oh, gizzle bear! Sacre dem gizzle bear, me see him une day, en le printems; big, grand felleu. Shoot him fusee; make him much blood; no kill him. Sacre dem bear, gizzle bear, him jump for me. 'Wa-r-r-h!' he say, (imitating the bear.) Bon Dieu! me no stay dare; me bein fast run; me abandonner la fusee; me climb une leetil pine. Sacre dem bear—vat you call him? Ah, oui, gizzle bear. Certes, monsieur, me parler bon Americàn, tel une naturel! Sacre dem bear, him come to tree; no climb him, —he too leetil. Look him all round, den; sacre dem bear, gizzle bear did. See fusee lie; pick him up; cock him fusee, sacre dem bear, gizzle bear did. Take him aim at me; snap him fusee tree time. Oh, mon Dieu! mon Dieu! Suppose him fusee been load! Tonnerre de batème! Him shoot me; him kill me dead! sacre dem bear, dem gizzle bear vould! Certes, monsieur; por le assuré, sacre dem gizzle bear, him kill me! en le vérité, monsieur, him kill me dead!"

"So," resumed I, "your reason for not carrying your gun loaded is, you are fearful that a bear might chance to get hold of it and shoot you!"

"Certes, monsieur; en le vérité! No carry gun load, sur le printems. Sacre dem bear get 'old of him, he shoot!"

Towards night, two of our party, who had gone in pursuit of buffalo, returned laden with meat, which, though poor, was far preferable to the lean venison we had fed upon for the last twenty-four hours.

The male buffalo, at this season of the year, is generally fatter than the female, unless it be one of the few barren cows that sometimes are found in large bands; but, neither is worth boasting of.

After our long fasting and indifferent fare for six entire days, it is not marvellous that we improved, with quickened zest, the present opportunity of feasting.

The day following, two parties started in quest of game,—one of which killed three bulls, at as many shots, within half an hour after leaving camp.

The other party also killed two, but, in securing one of them, they met with an exciting adventure.

Both animals were extended upon the ground, one entirely and the other apparently dead—the hunters, having butchered one of them, proceeded to the other, and were in the act of raising him to the right position for the commencement of operation. The old fellow, not relishing the like familiarity from new acquaintances, sprang to his feet, and made a plunge at the affrighted hunters, who only escaped the fatal charge by one of those admirable feats of quick dodging so often in requisition among mountaineers.

The bull, passing between them, fell head foremost against the ground, two or three feet beyond the spot they had occupied scarcely a second previous;—then rising, with glaring eyes and distended nostrils, and mouth foaming with blood and rage, he pursued one of them in hot chase, for a distance of several hundred yards. So close was the bull in a few leaps, that with a sweep of his horns he gored the hunter's back, tearing away his pantaloons and coat, and prostrating him upon all-fours at the edge of a deep ravine, down which he tumbled;—the enraged beast followed, but the force of an unbroken headway landed him, with a tremendous shock, against the opposite bank, far beyond the hunter. Improving the advantage thus gained, the latter escaped through the windings of the ravine, and ascended the bank, without the reach of his pursuer.

Having procured his rifle, after nine more shots had riddled the lights of the bull's carcase, the business of butchering was again commenced and terminated without further mishap.

Our stay at this camp was prolonged for three or four days.

The geological character of the vicinity corresponds very much with that previously remarked, and to describe it in full would seem too much like a repetition. I have, perhaps, said sufficient to give the reader a correct idea of the prominent characteristics of these parts, and hence, for the sake of brevity, shall hereafter forbear further notes upon this subject, unless some uniform change or striking peculiarity should call for a passing observation.

Prior to resuming our journey, a disagreement occurred between us relative to the proposed route.

Some were desirous of proceeding southward into the Plains of Laramie; thence, bearing eastward to Laramie river, following its valley to Fort Platte;—others were anxious to continue up the Platte to Sweet Water, or further, and from thence proceed as circumstances or inclination might suggest.

This difference finally resulted in a division of the party,—four in favor of the western, and three of the southern route,—myself being included with the former.

Selecting two pack-mules for the conveyance of provisions and camp-equipage, the day following we mounted our horses and were under way. With the exception of myself, the present party consisted of old and experienced mountaineers, well acquainted with the country and the nature of Indians. Though, in regard to the latter, little danger was apprehended at this season of the year, as the Sioux had not yet left their winter quarters, and they rarely traverse the vicinity of Sweet Water before the middle of May. Other tribes we might look upon as friendly. We, therefore, anticipated a safe and pleasant excursion.

During the day our course led over a rough undulating prairie, bounded on the right mostly by the river, and on the left by the mountains.

In the heads of valleys and ravines I noticed numerous withered stalks of the bread-root, (*psoralea esculenta*,) indicating its great abundance, and also an increased quantity of *absinthe*.

At night we encamped at the forks of a small stream called La Bonte's creek. Near the confluence of its waters with the Platte are the remains of a log cabin, occcupied by a trading party several years since.

The creek is tolerably well timbered, and the valley, through which it winds its way, affords many beautiful bottoms of rich soil. The rock in the vicinity disclosed a furruginous character, especially the sandstone.

Among the usual fruit-bearing shrubs and bushes, I here noticed the "service berry."

This kind of fruit is very abundant in the mountainons parts of Oregon, where it attains a size but little inferior to the common plum, and is highly esteemed for its superior flavor.

Leaving La Bonte's creek, we travelled by easy stages, for three successive days, and struck camp at the mouth of Deer creek.

Our course led over several beautiful streams, most of them well timbered with cottonwood and box-elder, and occasionally skirted by rich bottoms. Previous to reaching this point we followed along the Platte valley, for a distance of some twenty or thirty miles, which presented several fine bottoms of rich sandy soil upon either bank, together with numerous groves of cottonwood.

The face of the country is generally a succession of ridges and hollows, intersected by ravines and small streams of water.

At Deer creek, and for some distance before reaching it, the mountain chain to our left approaches within four or five miles of the river, rising abruptly to a height of from eight to fifteen hundred feet, with frowning brows and pine-clad summits.

Deer creek is one of the largest affluents of the Platte, from the south, between Sweet Water and Laramie. At this place it is about eight yards broad, with a smooth and transparent current that sweeps over a bed of rock and gravel. Its banks are well timbered with large cottonwoods, and present rich bottoms of alluvial soil, very luxuriant in grass.

Even this early in the season, the fresh grass of the vicinity affords tempting nourishment for our animals, and wishing to favor them as much as possible, we have concluded to remain a short time.

During the succeeding interval we were variously occupied in hunting, root-digging, and moccasin-making. The latter is a business in which every mountaineer is necessarily a proficient, and rarely will he venture upon a long journey without the appurtenances of his profession.

The process of *shoe-making* with him is reduced to its most simple form. He merely takes two pieces of buffalo (or any other suitable) skin, each being a little longer and wider than his foot, particularly towards the heel; these he folds separately, and lays them together parallel with the turned edges; then, rounding and trimming the sides, to render them foot-shaped, with an awl and the sinew of buffalo or other animal, or small strips of thin deer-skin, ("*whang*,") he sews the vamps from end to end,—then after cutting a tongue-like appendage in the upper side, midway from heel to toe, and stitching together the posterior parts, his task is done.

Having obtained a quantity of sap from a grove of box-elders near camp, we found it a sweet and pleasant liquid, and not inferior to that of maple. Sugar might be manufactured from it, with little trouble.

The leaves of this tree, as well as the general appearance of its wood, greatly assimilate those of maple, and, independent of its bushy tops and stunted, winding growth, it would be hard to tell the difference at a first glance.

Game was plenty on every side, both buffalo, deer, and elk, with some few bear.

The second day after our arrival, one of the latter, attracted by the scent of fresh buffalo meat, ventured within gun-shot of camp. Instantly the balls of four rifles were buried in his carcase. Aroused by this *feeling* salute, he rushed towards us at the top of his speed, when our horses, affrighted at the strange appearance, broke snorting away over the neighboring hills, and we ourselves took to trees as fast as possible.

In the midst of this general consternation a pistol ball, fired by one of the party, buried itself in the brains of our troublesome visitor and laid him prostrate.

He was one of a species common to the mountains, called the red bear, and must have weighed four or five hundred pounds. The fat upon his back was full three inches thick His skin when stretched would have compared in size to that of a buffalo, and the claws of his feet were full three inches long.

At this season of the year, when these animals first leave their dens, they are much the fattest,—a singular circumstance, if we remember the fact of their remaining holed up for the entire winter, without eating!

After butchering the greasy victim, and bringing our erratic horses back to camp, we regaled ourselves with an ample feast of bear's liver, heart, and kidneys, basted with fat,—a dish that epicures might well covet. Then, filling a large camp-kettle with portions of the "fleece" and ribs, we allowed it to boil till the next morning, and thus prepared another delicious entertainment, such as is rarely met with in any country other than this.

Bear meat, to be tender and good, should be boiled at least ten hours. This is probably the most preferable mode of cooking it, though a roast of the article is far from bad.

There are four several varieties of bear found in the Rocky Mountains and countries adjacent, viz.: The grizzly bear, the black, the red, and the white.

Of these, the grizzly bear stands pre-eminent in ferocity and strength. He will almost invariably flee at the sight or scent of a man, and seldom attacks any one unless wounded. When shot, he generally runs at full speed towards the sound, and woe to the unfortunate hunter who then comes in his way, unless fully prepared for a deadly encounter!

This animal reigns prince of the mountains, and every other beast within his wide realm acknowledges his supremacy.

Wolves and panthers dare not approach him, or disturb aught savoring of his ownership. Even the carcase of his prey, covered with the earth and rock his cautious instinct teaches him to heap upon it for preservation, is unmolested, though hundreds of wolves and panthers might be starving around.

Buffalo dread his presence far more than the dangerous approach of the hunter, and will sooner bring into requisition their swiftest powers of flight on such occasions. With great difficulty a horse can can be persuaded to go within any near distance of one of them, even when led, and then he will quail and tremble in every joint, from extreme terror.

In short, the grizzly bear stalks forth at pleasure, in his majesty and strength, lord of the wild solitudes in which he dwells, and none dares oppose him.

Some writers assert that bears will not prey upon dead carcases,—this is contrary to fact. I have often known them take possession of the carcases of animals, even when nearly putrid, and remain until they were devoured.

They frequently kill buffalo, horses, and cattle to gratify their taste for animal food, and, in such cases, always drag their prey to some convenient spot, and perform the task of burial by heaping upon it piles of rock or earth, to a depth of several feet, for protection against the voracity of other beasts of prey. It is not uncommon, even, that they drag the entire carcase of a full-grown bull a distance of several hundred yards, by the horns, for this purpose,—so great is their strength and so accute their sagacity.

THE GRIZZLY BEAR.—*Page* 158.

## CHAPTER XIV.

Desperate encounter with a grizzly bear, and extraordinary instance of suffering.—Close contest.—A comical incident.—Cross Platte.—Cañon camp.—Sage trees.—Mountain sheep, and all about them.—Independence Rock; why so called, and description of it.—Devil's Gate.—Landscape scenery.

THE adventure recorded in the preceding chapter called forth the rehearsal of many thrilling stories of frightful encounter with that proud monarch of the mountains, the grizzly bear. Two or three of these it may not be uninteresting to transcribe.

Several years since, an old trapper by the name of Glass, with his companion, while on an excursion, came upon a large grizzly bear.

Bruin, having received the salute of two rifles, as usual, rushed towards his uncivil assailants, who broke from him with all possible despatch. But Glass, stumbling, fell prostrate in his flight, and before he could recover his feet the infuriated beast was upon him.

Now commenced a death-struggle. The pistols of the hunter were both discharged in quick succession,—the ball of one entering the breast of his antagonist, and that of the other grazing his back.

Smarting and maddened by the pain of additional wounds, the bleeding monster continued the conflict with the fury of desperation,—tearing from the limbs and body of the unfortunate man large pieces of trembling flesh, and lacerating him with the deep thrusts of his teeth and claws.

Meanwhile the sufferer maintained, with his butcher-knife, an obstinate defence, though with fast waning effort and strength. Finally, enfeebled by the loss of blood, and exhausted from the extraordinary exertions of a desperate and unequal contest, he was unable to oppose further resistance, and quietly resigned himself to his fate.

The bear, too, with the thick blood oozing from his numerous wounds, and faint from the many stabs among his veins and sinews, seemed equally in favor of a suspension of hostilities; and, extending himself across the hunter's back, he remained motionless for two hours or more.

But now another enemy commences an assault upon his vitals—that enemy is death. In vain is defensive effort. In vain are all his struggles. He falls by the hunter's side a lifeless corse.

The setting sun had cast his lurid glare upon the ensanguined spot, as the comrade of the miserable Glass ventured near to ascertain the result of the fierce encounter.

There lay the body of his deserted friend, stretched out, apparently lifeless and half-torn to pieces; and, by its side, lay the carcase of that enemy, which had waged with it such murderous war, cold and stiffened in death!

Now, doubly terrified at his loneliness, but still governed by sordid motives, he stripped the former of his arms and every other valuable, then no longer needed (as he supposed) by their owner, and, mounting his horse, started immediately for the nearest trading post.

On his arrival he recounted the particulars of the fatal occurrence,—carefully concealing, however, his own criminal conduct. The story was accredited, and the name of Glass found place upon the long catalogue of those who had fallen a prey to wild beasts and savage men.

Six weeks elapsed and no one thought of the subject of our sketch as among the living. The general surprise, therefore, may be readily imagined, on opening the fort-gates one morning, at finding before them the poor, emaciated form of a man, half-naked, and covered with wounds and running sores, and so torn the fleshless bones of his legs and thighs were exposed to view in places! and how this astonishment was heightened on recognizing the person of Glass in the illy defined lineaments of his countenance—the very man so long regarded as the inhabitant of another world! A veritable ghost suddenly appearing upon the spot could not have occasioned greater wonder!

But, sensations of pity and commiseration quickly succeeded those of surprise, and the unhappy sufferer was conveyed within doors and received from the hands of friends that careful attention his situation so much required.

The story of his misfortunes was thrillingly interesting. When left by his companion for dead, he was in a state of unconsciousness, with scarcely the breath of life retained in his mangled body. But, the soft night-wind stanched his wounds, and a slight sleep partially revived him from his death-like stupor.

With the morning, the slight sensations of hunger he began to experience were appeased from the raw flesh of the carcase at his side; and, thus strengthened, by a slow and tedious effort he was enabled to reach a near stream and quench his thirst. Still further revived, he again crawled to the carcase at the demands of appetite.

In this manner he continued for three days, when the putrescent corse compelled him to abandon it.

Then it was he commenced his tedious return to the fort, (some seventy miles distant,) which he performed during an interval of forty successive days! The whole of this long stretch he crawled upon his hands and knees,—subsisting, for the meanwhile, only upon insects, such as chance threw in his way, but passing most of the time without one morsel with which to appease the gnawings of hunger or renew his wasted strength.

Yet, great as were his sufferings and intolerable as they may seem, he survived them all, and, by the kind attention of friends, soon recovered.

He still lives in the town of Taos, New Mexico, and frequently repeats to wondering listeners the particulars of this terrific and painful adventure.

One of our party, whose right hand was much disabled from the effects of a wound, now told his story.

For several years succeeding his first arrival in the Rocky Mountains, he had permitted no opportunity of killing any one of the various species of bear, common to these regions, to pass unimproved. Never did he think of fearing them, and was always the last to retreat in case of a charge.

When a bear appeared within any reasonable shooting distance of our hunter, it almost invariably fell a victim to his unerring aim. But, ere-long, this spirit of bold-daring proved the source of lasting regret to its possessor.

On the occasion alluded to, having shot at one of these animals, contrary to his usual good luck, he only wounded it.

The bear in turn now became the assailant, but received the contents of two pistols before it had time to advance far. Our hunter at this crisis sprang to a neighboring pine, which he commenced climbing. His pursuer, gaining the tree almost as soon, likewise began its ascent.

Here occurred a struggle between them—the man to force his way upwards, and the bear to prevent him. The former, drawing his butcher-knife, thrust it at the eyes and nose of his antagonist. Not fancying such *pointed* hints upon a delicate subject, Mr. Bruin caught hold of the hunter's hand, and, as an earnest of deep sensitiveness, crushed it between his teeth, —nor even then relinquished the gripe. Transferred to the left hand, the knife continued its work, till the sickening beast commenced sliding downward—dragging the poor hunter also to the ground. Both struck at the same time; but, at that instant, the knife of the latter pierced the heart of his antagonist, and laid him dead at his feet.

The unfortunate man, however, lost two of his fingers in the affray, and his hand was otherwise so much injured he has never since recovered its use.

Another story related at the same time, though not possessing the deep and thrilling interest of the preceding ones, partakes a little of the ludircous, and will doubtless amuse the reader.

The narrator a while since formed one of a trapping party, with which he proceeded to the Utah country. While there, on a certain occasion, having set his traps over night, he returned to examine them the next morning, in quest of beaver, and, to his surprise, one of them was missing. After cautiously examining the premises, under the impression that some lurking Indians had stolen his trap with its contents, he noticed the tracks of bears, near by, which served at once to unravel the whilom mystery of its disappearance.

He now began to muse upon his loss, as, without the missing trap, his set would be rendered incomplete, and, under present circumstances, the want of the thing was more than the worth of it. While thus ruminating, a slight noise, among neighboring cherry-bushes and cottonwood, caught his ear, which sounded like some one beating with two sticks.

This induced him to approach for the purpose of ascertaining the cause, when an opening revealed to view Mr. Bruin seated upon a log and holding to his face the missing trap, tightly clasped to his fore-paw.

The bear appeared to be regarding the strange instrument with close attention, as if to study into the principles of its construction;—now gazing at it endwise, then bringing its side in close proximity to his eyes; then turning it over to examine the opposite one;—now, he would essay its strength, and lightly taps it upon the log. But this is a painful operation,—he relinquishes it, and resumes his former grotesque movements.

Watching this curious performance, the trapper could scarcely retain his gravity, or master his fondness for the ludicrous sufficiently for the intended shot. He did, however, and the comedy was suddenly transformed to a tragedy, by leaving its actor struggling in death.

A light fall of snow during the last of our stay at Deer creek, rendered the ground quite muddy and soft; notwithstanding which we resumed our course early in the morning of the fourth day.

Continuing on, a ride of thirty miles brought us to the place where the Oregon trail crosses the Platte; and, after fording the river, we encamped upon the opposite side.

The stream, at this point, is about three hundred yards from bank to bank, and, at the time of our crossing it, swimming deep for a small portion of the way.

In ordinary stages, the water is but little over three feet deep, and the ford perfectly safe and practicable. The partial melting of the mountain snows had increased the size and velocity of its current, and rendered our passage slightly dangerous and difficult. The bed appeared to be rocky, and in some places rough,—requiring much caution in crossing waggons, to prevent them from overturning.

On the third day following, we arrived at another remarkable cañon, after travelling a distance of thirty-five or forty miles. Here, finding large numbers of mountain sheep, we were induced to remain a short time.

Our course for most of this distance was confined to the valley of the Platte, on account of the greater supply of wood found upon its banks.

Towards noon of the first day, we passed a point, called the "Red Buttes," at which the river cuts its way through a lofty ridge of hills. This passage left a considerable bank upon both sides, shut in by abrupt walls of red argillaceous sandstone, towering to the height of several hundred feet.

The soil was generally a mixture of clay and sand, and, in some places, afforded a reddish loam which appeared to be very rich.

A short ride from the "Red Buttes" took us across a beautiful stream, with a broad bottom, well timbered with cottonwood.

Large herds of buffalo were continually in sight upon the whole route.

Several miles previous to reaching the cañon, my notice was first attracted to the extraordinary size attained by the wild sage; it having merged its shrub-like appearance into that of trees varying from five to ten feet in height and from twenty to twenty-five inches in circumference at the root.

The magnificent dimensions of this herb are retained for a large extent of territory to the south and west of this vicinity. It is frequently made use of for fire-wood, and the prairies, in many places, are covered with beautiful groves of it,—perfuming the atmosphere and revelling in perennial verdure.

The cañon before referred to, is caused by the river passing through a chain of hills, for a reach of nearly half a mile.

## MOUNTAIN SHEEP.

The current is here shut in by banks of perpendicular rock, four or five hundred feet high, which sometimes overhang it, and leave a narrow space of scarcely two hundred feet for its bed. These consist principally of white cretaceous sandstone, soft and friable, and frequently present to view the appearance of regular mason-work.

During our stay we succeeded in killing five mountain sheep. Some of these were very large and quite fat.

The flesh of this animal is equal in flavor to that of buffalo. It is generally in good order, tender and sweet, and slightly assimilates our common mutton in taste.

The habits and appearance of mountain sheep resemble those of no other animal.

They select for their favorite habitation the rugged fastnesses of wild and inaccessible mountains. In the cold of winter, they descend to some of the numerous valleys that so beautifully diversify the scenery of these regions, where the verdure of spring so rarely fades; and, as the warm season advances, they commence their return towards the lofty snow-peaks, keeping even progress with spring and fresh flowers along the mountain-sides.

Theirs is a life of unbroken spring—beauty and grandeur are their dwelling place,—and, 'mid the awe-inspiring sublimity of nature's works, is their home. They gambol upon the fearful verge of the steep cliff, or climb its perpendicular sides, bidding defiance to all pursuers. There, secure from enemies, they rear their young, and teach them to leap from crag to crag in mirthful gaiety, or traverse the dizzy heights in quest of the varied sweets of changeful spring.

These animals are remarkably acute of sight, and quick of scent and hearing. The least noise or tainture of the air excites their attention and places them instantly upon the alert. Mounting upon some high rock, they will stand for hours in the same posture, gazing in the direction of the fancied danger. If fully satisfied of its reality, they abandon their position for another and a safer one, high among more rugged peaks, and often beyond the possibility of offensive approach. Their hue is so akin to that of the rocks which grace their range, they are with difficulty identified when standing motionless, and the hunter is constantly liable to mistake the one for the other.

In size the mountain sheep is larger than the domestic animal of that name, and its general appearance is in every respect dissimilar—excepting the head and horns. The latter appendage, however, alike belongs to the male and female. The horns of the female are about six inches long, small, pointed, and somewhat flat,—but those of the male grow to an enormous size. I have frequently killed them having horns that measured two feet and a half or three feet in length, and from eighteen to nineteen inches in circumference at the base.

These ponderous members are of great service to their owner in descending the abrupt precipices, which his habits so often render necessary. In leaping from an elevation he uniformly strikes upon the curve of his horns, and thus saves himself from the shock of a sudden and violent contusion.

The color of these animals varies from a yellowish white, to a dark brown, or even black. A strip of snowy whiteness extends from ham to ham, including the tail, which is short and tipped with black.

Instead of wool, they are covered with hair, which is shed annually. Their cry is much like that of domestic sheep, and the same natural odor is common to both.

It is extremely difficult to capture any of them alive, even while young, —and it is next to impossible to make them live and thrive in any other climate than their own. Hence, the mountain sheep has never yet found a place in our most extensive zoological collections.

Remaining three days at this place, we were again *en route*, and, bearing to the right, passed over a ridge of rough, rocky summits, and struck the valley of the Sweet Water. Continuing up the latter, a short ride brought us to the vicinity of a noted landmark of the country, known as Independence Rock, where we encamped.

The soil of the river bottoms is good, but the adjoining prairies are sandy and somewhat sterile.

The distance from this to the cañon is not far from twenty-three miles.

Independence Rock is a solid and isolated mass of naked granite, situated about three hundred yards from the right bank of the Sweet Water. It covers an area of four or five acres, and rises to a height of nearly three hundred feet. The general shape is oval, with the exception of a slight depression in its summit where a scanty soil supports a few shrubs and a solitary dwarf-pine.

It derives its name from a party of Americans on their way to Oregon, under the lead of one Tharp, who celebrated the fourth of July at this place,—they being the first company of whites that ever made the journey from the States, *via* South Pass.

The surface is covered with the names of travellers, traders, trappers, and emigrants, engraven upon it in almost every practicable part, for the distance of many feet above its base,—but most prominent among them all is the word "Independence," inscribed by the patriotic band who first christened this lonely monument of nature in honor of Liberty's birthday.

I went to the rock for the purpose of recording my name with the swollen catalogue of others traced upon its sides; but, having glanced over the strange medley, I became disgusted, and, turning away, resolved, "If *there remains no other mode of immortalizing myself*, I will be content to descend to the grave '*unhonored and unsung.*'"

The day following, a heavy fall of snow and sleet forced us to remain in camp, and the consequent muddiness of the route prolonged our stay still further.

The vicinity afforded an abundance of game and a sufficiency of dry fuel; it would, therefore, have been folly in us to care for wind or weather, detracting as did either so little from our comfort.

During this interval I rode into the prairie a short distance, in quest of game, and struck the river a few miles above camp, at a place where the stream cuts its way through a high ridge of hills, forming another cañon of three or four hundred yards in length and about forty broad, called the Devil's Gate, as I afterwards ascertained.

Its walls arose perpendicularly to a height of between four and five hundred feet, and consisted of trap rock, sandstone, and granite.

Dismounting, I ascended to the summit, where a grand and picturesque scenery burst upon the view.

Above, the broad valley of the Sweet Water stretched far away to the westward, bounded on either side by frowning mountains, that, towering to the height of fifteen hundred or two thousand feet, present their snowy summits in proud defiance of wind or storm, and laugh at the impotency of a summer's sun;—on the south, shaking their piny tops in scornful derision; and, on the north, with denuded crests of broken granite, challenging the lightnings of heaven and wooing its loudest thunders;—while further along, the clouds played in humble sportiveness around the base of the great chain dividing the waters of two oceans, nor dared ascend its dizzy heights to range amid eternal snow.

Below, in silent grandeur, arose to view the grantic mass that responds to the day-dawn of a nation's existence, surmounted by its lone pine, and bearing upon its broad register the sculptured names of the audacious disturbers of its solitude; and further yet, the parti-colored peaks of the Black Hills, now white with fresh-fallen snow, now darkened with clustering pines, seemed musing in modest retirement; while far around, in every spot accessible to discriminating vision, dense herds of grazing buffalo covered the prairie with their pall-like mantle of countless numbers.

It was indeed a magnificent prospect, and needed only the garnishing hand of spring to render it at as enchanting in loveliness as it was impressive in wild sublimity.

## CHAPTER XV.

Return route.—Oregon trail from Independence Rock through the South Pass.—Cross the Sweet Water and Platte.—Mountain Fowl.—Journey up Medicine Bow.—Dangerous country.—A fight with the Sioux.—The "Carcague."—A surprise.—Visit to the Crow village.—Number and character of the Crow nation—Selling a prisoner for tobacco.—Description of Laramie Plains.

PREVIOUSLY to leaving this place, considerable discussion arose relative to our future course.

The proposition was to continue up the Sweet Water valley to the dividing ridge at the head of Green river, and return by the same route;—*versus* the suggestion to cross the Sweet Water and proceed up the Platte to the confluence of a large tributary from the south; thence keeping by the valley of the latter stream as far as the Medicine Bow Mountains, return to the Fort by the way of Laramie river.

The fast melting of the snow, and anticipated difficulties, not to say dangers, consequent upon high water in the passage of creeks and rivers, influenced us to adopt the latter as the most advisable course.

Such was the final decision, and, the men with me being familiarly acquainted with every nook and corner of the adjacent country, I improved the opportunity to elicit from them all possible information relative to the Oregon route from this onward; and, never having personally travelled from Independence Rock to the head of Green river, it may not be out of place to lay before the reader a succinct statement of some of the items thus gleaned.

The distance from this point to the famous South Pass is but little over one hundred miles. The trail follows the Sweet Water to its source, keeping the river valley for most of the distance. This valley consists of an undulating prairie, (at intervals rough,) varying in width from the narrow limits of a few yards to the more ample dimensions of four or five miles.

Sometimes, the adjoining hills close in upon the river banks and force the trail among their rugged windings. In one place the road leads over a high stretch of table land for nearly a day's travel, when it again descends to the valley.

The stream, in places, is tolerably well timbered with cottonwood, oak, and aspen, and rolls over a rocky bed, with a clear and swift current.

The distance through the pass is about fifteen miles, and the ascent and descent are so gradual the traveller would scarcely notice the transition from the head of the Sweet Water to that of the Colorado. The hills at this point are low, and the face of the country rolling—but not rough, affording at all times a most excellent waggon road.

On the morning of the fourth day, we accordingly retraced our course, and, having traversed a rugged and hilly country for some ten or twelve miles, we camped in a small open prairie at the mouth of the Sweet Water.

During our ride we noticed several large bands of wild sheep, at intervals, gazing upon us from huge masses of granite that towered with isolated summits to a frequent altitude of sixty or one hundred feet.

The next morning, we crossed the Sweet Water a little above its mouth.

The ford was quite feasible, the stream being some ten yards wide and three or four feet deep, with a bed of sand and pebbles.

From this point, travelling up the Platte for about ten miles or more, we arrived opposite the creek previously alluded to, and, crossing at a shoal place a short distance above, camped in a grove of cottonwood and willows, at the delta formed by the confluence of the two streams.

There are several bottoms of very rich soil in this vicinity; but back from the river the country is rough and hilly.

Westward the Sweet Water mountains, distant some ten miles, showed their craggy peaks, and to the north and east the piny crests of the Black Hills burst upon the sight; while southward, a succession of high, rolling prairies opened to view a variety of romantic and beautiful scenery.

A CROW WARRIOR.— *Page* 169.

We remained at this place the two following days, for the purpose of hunting. Game of all kinds appeared in great abundance, particularly elk. At several points among the willows near the river were noticed fresh signs of beaver, and among the hills the recent marks of bear in digging for roots.

A large bird called the mountain fowl, quite common to these parts, was the occasion of some little curiosity, being the first of its species I ever saw. This bird is rather larger than our domestic hen, and of a grayish brown color. Little accustomed to the presence of man, it easily falls a prey to the hunter. Its flesh is tender and most excellent in flavor.

Having obtained a fresh supply of meat, we resumed our course.

Continuing up the right bank of the creek (which I have named Medicine Bow, for lack of a better term) and travelling by easy stages four successive days, we arrived at its head,—a distance of more than fifty miles above its junction with the Platte.

Many beautiful bottoms skirted the banks of this stream, which were well timbered with cottonwood, aspen, birch, willow, box-elder, and some few pines. The soil is generally of a reddish loam, and the luxuriant size of the dead grass, together with the rank verdure of the present season, gave evidence of its richness and fecundity.

I was pleased to observe not a few wild flowers, of rare beauty, in full bloom, lending their fragrance to the breath of spring, and blushing at the admiration challenged by their loveliness.

On the right lay a broad expanse of undulating prairie, covered with stately clusters of *absinthe*, and disclosing every variety of soil, from the rude sterility of an African desert to the rich productiveness of a garden;—on the left, the mountains, increasing in altitude, jutted their craggy sides in close proximity to the creek—now disclosing immense piles of granite, with red argillaceous, grayish micaceous, dark ferruginous, and white calcareous sandstone, limestone, and coarse-grained conglomerates, naked and variegated with almost every diversity of color,—and now, surmounted by stunted pines and cedars, or towering balsam, hemlock and pinion; and in front, the lofty peaks of Medicine Bow, rearing their snowy heads beyond the clouds, opposed an eternal barrier to further prospect.

As we passed along, I noticed three or four small branches that emptied into the creek from the opposite side, and, just before reaching our present encampment, we crossed three others from the right, all of them well timbered and graced by rich valleys and *prairillons*.

This section of country, being the great war-ground between the Sioux and Chyennes on the one side, and the Snakes and Crows on the other, is considered dangerous, particularly from May till November of each year. During that time it is extremely unsafe for a white man to venture within its confines, unless protected by a strong force.

A small creek at our right, became the scene of a bloody tragedy two months subsequent to our visit.

Three trappers, with whom I became acquainted upon my return to the Fort, tempted by the abundance of fur-bearing game common to the vicinity, came here for the purpose of making a summer hunt. While successfully pursuing their occupation, unsuspicious of immediate danger, they were suddenly surrounded, early one morning, by a war-party of Sioux, whose first salute was a discharge of fire-arms, accompanied by a shower of arrows and the sharp thunder of deafening yells.

Two of them fell dead. The remaining one retreated to a hollow tree, close at hand, into which he crawled; and, though severely wounded, maintained from it an obstinate resistance till near sundown,—keeping at bay the whole host of savage assailants, and thinning their numbers, one by one, with the deadly discharge of his unerring rifle.

Six warriors lay stiffened in death, and as many more had felt the burning smart of wounds,—one of the latter having had his tongue shot out, close to its roots!—and still he continued the unequal contest.

His triumph would have been complete had not the remorseless crew, as a last resort, set fire to the woods and burned him from the shell-like fortress from which they could not drive him.

He fell with his companions, mingling his own blood with that of their murderers; and the scalps of the three were treasured among the horrid trophies of savage victory.

Of these unfortunate men, one, named Wheeler, was a Pennsylvanian; another, named Cross Eagle, was a Swede; and the third, name not remembered, was a native of France. They were men of noble hearts and much esteemed by all who knew them.

In the neighborhood I noticed many indications of coal, of which there appeared to be extensive beds, as well as iron and mineral salts.

Continuing on, a short ride brought us to the pass-trail, following which, after travelling a few miles by a road intercepted by frequent ravines between a defile of mountains, we were finally ushered into the broad prairie, opening eastward, known as the Plains of Laramie.

The mountains upon both sides were heavily coated with snow, which intruded to the trail, while groves of pine and aspen relieved the eye in scanning their rough escarpments.

The prevailing rock appeared to be a compact red granite, with occasional strata of sandstone.

While winding among the ravines and aspen groves, we obtained an indistinct view of a strange-looking, dark-colored animal, that my companions pronounced a "*carcague*."

Of the character, or even the existence of such a creature, I cannot speak from positive knowledge—this, if one, not being sufficiently near for a scrutinizing observation, and no other of its kind ever came in my way; but, in answer to inquiries, I am enabled to give the following description,—for the correctness of which, however, I will not vouch, though, for my own part, inclined to accredit it.

The "carcague" is a native of the Rocky Mountains, and of a family and species found in no other part of the world as yet known. He seems a distinct *genus*, partaking the mixed nature of the wolf and bear, but is far more ferocious than either.

His color is a jet black, hair long and coarse, and body trim and slender. His head and neck are like those of a wolf, but his tail and feet assimilate he bear, and his body presents the marked qualities and appearance of both.

In size, he is considerably larger than the common cur-dog, and is more agile in his movements. Unlike the bear, he will not run from the presence or scent of man, and regards the "lord of creation" with neither fear nor favor. Hence he is looked upon as a creature much to be dreaded by all who are anywise conversant with his character and existence.

The representatives of his family are seldom met with, which affords the principal reason why so little, comparatively, is known of his nature and habits.

If the information contained in the above description is correct, (and that it is so, I have not the least doubt,) the "carcague" presents, either the extraordinary phenomenon of the creation of a new race of wild beasts, or, the living relics of an order now almost extinct; and, whether he be the one or the other, his existence is vested with deep interest to all lovers of the marvellous.

An old trapper related the following story, soon after the incident above noticed, which will serve to give some idea of this ferocious animal:

A party of hunters, at their night camp, were seated around a large fire, at whose side were fixed several pieces of meat, *en appolas*, for the purpose of roasting. All were waiting patiently the kind office of the fire in the preparation of their longed-for suppers, when, attracted by the fumes of the cooking viands, a "carcague" came bounding from the mountain-side, directly over their heads, and made for the roasts, with which he disappeared before even a shot could be fired in their defence.

Thus bold and daring is their nature, and so little is their regard for the presence of man.

Bearing southward, in the course of a few miles we came to a large creek, and camped early in the afternoon, near the base of a lofty mountain of the Medicine Bow range.

In this vicinty were the relics of three Indians forts. On the banks of the stream was an abundance of timber of various kinds; the bottoms were broad and of a rich soil, shut in by abrupt acclivities that lead to the arid plains through which the creek traces its way.

Game appeared in great abundance in all directions, and seemed more than usually tame and accessible.

Soon after camping, three of us went in quest of a fresh supply of eatables, and, towards night, returned with the choice portions of a buffalo and a black-tailed dear.

The valley also afforded large quantities of wild onions, which were shooting forth with singular luxuriance.

We passed the night in quiet slumber, neither of us dreaming of the possible existence of human beings, other than ourselves, within a less distance than one hundred miles.

In the morning, however, we were awakened by the wild yell of savages, and, on looking to ascertain the cause, saw a dense throng of painted monsters surrounding us, who were whooping, screeching, and dancing in a most terrific and fantastic manner. Seizing our guns, we levelled at the foremost of them, who immediately sheathed their bows and made the sign of friendship and their nation.

They were Crows, and, having discovered us the afternoon before, now came for a morning call.

The chief of the band bore the name of Little Robber, and was a large, portly, well-made man, as, in fact, were all his party. He was recognized by one of us as an old acquaintance, and was greeted as such, when several of his people came forward to shake hands, and we were soon on most friendly terms.

They informed us, by means of signs, that they were advancing against the Sioux, and their village was encamped upon a neighboring creek, a little to the right,—after which they insisted upon our accompanying them to it.

Not waiting for further ceremony, they drove up our horses and commenced saddling them. Supposing it useless to resist, we yielded compliance to their wishes, and, in about an hour's ride, came to the village. Here we were inducted to the chief's lodge, where commenced a series of feastings peculiar to Indians on occasions like this.

The Crows are a nation living upon the waters of the Yellow-stone, at a distance of about four hundred miles west-northwest of Fort Platte. Their number embraces not far from four hundred and fifty or five hundred lodges, being something near four thousand men, women, and children.

Ten or twelve years since they were enemies to the whites, but, more recently, have been on friendly terms.

They never kill or injure the white man who comes within their power, and rarely take from him anything without returning for it an equivalent. For instance,—they may take his robe, horse, or gun; but, in that case, they will return another robe, horse, or gun; acting upon the principle that "exchange is no robbery," even though it be compulsory.

Less contaminated by intercourse with the whites than most mountain tribes, they will tolerate the importation of liquor among them upon no consideration, not even by traders for their own individual use. Whenever it is ascertained that any one in their vicinity, whether white man or Indian, is in possession of that article, they take it from him, if necessary, by force, and pour it upon the ground.

Their bitter hatred of this vile stuff, is said to have resulted in the following strange manner:

The whites, as usual, came first among them bringing alcohol; and, at a feast given to the chiefs, soon after, several of the latter became intoxicated from too lavish potations of the new and curious drink.

In common with inebriates of civilized society, they acted very foolishly, and, on appearing before their people, the drunken chiefs became the subject of ridicule. This so shamed them, that, upon the return of sobriety, they could not be persuaded to taste another drop, and thereafter made use of their united influence to prevent its introduction and sale.

Ever since the above occurrence, alcohol has received, from the Crows, the appellation of "*Fool's Water*," a term at once attesting their nice moral discernment and good sense.

Several years since, a missionary, on visiting them, began through an interpreter to rehearse the story how sin first came into the world, and how all men had become bad—whether white or red.

THE CROW CHIEF MAKING A SPEECH. — *Page* 175.

Thus premised, he proceeded to explain the great truths of Christianity, and averred that he had come to do them good, and to tell them how to be happy; asserting that, unless they listened to him and worshipped the Good Spirit in the manner he pointed out, they could never, at death, reach that happy country into which good people alone find admittance.

One of the chiefs upon this arose and made the following reply:

"My white brother is a stranger to us. He talks bad of us, and he talks bad of his own people.

"He does this because he is ignorant. He thinks my people, like his, are wicked. Thus far he is wrong!

"Who were they that killed the very good man of whom he tells us? None of them were red men!

"The red man will die for good men, who are his friends;—he will not kill them!

"Let my pale-face brother talk to the white man—his own people—they are very bad. He says, he would do us good! He does no good to chide us and say we are very bad.

"True we are bad; and were we bad as the pale-faces it would become us to listen to him!

"Would my brother do us good? Then, let him tell us how to make powder and we will believe in the sincerity of his professions;—but let him not belie us by saying we are bad like the pale-faces!"

These Indians rarely kill the women and children of an enemy when in their power, and, in this particular, they show themselves unlike most of the wild tribes found on the American continent.

They are a brave and noble people, prosecuting their endless hostilities against the Sioux and Blackfeet, (the only nations with whom they are at variance,) not so much to gratify an innate love for war, as from a just hatred of the meanness of those they war against.

In the summer of 1842, a war-party of some two hundred Crows invaded the Sioux country by way of Laramie pass, and penetrated as far as Fort Platte, and beyond, in pursuit of their enemy.

A few miles above the Fort, having met with a lone French engagé, who was rather *green* in all that pertains to Indians as well as some other things, they began by signs to enquire of him the whereabouts of the Lacotas, (the sign for them being a transverse pass of the right front-finger across the throat.)

The poor Frenchman, mistaking this for the avowed intention of *cutting his throat*, commenced bellowing *a la* calf, accompanying the music by an industrious appliance of crosses in double-quick time—not forgetting to make use of sundry most earnest invocations of the blessed Virgin to graciously vouchsafe to him deliverance from impending danger.

The Indians, perceiving his strange conduct to be the result of fear, felt disposed to have a little fun at his expense; so, mounting him upon a horse, they bound his hands and feet and guarded him to a post of the American Fur Company as a prisoner.

The Fort gates being closed against them, they demanded admittance on the plea of wishing to trade.

"What would you buy?" asked the commandant.

"Tobacco."

"What have you brought to pay for it?"

"A white man."

"A white man?" exclaimed the former; "at what price?"

"Oh, he is not worth much. A plug of tobacco is his full value!" continued the warriors.

The commandant now began to understand the joke; and, on recognizing the prisoner as an employee of the other Fort, he told them they might possibly find a market for him at the next post, but for his own part he was not disposed to purchase.

The Indians then paraded around the Fort, and, after saluting its inmates with three deafening whoops, proceeded at full charge towards Fort Platte.

When arrived, having prostrated two scaffolds of dead Sioux by the way, they informed the person in charge, that they had brought back one of his men, and claimed from him a plug of tobacco for their trouble. The circumstances attending this request were of so comical a nature, the commandant felt disposed to humor the joke, and gave the tobacco, upon which they immediately left in pursuit of their enemies.

Having remained prisoners to the hospitality of these Indians for two days and a half, we were at length permitted again to resume our journey.

Following the creek downwards for the two days next succeeding, and then bearing to the left, after a ride of some twelve miles, we struck Laramie river at a point which presented broad bottoms upon each side with an abundance of timber; here we remained encamped till the subsequent day.

In journeying thus far, we passed over a sufficient extent of this broad expanse to give a general description of it, from personal observation coupled with information derived from others more experienced.

The Plains of Laramie are bounded north and east by the Black Hills, south by a ridge of naked elevations, (composed of soft, arenaceous rock and terrene limestone, embedded in marl and white clay, sterile and almost entirely destitute of vegetation,) and west by the Medicine Bow Mountains.

This section includes an area one hundred and sixty miles long by seventy broad.

The northern portion of it is a high plateau, almost destitute of springs or streams of water, having a mixed soil of clay and sand, producing the grass and other peculiarities incident to the grand prairies. Westerly, it is composed of red sand and gravel, tolerably fertile and abundant in rocky fragments. The southern portion is watered by a number of streams that rise in the Medicine Bow Mountains and flow eastward; some of them pouring their waters into Laramie river, and others losing themselves in the sand.

Towards the southwestern extremity, at the base of a lofty, isolated mountain, is a salt lake of considerable dimensions. Several other lakes are also found adjacent to the Medicine Bow Mountains, whose waters are strongly impregnated with mineral salts.

In numerous places the surface, for small distances, is entirely naked and whitened with saline efflorescences, that vie in their appearance with the unspotted purity of fresh-fallen snow.

The Laramie river* traces its way through the whole extent,—rising in the southern extremity of the Medicine Bow Mountains and in the desolate highlands that form the dividing ridge between its own and the waters of Càche a la Poudre, and, after flowing a distance of some three hundred miles, discharges itself into the Platte.

Upon this river and its branches are many beautiful bottoms of rich alluvial soil, well adapted to cultivation, varying from five to ten miles in length, and from two to five in breadth. These bottoms are to some extent well supplied with timber, consisting of ash, elm, cottonwood, box-elder, and willow, while the adjacent mountains and hills afford pine, cedar, and balsam.

Of the various kinds of wild fruits and berries are found cherries, plums, currants, gooseberries, service-berries, buffalo-berries, and some few grapes; among its vegetables and roots are the bread-root, pomme blanc, onions, and commote.

Its prevailing rock is sandstone, (gray micaceous, brown argillaceous, red granitic, and ferruginous,) limestone, (siliceous, testaceous, fossiliferous, and terrene,) and red granite, with various conglomerates and heavy boulders of fragmentary and transition rock.

Among the mineral productions incident to this region are salt, sulphur, soda, magnesia, nitre, alum, coal, iron, copper, and gold, (the latter only in small quantities.) Among its game is embraced nearly every variety found in countries adjacent to the mountains.

The high prairies skirting the tributaries of the Laramie, though favored with many valleys of fertile soil, are fit only for grazing purposes, on account of their general aridity and scarcity of water; a fault, by the way, too common with a large proportion of that vast extent of territory from the neighborhood of our western frontiers almost to the very shores of the Pacific.

*This river received its present name from one Joseph Laramie, a French trapper, who was killed near its mouth, several years since, by the Indians.

## CHAPTER XVI.

Sibille's-hole.—Novel bitters.—Chugwater.—Gold.—Curiosity.—Affairs at the Fort.—Amusements.—Gambling among squaws, and games played.—Squaw dresses, and riding fashion.—Items of interest to the curious, proving the intercourse of the ancient Romans with the people of this continent.

On resuming our course, we soon after struck into a lodge-trail leading to the Platte by way of Sibille's creek;—following this we travelled over an undulating and sandy prairie for about ten miles, and came to a chain of rugged mountains, bearing from north to south, through which we passed, by a tedious and circuitous route, for a considerable distance, winding among rocks and narrow defiles of naked hills, till we were finally ushered into a beautiful opening facing the east, known as Sibille's-hole.

This valley is situated at the confluence of two small streams, heading in the adjoining mountains, that unite to form Sibille's creek.

It is shut in upon three sides by lofty ridges, many hundred feet high, consisting of immense piles of earthy limestone and marl, whose rough, naked sides, ornamented with occasional dwarf-pines, cedars, or fruit-bearing shrubs, present a wild and romantic scenery.

The valley is four or five miles in length and of variable width, with a strong, black soil, affording a goodly supply of timber.

The season was further advanced in this than in any other place we had yet visited. Several specimens of wild flowers were in full bloom, belading the soft air with their sweetest odors. The grass too had attained a height of some three inches, and furnished a most sumptuous entertainment for our jaded animals, which they were nowise backward to accept.

Wishing to afford them an opportunity to recruit their strength, we remained encamped the two following days.

During the interval we were successful in killing two very fat bulls, and were thus enabled to renew the series of feasting which had graced the greater part of our journey.

I here became for the first time acquainted with a kind of beverage very common among mountaineers. The article alluded to may with much propriety be termed "bitters," as the reader will readily acknowledge on learning the nature of its principal ingredient.

It is prepared by the following simple process, viz: with one pint of water mix one-fourth gill of buffalo-gall, and you will then have before you a wholesome and exhilarating drink.

To a stomach unaccustomed to its use it may at first create a slightly noisome sensation, like the inceptive effects of an emetic; and, to one strongly bilious, it might cause vomiting;—but, on the second or third trial, the stomach attains a taste for it, and receives it with no inconsiderable relish.

Upon the whole system its effects are beneficial. As a stimulent, it braces the nerves without producing a corresponding relaxation on the cessation of its influence; it also tends to restore an imparèd appetite and invigorate the digestive powers.

As a sanative, it tends to make sound an irritated and ulcerated stomach, reclaiming it to a healthful and lively tone, and thus striking an effective blow at that most prolific source of so large a majority of the diseases common to civilzed life.

From what I have seen of its results, I consider it one of the most innocent and useful medicines in cases of dyspepsy, and will hazard the further opinion, that, were those laboring under the wasting influences of this disease to drink *gall-bitters* and confine themselves exclusively to the use of some *one* kind of diet, (animal food always preferable,) thousands who are now pining away by piecemeal, would be *restored to perfect soundness*, and *snatched from the very threshold of a certain grave* which yawns to receive them!

Resuming our course, we continued down Sibillis creek to its junction with the Laramie; then, following the course of that river, in the afternoon of the third day we arrived at Fort Platte, after an absence of nearly two months,—having travelled, in the interval, a distance of more than five hundred miles.

To give a general description of the country passed over during the concluding part of our journey, would seem too much like a recapitulation of previous remarks.

Our observations in reference to the river and creek bottoms, may be again correctly applied; as may, also, those relative to the timber, and the geological character of the adjoining prairies.

Several miles above the Fort we crossed the Chugwater, a large affluent of the Laramie, from the right. This creek takes its rise in a wild and desolate section of the Black Hills, near the head of Horse creek.

Thirty miles or more of its way is traced through a dreary wilderness of rock, sand, and clay, almost entirely devoid of vegetation.

This region, it is said, affords gold; and, indeed, I have received frequent assurances that that valuable metal has been procured, in small particles, from among the sand of the creek-bed.

This region also claims many natural curiosities, of which I may take occasion to speak more particularly hereafter;—one, however, situated upon Chugwater, here seems more appropriately to demand a passing notice.

It consists of a columnar elevation of sandstone and marl, towering aloft to the height of several hundred feet, like the lone chimney of some razed mansion,—standing as the melancholy monument of the ruins that surround it.

This singular pile of rock and earth is nearly of a quadrangular form, quite regular in its structure, and compares very nearly with the "Chimney" below Scot's Bluff, in its general outlines. It stands within a short distance of the east bank of the Chugwater, and gives the creek its present name.*

Our arrival at the Fort dated the 26th of April. The boat being completed, all things, save the spring rise, were in readiness for the intended voyage.

This craft was put together in regular ship-shape, and finished in a workman-like manner. She measured fifty feet keel by thirteen beam, and, without her lading, drew but an inch and a half of water. Her intended burthen was between two and three tons. While admiring her beauty and symetry, little did I think of the sufferings in store for me with her hardy crew.

Several important changes had taken place during our absence. The Fort with its fixtures now claimed different owners, and was occupied by the men of two companies besides our own. This swelled the present number to some forty or fifty, and afforded quite a lively scene.

Now was an interval of leisure to all hands, and the time, unemployed in eating and sleeping, was passed in story-telling, ball-playing, foot-racing, target-shooting, or other like amusements.

Several, forming themselves into a club for forensic debate, secured a prolific source of entertainment, for the time being. A partner in one of the trading firms, whose men were now stationed at the Fort, made himself quite conspicuous as a participator in these discussions.

He was very self-important and conceited, and not a little ignorant withal, and with regard to temperance, being uniformly about "three sheets in the wind," and the other *fluttering*, his spoutings were an exhaustless fund of laughter.

At his request, in order to render the exercises more *spirited*, the merits of the arguments presented were decided upon by a committee of three, and the speakers decided against, sentenced to *liquorize* the club.

The treating, however, was always on one side; for, as the whole business was an affair of sport, the committee of arbitration generally had this primary object in view while pronouncing their decisions. When these were averse to our orator, he of course paid the forfeit as an affair of debt; and when favorable to him, he was equally prompt in proferring a common treat, exultatory upon his fancied success.

My own part in this performance was that of a mere looker-on, but it required of one more than my usual self-mastery, to retain his gravity under the potent influences of so ludicrous an exhibition.

Other matters of interest, however, occurred at this time, and, as they tend to throw some light upon Indian habits and customs, perhaps the reader will not look upon it as altogether out of place for me to notice them.

* The word "Chug" implies chimney; of the derivation of the term, however, I am ignorant.

At the two Forts in this neighborhood were some ten or twelve squaws, married to the traders and engagés of the different fur companies. These ladies were in the habit of meeting, occasionally, for gambling purposes. In this they acted as systematically as the most experienced black legs of a Mississippi steamboat; if they failed to play as high, it was only for the lack of means.

Ball-playing was one of the games upon which heavy bets were made. The instrument used in this amusement consisted of two globular forms, about two inches each in diameter, which were attached by a short string. The play-ground was the open prairie in front of the Fort, and embraced an area of nearly a mile in extent.

As the initiatory step, each party, composed of equal numbers, selected an equal amount of valuables, consisting of beads, scarlet, vermilion, rings, awls, shells, &c., which were placed in two piles about half a mile apart, and equi-distant between them was placed the ball. Each gamestress, armed with her club, then repaired to the spot, and the opposing parties arrayed themselves, the one facing the other with the ball between them. At a given signal they all strike—the one party striving to propel it towards its own valuables, and the other to force it in a contrary direction. The party propelling it to its own pile, wins, and becomes entitled to both.

As success in this game depends more upon fleetness of foot than skill in striking, a large party of squaws, thus engaged, opens to the beholder a rich scene of amusement.

Another game is still more extensively practised among them. This is somewhat upon the principle of dice, though different in its details.

Six plum-stones, smoothly polished, and marked with various parallel, triangular, and transverse lines, are thrown loosely into a small, plate-like basket, around which the players are seated with their stores of trinkets. The leader then receives the basket in one hand, and, briskly moving it to change the position of the dice, suddenly strikes it upon the ground, tossing the plum-stones from their places and catching them in their descent.

The amount won depends upon the number of triangular and transverse lines left uppermost.

The loser, having paid the forfeit, next takes the basket and describes the same movements, receives her winnings in like manner, and returns it to her opponent,—and so on alternately.

Much cheating and trickery are practised in this game.

The game of hand, for a description of which the reader is referred to a previous marginal note, is also a favorite play with squaws as well as men. Large parties of both sexes not unfrequently engage in this amusement, and many a poor Indian loses his all by the operation.

Speaking of squaws reminds me of not having previously described their dress and appearance.

The dress of a squaw is scarcely less simple than that of an Indian. Two pieces of skin, sewed together in a bag-like form, (of sufficient size to envelope the body from neck to knee, leaving an aperture for the former with the arms,) constitute her gown, which is completed by two other pieces of skin sewed from neck to waist so as to fall loosely upon the arms as far as the elbow; then, with leggins of thin deer or antelope skin, garnished moccasins, and a painted robe, you have before you the full rig of a mountain squaw.

Some of the younger ones, however, flaunt dresses quite tastefully ornamented, with full capes and fringe-works, garnished with beads and porcupine-quills, that present a wild, fantastic appearance, not altogether estranged to beauty.

A squaw prides herself much upon the number of rings in her ears and upon her fingers, as well as the taste displayed in plaiting her hair and beautifying her face.

Women, in savage alike with civilized life, are vested with a good supply of pride and vanity in their composition,—all, fond of show and gaudy equipage. But the mountain squaw, next to ornaments, displays the most vanity in the gay caparison of her riding horse, and the splendid trappings of his saddle. Both of them are fancifully garnished with beads and paint, and bestrung with various trinkets, that impart a tinkling sound, as they strike each other at every movement, and fill the rider's ears with that wild and simple music so consonant to her feelings and thoughts.

Men and women practise the same mode of riding, (astride,) and a squaw is as much at home on horseback as the most experienced cavalier.

This fashion is properly considered unbecoming for ladies of civilized countries; yet, improper as it may seem, it is quite common with the ladies of New Mexico.

As my subsequent travels in the countries bordering upon the Rocky Mountains preclude the opportunity of speaking connectedly of the Sioux nation, I cannot forego the present occasion for presenting to the curious, some few items relative to the language of these Indians, that tend to shed no small amount of light upon the ancient history of the American continent.

There are several remarkable peculiarities in the Sioux language, that cannot fail to prove interesting and satisfactory, so far as they go, to all lovers of antiquarian research.

The first of these consists in the striking similarity observable in its general structure to that of the ancient Romans, when the two are carefully compared with each other.

In regard to the arrangement of words and the construction of sentences, they are both governed by the same fixed laws of euphony, irrespective of the relative position otherwise maintained by the different parts of speech. It will be observed that the leading purpose of the speaker of either language is, to avoid a harsh and inharmonious intermingling of words, such as would grate upon the ear when pronounced in an abrupt connection; and, by so doing, to give a smooth and musical turn to the expression of his ideas.

The few brief sentences, hereto subjoined in the same order as they occur in the original, accompanied by the translation of each word as it appears, will serve to illustrate this matter more fully:

| LATIN. | SIOUX. |
|---|---|
| Invictum animi robur ostensit. | Tepe nea-tour toocta? |
| Invincible of mind strength he displayed. | Lodge your own where is it? |
| Omnia delicarum instrumenta e | Mea warchee muzarka nea-tour. |
| All of delicacies the intruments from | I want gun your own. |
| castris ejecit. | Kokepa warneche wecharcha ha. |
| camp he cast. | Afraid nothing the man is. |
| Non amo nimium diligentes. | Minewarka appello warktashne ha |
| Not I love overmuch the careful. | Medicine-water I say not good is. |

A mere glance at the foregoing will at once show the constructional similarity between the two; and, to illustrate the proposition still farther, I here subjoin yet other proofs of a more important relationship:

| LATIN. | SIOUX. |
|---|---|
| Appello, (pres. ind., 1st per. sing.; inf. appellàre,) *I declare, I proclaim.* | Appello, *I declare, I proclaim, I tell, I make known.* |
| Bestia, *a wild beast.* | Beta, *a buffalo.* |
| Cæca, *uncertain, ambiguous, confused, rash.* | Ceicha, *bad, disorderly, unsound.* |
| Cogor, *one who collects, brings together, compels, forces, or heaps up.* | Cogor, *a maker of anything, a manufacturer, one who produces a thing by an ingenious arrangement of materials.* |
| Mea, (meus, a, um,) *of or belonging to me.* | Mea, *I, myself, me.* |
| Mena, *a narrow sharp fish.* | Mena, *a knife.* |
| Ne, (this when affixed to a word or a sentence gives it a negative signification,) *no, not.* | Ne, (this word is used precisely the same as in Latin, and has a similar meaning,) *not.* |
| Papæ, *rare, excellent, wonderful.* | Papa, *meat, flesh used for food.* |
| Pater, *father.* | Pater, *fire.* |
| Pes, *the foot.* | Pea, *the foot.* |
| Taurus, *a bull.* | Tau, (or tah,) *a bull.* |
| Tepor, *warmth.* | Tepe, *a lodge.* |
| Tuor, (tui, tutus sum,) *to look, to see.* | Tula, (astonishment,) *look! see there!* |

I might pursue this comparison to a yet greater extent, were my knowledge of Sioux sufficiently full and critical for the task, (for I have a firm confidence that many other similarities might be pointed out, quite as glaring in their character as any of the above;) but, enough, I trust, has already been said to fortify the position so largely warranted by the premises, to wit: that in former ages the Romans maintained a foothold upon the American continent, and had *intercourse* with this nation, either by arms or by commerce.

The argument drawn from the foregoing is still further strengthened, when we take into consideration the fact, that language is constantly varying in its form, and changing the meaning and pronunciation of its words, as time progresses. To exemplify this more clearly and forcibly, let the reader compare the works of standard English authors of the present day with those of the like not more than five hundred years since, and he will readily acknowledge the palpable indications of progressive change.

If so short an interval has produced a transformation so bold in a written language, what might we look for in one spoken only?

But, an interval of three times five hundred years has passed since the Romans and the Sioux held intercourse with each other, and we yet find the general structure of the two languages strikingly similar, and several of their words identical in meaning and pronunciation! And, though the latter observation fails in some cases, even this, so far from proving anything averse to the position before assumed, serves to strengthen it.

The word *pater*, for instance, pronounced alike in both languages, differs in signification; being used in the one to imply *father*, in the other *fire*. This apparent discrepancy of meaning may be explained in a few words. The Sioux are accustomed to venerate the *sun* as one of the more especial manifestations of the Divine Essence, who is regarded as the FATHER or creator of all things; and it, being the great source of light and heat, is naturally looked upon as an immense body of fire. Thus, in the course of ages, the term became perverted in its meaning and application, and, instead of being used to express the sun, or Great Spirit, the father of all, it now only implies the simple element of fire, an emanation from the sun.

So in relation to the Latin word *tepor*, *warmth*, and the Sioux word *tepe*, *a lodge*. The lodge is employed in winter to retain the heat within itself, and exclude the cold air; nor is it wonderful that, in the progress of years, the term *tepor*, or *tepe*, should become the only one by which a lodge is known.

The word *mena*, is also pronounced the same in both, though different in its signification; meaning, in Latin, a narrow sharp fish, and, in Sioux, a knife. In explanation of this, I would barely refer to the similarity of shape between a knife and a narrow sharp fish.

The relationship disclosed between these two languages is seemingly too close and significant to be attributed to mere chance or accident, and can be in no other way satisfactorily accounted for, than by admitting the correctness of the premises before quoted.

But this position, curious as it may seem to some readers, and impregnable as it must doubtless prove, has other weapons to protect it at command; and, ere dismissing the subject, I will briefly notice some of them.

It is by no means a conjecture of recent origin, that the ancient Romans did actually colonize portions of the American continent. The industrious researches of antiquarians have long since brought to light many items which prove and strengthen it, though none of them so tangible and obvious as those previously noticed.

Several obscure hints of the existence of extensive Roman colonies planted westward of the Pillars of Hercules, (doubtless alluding to the American continent,) have been detected in the writings of ancient authors yet extant; but still further proof is afforded in the relics of temples, cities, roads, and fortified camps, long since discovered in Peru, Mexico, and the United States, which strongly savor of Roman origin.

The ancient works at Marietta, Ohio, have been regarded, by not a few, as the offspring of Roman industry and military science,—and various other remains, that signalize the Mississippi valley, point quite plainly to this nation for a parentage. But a proof, still more conclusive than any yet adduced, is afforded by the discovery of a genuine Roman coin, in the State of Missouri, several years since.

Taking all these corroborative circumstances in connection, the fact that Roman colonies *did* exist, to some extent, upon this continent in past ages, must be regarded as placed beyond successful controversy.

## CHAPTER XVII.

Singular exhibition of natural affection.—Embark for the States.—Scarcity of provisions and consequent hardship and suffering.—Extraordinary daring of wolves.—Difficulties of navigation.—Novel diet.—Fishing.—A fish story, and another to match it.—A bull story.—Hard aground and dismal situation.—Extreme exposure.—Cold, hungry, and wet.—Again afloat.—Re-supply of provisions.—Camp on fire.—A picture of Platte navigation.—Country north of river.—Adventure with a bull.—Indian benevolence.—Summary of hardships and deprivations.—Abandon voyage.

Soon after our return, one of the hunters came in from a short excursion followed by a buffalo calf, which appeared as tame and docile as if always accustomed to the presence of man.

This incident first brought to my knowledge a remarkable peculiarity in the nature of these animals,—viz: the strength of affection existing between the mother and her offspring.

The buffalo will never desert her calf, except in cases of imminent danger, and then, never for a long time;—she is certain to return promptly in search of it, even at the hazard of her own life. The calf, on the other hand, exhibits an equal, or rather superior, love for its mother.

If she, to whom he owes his birth, falls a prey to the relentless hunter, he deserts her not, but lingers near her lifeless carcase, till the butcher-knife performs its office, and the reeking flesh belades the pack-horse;—nor then, even, does he leave her.

As the honored relics are borne away, he not unfrequently follows on, mournfully, regardless of aught else, as if saying, "Where thou goest let me go, and now thou art dead, I would live no longer." There is something touchingly beautiful in such exhibitions of natural affection on the part of dumb brutes.

*May 7th.* Availing ourselves of a slight rise of water, we embarked on our meditated voyage to the States.

The boat was freighted with some sixty packs* of robes, and provisions for four weeks. A barge belonging to another company, also in readiness, started with us, and we all flattered ourselves with the hope of a speedy and pleasant trip.

The two boats numbered a united crew of eleven men,—mine consisting of five, and that of our consort counted six.

*A pack of robes generally embraces ten skins, and weighs about eighty pounds.

Slipping cable, we glided midway of the stream, and gave a parting salute to the friends who lined the shore, accompanied by a loud hurra and waving of hats, deeply responded to by them,—and even tears coursed their way a down the dusky visages of our voyageurs, when mindful of the fate separating them—perhaps forever!

The crews now struck up a merry song, while the dripping oars, as they spurned the crystal waters, responded their time in measured strokes.

As we passed swiftly along and were fast receding from within hailing distance of the Fort, an old mountaineer, who stood gazing upon us, exclaimed, "Ah, boys; you can sing now, but your tune will be altered erelong!"

This strange announcement, though a riddle at the time of its utterance, soon began to more than verify itself, and often did we repeat the remark, "Well, sure enough, our tune has changed."

Moving along prettily during the day—sometimes floating with the current then again plying oars,—we reached the mouth of Horse creek; and, passing on a short distance, lay to for the night.

The day following we again pushed off; but, after proceeding ten or twelve miles, the water became so shallow, we were compelled to lay by to await a further rise, and struck camp in a small grove of cottonwood upon the right bank of the Platte, a short distance above Scott's Bluff. Here we remained for some two weeks.

The crew of our consort being poorly supplied with provisions, we divided our own with them, and, at the expiration of a few days, were left entirely destitute.

From this on, we were dependent solely upon such game as chance threw in our way,—sometimes starving for two or three days, and then feasting for a like interval, upon the products of successful hunting.

To us was a tedious lot,—there being no game in the country, save perchance a few straggling bulls, and they rarely within less distance than ten or twelve miles. Our hunting excursions often led further than that, and when we were so fortunate as to kill, the proceeds were borne upon our backs to camp. We became so accustomed to packing in this manner, it was thought no extra burthen for an individual to carry upwards of a hundred pounds of fresh meat at a single load, some ten or twelve successive miles, over an open, sandy prairie, and beneath the scorching rays of an almost vertical sun.

So far from regarding it a task, we esteemed it a pleasure, and were glad to appease the cravings of appetite even at so small a sacrifice of comfort and convenience.

The reason for the scarcity of all kinds of game in the vicinity of the river at this time, was the recent burning of the prairie upon both sides, for many miles back, leaving not even the vestige of vegetation for the subsistence of any graminivorous animals.

This we found to be the case nearly the entire distance to the forks.

During the latter part of our stay at this camp, it rained almost incessantly; we also encountered a severe snow storm.

The winds were usually high, and frequently blew with hurricane-violence.

A pack of hungry wolves, attracted by the scent of camp, were our regular nocturnal visitors, and proved a constant source of annoyance. On one occasion they carried off a bake-kettle to a distance of several hundred yards;—at another time, they took away a tin-pan, which we never afterwards recovered;—and, stranger yet, one night these piratical pests stole a fur cap from off my head while I was sleeping, and in the morning, after a diligent search, no trace of it could be found.

The river having slightly risen, we again loosed cable, and, after toiling all day, and tugging with might and main, by hand-spikes and levers,—twisting, screwing, and lifting, now in water up to our necks, and now on dry sand-bars, we succeeded in dragging, or rather carrying, our craft for a distance of about five miles, and again lay by for four succeeding days to await a still further rise.

Upon the opposite side of the river was a bald-eagle's nest, with two half-grown fledgelings. One of our party, ascending the tree, captured the young ones, and we had a fine meal from their carcases. A wood-duck's nest, containing some twelve eggs, near by, afforded a seasonable repast,—and, in hunting for game, we came upon the nest of a wild goose, as well as those of numerous ravens among the neighboring cottonwoods and willows, which we subjected to such forced contributions as appetite demanded.

A portion of the interval was employed in fishing, but with poor success, the fish of the Platte being nearly all of them small, and not very plentiful even, at that.

An old Franco-Canadian, of our crew, here favored us with, perhaps, a little the biggest fish story of any told at the present day.

He had been down the Missouri on several occasions in boats connected with the fur trade. On one of these voyages, while in the act of reaching over the boat-side for a drink of water, he dropped his cup, which immediately sank to the bottom of the river and was lost.

Three years afterwards he again passed the same place, with hooks and lines attached to the boat-stern for the purpose of catching fish as he glided along.

A large cat-fish, attracted by the tempting bait borne upon the hook, greedily swallowed it, and, in a trice, found himself translated to a new and strange element.

The creature was so heavy, it took two men to pull him into the boat, while his gigantic proportions astonished all beholders.

But the most surprising thing was revealed on opening him;—there, snugly stowed away in one corner of the monster's capacious maw, reposed the identical cup our *voyageur* had lost, three years before, with his name and the date marked upon it!

"Pooh! Gumbo," said an old sailor, "I can beat such stories as that, all day.

"Why, fellow, on my last trip from Liverpool to New York, a shark followed the ship for a long time, picking up such bits of bread and meat as were thrown into the sea.

"Our steward was a very careless fellow, and, in shaking the tablecloth, he would frequently drop overboard the knives and forks and spoons, and received from the captain several floggings on that account. He was even accused of stealing them, but strongly protested his innocence of the latter charge.

"Among our passengers was an old whaleman, who, being very expert in the use of the harpoon, took it into his head one day to victimize the shark. After several ineffectual attempts, he finally succeeded in forcing his instrument through the monster's vitals, and drew the lifeless carcase alongside.

"The piratical cruiser was so thundering big, it took eight men with tackles to raise it on board;—it must have weighed at least sixteen hundred pounds! The body of the greedy creature was then laid upon deck, and on opening it all were astonished! What do you think was found, Gumbo?"

"Sacre sharp! Certes me tink dey fine de spoon, de fork an de knife' Him shark no follow de ship for nottin."

"Well, boys, what do you all suppose was found?"

"Indeed, we could'nt say."

"Guess,"

"The knives and spoons, of course.'

"You are wrong, to a man."

"What, in the name of reason, could it have been? Do tell—we give it up."

"Hang me, if you aint a bright set of fellows!—Can't guess a thing so easy? Why, if I must tell you—'twas guts,—only guts—nothing in the world but *guts!*"

"Look here, Jack," said one of the listeners, advancing towards him hat in hand, "you can take this. We'll be quite likely to remember hereafter that fish generally carry their guts inside!"

The old Frenchman looked rather crest-fallen at the curious manner in which his extraordinary fish story had been matched,—but felt little disposed to yield his laurels without an effort to retrieve them,—so, calling to aid his recollections of the marvellous, he again commenced.

Several years ago, while in the employ of the American Fur Company, our hero and another man were sent expresses to a distant post. It was winter; and they travelled on foot, depending for daily subsistence upon such game as chance brought in their way. Their course lay through an open and cheerless prairie, covered with snow, and the journey occupied nearly a month.

Having been *en route* some five or six days, their ammunition began to fail in the item of lead,—and only two bullets were left. Their condition now became extremely desperate, as there was no way of procuring a re-supply,—and anticipated starvation stared them in the face.

Determined to eat as long as the means of subsistence remained, their last balls were shot away in killing a buffalo bull. After furnishing themselves from his carcase with a large supply of meat for present and future use, our hero proceeded to cut a few locks of hair from off the creature's head, for the purpose of stuffing his moccasins.

"Bon Dieu! Vat you tink me fine? You no can tell all day! Me no ask you guess. Bon Dieu! c'etre admirable. Me fine forty ballas, in he head. Me get 'em out. Sacre tonnerre! den me had him sufficient la poudre and la ballas for de route! No go hungry une leetil bit!"

On the fifth day subsequent, we again launched forth into the stream, and after a series of most extraordinary exertions, (being obliged to lighten our boat several times, by carrying its loading on shore, and reloading as often, thus to enable us to lift it over sand-bars,) we succeeded in getting it some three miles, and finally became safely moored in the middle of the river, from which it was impossible to extricate ourselves either by going backwards, forwards, or sidewise—with or without a cargo.

Here we remained for three days, and experienced, during the interval, a continuous fall of rain and sleet, which rendered the weather dismal and our own situation disagreeable in the extreme.

A cáche of liquor having been made, fifteen or twenty miles distant, by a trader connected with our consort, a month or two previous, unforbidding as was the weather, the crew could not rest content until the hidden treasure was among them.

Improving the opportunity presented by a slight suspension of the storm, one morning two of them started to procure it. Soon after it commenced snowing and raining, accompanied by a fierce, cutting wind and all the withering bleakness of a winter's blast.

Still keeping on, however, they obtained the cáche, and returned with it towards the boat.

But night shut in upon them by the way, and a thrice dreary night it was. Being too drunk to navigate, they lost their course and were forced to camp in the open prairie, without wood or aught else of which to build a fire, or even a robe to cover or a rock to shelter them from the chill wind and peltings of the pitiless storm.

Half-frozen with cold and wet to the skin, they lay upon the muddy ground and passed the interval, not in sleep, but in a state of drunken stupor, produced by inordinate draughts upon the contents of their keg.

On the next morning they reached the boat,—a beautiful looking couple, as might well be supposed! Covered with mud from head to foot, their clothes were wringing wet, and their faces bloated and swollen almost to twice their natural size. So complete was the transformation, they were scarcely recognizable as the same persons.

But, regardless of hardship and suffering, they stuck to the liquor-keg and brought it with them as proof of their triumph.

And now commenced a scene of drunken revelry, which, despite my efforts to prevent it, soon communicated itself to both crews, and continued without intermission till the stock on hand was exhausted.

The lack of a fire by which to warm ourselves, contributed materially to the misery of our present condition; there being no wood procurable for that purpose within five or six miles of either shore, and having none on board, we were compelled to endure the dreary interval as best we could.

But another evil came pressing upon our already heavy load through the entire exhaustion of provisions, and the last of our stay was made twice forlorn by cold and fasting.

The gloomy reality of this situation may be thus briefly summed up;—we were fast aground in the middle of a river, three-fourths of a mile from either shore, confined to the narrow limits of a few feet, exposed to the merciless peltings of a chill storm of rain and sleet, with only a thin lodge skin to shelter us, without fire to warm or dry ourselves by, and, worse than all, destitute of the means of appeasing the gnawings of hunger.

But, forbidding as the picture may seem, it proved only the commencement of a long series of suffering and deprivation, more intensely dreadful in its nature, that was yet held in reserve for us.

On the forenoon of the fourth day the storm abated, and, favored with a slight rise of water, by dint of extraordinary effort we finally succeeded in getting afloat, and gained the right shore after pulling our craft over sand-bars for a distance of two miles.

All hands now turned out in search of game, one of whom returned, towards night with an antelope, providing us with a needful supply of food for the time being.

The next day, forcing our craft onward for six or eight miles, we brought to upon the left shore, where, after a short excursion among the hills, two other antelope were brought in, which furnished us with a further supply of provisions.

The day following we continued our voyage till towards noon, when a high wind compelled us again to lay by under the lee of a small island.

Here, towards night, having spread our robes near the camp fire, while all hands were busy at the boat, a sudden gust of wind bore the sparks among the dry grass, and in an instant the whole island was one sheet of flame! robes, blankets, and all, were almost entirely destroyed, notwithstanding our prompt efforts to save them.

Continuing on, the next morning we forced our boat, or rather *carried* it, down stream for about fifteen miles,—wading the river for nearly the whole distance.

Our mode of voyaging was pretty much the same, each day of its continuance. Sailing was out of the question.

Not unfrequently we were obliged to unload five or six times in the course of a few hours, in order to lift the boat over high sand-bars,—carrying its cargo upon our backs through the water a half-mile or more, to some dry place of deposit for the mean time; then returning it in the like tiresome manner,—now in water up to our arm-pits,—then scarcely enough to cover the sand of the river bed.

As for a channel there was none, or rather, there were so many we were at a continual loss which to choose.

Now, gliding along merrily for a mile or two, we are brought to a halt by the water scattering over a broad bed, and find ourselves snugly "*pocketed*," with no other means of extrication than by backing out; then, wading against a swift current, we retrace our steps for a like distance, and try another *chute*, perhaps with no better success;—then, again, conveying our landing to the nearest point of land, by means of hand-spikes and levers, (requiring an exercise of the utmost strength,) we force our empty craft over the shoals, and again load it, perhaps, to re-act the same scene in a brief interval.

Sometimes we were obliged to travel (for such navigation as this was tenfold worse than travelling) four of five miles to make one mile headway. By crossing and re-crossing a river varying in width from one to two miles—first advancing, then retreating; now taking to the right, then to the left; now transverse, and then oblique, we wasted our time, strength, and patience, in labor to little or no purpose. No one, unless practically experienced, can have a correct idea of the beauties of such a voyage.

Towards night, attracted by the appearance of a couple of bulls among the sand-hills, we brought to upon the left shore, and succeeded in killing one of them.

A high wind the day following kept us encamped and afforded another opportunity for hunting.

Improving the occasion to explore the country northward, and obtain, if possible, some correct conception of its general character, a jaunt of four or five miles, over the bottom of rich alluvial soil skirting the river, ushered me into a high rolling prairie, partaking of the mixed nature of the garden and desert.

The hills, in many places, were piles of sand or sun-baked clay, with scarcely a shrub or spire of grass to hide their nude deformity, while the space between them sported a rich soil and luxuriant vegetation, and was clothed in the verdure and loveliness of spring, and adorned with blushing wild-flowers in full bloom.

Further on were yet higher summits, surmounted by pines and cedars, raising their heads in stately grandeur far above the sweet valleys at their feet.

Taken together, the scenery was not only romantic and picturesque, but bewitching in its beauty and repulsive in its deformity.

The prevailing rock was a dark, ferruginous sandstone, and argillaceous limestone, interspersed with conglomerates of various kinds.

Proceeding to a distance of about fifteen miles from the river, in hopes of finding game, I encountered nothing save a solitary band of wild horses, that fled across the sand-hills with the fleetness of the wind on my appearance, after which I returned to the boat much fatigued from the excursion.

Our other hunters had also returned; but neither of them with better success than myself.

The subsequent morning we again renewed our voyage. Soon after, an old bull presenting himself upon the river bank, we landed, and one of the crew approached him from the water-edge.

The old fellow, unconscious of the danger which threatened, permitted the hunter to advance till within three or four yards of him. The sharp crack of a rifle-shot first awoke him to a sense of his situation, when, reeling, he plunged headlong from the steep bank into the river. Our marksman, in an effort to dodge the falling beast, tumbled backwards into swimming water—lost his gun, and came very near being drowned.

The bull made halt at a sand-bar, near by, and received nineteen shots in his carcase before he could be dispatched.

When killed, his hams were found half eaten by wolves, and his whole body otherwise so badly mangled we left it unbutchered.

In the afternoon, having pursued our way eight or ten miles, we lay by for the night.

A high wind and rain during the three succeeding days prevented further progress, and in the interval our provisions became again exhausted.

While here, observing two Indians in the distance, running buffalo, I took three men and started to meet them. On coming up, we found an old Indian with his son engaged in butchering. Announcing the object of my visit to be the procurement of meat, they listened without a reply, but continued their operations,—laying the selections in two separate heaps.

When finished, the old man led up his horse, and, pointing to an assorted pile, told me it was mine, and the animal also should be at my service to convey it to camp.

His village, he remarked, was a long distance over the hills, on the watch for Pawnees, and though in a directly opposite course from us, he loved the white man and would give him meat and a horse to carry it.

Accepting the offer of the generous-hearted savage, I took the heavy-laden horse and returned to the boat,—the owner following to regain his beast. When arrived, he hinted at no remumeration for his kindness, and mounting his horse, would have left for his village.

Where will you find among civilized people men thus generous and obliging? Such cases are indeed rare. The savage here proved himself of more noble principles than nineteen-twentieths of his enlightened and christianized brethren, whose religion teaches them to love their neighbor as themselves, and do to others as they would like to be done unto!

Unwilling that such disinterested kindness should go unrewarded, I made the old man some trifling presents, which he accepted with great pleasure, and, pressing his hand to his breast, exclaimed: "Chanta-ma warstaello!" (my heart is good!) and, shaking hands with the company, put whip to his horse and was soon out of sight.

It is useless to notice the particular progress of each day, or to state how many times we unloaded in the interim—how often we crossed the river, or how far we carried our boat by main strength; these things have been already laid before the reader sufficiently to give him some faint idea of the intolerable hardships and sufferings we were compelled to undergo. Each day was but a repetition of the toils and struggles of the preceding one.

Neither would it be interesting to state the especial half-day, day, or successive days we went without eating, meanwhile; suffice it to say, the morning of the 10th of June found us at the mouth of a small creek upon the right shore, about two hundred miles below the Fort,—having been thirty-five days *en barquette*, and without eating for full one third of that time! The expected spring rise had failed, and the river was very low and still falling, so that there was no possible chance of conveying our cargo to the States, as the most difficult part of the voyage lay yet before us. I accordingly abandoned all thoughts of the latter, and adopted such other arrangements as my judgment suggested upon the premises.

## CHAPTER XVIII.

Hunting excursion.—Thirst more painful than hunger.—Geological observations.—Mournful casualty.—Sad scene of sepulture.—Melancholy night.—Voyage in an empty boat.—Ruins of a Pawnee village at Cedar Bluff.—Plover creek. Câcne Grove.—Thousand Islands.—Abandon boat.—Exploring company.—A horrible situation.—Agony to torment.—Pawnee village.—Exemplary benevolence of an Indian chief.—Miserable fourth of July.—Four days starvation.—Arrival at Council Bluff.—Proceed to Independence.

For two days preceding we had been without eating, and our first effort was to procure a re-supply of provisions. Both crews started out with their rifles in pursuit of game, though not the foot-print of any living creature appeared to excite even the faintest hope of success.

Still, however, we kept on, determined not to despair so long as the use of legs remained to us.

Having travelled some fifteen miles, chance threw in our way a doe-elk with her fawn, which the unerring aim of a rifle speedily laid dead before us. Soon as opened, the liver disappeared at the demands of voracious appetites, and next to it the marrow bones and kidneys.

The process of cooking was then commenced over a fire of *bois de vache,* which was continued till each stomach was abundantly satisfied. But, here another enemy assumed the place of hunger, and one far more painful in its nature. There was not a drop of water to allay our thirst short of the river, fifteen miles distant,—over an open sand-prairie and beneath the scorching rays of a vertical sun.

I can endure hunger for many days in succession without experiencing any very painful sensations,—I can lie down and forget it in the sweet unconsciousness of sleep, or feast my imagination upon the rich-spread tables of dreams ;—but not so with thirst. It cannot be forgotten, sleeping or waking, while existence is retained. It will make itself known and felt ! It will parch your tongue and burn your throat, despite your utmost endeavors to thrust it from memory !

Each one shouldering his burden from the carcase, we took up our line of march for the boat, where, arriving in four or five hours subsequently, we quenched our burning thirst in the water of the thrice welcome stream.

The country, travelled over during this excursion, for the first ten or twelve miles, was a level plain, presenting a thin vegetable mould with a luxuriant growth of grass and herbage, upon a substratum of sand and gravel.

The remainder of our route led through a ridge of hills, many of them naked, others clothed with grass and ornamented with pines ;—between the *tumuli* were many beautiful *vallons,* gorgeously decked with wild-flowers in full bloom, and arrayed in mantles of living green ; while thick clusters of fruit-bearing trees and shrubs attested the general fecundity and lent their enchantment to the scene.

17

Beyond this a gentle acclivity, that led to the high prairies, spread before the beholder a wilderness of verdure, without one moving object to relieve its cheerless monotony.

The boats were unloaded on our return and their contents placed in a compact pile upon shore, over which were spread two thicknesses of lodge-skin, to protect it from the weather. Other necessary arrangements were soon completed. Two men being selected to remain with the robes, two were dispatched to the Fort, while the remainder with myself were to make our way to the States, if possible, in an empty boat.

Everything was put in order for departure the next morning, and a gloomy feeling pervaded each mind as the hour approached that was to separate a band so closely united by mutual sufferings, toil, and deprivation.

Those selected to accompany me were congratulating themselves on the prospect of soon reaching the termination of their arduous and eventful expedition, among the friends and acquaintances of other days; and none were more happy in the anticipation of this hoped for *finale*, than was a lively French youth, named Prudom.

Notwithstanding the general tendency of circumstances was to produce feelings of melancholy, his voice rang loud in announcing the varied plans of amusement and pleasure, that were to be realized upon his arrival at home.

For this day, so far at least, he had been the *petit garçon* of the company; and, it was frequently remarked, as his quaint expressions and sallies of wit burst upon the ear, "What in the world is the matter with Prudom?"

His good nature and kindness of disposition had won the esteem of all acquainted with him, while his cheerfulness and fortitude at all times contributed much to render tolerable the dreariness of our forlorn condition.

A little before night, the company indulged in a general cleansing, accompanied by a shave and change of clothes. Prudom was among the number, for whom an intimate friend officiated as barber;—the operation finished, he jokingly remarked:

"Well, Tom, I suppose this is the last time you'll ever shave me!"

Little did the poor fellow think how soon his words were to be verified. Seizing his rifle he stepped on board the boat, and, stooping to lay it by, exclaimed, "Here's the game!"

The words were scarcely uttered, when the gun-lock, coming in sudden contact with the boat-side, discharged the piece and shot him through the heart! He staggered, faltering forth "Mon Dieu!" and fell dead at my feet!"

A thrill of horror struck every nerve on witnessing this tragical event. If we had previously felt melancholy, we now felt dismal and wobegone. He, who five minutes since was the very soul of cheerfulness and mirth, now lay a lifeless corpse! How true it is, we "know not what a day or an hour may bring forth."

The sun was just setting as we commenced digging a grave in which to deposite all that remained of our friend and companion.

The task was a sad one, and as tedious as it was sorrowful. We had neither shovel nor pick-axe, and were compelled to dig it with our butcher knives and hands.

The pale-moon, new-risen, shed her sombre light over the dismal realms of Solitude, and an intervening cloud cast its pall-like shaddow upon the scene of sepulture, as we laid low the corse in mother dust. No shroud covered—no useless coffin enclosed it,—a grave was the only gift within the power of friendship to bestow! A thin coating of earth succeeded by a layer of stones and drift-wood, and that again by another earth-coat, was its covering,—then, the mournful task was done,—a tear dropt to the memory of poor Prudom, and his body left to slumber in its narrow prison-house, till the sound of the last trump shall wake the dead to judgment.*

That night to us was a more painful one than any we had passed. A feeling of superstitious awe, mingled with thrilling sensations of grief and thoughts of our own miserable condition, occupied each mind and usurped the soothing powers of sleep. The dolesome howlings of the prairie-wolf, and hootings of the midnight owl, borne upon the listening air, kept sad condolence with our musings, and gave increased momentum to the pressure that crushed our spirits. Who could sleep, amid such scenes and surrounded by such circumstances?

The rising sun of the morrow brought the hour of separation, and exhibited upon every face the same downcast look, prefiguring the inward-workings of a mind absorbed in the melancholy of its own thoughts.

My party consisted of six, some of whom were selected from the crew of our consort. We all embarked in one boat, taking with us a small quantity of robes, (our own individual property,) and a portion of the provisions at camp.

Our voyage for a few days succeeding, was performed without much difficulty, except in the article of food—for, from this onward, till we finally reached the settlements, (an interval of twenty-eight days,) we were without eating full one half of the time!

Proceeding some thirty miles, we overtook the American Fur Company's barges, three in number, the crews of which were struggling on in vain effort to reach the States. We glided past them with a loud huzza, and rallied the poor, toiling *voyageurs*, upon the futility of their exertions.

Five or six days subsequently, we were, in turn, overtaken by them;—they, like ourselves, abandoning all hope of accomplishing the objects of their voyage, had left their freight at Ash creek, under guard—and, from that on, became our *compagnons de voyage*.

The only game previous to reaching the forks of the Platte—a distance of some two hundred miles—was now and then an antelope, with a few straggling deer. Our subsistence, meanwhile, was principally upon "*greens,*" and such roots as we had time and opportunity to gather.

The country was pretty much of a uniform character, with that previously described. The rich alluvion of the river bottom reposed upon a varied substratum of sand, marl, gravel, and clay.

* On my return the ensuing fall, I learned that the body of the unfortunate young man had been disinterred by wolves and devoured.

I noticed several varieties of clays in the river banks exposed by the attrition of the water—of these were the white, red, black, yellow, blue, and green.

The white clay is much used by the Indians in cleaning skins and robes; an operation performed by mixing it with water till the compound assumes the color and about four times the consistency of milk, when it is applied to the surface of the article in hand; the robe or skin thus washed, after being thoroughly dried in the sun, is rubbed until it becomes soft and pliable from friction, and the grosser particles of the preparation are loosened and removed.

By this simple process skins assume a milky whiteness, and every spot of grease or dirt is made to disappear.

All kinds of skin may be thus cleansed, and will readily attain an unsoiled purity, surpassing that originally possessed. Red, yellow, black, blue, or any other kind of clay, may be used for like purposes, and will readily impart to the cleansed articles their own color.

In case a single application is insufficient, repeat the process for two or three times, and there can be no possible failure in the result, provided the clay is pure and good.

Some twenty miles above the Forks, we passed a ridge of rocky hills exhibiting layers of limestone and sandstone in bold escarpments, that jutting into the river from the right, formed a high embankment covered with pines and cedars, known as Cedar Bluff.

At the upper side of this point stood the remains of an old Pawnee village, which had been deserted by its inhabitants immediately after the bloody battle between that nation and the Sioux, at the mouth of Ash creek.

The bottom, for several miles above, is rarely excelled in fertility. The islands are generally timbered, but the river banks upon both sides are almost entirely destitute of trees of any kind.

From Cedar Bluff, in about eight miles, we came to the mouth of a large and beautiful creek, forcing its way, with a clear and rapid current, from the high rolling prairies to the north. This presented the appearance of being skirted with broad and fertile bottoms, well supplied with timber among the hills. Though vested with some importance on account of its size and locality, it is as yet nameless—the abundance of plovers in its vicinity at the time of my passing, suggested the term "Plover creek" as a proper appellation.

Five or six miles further on, we came to a large grove of cottonwood upon the right shore. Here, some five years since, a company of traders, while descending the Platte in boats loaded with furs, made cáche of one hundred and sixty packs of robes, which they were compelled to leave on account of the low stage of the water. The luckless party, after enduring great hardships, arrived in the States; but their cáche was subsequently plundered by Pawnees.

The confluence of the North and South Forks made but little perceptible difference in the size of the river. From the junction, in five days' time we reached the vicinity of Grand Island, about two hundred and twenty miles from the nearest white settlements.

The high prairie upon the north shore, between the above points, is generally sandy. The river presents numerous clusters of islands, most of which are heavily timbered and clothed with luxuriant growths of vegetation. The soil is of a deep, sandy loam, and well adapted to cultivation. I noticed upon them several choice wild flowers of rare beauty.

We experienced great difficulty in forcing our boats through a large group, called the "Thousand Islands," that thickly studded the river for some ten miles, and, before clearing them, found our passage completely blockaded.

Having consumed an entire day in vain effort to proceed, we were at length compelled to abandon the idea. The water was constantly falling, and our condition hourly becoming worse. This forced upon us the *dernier resort* of performing the remainder of our arduous journey on foot.

Accordingly, making cáche of the personal property with us, we sunk our barges in a deep hole near by, threw all extra clothing into the river, and, each selecting a robe with as much meat as he could carry, we commenced our weary tramp.

The property thus disposed of was of the value of several hundred dollars. Among other articles left in cáche, were arms and tools of various kinds.

No one would now carry a gun,—as we were to pass through a section of country destitute of game, and, being obliged to travel with all possible despatch to avoid starvation, good policy prompted us to dispense with every unnecessary encumbrance. For myself, however, I was unwilling to relinquish my rifle, and determined to take it with me.

There were fourteen of us, including the *coups de barquette* of the American Fur Company; and, as we trudged along at a pace enfeebled by a series of cruel hardships, fatigue, and starvation,—with provisions and beds bound in close bundles and strapped to our backs,—half-naked, long-bearded, careworn, and haggard,—we looked like the last remnants of hard times!

The 28th of June dated the commencement of this last stage of our tiresome pilgrimage.

Having travelled some ten or twelve miles, we espied a camp of whites a short distance in advance, and were observed by them almost at the same time. Our appearance created an evident consternation,—their horses were driven in with great speed, and their guns stripped ready for action, while our or five men, mounted upon fleet chargers, rode out to reconnoitre.

On ascertaining the cause of their alarm to be only a handful of unarmed men, they ventured up, and were saluted with the cordiality of old acquaintances, so rejoiced were we at the sight of anything savoring of the endearments of home and civilization.

The company proved one in the employ of the United States Government, under the command Lieut. J. C. Fremont, of the Corps of Topographical Engineers, on an expedition for the exploration and survey of the country laying between the Missouri river and the mountains.

The commandant seemed a gentleman of urbanity and intelligence, and politely furnished us with all the passing news of the day preceding his departure from the States.

Our smokers and tobacco-chewers, who had been for sometime without the *sina qua non* of the mountaineer, now procured a re-supply for the indulgence of their filthy and unnatural taste.

Leaving our new-found friends, we continued on for a few miles, and halted a brief interval under the shade of a cottonwood grove. While thus reclining upon the green grass, what was our surprise at seeing three Indians, who appeared suddenly in our midst extending their hands to greet us!

They belonged to a war-party of Chyennes,—had been to the Pawnees, and were now on their return, with three horses captured from the enemy.

Continuing our course, towards sundown I began to find my rifle rather cumbersome, and, yielding to the advice of all hands, threw it away.

Having travelled till late at night, we laid ourselves down in the trail for repose;—the musquetoes, however, together with the heat, were so annoying, sleep was impossible.

I never in my life before was so tortured by these relentless persecutors. Their sting was far more tolerable to me than the unending hum of their music. To exterminate them was a hopeless task, for, at the death of one, fifty would come to its funeral,—and to submit quietly to their rapacity and be eaten up alive by such loving friends, was more than human flesh and blood could endure.

For three hours I lay, sweltered by the heat and pierced by the hungry myriads that swarmed around, until my agony became so great it obtained the mastery of reason, and I was scarcely self-conscious whether a being of earth or an inhabitant of the realms of woe.

In the height of my phrenzy I fancied four demons had hold of the extremities of my robe, and were fiercely dragging me over a prairie of sharp rocks, that tore my flesh at every bound. The remainder of the party suffered equally with myself, and none of them were permitted to close their eyes that night.

*June 29th.* We started at early day, and pursued our journey till ten o'clock, which brought us to the foot of Grand Island,—a distance of *sixty miles* from the place of our adventure with the Indians during the previous afternoon. Here we indulged in a slight repast, and, reclining upon the grass, enjoyed a few hours' sleep, despite the continued annoyance of musquetoes.

On arousing to resume the painful march, our legs were found in a very unenviable plight, and almost refused to sustain the accustomed burthen. Our feet, also, (softened and made tender by the mollifying effects of the water, to which they had been so long familiar, and, unused to the offices now newly forced upon them,) were sore and swollen to a frightful size. From this on, our journey was most intensely painful.

But, notwithstanding all, we were compelled to keep moving, though our progress seemed more like the passage of Mahomet's "bridge of swords" than aught else imaginable.

*July 2d.* This morning our stock of provisions was entirely exhausted, and yet a long distance intervened between us and the settlements.

Towards night, however, chance brought us in the way of a plentiful supper, by our encountering the Pawnee village on its way to the buffalo range. We were entertained by the head chief in a hospitable manner, who furnished us bountifully with boiled corn and mush; and we were also invited into several shantees with the same kind intention.

The Pawnee chief (Red Eagle, if my recollection serves me right) was a generous old fellow, aged some sixty years. His benevolence was truly exemplary, as his conduct well attested. My moccasins, being much worn by long usage, exposed to the ground the bottoms of my feet. This was no sooner discovered by the noble-hearted old man, than he pulled off his own (a pair of new ones) and gave them to me!

What white man would have done the like? And this was done by the poor Indian, not from the expectation of reward, but through the promptings of an innate benevolence! A small tin-cup, taken with me thus far, was the only return in my power to make.

Leaving the village a little before sundown, we encamped for the night near the houses recently occupied by these Indians, after having travelled seven or eight miles. Their buildings are coniform, and constructed of earth and timber, very similar to those of the Kansas tribe, described in a previous chapter.

Several years ago, the Pawnees were a numerous and powerful nation, possessing an extensive territory, and occupying five large towns, viz: one upon the Republican branch of the Kansas river, one at the forks of the Platte, one south of the Arkansas near the Cumanche country, one on Loup creek, and one some ninety miles above the mouth of the Platte. These several divisions were known by the terms of Pic, Mahah, Republican, Loup, and Grand Pawnees. The Riccarees, speaking the same language, may also be reckoned a fraction of this tribe. The five villages before named are now reduced to two, i. e. on Loup creek and above the mouth of the Platte.

The whole number of the Pawnee nation, exclusive of the Riccarees, probably does not exceed six thousand souls. All of the western tribes being at war with them, their numerical strength is continually diminishing.

Slight advances have been made towards improving the condition of this nation, but, as yet, with little apparent success. A farmer, blacksmith, and schoolmaster are provided them under the patronage of the U. S. Government, and a missionary is also stationed among them by the American Board of Foreign Missions.

They raise corn* and other vegetables, but their principal dependence for subsistence is upon the proceeds of hunting. Their general character is stamped with indolence, treachery and cowardice, for which they have become famous, not only among the whites, but also among their rude neighbors,—having thus attained the hatred of both.

*July* 3*d*. This morning we parted company, and each of us undertook to make his way to Council Bluff according to the best of his ability. Being entirely destitute of food, it became us to urge our course with all possible dispatch.

---

*I noticed one cornfield, near the village, that contained sixty acres or more, and in appearance savored much of civilized agriculture.

*July 4th.* Accompanied by two others, in an equally forlorn condition, the "glorious fourth" finds me plodding along, over an open prairie, beneath the scorching rays of a summer's sun, unarmed, half-naked, with a shouldered pack, and not having had a morsel to eat for the past two days.

It is now I think of the festal boards and scenes of good cheer so omnipresent upon Freedom's birth-day in the land of my nativity! Mine is a mode of celebrating Independence, that I care not ever again to observe.

On the 6th we reached the Ottoe mission and obtained food, after an abstinence of four successive days.

Early in the morning of the 7th we arrived at Council Bluff on the Missouri, eight miles above the mouth of the Platte, and nearly four hundred above Fort Leavenworth. In the course of the day following our whole party came in, one after another—some of whom had become so weakened by hardship and deprivation they could scarcely move a dozen yards without stumbling!

Having remained a few days at Council Bluff to recruit our strength, we procured canoes and descended the Missouri. The 21st inst. found me at Independence, Mo., after an absence of nearly nine months,—having consumed seventy-five days upon my return voyage, and, in the meantime, experienced a series of suffering and misfortunes seldom equalled and rarely surpassed.

## CHAPTER XIX.

The country between the Pawnee village and Bellevieu, and from that to Fort Leavenworth.—Leave Independence for the Mountains.—Meet Pawnees.—Indian hospitality.—Journey up the South Fork Platte.—Fort Grove.—Beaver creek.—Bijou.—Chabonard's camp.—Country described.—Medicine Lodge.—The Chyennes; their character and history.—Arrive at Fort Lancaster.—Different localities in its neighborhood.—Fatal Duel.—Ruins.

THE country travelled over from the Pawnee village to Council Bluff (or Bellevieu, as more recently called) is generally possessed of a rich, clayey soil, which is well adapted to cultivation.

Large quantities of timber skirt the streams, that include all the varieties found in the States. The landscape is beautifully undulating, and, at the time of our passing it, was covered with a luxuriant growth of vegetation, (the grass being frequently waist high,) and ornamented by rare specimens of wild flowers.

The Pawnees, Ottoes, and Omahas possess the whole extent of this territory, which embraces much valuable land within its limits. That north of the river and adjacent to Bellevieu is owned by the Pottowatomies, who also claim to the boundary between Iowa and Missouri.

INDIAN SAGACITY IN HUNTING. — *Page 203.*

The Kickapoos, Iowas, Sacs, and Foxes occupy the country south of the Missouri, from the mouth of the Platte to Fort Leavenworth.

All of this interval possesses a fertile soil, is well watered and passably well timbered. A more particular description of it, however, does not properly come within the limits of this work.

Upon my arrival at Independence, affairs were in a rather confused state. Times were hard and all kinds of business at their lowest ebb. The company for which I had acted had become bankrupt, and left me a loser to no inconsiderable amount. But, notwithstanding this unfavorable aspect of things, I decided upon returning to the Mountains for the purpose of visiting the different regions adjacent to them.

Acting upon this resolution, I expended the means at my immediate command for the procurement of an outfit; — and the beginning of August saw me again *en route*, accompanied by two experienced mountaineers — all of us mounted upon hardy mules and well provided for the journey before us.

The first four or five days subsequent, our progress was much impeded by successive rains, that rendered the road muddy and ourselves uncomfortable. We were necessitated to raft the Wakarousha, and the Kansas was so swollen it was forded with great difficulty, — the water frequently covering the backs of our animals.

From that onward we enjoyed pleasant weather and journeyed without further interruption; — nothing occurred worth note, till we reached the Pawnee range, near the head of Big Blue.

One morning, while travelling along unconcernedly and at our leisure, having as yet observed nothing to excite our apprehensions, a Pawnee suddenly made his appearance directly in front of us.

Such a customer had we been aware of his proximity, would have been most carefully avoided, in a place so dangerous as this; but, as he had first discovered us, it was now too late to give him the slip, and we accordingly permitted his approach, greeting him in a friendly manner.

He immediately informed us that the whole country was full of his people returning from their summer-hunt, and he invited us to accompany him to the village. This we declined, being unwilling to trust either him or his people.

Observing several other "shaved heads" hurrying towards us from over the adjoining hills, we struck camp and prepared for the expected rencounter. Upon coming near, however, they appeared friendly and were most of them unarmed. Again we were urged to visit the village.

After waiting an hour or more, we resumed our course, still followed by the unwelcome visitors. A ride of scarcely a half mile brought us to the top of a hill, and, to our surprise, placed us in the immediate precincts of the village, — too far advanced for a retreat.

The entire population was instantly in motion, and came crowding towards us upon every side. Pushing boldly forward, we were received by the same kind-hearted old chief of whom I had occasion to speak in the preceding chapter. On recognizing me, I was welcomed with great cordiality, and we were forthwith conducted to his shantee and sumptuously entertained upon the choicest in his possession.

Our camp-equipage and other articles were all safely disposed of, and nothing conducive to our pleasure or comfort was left unattended to. During our entire stay, we were beset with invitations to feasts which were prepared expressly for us by these hospitable villagers, who appeared displeased whenever we declined their acceptance.

The old chief brought forward his little grandson to shake hands with us—remarking, that he would teach his children like himself to love the Americans.

A small sack filled with papers was then laid before me for perusal. They consisted of recommendations, speaking in very flattering terms of the bearer, Red Eagle, and belauding his kindness and liberality. Most willingly would I have complied with his request, and made "the paper talk" for him, but the means were not at hand.

The kind-hearted old man presented us each a pair of moccasins and urged our stay till the next morning,—adding: "Some of my men are bad, and my heart is sick for them. Should you go before sleep, they might follow and rob you. When the morrow's sun has newly risen above the prairie, they will have left their foot-prints in the homeward trail, and my white brothers may pass unmolested. But, if you will not rest beneath the shade of the Red Eagle, wait till the day-king is low, then ride fast till the night is old, and thus may you avoid the evil ones who would injure you."

This advice seemed so reasonable, we consented to remain till late in the afternoon, when, driving up our animals, we made preparations to start.

Every article belonging to us was faithfully returned by the old man, who ordered for us a present of buffalo meat. Several large pieces were accordingly brought by different individuals, of excellent quality, and in quantity more than we could well carry.

This was all a free gift,—no one even hinted at a compensation. Where will you find among civilized man generosity and hospitality equal to this?

Willing to reward such exemplary conduct, we presented the liberal donors with a small supply of sugar, coffee, and tobacco; and, to our host, we gave a knife and some other trifling articles, all of which he received with evident gratification.

Bidding the noble chieftain adieu, we pursued our course in accordance with his direction,—travelling nearly all night.

Early the next morning we struck the Platte, and, in the afternoon, reached the point at which myself and others had abandoned our boats.

On visiting the cache made at that time, not a thing remained;—it had been robbed by the Pawnees, in all probability, as the island was covered with the tracks of men and horses. But what afforded still more conclusive evidence, was the site of a recent Pawnee encampment within some four hundred yards of the place.

The next morning brought us to the buffalo range, and our fare was one of continued feasting from that onward.

Three days subsequently we came to the forks of the Platte, and continued up the south branch, with the design of proceeding to New Mexico by way of Fort Lancaster.

## MEETING AGAIN.

Here we entered a stretch of territory not as yet brought before the reader's notice.

Passing on, a ride of between fifty and sixty miles brought us to a large grove of willows at the mouth of a sand-creek, where we remained the day following.

The vicinity contained the relics of three or four Indian forts, constructed of logs,—one or two of which were in an almost entire state of preservation, and afforded a correct illustration of Indian military genius. Their forms were oval, and the roofage so complete, we were amply sheltered in one of them from a heavy shower which fell during our stay.

From this point (properly denominated Fort Grove) to the forks, the country is rather sterile and rolling, with the exception of the river bottoms, which, as usual, are possessed of a rich soil and vary in width from one to five miles. There is scarcely a tree, worth naming, upon either bank of the river for the whole extent.

The expanse lying to the northward is quite broken and hilly, with some few pines and cedars at the heads of ravines.

Previous to leaving Fort Grove I experienced an attack of the fever and ague, which recurred, at intervals of once in two days, until we reached Fort Lancaster.

Resuming our journey, a ride of some ten miles brought us to the mouth of Pole creek, a large affluent of the right shore. This is a clear and handsome stream, running through a rich valley of considerable width. Its entire course affords but very little timber, and the prairie upon either side is generally sandy and barren.

Journeying on about seventy-five miles further, we came to a large stream called *la Fouchett aux Castors*, or Beaver Fork.

This creek heads in the highlands between the Platte and Arkansas, and traces its course through a sandy country, varied by diminutive hills of clayey soil, for a distance of nearly two hundred miles. It presents many beautiful bottoms of a rich vegetable mould, with here and there small clusters of timber.

Some forty or fifty miles above Beaver creek, we crossed Bijou, another large affluent of the left shore. The water at the mouth of this stream was shallow, dispersing itself in several small channels, over a bed of gravel and quicksand, about four hundred yards wide, and enclosed by abrupt banks of clay and sand.

For several miles above its junction with the Platte no timber appears; but further on, many large groves relieve the eye, and invite the traveller to their shade, while broad meadows and rich bottoms, clothed with grass and flowers, cheer the beholder and delight his fancy.

*Aug. 30th.* A ride of ten or fifteen miles, from this point, brought us to a camp of whites, in the employ of Bent and St. Vrain, occupying a small island in the Platte. They were guarding a quantity of robes with which they had attempted to descend the river, but were unable to proceed further on account of low water.

I was much gratified at here meeting an old acquaintance, with whom I had passed a portion of the previous winter upon White river

The camp was under the direction of a half-breed, named Chabonard, who proved to be a gentleman of superior information. He had acquired a classic education and could converse quite fluently in German, Spanish, French, and English, as well as several Indian languages. His mind, also, was well stored with choice reading, and enriched by extensive travel and observation. Having visited most of the important places, both in England, France, and Germany, he knew how to turn his experience to good advantage.

There was a quaint humor and shrewdness in his conversation, so garbed with intelligence and perspicuity, that he at once insinuated himself into the good graces of listeners, and commanded their admiration and respect.

The country, between Fort Grove and Cabonard's camp, with the exception of the river bottoms, (which were quite fertile and occupied an area, upon both banks, varying in width from one hundred yards to five miles,) is slightly undulating, and presents two uniform characteristics,—one, a thin clayish loam upon a substratum of sand and gravel, and the other a sandy surface, often entirely destitute of vegetation, save, perchance, a few scattering spires of coarse grass and a species of prickly burr.

Various specimens of *cacti* are found in every direction, and prove a frequent source of vexation to the traveller. The landscape discloses a scene of dreary sterility,—more to be accounted for by the dryness of the climate than any natural defect in the soil.

The river upon both sides is nearly destitute of timber, and we were frequently compelled to use *bois de vache* for cooking purposes. There is also a scarcity of rock,—though, in the neighborhood of Bijou, I observed a kind of grayish sandstone, exposed to view in the beds of ravines; and, directly opposite Chabonard's camp, the action of the waters had formed a steep wall, some thirty or forty feet high, which disclosed a large bed of sandstone and slate, with earthy limestone.

A few miles above Beaver Fork, we obtained a distinct view of the main ridge of the Rocky Mountains with the snowy summit of Long's Peak, distant some sixty or sixty-five miles. They appeared like a pile of dark clouds just rising from the verge of the horizon, and could be identified only by their uniform and stationary position.

From the time of first entering the buffalo range till we reached Bijou creek, our entire course was beset with dense masses of those animals, which covered the river bottoms and prairies in all directions, far as the eye could reach. Our usual practice was to kill one every day, and select from its carcase the choice portions so well known and highly appreciated by mountaineers; and, calling to aid the varied modes of cooking peculiar to hunters, surely never did epicures fare better than we.

A few miles above Beaver creek we passed the site of a recent Indian encampment, where was yet standing the frame-work of a medicine lodge, erected by the Chyennes and Arapahos for the performance of their religious rites and ceremonies. This was made of light poles, describing an amphitheatre with a diameter of some fifty feet. In form it was much like the pavilion of a circus, and of sufficient dimensions to contain several hundred individuals.

I shall take occasion in subsequent pages to speak of medicine-making, and would refer the reader to that part for an explanation of the peculiar purposes for which the medicine lodge is constructed.

The river at Chabonard's camp is reduced fully one half in width, compared with its size at the forks. The current is also clearer and more rapid. Its banks and islands are much better timbered, and its general appearance indicates an approach to the mountains.

About noon we bade farewell to our new friends, by whom we had been kindly entertained, and resumed our journey, accompanied by my whilom companion and two others,—increasing our number to six.

Towards sundown, coming to a small village of Chyennes, we passed the night in the lodge of a chief, called the Tall Soldier. Our host treated us with much civility, but in this he appeared actuated only by selfish motives, and with the sole view of extorting a more,than fourfold equivalent by way of presents.

We were also continually harassed by beggars from all quarters, and gladly availed ourselves of the first dawn of the ensuing morning to pass on, and thus escape their importunities.

The Chyennes at this time occupy a portion of the Arapaho lands, bordering upon the South Fork and its affluents.

Some six or eight years since, they inhabited the country in the vicinity of the Chyenne and White rivers and the North Fork of Platte, from whence they were driven by the hostile incursions of the Sioux, who now hold in quiet possession the whole of that territory.

This tribe, in general appearance, dress, and habits, assimilates most of the mountain and prairie Indians, with the single exception, perhaps, of being meaner than any other. They are certainly more saucy as beggars, and impudent and daring as thieves, than any other I ever became acquainted with.

Formerly they were a much better people, but the contaminating effects of intercourse with the whites have made a disposition, naturally bad, immeasurably worse. Contrary to Indian character in general, they are treacherous and unworthy of trust, at all times and in all places.

Their history contains a small speck of romance, which may not prove altogether uninteresting to the curious.

The Chyennes, at the present time, number about four hundred lodges, and claim some eight hundred warriors. The tribe is composed of two divisions, viz: the Chyennes and Gros Ventres,—both speaking the same language and practising the same designation of nationality, shown in sundry transverse scars upon the left arm.

Neither of these divisions know their origin, but tell the following curious story of their first intercourse with each other.

Many years since, the Chyennes, while travelling from a north country, discovered the Gros Ventres, who were also upon a journey. As usual among strange tribes, both parties rushed to the attack, and a bloody battle would undoubtedly have been the result, had it not been stayed by the mutual discovery of an identity of language. Upon this, hostility at once gave place to friendship, and the two parties negotiated an immediate union. Since then they have been considered as one nation.

What is most singular in this occurrence, neither the Gros Ventres nor Chyennes could trace any previous connection or intercourse with each other, or knowledge of their individual existence.

This tribe has made no advances in civilization, and most probably will make none for many years to come. Their roving and unsettled habits prove an obstacle, almost insuperable, to any efforts that may be undertaken for their improvement.

They are generally accounted friendly to the whites, but friendship like this is essentially of a dangerous character.

Continuing our journey, the evening of Sept. 2d brought us to Fort Lancaster, after an interval of twenty-six days, during which we had travelled not far from seven hundred and twenty miles.

Our route from Chabonard's camp to this point, for the most part, led along the valley of the Platte, which resembled a garden in the splendor of its fields and the variety of its flowers.

A ride of four or five miles took us across the dry bed of a large sand-creek, four or five hundred yards wide, known as the Kuyawa. The banks of this *arroyo* are very steep and high, disclosing, now and then, spreads of beautiful bottom lands with occasional groves of cottonwood. At this season of the year its waters are lost in the quicksand and gravel.

We also passed the mouths of three large affluents of the right bank of Platte, severally known as Crow creek, Cache a la Poudre, and Thompson's Fork.

These creeks rise in the adjoining mountains, and, with the exception of Crow creek, trace their way with clear and rapid currents, from two to three feet deep and sixty feet wide, over beds of sand and pebbles. Their valleys are broad, rich, and for the most part well timbered.

Timber increases in quantity, upon the Platte and its affluents, as the traveller approaches the mountains, and the soil gradually loses that withering aridity so characteristic of the grand prairie.

Twelve miles below Fort Lancaster we passed Fort George, a large trading post kept up by Bent and St. Vrain. Its size rather exceeds that of Fort Platte, previously described; it is built, however, after the same fashion,—as, in fact, are all the regular trading posts in the country. At this time, fifteen or twenty men were stationed there, under the command of Mr. Marsalina St. Vrain.

Six miles further on, we came to a recently deserted post, which had been occupied the previous winter and summer by Messrs Lock and Randolph.

One of our party, a whilom engagé of this company, informed me of its principals' becoming bankrupt, through mismanagement and losses of various kinds;—he stated, that, in May last, their entire "cavalliard," consisting of forty-five head of horses and mules, had been stolen by the Sioux Indians; this, in connection with other bad luck—together with the depreciated value of furs and peltries, the failure of a boat-load of robes to reach the States, the urgent demands of creditors, &c., had caused them to evacuate their post and quit the country.

A short distance above this, at a point of timber occupying a large bottom, had been the scene of a fatal duel the previous winter, between two whites by the names of Herring and Beer. On my first arrival in the country I had become acquainted with both of the actors, and felt much interested in the details of the bloody affair as related by one present at the time of its unfortunate occurrence. The difficulty between them related to a Mexican woman from Taos,—the wife of Herring.

Backed by a number of personal friends, and anxious to obtain the lady from her husband, the former had provoked a quarrel and used very insulting language to his antagonist. This was received with little or no reply, but soon, however, resulted in a challenge which was promptly accepted.

The preliminaries were arranged in confident expectation of killing Herring, who was considered a poor marksman, especially at an off-hand shot. The weapons selected by Beer were rifles, the distance fifty yards, the manner off-hand, and the time of shooting between the word fire and three. The two met, attended by their friends, at the time and place agreed upon,— at the word "*fire*," the ball of Beer's rifle was buried in a cottonwood a few inches above the head of his antagonist,—at the word "*three*" the contents of Herring's rifle found lodgement in the body of Beer, who fell and expired in a few minutes.

Between this point and Fort Lancaster, I noticed the ruins of another trading post, much dilapidated in appearance, and nearly levelled with the ground.

Passing along, I could not refrain from musing upon the frequent deeds of mischief and iniquity that had originated within them, in connection with the infamous liquor traffic. Ah, thought I, were those bricks possessed of tongues, full many a tale of horror and guilt would they unfold, to stand the listener's "hair on end," and make his blood run cold! But, lost in silent unconsciousness, they refuse to speak the white man's shame!

## CHAPTER XX.

Old acquaintances.—Indian murders.—Mode of travelling in a dangerous country.—Mexican traders.—Summary way of teaching manners.—Fort Lancaster and surrounding country.—Resume journey.—Cherry creek and connecting observations.—Sketch of the Arapahos, their country, character, &c.—Camp of free traders.—Blackfoot camp.—Daugherty's creek.—Observations relative to the Divide.—Mexican cupidity.—Strange visitors.—The lone travellers.—Arrive at the Arkansas.—General remarks.—Curious specimens of cacti.—Fontaine qui Bouit, or Natural Soda-fountain.—Indian superstition.—Enchanting scenery.—Extraordinary wall of sandstone.

At Fort Lancaster I was gratified by meeting with several acquaintances of the previous winter, two of whom had been comrades during a part of my unfortunate and adventurous voyage down the Platte.

My appearance created no little surprise and pleasure, on all sides. Queries of various kinds were industriously plied, relative to the latest news from the States, and also in reference to the miseries and hardships undergone during the interval of my absence. The dangers of our mode of travelling were freely expatiated upon, and numerous instances of recent Indian hostilities cited to prove our "fool daring."

Among the latter was an outrage perpetrated by the Chyennes, only two weeks previous, in the murder of three white men,—one of whom was the oldest trapper in the mountains, and had been for some time engaged in the fur trade.

The murderers had the impudence to ask a scalp-feast from the commandant of the Fort, according to custom in case of overcoming their enemies in battle! The hair, however, being recognized as that of a white man, no feast was given. When accused of the murder, they apologized by saying the poor fellow was suffering greatly at the time from recent wounds, and they had killed him out of pity!

In our mode of travelling, we always used due precaution to avoid surprise and attack. This is easily done, while among buffalo, by noticing their movements,—as these animals invariably flee across the wind upon the approach of man, and neither Indians nor whites can traverse their range without setting the whole country in motion.

We observed another plan of caution by frequently ascending some eminence, and scanning the wide expanse, far and near.

Our general practice was to travel till night, and camp without fire in the open prairie, thus precluding the possibility of being discovered, even though in the immediate vicinity of Indians.

A party of three or four men can pass through a dangerous country and avoid coming in contact with enemies, provided they exercise a needful vigilance much more easily than one of larger numbers. With a large company too much dependence is reposed in each other, which soon results in individual carelessness and neglect. Added to this, they are apt to rely upon their numerical strength, and, forgetting this simple truism, that "caution is the parent of safety," rush into danger when they are least aware of it. It thus occurs that large parties are more liable to surprise than smaller ones, and more frequently suffer losses from the depredations of prowling enemies.

On the contrary, where but three or four individuals are travelling together, they trust exclusively to their own personal vigilance. Keenly alive to every suspicious appearance, they seldom fail to discover the presence of danger without exposing themselves, and may avoid it by a timely retreat or change of course.

There is little risk in an open prairie, in case an enemy is first seen by the party wishing to shun his presence;—they have only to manœuvre in such a manner as to elude observation, (a thing not often difficult,) and all is safe. In subsequent travels through dangerous countries I have always acted upon these suggestions, and never yet found them to fail.

Some twelve or fifteen Mexicans were at this time present at the Fort. They constituted a trading party from Taos, escorting a caravan of pack-horses and mules, laden with flour, corn, bread, beans, onions, dried pumpkin, salt, and pepper, to barter for robes, skins, furs, meat, moccasins, bows and arrows, ammunition, guns, coffee, calico, cloth, tobacco, and old clothes, which were to compose their return freight.

A worse looking set was here presented than that previously described in the second chapter of this volume. Some of them were as black as veritable negroes, and needed only the curly hair, thick lips, and flattened nose, to define the genuine Congo in appearance. A more miserable looking gang of filthy half-naked, ragamuffins, I never before witnessed.

Their cargoes had already been disposed of at various prices, according to circumstances. Flour and meal were sold at from four to six dollars per *fanega*, (one hundred and twenty pounds,) and other articles at like prices. Their first asking price was at the rate of twenty dollars per *fanega*; but an affray which occurred with a small party of Americans, immediately upon their arrival, had made these *produce merchants* much more reasonable in their demands.

The particulars of the affair were rather disgraceful to both parties. The Americans, anxious to purchase a quantity of flour, offered to take it at the asking price, provided the Mexicans would receive their pay in robes of a rather indifferent quality. This the latter refused and a dispute arose, when insulting language was used on both sides, coupled with threats of mutual injury.

The Mexicans retired a short distance and camped,—soon after the Americans, four in number, rushed among them and drove off their entire *cavallard*, containing twenty head of horses and mules. The Mexicans seized their arms for resistance, and the *commandante* advancing demanded of the nearest assailant:

"Que quiere, cabellero?" (what do you want, sir?)

"Yo tenga lo caballardo,—porque dicirme esta?" (I have your horses,—why do you ask?)

"Carraho, Americanâ!" said the Mexican, levelling his gun at the speaker. In an instant a pistol-shot from the latter laid him prostrate,—the ball entering his chest near the heart. No further resistance was offered, and the assailants retired with their booty.

The next morning, however, they returned, and the two parties compromised the matter by certain conciliatory arrangements, which resulted in the Americans giving up the captured animals, on condition that the Mexicans should in future be less insolent and conduct their trade on more reasonable terms.

The wounded man recovered in three or four weeks, and was now ready to accompany his party on their homeward-bound journey.

A large number of Mexicans are employed at the different trading posts in this vicinity. They prove quite useful as horse-guards, and also in taking care of cattle and doing the drudgery connected with these establishments.

Their wages vary from four to ten dollars per month, which they receive in articles of traffic at an exhorbitant price;—viz: calicoes, (indifferent quality,) from fifty cents to one dollar per yard; blue cloth, from five to ten dollars per do.; powder, two dollars per lb.; lead, one do. do.; coffee, one do. do.; tobacco, from two to three do. do.; second hand robes, two dollars apiece,—and everything else in proportion.

Their wages for a whole year, in actual value, bring them but a trifling and almost nameless consideration. Notwithstanding, these miserable creatures prefer travelling four hundred miles to hire for such diminutive wages, rather than to remain in their own country and work for less. They know of no better way to get a living, and are, therefore, happy in their ignorance, and contentedly drag out a wretched existence as best they may.

After a period of service they generally return home laden with the paltry proceeds of their toil, and, yielding to the impulses of custom, a single *fandango* is sufficient to leave them penniless like the squalid crowd with whom they mingle.

A week's stay at the Fort restored me to health and soundness from the debilitating effects of the fever and ague, without a resort to medicine. This disease (the first and only attack of which I ever experienced) had made fearful inroads upon my strength during the short interval of its continuance, and rendered me unfit for travelling;—but, a change of climate and the inhalation of the pure mountain air effected a permanent and speedy cure, in a much less time than I had reason to expect.

Fort Lancaster occupies a pleasant site upon the south bank of the Platte river, about nine hundred miles from its mouth, and seven hundred and twenty from Independence, in lat. 40° 12' 25" north, long. 105° 53' 11" west from Greenwich. The distance from this point to the dividing ridge of the Rocky Mountains is about thirty-five miles, and from Taos, in New Mexico, between three and four hundred miles.

Long's Peak with its eternal snow appears in distinct view to the westward, and imparts to the sunset scenery a beauty and grandeur rarely witnessed in any country. This peak is one of the highest of the mountain range, being upwards of 13,500 feet above the level of the Gulf of Mexico, and issues from its eastern side the waters of the Atlantic, and from its western the tributaries of the Pacific.

Between the mountains and the Fort, the prairie is generally level, though slightly undulating in places ;—it is possessed of a tolerable soil, composed of clay and gravel, ever and anon spreading before the traveller rich valleys, decked with sweet flowers and lusty herbage.

The country eastward is rolling, sandy, and sterile; and, with few exceptions, presents little to attract the eye or please the fancy.

The Platte bottoms, above and below, are quite heavily timbered and afford an abundance of grass of various kinds. The soil is of a black, deep loam, very rich and well adapted to cultivation.

The business transacted at this post is chiefly with the Chyennes, but the Arapahos, Mexicans, and Soux also come in for a large share, and contribute to render it one of the most profitable trading establishments in the country.

*Sept. 10th.* Arrangements being completed for resuming my journey, I left Fort Lancaster in company with four others, intending to proceed as far as Taos in New Mexico. We were all mounted upon stout horses, and provided with two pack-mules for the conveyance of baggage and provisions.

Following the trail leading from the Platte to the Arkansas, or *Rio Napeste*, we continued our way some thirty-five miles, and halted with a camp of free traders and hunters, on Cherry creek.

This stream is an affluent of the Platte, from the southeast, heading in a broad ridge of pine hills and rocks, known as the "Divide." It pursues its course for nearly sixty miles, through a broad valley of rich soil, tolerably well timbered, and shut in for the most part by high plats of table land,—at intervals thickly studded with lateral pines, cedars, oaks, and shrubs of various kinds,—gradually expanding its banks as it proceeds, and exchanging a bed of rock and pebbles for one of quicksand and gravel, till it finally attains a width of nearly two hundred yards, and in places is almost lost in the sand. The stream derives its name from the abundance of cherry found upon it.

The country passed over from the Fort to this place, is generally sandy, but yields quite a generous growth of grass. We passed, in our course, the dry beds of two transient creeks, one eight, and the other fifteen miles from the Fort.

Our route bore nearly due south for twenty miles, following the Platte bottom to the mouth of Cherry creek, thence southeast, continuing up the valley of the latter. The Platte presented heavy groves of timber upon both banks, as did also its islands, while its bottoms appeared fertile.

The mountains, some fifteen miles to our right, towering aloft with their snow-capped summits and dark frowning sides, looked like vast piles of clouds, big with storm and heaped upon the lap of earth; while the vapor-scuds that flitted around them, seemed as the ministers of pent up wrath, in readiness to pour forth their torrents and deluge the surrounding plains, or let loose the fierce tornado and strew its path with desolation.

Three or four miles before reaching our present camp, we passed a village of the Arapahos on its way to the mountains, in pursuit of game

With this the reader is introduced to that nation for the first time, which affords me occasion to speak of them more particularly.

The Arapahos are a tribe of prairie Indians, inhabiting the country bordering upon the South Fork of the Platte and Arkansas rivers.

Their territory embraces an extent of about forty-five thousand square miles, a portion of which is well watered and interspersed with numerous fertile spots. Timber is rarely found, except in the creek bottoms and among the mountains. A large section of it, however, is dry, sandy, and sterile, and almost entirely timberless and destitute of water. The game of these regions includes all the varieties common to the mountains, which are quite abundant. The territory also possesses large mineral resources, and includes among its stores of hidden wealth, gold, silver, copper, lead, iron, coal, soda, nitre, salt, and sulpher, with vast beds of gypsum.

This nation boasts some five hundred and twenty-five lodges, numbering not far from four thousand souls. In appearance, as well as manners and customs, they assimilate the Sioux and Chyennes. Their insignia of nationality is a tattooed breast, by which they are distinguished from neighboring tribes. They afford to the observer the rare instance of increasing numbers in an Indian population.

The Arapahos since their first treaty with the whites, some fifteen years ago, have maintained terms of the strictest friendship on their part. They have never been known to kill or even injure a white man in the interval, and rarely to steal from him any article of value. They seem to take pleasure in the bestowment of kindness and hospitality upon such whenever in their power, but commonly in expectation of reward, and are exceedingly annoying as beggars.

These Indians, though brave, are less warlike than contiguous tribes,—being at variance only with the Utahs and Pawnees, whose countries are severally invaded as occasion serves, and often with success.

They possess considerable taste for trafficing, and regularly meet the Sioux, Chyennes, Cumanches, and Kuyawas for that purpose, and many of them know how to drive as good a bargain as the most expert Yankee.

Notwithstanding the many good qualities possessed by them, they are inferior to their neighbors in morality. The Sioux and Chyennes are far more chaste, and never indulge in the low practices common with the Arapahos. Virtue with the former is guarded by the strictest vigilance and jealousy, while with the latter it is made the minister of lust and is prostituted for a paltry bribe.

As yet no effort has been made for their improvement, though I regard them as more susceptible of civilization than any other of the prairie tribes. They appear to be great admirers of the manners, customs, arts, and mode of living prevalent among the whites, and only lack the requisite instruction to become their successful imitators.

The camp at which we are at present located consists of four lodges,—three of whites, and one of Blackfoot Indians.

Each of the whites has his squaw wife, and the usual accompaniment of ruddy faced children. In regard to the latter, I must say they were more beautiful, interesting, and intelligent than the same number of full-bloods,—either of whites or Indians.

A BLACKFOOT CHIEF. — *Page* 214.

These men were living after the fashion of their new-found relatives, and seemed to enjoy themselves as well as circumstances would admit. They had a number of horses, with the requisite supply of arms and ammunition,—the sure sources of wealth and comfort in a country abounding with game.

The Indian family were relatives by marriage, and were one of some fifteen lodges of Blackfeet among the Arapahos, who forsook their own nation, on account of its uncompromising hostility to the whites. Quite a number of these Indians have also joined the Sioux and Nesperces, for a like reason.

We were entertained very kindly by our new friends who spared no effort to render our stay agreeable. Among the delicacies set before us, was one deserving of notice,—it consisted of the fruit of prickly pears (*cacti*) boiled in water for some ten or twelve hours till it became perfectly soft, when it was compressed through a thin cloth into the fluid in which it had been boiled. This forms a delicious variety in mountain fare, and one highly stimulating and nutritious.

The immense quantities of *cacti* fruit found near the mountains, at the proper season, render the above an entertainment not uncommon.

*Sept.* 13*th.* Again under way; after a ride of fifteen miles, night finds us at Blackfoot-camp, snugly chambered in a spacious cave, to avoid the disagreeable effects of a snow-storm that comes upon the reluctant prairie with all the withering keenness of winter.

The cave affording us shelter is formed in an abrupt embankment of limestone, that marks the eastern limits of a beautiful valley through which a small affluent of Cherry creek traces its way. The floor is of dry gravel and rock, about fifty feet long by fifteen wide, while upon one side a crystal spring presents its tempting draughts. Thus chambered, a small fire soon rendered us comfortable and happy, notwithstanding the dreary weather without.

Our course during the day bore southward, and led from the valley of Cherry creek to an interesting plateau, furrowed at intervals by deep cañons, enclosing broad bottoms of rich alluvion, and ridged upon either hand by high hills of pine and ledges of naked rock.

The streams are generally timberless,—the soil of the highlands is of a red, clayey mould, and quite fertile. Instead of the aridity incident to the neighboring prairies, it is usually humid.

The country hereabouts, for an extent of upwards one thousand square miles, is much subject to storms of rain, hail, snow, and wind,—and it is rarely a person can pass through it without being caught by a storm of some kind. I can account for this in no other way than by supposing it has some connection with the vast quantities of minerals lying embedded in its hills and valleys.

*Sept.* 14*th.* Morning was ushered in with a pleasant sunshine, that soon caused the snow of the past night to yield beneath its melting influences.

When on the point of raising camp, an old grizzly bear made her appearance with *three* cubs. An effort to approach her proved futile,—she, having snuffed the closeness of danger with the breeze, made a hasty retreat with her offspring.

I allude to the above incident for this reason, that it is generally supposed the bear produces but two at a birth.

Continuing our journey till late at night, we reached an affluent of *Fontaine qui Bouit*, called Daugherty's creek, after travelling a distance of some thirty miles. Here we remained for three or four days, to procure a further supply of provisions.

The route from Blackfoot-camp, for the most part, led over a rough country, interspersed with high piny ridges and beautiful valleys, sustaining a luxuriant growth of vegetation, which is known as the Divide.

This romantic region gives rise to several large tributaries both of the Platte and Arkansas, and furnishes the main branches of the Kansas. Its geological classifications consist of sandstone, limestone, granite, and cretaceous rock. Large quantities of silex are also found, together with many interesting specimens of petrifaction that principally consist of pine wood; these, in many cases, exhibit the tree in its perfect shape, with all the grains and pores that marked its growth.

A ride of three hours took us past the heads of Bijou and Kuyawa, whose clear and swift currents, confined to narrow beds, here presented a striking contrast to those remarked at their confluence with the Platte.

Continuing on a few miles, we reached Black Squirrel creek, an affluent of the Arkansas; and from thence, after a brisk trot for some fourteen miles over a nearly level prairie, we came to our present camp.

Our place of stay was in sweet little valley enclosed by piny ridges. The entrance leading to it is through a defile of hills from whose rugged sides protrude vast piles of rock, that afford a pass of only fifty or a hundred yards in width. An abundance of grass greets the eye, arrayed in the loveliness of summer's verdancy, and blooming wild-flowers nod to the breeze as enchantingly as when the fostering hand of spring first awoke them to life and to beauty.

The creek derives its name from Daugherty, a trader who was murdered upon it several years since. At the time he was on his way to the Arkansas with a quantity of goods, accompanied by a Mexican. The latter, anxious to procure a few yards of calico that constituted a part of the freight, shot him in cold blood, and hastened to Taos with his ill-gotten gains, where he unblushingly boasted of his inhuman achievement.

My excursions among the hills brought before me many interesting geological specimens, mostly such as characterize the Divide. I noticed two or three extensive beds of stone coal in the vicinity of the creek, with an abundance of nitre and other mineral salts.

Having killed three fine cows during the five days we remained at this place, the scent of fresh meat attracted an old bear and her cub, which, in the expectation of a choice repast, were induced to pay us a night visit.

We were quietly reposing at the time, nor dreamed of the ungainly monsters within camp, till their harsh growls grated upon our ears and raised us each to a speedy consciousness. Instantly every rifle was clenched and levelled at the unwelcome intruders, and two discharges bespoke their warm reception. The bears, not fancying this new test of friendship, quickly withdrew and permitted us to resume our slumbers.

Fitzpatrick and Van Dusen, two old mountaineers, passed our encampment, in the interim, on their way to the States. Having devoted a number of years to the business of trapping, few possess a more intimate knowledge of this country than they. The former of these gentlemen was on his return from Oregon with dispatches for the U. S. Government, and had acted as pilot for a party of emigrants to that territory during the previous summer. After conducting his charge to their place of destination, he and his companion had travelled thus far alone,*—a distance of more than one thousand miles.

*Sept.* 19*th*. Leaving Daugherty's creek we resumed our course, and reached the Arkansas the next day, about noon. Here we encamped in a small grove of cottonwood upon the right bank, a few miles above the mouth of Fontaine qui Bouit.

In gaining this point we travelled some forty-five miles, mostly over a sandy prairie, slightly undulating to the leftward, but, to the right, describing the waves of a tempest-tossed ocean.

Its general character is sterility; the grass gowing thinly and being of a coarse kind, with the exception of that of the creek bottoms, which affords several varieties of a lusty size, mingled with occasional spreads of prele— a choice article for the subsistence of horses and mules.

In passing along, I observed a new species of the *cacti* family, that grew in a shurb-like form to a height of five or six feet. Its stalk was round and fully an inch in diameter.

This made the fourth variety of *cactus* noticed during the past few days. Of these, two resemble the common "prickly pear" in their appearance. Another species, however, was egg-shaped, bearing a fruit much like the cranberry in color and form. At the proper season, it also produces a beautiful red flower, that emits a most agreeable perfume, in some measure atoning for its dreaded intrusion upon the path of the wayfarer.

*Fontaine qui Bouit*, or the Boiling Fountain, is the name bestowed upon a considerable stream that heads under Pike's Peak, in lat. 38° 52' 10" north, long. 105° 22' 45" west from Greenwich, and pursues a southerly course till it unites with the Arkansas.

This name is derived from two singular springs, situated within a few yards of each other at the creek's head, both of which emit water in the form of vapor, accompanied with a hissing noise—the one strongly impregnated with sulphur and the other with soda.†

* Before reaching the States, however, he was robbed of everything in his possession by a war-party of Pawnees, whom he had imprudently suffered to obtain the advantage. He would, doubtless, have been killed had it not been for the determined courage of Van Dusen. The latter, seizing his rifle, levelled it at the foremost and thus deterred a further advance; then, by an adroit movement, breaking from them, set pursuit at defiance through his fleetness of foot.

The Pawnees, now well aware that further outrages would be made known and become a subject of investigation by the U. S. Government, forbore their designs, and returned to Fitzpatrick his gun and one mule, with which he accomplished the remainder of his journey alone. Van Dusen, having succeeded in reaching Bent's Fort on the Arkansas, reported his companion as killed by them.

† Capt. Fremont, who visited Fontaine qui Bouit in the summer of '43, has furnished the following analysis of an incrustation with which the water of this spring has

The soda water is fully as good as any manufactured for especial use, and sparkles and foams with equal effervescence. This spring, though at present cool, is said to have been formerly quite the reverse. Some twenty years since, the heat was sufficient to cook flesh in an half hour's time, if submerged in its waters.

The Arapahos regard this phenomenon with awe, and venerate it as the manifestation of the immediate presence of the Great Spirit. They call it the *Medicine Fountain*, and seldom neglect to bestow their gifts upon it whenever an opportunity is presented.

These offerings generally consist of robes, blankets, arrows, bows, knives, beads, moccasins, &c., which they either throw into the water or hang upon the surrounding trees. Sometimes a whole village will visit the place for the purpose of paying their united regard to this sacred fountain.

The scenery of the vicinity is truly magnificent. A valley several yards in width heads at the springs, overlooking which from the west in almost perpendicular ascent tower the lofty summits of Pike's Peak, piercing the clouds and revelling in eternal snow, at an altitude of 12,500 feet above the level of the sea.

This valley opens eastward, and is walled in upon the right and left, at the mountains' base, by a stretch of high table land, surmounted by oaks and stately pines, with now and then an interval displaying a luxuriant coating of grass. The soil is a reddish loam, and very rich. The trees which skirt the creek as it traces its way from the fountain are generally free from under-brush, and show almost as much regularity of position as if planted by the hand of art. A lusty growth of vegetation is sustained among them to their very trunks, which is garnished by wild flowers, that, during the summer months, invest the whole scene with an enchantment peculiar to itself.

The climate too is far milder in this than in adjoining regions, even of a more southern latitude. 'Tis here "summer first unfolds her robes, and here the longest tarries." The grass, continuing green the entire winter, here first feels the genial touch of spring. Snow seldom remains upon the ground to exceed a single day, even in the severest weather, while the neighboring hills and prairies present their white mantlings for weeks in succession.

As the creek emerges from the mountains, it increases in size by the accession of several tributaries, and the valley also expands to a width of

covered a piece of wood; and, though probably not a fair test, it will afford the reader some idea of its mineral properties:

| | |
|---|---|
| Carbonate of lime | 92, 25 |
| Carbonate of magnesia | 1, 21 |
| Sulphate of lime } | |
| Chloride of calcium } | 23 |
| Chloride of magnesia } | |
| Silica | 1, 50 |
| Vegetable matter | 20 |
| Moisture and loss | 4, 61 |
| | 100, 00 |

three or four miles, retaining for a considerable distance the distinguishing traits before described.

The vicinity affords an abundance of game, among which are deer, sheep, bear, antelope, elk, and buffalo, together with turkeys, geese, ducks, grouse, mountain-fowls, and rabbits.

Affording, as it does, such magnificent and delightful scenery; such rich stores for the supply of human wants, both to please the taste and enrapture the heart; so heaven-like in its appearance and character, it is no wonder the untaught savage reveres it as the place wherein the Good Spirit delights to dwell, and hastens with his free-will offerings to the strange fountain, in the full belief that its bubbling waters are the more immediate impersonation of Him whom he adores.

But, there are other scenes adjoining this, that demand a passing notice. A few miles above Fontaine qui Bouit, and running parallel with the eastern base of the mountain range, several hundred yards removed from it, a wall of coarse, red granite (quite friable and constantly abrading) towers to a varied height of from fifty to three hundred feet.

This wall is formed of immense strata, planted vertically and not exceeding eight feet in thickness, with frequent openings—so arranged as to describe a complete line.

The soil in which they appear is of a reddish loam, almost entirely destitute of other rock, even to their very base.

This mural tier is isolated, and occupies its prairie site in silent majesty, as if to guard the approaches to the stupendous monuments of nature's handiwork that form the back-ground, disclosing itself to the beholder for a distance of more than thirty miles.

## CHAPTER XXI.

Vicinity of the Arkansas.—Settlement.—The Pueblo.—Rio San Carlos, its valleys and scenery.—Shooting by moonlight.—Taos.—Review of the country travelled over.—Taos; its vicinity, scenery, and mines.—Ranchos and Rancheros.—Mexican houses; their domestic economy, and filth.—Abject poverty and deplorable condition of the lower classes of Mexicans, with a general review of their character, and some of the causes contributing to their present degradation.—The Pueblo Indians and their strange notions.—Ancient temple.—Character of the Pueblos —Journey to the Uintah river, and observations by the way.---Taos Utahs, Pa-utahs, Uintah and Lake Utahs.---The Diggers; misery of their situation, strange mode of living, with a sketch of their character.---The Navijos; their civilization, hostility to Spaniards, ludicrous barbarity, bravery, &c., with a sketch of their country, and why they are less favorable to the whites than formerly.

THE Arkansas at this point is a clear and beautiful stream, about one hundred and fifty yards wide. It flows over a bed of rock and pebbles, with a rapid current, averaging two feet in depth. Its southern bank is steep and inducts to a high sandy prairie, which present a somewhat sterile and denuded appearance. The northern shore affords a wide bottom of black loam, generally fertile, and timbered with occasional groves of cottonwood. Beyond this a high undulating prairie, presenting now and then a cluster of pines and cedars, leads off to the neighboring mountains.

The river above, for a distance of some forty miles, possesses many beautiful valleys, well timbered, and a rich soil, until the traveller arrives at the place where it makes its entrée from the lofty mountain chain in which it heads.

The land indicates a fitness for agricultural purposes, and holds out strong inducements to emigrants. A small settlement of whites and half-breeds, numbering fifteen or twenty families, has already been commenced about thirty miles above the mouth of Fontaine qui Bouit under quite favorable auspicies. The only fears entertained for its success, are on account of the Indians.

Many other localities in this vicinity are equally inviting were it not for the character and habits of the surrounding natives.

At the delta, formed by the junction of Fontaine qui Bouit with the Arkansas, a trading fort, called the Pueblo, was built during the summer of 1842. This post is owned by a company of independent traders, on the common property system; and, from its situation, can command a profitable trade with both Mexicans and Indians. Its occupants number ten or twelve Americans, most of whom are married to Mexican women, while everything about the establishment wears the aspect of neatness and comfort.

*Sept. 22d.* Crossing the Arkansas, I for the first time set foot upon Mexican soil.

Taking the Taos trail, we continued our way for ten or twelve miles and came to the Rio San Carlos. Here the abundance of deer and turkeys was too great a temptation to be resisted, and we remained several days to bestow upon them that attention our appetites demanded.

The country adjacent is very romantic and beautiful. The hills, enclosing the valley of the San Carlos upon both sides, are high and precipitous,—affording numerous groves of pine, pinion,* and cedar. Interspersed among them are frequent openings and *prairillons* of rich soil and luxuriant vegetation. The valley is narrow, but fertile and well timbered.

Near the head of the river is a broad area, known as Fisher's-hole, bounded upon all sides by rugged hills and mountains, inaccessible except by a circuitous pass leading into it from the south. The stream forces its egress through a ledge of dark-colored rock, several hundred feet in altitude, leaving vertical walls upon each side for a long distance, that frequently overhang the gurgling waters sweeping at their base.

---

* This tree is a species of pine, quite common in New Mexico, California, and some parts of the mountains. It yields a kind of nut similar to that of the beech, which is esteemed as an article of food. Wild turkeys delight to frequent groves of this timber, and will thrive in an extraordinary manner upon pinion-nuts.

This valley contains more than a thousand acres of choice land, well supplied with timber from the heavy pine forests surrounding it.

The prevailing rock is granite, sandstone, limestone, and lias, with occasional conglomerates of various kinds. I noticed strong indications of copper and other minerals; and the general appearance of the country led me to conclude it to be one possessed of vast stores of hidden wealth.

While here, we were quite successful in replenishing our stock of provisions.

My experiments in turkey-hunting made me a proficient shot by moonlight, a feat which adds materially to the sport. This is done by manœuvring so as to have the turkey in a direct line between the marksman and the moon, causing its shadow to fall upon his face,—then, raising his rifle to a level from the ground upwards, the instant the sight becomes darkened he fires, and, if his piece be true, seldom fails to make a centre shot.

The most feasible mode of hunting turkeys is to watch their roosting places at night; and, after the moon attains the required position, they may be killed by dozens in the above manner. They rarely leave their roosts on account of the firing; but remain, half stupified with affright, while they are picked off one after another by the practised hunter.

*Sept. 25th.* Again resuming our journey, we reached Taos on the 1st of October.

Our stay at this place was prolonged for several days, during which time we took boarding with a Mexican lady, the widow of an American trader.

The country travelled over *en route*, from the San Carlos to Taos is very rough and mountainous, but variegated by many fertile valleys skirting the numerous tributaries of the Arkansas and del Norte.

The trail crosses several of the latter streams, for the most part bearing an easterly course; among which are the Cornua Virda, Huaquetore, Timpa, Apache, and Pischepa.

These creeks frequently pass through deep cañons of sandstone and limestone for a distance of several miles together,—disclosing upon all sides a wild and romantic scenery. The great fault with the valleys is a lack of timber; the hills, however, are generally supplied with pine, piñion, and cedar, which, in a measure, atones for the above deficiency.

On leaving the Pischepa, a reach of little more than one *jornada* (day's travel) leads over the mountain range, separating the waters of the Arkansas and del Norte, at a point bearing a short distance to the left of two famous landmarks, called the Spanish Peaks.

Here the traveller is at once ushered into the valley of Taos; and, continuing on, in a brief interval finds himself surrounded by a clan of half-naked Mexicans.

Taos proper embraces several fertile lateral valleys bordering upon the del Norte, and three small affluents from the east and is supposed to contain a population of some ten thousand, including Indians, Moors, Half-breeds, Mulattoes, and Spaniards. It is divided into several precints, or neighborhoods, within short distances of each other, among which Arroyo Hondo is the principal.

This section of country is very romantic, and affords many scenes to excite the admiration of beholders. It is shut in by lofty mountains, upon three sides, that tower to an altitude of several thousand feet, now presenting their pine-clad summits among the clouds, now with denuded crests defying the tempest; and then peering skyward to hold converse with the scathing blasts of unending winter.

The mountains are rich in minerals of various kinds. Gold is found in considerable quantities in their vicinity, and would doubtless yield a large profit to diggers, were they possessed of the requisite enterprise and capital. At present these valuable mines are almost entirely neglected, —the common people being too ignorant and poor to work them, and the rich too indolent and fond of ease.

The Mexicans possess large *ranchos* of sheep, horses, mules, and cattle among the mountains, which are kept there the entire year, by a degraded set of beings, following no business but that of herdsmen, or *rancheros.*

This class of people have no loftier aspirations than to throw the *lasso* with dexterity, and break wild mules and horses.

They have scarcely an idea of any other place than the little circle in which they move, nor dream of a more happy state of existence than their own. Half-naked and scantily fed, they are contented with the miserable pittance doled out to them by the proud lordlings they serve, while their wild songs merrily echo through the hills as they pursue their ceaseless vocations till death drops his dark curtain o'er the scene.

There are no people on the continent of America, whether civilized or uncivilized, with one or two exceptions, more miserable in condition or despicable in morals than the mongrel race inhabiting New Mexico. In saying this, I deal in generalities; but were I to particularize the observation would hold good in a large majority of cases.

Next to the squalid appearance of its inhabitants, the first thing that arrests the attention of the traveller on entering an Mexican settlement, is the uninviting mud walls that form the rude hovels which constitute its dwellings.

These are one story high and built of *adobies*, with small windows, (like the port-holes of a fortification,) generally without glass. The entrance is by an opening in the side, very low, and frequently unprotected by a door. The roof is a terrace of sod, reposing upon a layer of small logs, affording but poor protection from the weather.

The interior presents an aspect quite as forbidding;—the floors are simply the naked ground,—chairs and tables are articles rarely met with. In case of an extra room, it is partitioned off by a thin wall of mud, communicating with its neighbor through a small window-shaped aperture, and serves the double purpose of a chamber and store-house.

A few rags, tattered blankets, or old robes, furnish beds for its inmates, who, at nightfall, stow themselves away promiscuously upon the ground or in narrow bins, and snooze their rounds despite the swarms of noxious vermin that infest them, (companions from which they are seldom free,

## ABJECT CONDITION OF MEXICANS.

whether sleeping or waking,—and afford them, perhaps, in greater number and variety of species than any other known people.)

But, before the picture is complete, we must be indulged in a brief sketch of their kitchen economy.

Knives, forks, spoons, and plates, seldom grace the board of a Mexican in common circumstances. A single pot of earth, a knife, two or three trenchers, and as many water-gourds, constitute almost the entire kitchen furniture of the lower classes;—a kind of gruel (*tolle*) made by stirring a few handfuls of flour into boiling water or milk, is their principal subsistence.

Meat finds no place upon their larder,—it being an article too costly for ordinary food, as the sheep and cattle of the country are owned by the wealthy, and by their exorbitant demands placed beyond the means of the commoner. Wood too, being two *rials* (25 cents) per mule-load, is seldom used in the large towns for other than culinary purposes.

During the winter months, these filthy wretches are seen, day after day, basking at the sunny side of their huts, and bestowing upon each other certain friendly offices connected with the head, wherein the swarming populace of the pericranium are had in alternate requisition.

The entire business of the country is in the hands of the rich, upon whom the laboring classes are mainly dependant for support; and, as a natural consequence, the rich know no end to their treasures, nor the poor to their poverty.

The common laborer obtains only from four to six dollars per month, out of which he must feed and clothe himself. In case he runs in debt beyond his means, he is necessitated by law to serve for the required amount, at two dollars per month;—thus, once in debt, it is almost impossible ever to extricate himself.

But a thing adding still further to his load of misfortunes is the high price set upon the necessaries and comforts of life. This ranges as follows: coffee, from 37½ to 50 cts. per lb.; sugar, from 18 to 25 cts. per do.; calico, from 25 cts. to $1 per yd.; domestic, 25 to 50 cts.; broadcloths, from $10 to $20, and every thing else in proportion.

Under such circumstances, it is scarcely marvellous that we find the Mexican in his present low state of degradation.

Having faintly depicted the real condition of a large majority of the degenerate inhabitants of New Mexico, it will be expected of me to say something of their intelligence and morality; and here a still more revolting task awaits my effort.

Intelligence is confined almost exclusively to the higher classes, and the poor "*palavro*" comes in for a very diminutive share.

Education is entirely controlled by the priests, who make use of their utmost endeavors to entangle the minds of their pupils in the meshes of superstition and bigotry. The result of this may be plainly stated in a few words:—

Superstition and bigotry are universal,—all, both old and young, being tied down to the disgusting formalities of a religion that manifests itself in little else than senseless parade and unmeaning ceremony,—while a large majority can neither read nor write.

These conservators of intelligence and morals are often as sadly deficient in either as those they assume to teach. Gambling, swearing, drinking, Sabbath-breaking, and sundry other vices, are the too frequent concomitants of their practice;—under such instructors, who can fail to foresee the attendant train of evils? The abject condition of the people favors the impress of unsound instruction and deteriorating example, reducing public morals to a very low ebb.

Property and life are alike unsafe, and a large proportion of the whole community are little other than thieves and robbers. Profanity is their common language. In their honesty, integrity, and good faith, as a general thing, no reliance should be placed. They are at all times ready to betray their trust whenever a sufficient inducement is presented.

With the present of a few dollars, witnesses may be readily obtained to swear to anything; and a like bonus placed in the hands of the *Alcaldi* will generally secure the required judgment, however much at variance with the true merits of the cause.

Thus, justice becomes a mere mockery, and crime stalks forth at noonday, unawed by fear of punishment, and unrebuked by public opinion and practice.

But fear, in most cases, exercises a far more controlling influence over them than either gratitude or favor. They may be ranked with the few exceptions in the family of man who cannot endure good treatment. To manage them successfully, they must needs be held in continual restraint, and kept in their place by force, if necessary,—else they will become haughty and insolent.

As servants, they are excellent, when properly trained, but are worse than useless if left to themselves.

In regard to the Mexican women, it would be unfair to include them in the preceding summary.

The ladies present a striking contrast to their countryman in general character, other than morals. They are kind and affectionate in their disposition, mild and affable in their deportment, and ever ready to administer to the necessities of others. But, on the score of virtue and common chastity, they are sadly deficient; while ignorance and superstition are equally predominant.

One of the prime causes in producing this deplorable state of things may be attributed to that government policy which confines the circulating medium of the country within too narrow limits, and thus throws the entire business of the country into the hands of the capitalist.

A policy like this must ever give to the rich the moneyed power, while it drains from the pockets of the poor man and places him at the mercy of haughty lordlings, who, taking advantage of his necessity, grant him but the scanty pittance for his services they in tender compassion see fit to bestow.

The higher classes have thus attained the supreme control, and the commoners must continue to cringe and bow to their will. In this manner the latter have, by degrees, lost all ambition and self-respect,—and, in degradation, are only equalled by their effeminacy.

Possessed of little moral restraint, and interested in nothing but the demands of present want, they abandon themselves to vice, and prey upon one another and those around them.

Acting upon the principle, that "necessity knows no law," they know no law for necessity, and help themselves without compunction to whatever chance throws in their way.

To this we may also look for a reason why the entire country is so infested with banded robbers, that scour it continually in quest of plunder. Mankind are naturally vicious; and, when necessity drives them to wrong for the procurement of a bare subsistence, they are not slow to become adepts in the practice of evil.

A few miles to the southeast of Taos, is a large village of Pueblos, or civilized Indians. These are far superior to their neighbors in circumstances, morals, civil regulations, character, and all the other distinguishing traits of civilization.

This race are of the genuine Mexican stock, and retain many of their ancient customs, though nominally Catholic in their religion.

Cherishing a deep-rooted animosity towards their conquerors, they only await a favorable opportunity to re-assert their liberty.

They live in houses built of stone and earth, and cultivate the ground for a subsistence,—own large herds of cattle, horses, and sheep,—while their women spin and weave, with no small pretentions to skill.

Among their peculiarities is the belief, still entertained by many of them, that Montezuma, their former emperor, will yet return from the Spirit Land, and, placing himself at the head of his people, enable them to overcome the despoilers of his ancient dominions.

In this strange faith a fire was kept burning without intermission, from the death of Montezuma till within ten years past, (a period of nearly three centuries,) as a beacon-light to mark the place for his appearing.

This fire was sustained by an ancient order of priests ministering at a temple of unknown age, the ruins of which, it is said, are yet to be seen two miles back from St. Miguel, in a very good state of preservation. By verbal descriptions received from those who have visited them, I am led to infer that they afford many curious and interesting evidences of Mexican grandeur and tend to shed much light upon their former history and religion.

The sculpture is said to represent men and animals of different kinds, in many strange varieties of shape and posture; among them are beasts, birds, and reptiles, some of which are of unknown species.

The workmanship is rather rude and without much regard to uniformity or proportion of parts, yet possessing a wild beauty and harmony peculiar to itself alone, that at once strikes the beholder with feelings of pleasing wonder.

I had cherished the intention of visiting personally these strange relics of the past, but was induced to defer it for a more convenient opportunity than the present; and, finally, from my subsequent connection with the Texans, I abandoned it altogether.

The Pueblos number a population of several thousand, and are scattered over a considerable extent of territory. They bestow much attention to the inculcation of good morals in the minds of their children; and, in portraying the pernicious effects of evil-doing, frequently admonish them in a quaint and expressive manner,—" If you do thus and so, you will become *as bad as a Spaniard !"*—This seems to constitute, in their opinion, the grand climax of everything vile and degrading.

They are represented as humane and brave, and strictly honest and upright in their dealings. Their women too are chaste and virtuous, and in this respect present a very favorable contrast to their fairer and more beautiful sisters of Spanish extraction.

A small party from a trading establishment on the waters of Green river, who had visited Taos for the procurement of a fresh supply of goods, were about to return, and I availed myself of the occasion to make one of their number.

On the 7th of October we were under way. Our party consisted of three Frenchmen and five Spaniards, under the direction of a man named Roubideau, formerly from St. Louis, Mo. Some eight pack-mules, laden at the rate of two hundred and fifty pounds each, conveyed a quantity of goods;—these headed by a guide followed in Indian file, and the remainder of the company mounted on horseback brought up the rear.

Crossing the del Norte, we soon after struck into a large trail bearing a westerly course; following which, on the 13th inst. we crossed the main ridge of the Rocky Mountains by a feasible pass at the southern extremity of the Sierra de Anahuac range, and found ourselves upon the waters of the Pacific.

Six days subsequent, we reached Roubideau's Fort, at the forks of the Uintah, having passed several large streams in our course, as well as the two principal branches which unite to form the Colorado. This being the point of destination, our journey here came to a temporary close.

The intermediate country, from Taos to the Uintah, is generally very rough and diversified with rich valleys, beautiful plateaux, *(tierras templadas,)* arid prairies, sterile plains, *(llanos,)* and denuded mountains.

We usually found a sufficiency of timber upon the streams, as well as among the hills, where frequent groves of pinion, cedar, and pine lent an agreeable diversity to the scene. Game appeared in great abundance nearly the whole route,—especially antelope and deer.

The prevailing rock consisted of several specimens of sandstone, puddingstone, and granite, with limestone, (fossiliferous, bituminous and argillaceous,) and basalt.

This territory is owned by the Utahs and Navijo Indians.

The former of these tribes includes four or five divisions, and inhabits the country laying between the Rio del Norte, the Great Salt Lake, and the vast desert to the southward of it. These different fractions are known as the Taos, Pa-utah, Digger, and Lake Utahs, numbering in all a population of fifteen thousand or more, and exhibiting many peculiarities of character and habits distinct from each other.

The Taos Utahs are a brave and warlike people, located upon the del Norte a short distance to the northwest of Taos. These subsist principally by hunting, but raise large numbers of horses. They are generally treacherous and ill-disposed, making alike troublesome neighbors to the Spaniards and dangerous opponents to the whites, whenever an opportunity is presented.

The Pa-utahs and Lake Utahs occupy the territory lying south of the Snakes, and upon the waters of the Colorado of the west, and south of the Great Salt Lake.

These Indians are less warlike in their nature, and more friendly in their disposition, than the Taos Utahs. The persons and property of whites, visiting them for trade or other purposes, are seldom molested; and all having dealings with them, so far as my information extends, unite to give them a good character.

They rarely go to war, and seem content to enjoy the blessings of peace, and follow the chase within the limits of their own hunting grounds.

The Diggers, or rather a small portion of them, are a division of the Utah nation, inhabiting a considerable extent of the barren country directly southwest of the Great Salt Lake. They are represented as the most deplorably situated, perhaps, of the whole family of man, in all that pertains to the means of subsistence and the ordinary comforts of life.

The largest (and, in fact, almost the only) game found within their territory, is a very small species of rabbit, whose skins sewed together constitute their entire clothing. The soil is too barren for cultivation, sparsely timbered, and but illy supplied with water. The consequence of these accumulated disadvantages is, that its unfortunate inhabitants are left to gather a miserable substitute for food from insects, roots, and the seeds of grass and herbs.

In the summer months they lay in large supplies against the approach of winter,—ants furnishing an important item in the strange collection.

These insects abound in great numbers, and are caught by spreading a dampened skin, or fresh-peeled bark, over their hills, which immediately attracts the inquisitive denizens to its surface; when filled, the lure is carefully removed and its adherents shaken into a tight sack, where they are confined till dead,—they are then thoroughly sun-dried, and laid away for use.

In this manner they are cured by the bushel. The common way of eating them is in an uncooked state. These degraded beings live in holes dug in the sand near some watercourse, or in rudely constructed lodges of *absinthe,* where they remain in a semi-dormant, inactive state the entire winter,—leaving their lowly retreats only, now and then, at the urgent calls of nature, or to warm their burrows by burning some of the few scanty combustibles which chance may afford around them.

In the spring they creep from their holes, not like bear—fattened from a long repose—but poor and emaciated, with barely flesh enough to hide their bones, and so enervated, from hard fare and frequent abstinence, that they can scarcely move.

So habituated are they to this mode of life from constant inurement, they appear to have no conception of a better one.

Their ideas and aspirations are as simple as their fare. Give them an occasional rabbit, with an abundance of ants, seeds, and roots, and they are content to abide in their desert home and burrow like the diminutive animal they hunt.

They entertain great dread of the whites, whose power to do them harm they have learned on several occasions by bitter experience. These painful lessons have generally been inculcated as follows: impelled by hunger, these miserable creatures have sometimes attempted to kill the animals of trapping parties; and the trappers, in order to prevent a repetition of such occurrences, have been accustomed to shoot down their rude assailants without mercy.

Since the practice of this summary mode of chastisement has obtained, those able to run will flee with the utmost consternation on the approach of a party of whites,—leaving the feeble and infirm in the rear, who employ their most piteous supplications and moving entreaties for mercy.

These Indians possess a capacity for improvement, whenever circumstances favor them. I have seen several, both of men and women, taken from among them while young, who, under proper instruction, had made rapid progress, and even disclosed a superiority of intellect, compared with like examples from other nations,—a fact contributing much to prove that mankind need only to be placed in like conditions by birth and education to stand upon the same common level.

Most of them are represented as inoffensive in their habits and character,—never going to war, and rarely molesting any one that passes through their country.

Their arms are clubs, with small bows and arrows made of reeds—affording but a poor show of resistance to rifles, and a dozen mountaineers are rendered equal to a full army of such soldiers.

The Navijos occupy the country between the del Norte and the Sierra Anahuac, situated upon the Rio Chama and Puerco.—from thence extending along the Sierra de los Mimbros, into the province of Sonora.

They are a division of the ancient Mexicans that have never yet fully succumbed to Spanish domination, and still maintain against the conquerors of their country an obstinate and uncompromising warfare.

Like their ancestors, they possess a civilization of their own. Most of them live in houses built of stone, and cultivate the ground,—raising vegetables and grain for a subsistence. They also grow large quantities of horses, cattle, and sheep—make butter and cheese, and spin and weave

The blankets manufactured by these Indians are superior in beauty of color, texture, and durability, to the fabrics of their Spanish neighbors. I have frequently seen them so closely woven as to be impervious to water, and even serve for its transportation.

The internal regulations of this tribe are represented, by those more intimately acquainted with them, as in strict accordance with the welfare of the whole community. Lewdness is punished by a public exposure of the culprit; dishonesty is held in check by suitable regulations; industry is encouraged by general consent, and hospitality by common practice.

In their warfare with the Spaniards, they frequently exhibit a strange mixture of humanity and ludicrous barbarity.

They never kill women or children when in their power, but retain them as prisoners. The men, however, are invariably dispatched.

But in the latter, a comedy not unfrequently precedes the tragedy which closes the scene. Taking their cue from the passionate fondness of the Spaniards for dancing, at times, when any one of these unfortunate wretches falls into their power, they form a ring around him, and provided with switches, compel him to dance until from exhaustion he can do so no longer, after which he is unfeelingly butchered. His cruel tormenters continue singing, as they force him to *dance his own deathdirge*, and laugh at his faltering steps.

As warriors they are brave and daring, and make frequent and bold excursions into the Spanish settlements, driving off vast herds of cattle, horses, and sheep, and spreading terror and dismay on every side. As diplomatists, in imitation of their neighbors, they make and break treaties whenever interest or inclination prompts them.

The Navijo country is shut in by high mountains, inaccessible from without, except by limited passes, through narrow defiles well situated for defence on the approach of an invading foe.

Availing themselves of these natural advantages, they have continued to maintain their ground against fearful odds, nor have they ever suffered the Spaniards to set foot within their territory as permanent conquerors.

The valleys of the Chama and its tributaries are said to be unrivalled in beauty, and possessed of a delightful climate, as well as an exuberant fertility of soil. In these valleys winter is comparatively unknown and vegetation attains an extraordinary size. The mountains abound with game, and are rich in all kinds of minerals. Some of the most valuable gold mines in Mexico are supposed to be held by the Navijos. I have conversed with several Americans who have travelled to considerable extent in the territory of these Indians, and all unite to speak of it in most flattering terms.

The Catholics maintain numerous missions among them, and have succeeded in propagating their peculiar religious notions to some extent, notwithstanding their continued hostilities with the Spaniards.

The Navijos are generally friendly to the Americans visiting them; but were formerly much more so than at present. This partial estrangement may be attributed to the depredations of a party of Americans, under the lead of one Kirker, who were employed by the governments of Santa Fe and Chihuahua, to oppose their incursions. This was done with great success—the mercenaries despoiling their property, butchering their warriors, and bearing off men, women, and children, as captives to be sold into slavery.

## CHAPTER XXII.

Uintah trade.---Snake Indians; their country and character.---Description of Upper California.---The Eastern Section.---Great Salt Lake and circumjacent country.—Desert.—Digger country, and regions south.—Fertility of soil.—Prevailing rock and minerals.—Abundance of wild fruit, grain, and game.—Valley of the Colorado.—Magnificent scenery.—Valleys of the Uintah and other rivers.—Vicinity of the Gila.—Face of the country, soil &c.—Sweet spots.—Mildness of climate, and its healthiness.—The natives.—Sparsity of inhabitants.---No government.---All about the Colorado and Gila rivers.—Abundance of fish.—Trade in pearl oyster-shells.—Practicable routes from the United States.

In preceding remarks relative to regions coming under present observation, I have confined myself to generalities, for the reason, that less interest is felt by the American public, in a minute description of the rivers, mountains, valleys, etc., so far within the limits of Mexico, than in one connected with U. S. Territories; consequently the reader must rest contented with greater conciseness in subsequent pages, until he is again introduced to the interesting localities of his own country.

Roubideau's Fort is situated on the right bank of the Uintah, in lat. 40° 27' 45" north, long. 109° 56' 42" west. The trade of this post is conducted principally with the trapping parties frequenting the Big Bear, Green, Grand, and the Colorado rivers, with their numerous tributaries, in search of fur-bearing game.

A small business is also carried on with the Snake and Utah Indians, living in the neighborhood of this establishment. The common articles of dealing are horses, with beaver, otter, deer, sheep, and elk skins, in barter for ammunition, fire-arms, knives, tobacco, beads, awls, &c.

The Utahs and Snakes afford some of the largest and best finished sheep and deer skins I ever beheld,—a single skin sometimes being amply sufficient for common sized pantaloons. These skins are dressed so neatly as frequently to attain a snowy whiteness, and possess the softness of velvet.

They may be purchased for the trifling consideration of eight or ten charges of ammunition each, or two or three awls, or any other thing of proportional value. Skins are very abundant in these parts, as the natives, owing to the scarcity of buffalo, subsist entirely upon small game, which is found in immense quantities. This trade is quite profitable. The articles procured so cheaply, when taken to Santa Fe and the neighboring towns, find a ready cash market at prices ranging from one to two dollars each.

The Snakes, or Shoshones, live in the eastern part of Oregon and in Upper California, upon the waters of the Great Snake and Bear rivers, and the two streams which unite to form the Colorado.

They are friendly to the whites, and less disposed to appropriate to their own use everything they can lay hands on, than some other tribes. They seldom go to war, though by no means deficient in bravery,—frequently resisting with signal success the hostile encroachments of the Sioux and Chyennes. Rich in horses and game, they likewise include within their territory many interesting and beautiful localities, as well as some extraordinary natural curiosities.

One division of this tribe is identified with the Diggers in habits and mode of living,—the same causes operating in each case to produce the same results. Another division is identified with the Crows, and yet a third one with the Utahs,—numbering in all not far from twelve thousand.

Being less migratory in their habits, and more tractable in their disposition than those of their eastern brethren demontés, they are far more susceptible of civilization and improvement; though, as yet, nothing has been done for their benefit. The missionary might here find an encouraging field for his philanthropic exertions.

With the passage of the mountain chain, noticed in the preceding chapter, the reader is inducted to the northeastern extremity of California. My intention of visiting the interior of this interesting province of the Mexican Republic was frustrated through the lack of a convenient opportunity for its prosecution; but, as the public mind, during the past few years, has been so much occupied with subjects connected with this country, I am unwilling to pass on without presenting a brief description of it, obtained from sources upon which full reliance may be placed.

The following sketch, coupled with my own observations, is carefully arranged from information derived from indviduals encountered during my stay in this country, some of whom had travelled over most of it, and others had resided for years within its confines.

On referring to the map, a large extent of country will be noticed, bounded upon the north by Oregon, east by the Rocky Mountains, south by the Lower Province and Gulf of California, together with the Rio Gila which separates it from Sonora, and west by the Pacific, situated between parallels 32° and 42° north latitude, which is now known as Upper California.

This embraces an extent of nearly 450,000 square miles, and is walled in for the most part upon the north and east by lofty mountains, impassable except at certain points; while upon the west and south its vast stretch of sea-coast, navigable rivers, and commodious harbors open it to the commercial intercourse of all nations.

The entire country is more or less broken by hills and mountains, many of them towering to a height of several thousand feet above the level of the sea, whose summits, clothed with eternal snow, overlook the valleys of perennial verdure that so frequently lie around them. The most noted of these is the California, or Cascade range, which, by intersecting the province from north to south, separates it into two grand natural divisions, properly denominated Eastern and Western California.

The above range, though higher than the principal chain of the Rocky Mountains, is passable at various points. It is situated inland from the

20*

Pacific at distances varying from one hundred and fifty to four hundred miles, tracing its way with diminished altitude adown the isthmus that forms the Lower Province.

Owing to its locality, a description of the Eastern Division seems to come naturally the first in order.

This section is watered principally by the Colorado, Gila, and Bear rivers, with their numerous tributaries, and has also several lakes in various parts of it, prominent among which is the Great Salt Lake near the northern boundary.

This large body of water is nearly one hundred and fifty miles long by eighty broad; and, though the receptacle of several large rivers, has no visible outlet, and hence is supposed by many persons to hold subterranean connection with the Ocean. Its waters are so strongly impregnated with salt, incrustations of that mineral are frequently found upon its shores.

Towards the northern extremity an island makes its appearance, from whose centre a solitary mountain rises in proud majesty for nearly a thousand feet above the circumfluent waters; its craggy sides, naked and desolate, with whitened surface, now inspire the beholder with feelings of awe, while its bounding streamlets, skirted with verdant openings and diminutive trees, strike the eye pleasantly, as the sheen of their waters falls upon the vision and engenders commingled sensations of delight and admiration.

Viewed from the northern shore, this island seems not more than twelve miles distant; a deception caused by the extraordinary purity of the atmosphere. Several attempts to reach it, however, by means of canoes, have proved futile, owing to its great distance the dangerous state of navigation.

It is thought by many persons that still other islands of larger dimensions occupy the centre of the lake, and not without some show of reason; there is ample room for them, and, although this vast body of water has been circum-traversed per shore, it has never yet been otherwise explored by man *

The largest of the rivers that find their discharge in this vast saline reservoir is the Big Bear, a stream which rises near the South Pass, and, following its meanderings, is about two hundred and fifty or three hundred miles in length. It rolls leisurely on with its deep sluggish volume of waters, measuring some two hundred yards wide at its mouth, and deposites its willing tribute into the bosom of this miniature ocean, while four or five other fresh water affluents from the east and south make a like debouche without increasing its size or diminishing its saltness.

The valleys of these streams possess a very rich soil and are well timbered. The landscape adjacent to the lake is diversified with marshes, plains, highlands, and mountains, affording every variety of scenery. The soil is generally fertile and prolific in all kinds of vegetation as well as fruits indigenous to the country.

---

* Recently, however, Capt. Fremont reports his having succeeded in reaching the island nearest to the northern shore, but he was unfortunately prevented a further exploration. In his account of this he makes no mention of trees or streams of water upon the mountain. I have described it only as it appears when viewed from the main land.

Timber also abounds in sufficient quantity for all necessary purposes Game too is found in great abundance, particularly deer and elk; and, taken as a whole, the vicinity of the Great Salt Lake holds out strong inducements to settlers, and is capable of sustaining, as it will no doubt ultimately possess, a dense population.

Forty or fifty miles west and south from this the traveller is inducted to the vast expanse of sand and gravel, lying between lat. 35° and 40° north, which is almost entirely destitute of both wood and water.

This reach is upwards of three hundred miles in length and nearly two hundred broad. It is impassable at all seasons of the year on account of its extreme dryness and lack of suitable nourishment for animals; and even a trip from Santa Fe to Western California, by the regular trail, is rarely undertaken except in the fall and spring months, at which time the ground is rendered moist by annual rains and the transient streams venture to emerge from their sandy hiding places.

The Digger country, of which I have taken occasion to speak in connection with its unfortunate inhabitants, lies upon the eastern and southern extremities of this desolate waste, and presents an aspect little less forbidding.

As a general thing the landscape is highly undulating and varied with conical hills, some of which are mere heaps of naked sand or sun-baked clay of a whitish hue; others, vast piles of granitic rock, alike destitute of vegetation or timber; while yet others are clothed with a scanty herbage and occasional clusters of stunted pines and cedars.

Now and then a diminutive *vega* intervenes in favorable contrast to the surrounding desolation, greeting the beholder with its rank grasses, mingled with blushing prairie-flowers. But such beauty-spots are by no means frequent.

The watercourses are mere beds of sand, skirted with sterile bottoms of stiff clay and gravel, and afford streams only at their heads, while, for nearly the entire year, both dew and rain are unknown. Vegetation, consequently, is sparse and unpromising, and the whole section of necessity remains depopulated of game.

It is needless to say such a country can never become inhabited by civilized man.

Between the Colorado river and the California mountains, south of the cheerless desert above described, the prospect is far more flattering. The hills are of varied altitude and are usually clothed with grass and timber; while comparatively few of them are denuded to any great extent. The landscape is highly picturesque and pleasingly diversified with mountains, hills, plains, and valleys, which afford every variety of climate and soil.

This section is principally watered by the Rio Virgen and lateral streams; and, though little or no rain falls in the summer months, the copiousness of nightly dews in some measure make up for this defect.

The superfice of the valleys ranges from one to three feet in depth, and generally consists of sedimentary deposites and the debris of rocks, borne from the neighboring hills by aqueous attrition, which, mingled with a dark-colored loam compounded of clay and sand, and various organic and vegetable remains, unite to form a soil of admirable fecundity, rarely equalled by that of any other country.

The hills, however, are unfit for cultivation to any great extent, owing to their common sterility as well as the abundance of rock in many parts; yet they might serve a good purpose for grazing lands.

The prevailing rock is said to be sandstone, limestone, mica slate, trap, and basalt; the minerals, copper, iron, coal, salt, and sulphur.

Game exists in great abundance, among which are included antelope, deer, (black and white-tailed,) elk, bear, and immense quantities of waterfowls; large herds of wild horses and cattle, also, are not unfrequently met with.

Timber is usually a scarce article, which constitutes one grand fault in the entire section of Eastern California. This evil, however, is partially remedied by a mild climate, and only a comparatively small amount of wood is required for building, foncing, and fuel.

Fruits of all kinds indigenous to the country, particularly grapes, are found in great profusion, and those native only to the torrid and temperate zones may also be successfully cultivated.

Among the grasses, grains, and vegetables growing spontaneously in some parts, are red-clover and oats, (which atttain a most luxuriant bulk,) flax and onions; the latter not unfrequently equalling in size the proudest products of the far-farmed gardens of Wethersfield.

We are now naturally led back to the Colorado, and the country lying between it and the Sierra de los Mimbros range, on the east. This division embraces much choice land in its valleys, but the high grounds and hills present much of the dryness and sterility incident to the grand praries.

The valley of the Colorado averages from five to fifteen miles broad, for a distance of nearly two hundred miles above its mouth.

Further on, the passage of the river through high mountains and *tierras templadas* (table lands) presents an almost continuous gorge of vertical and overhanging rocks, that, closing in upon the subfluent stream at a varied height of from fifteen to six hundred or even a thousand feet, afford only an occasional diminutive opening to its waters.

This vast cañon is said to extend for five or six hundred miles, interrupting the river with numerous cataracts, cascades and rapids, and opposing to its swift current the sharp fragments of severed rocks thrown from the dizzy eminences, as breakers, by which to lash the gurgling waters and depict the more than tempest-tossed foam and maddened fury of old ocean!

In some places the impending rocks approach so near to each other from above, a person may almost step across the vast chasm opening to view the foaming river, half obscured in perpendicular distance and dimmed by the eternal shadows of thrice vertical walls.

This superbly magnificent scene continues nearly the entire extent, from the head of the Colorado valley to the boundary between Oregon and California.

The table lands and mountains on both sides, as a whole, disclose a dreary prospect. Now, the traveller meets with a wide reach of naked rock paving the surface to the exclusion of grass, shrubs, or tree,—now, a narrow fissure, filled with *detritus* and earth, sustains a few stunted pines,—now, a spread of hard sun-baked clay refuses root to aught earth-growing,—now, a small space of saline efflorescences obtrudes upon the vision its snowy incrustations, alike repulsive to vegetable life;—then, comes a broad area clothed with thin coarse grass; an opening *vallon* next greets the eye in the generous growth of its herbage and the fertility of its soil; a beautiful grove of stately pines, cedars, and pinions, rises in the back ground; a still larger, more expansive, and thrice lovely valley, skirts the banks of some bounding stream, and delights the fancy with its smiling flowers and luxuriant verdure.

Here, a huge mountain rears itself in majesty—now, piling heaps upon heaps of naked granite, limestone, sandstone, and basalt, variegated and parti-colored,—now, thickly studded with lateral pines, cedars, pinions, and hemlocks,—then, again denuded, till at last its sharpened peaks pierce the clouds while storms and tempests in their wild orgies haste to do it reverence. There, a lesser, coniform elevation of the continuous chain, is mantled in living green; while perhaps by its side, another pains the eye with the well defined lineaments of desolation.

A country of this description occupies nearly the whole interval from the two main branches of the Colorado to the dividing ridge of mountains.

The valleys of the Uintah, and several other affluents within its limits, however, are broad, fertile and tolerably well timbered. Grass continues green nearly the entire winter, and game of all kinds common to the mountains, excepting buffalo, is abundant. The valley soils are well adapted to cultivation, and might sustain a large population.

We come now to the southeastern extremity of the province, bordering upon the Rio Gila which separates it from Sonora, and lying between the Colorado and the Sierra de los Mimbros range.

This stretch, though less fertile as a general thing, partakes of much the same characteristics as that upon the opposite side of the Colorado, and upon Rio Virgen, south of the Digger country, which was so fully described upon a former page. The soil, however, is not generally so sandy, and the landscape is far more rough and broken. The bottoms of the Colorado and Gila, with their tributaries, are broad, rich, and well timbered. Everything in the shape of vegetation attains a lusty size, amply evincing the exuberant fecundity of the soil producing it.

There are many sweet spots in the vicinity of both these streams, well deserving the name of earthly Edens. Man here might fare sumptuously, with one continued feast spread before him by the spontaneous products of the earth, and revel in perennial spring or luxuriate amid unfading summer.

Yet, notwithstanding the other attractions held out, game is much less plentiful in this than in other parts,—probably owing to the warmth of the climate.

Winter is unknown, and the only thing that marks its presence from that of other seasons, is a continuation of rainy and damp weather for some two or three months. All the wild fruits and grains indigenous to the country are found here in profuse abundance.

The entire Eastern Division of Upper California possesses a uniformly salubrious and healthful atmosphere. Sickness, so far as my knowledge extends, is rarely known.

The natives, for the most part, may be considered friendly, or at least, not dangerous. Some of them, in the neighborhood of the Gila and the Gulf of California are partially advanced in civilization, and cultivate the ground, raising corn, melons, pumpkins, beans, potatoes, &c.

These live in fixed habitations, constructed of wood, and coated with earth, in a conical form, much like Pawnee huts.

The condition and character of these tribes present most flattering inducements for missionary enterprise; and, should efforts for their amelioration be put forth by zealous and devoted men, (and meet with no counteracting opposition from the united influence of the Mexican Government and the narrow minded bigotry of an intolerant clergy and priest-ridden people,) a glorious fruition of their most sanguine hopes might soon be expected.

There are no settlements of either whites or Mexicans, to my knowledge, throughout the whole extent of this territory. Indians may, therefore, be considered its only inhabitants, other than the strolling parties of trappers and traders that now and then travel it, or temporarily establish themselves within its limits. Of course then the Eastern Division of Upper California must be considered without a people or a government.

The Rio Colorado rises in the U. S. territory about lat. 42° 30′ north, interlocking with the head waters of the Columbia, Missouri, Platte, and Arkansas, and empties into the Gulf of California near lat. 32° north. Following its windings it is some twelve or fifteen hundred miles in length. This stream with its numerous tributaries is the only river worth naming in Eastern California, and, to a great extent, serves to water that country. Owing to the rapidity of its current and its frequent falls and cascades, the navigation is entirely destroyed, till within about one hundred miles of its mouth, at the head of tide water; from this on no further interruption occurs, and the depth is sufficient for vessels bearing several hundred tons burthen.

The Gila is properly a river of Sonora, though commonly regarded as the northern boundary of that province. It rises in the Sierra de los Mimbros, near lat. 33° 25′ north, long. 106° 15′ west from Greenwich, and pursues a west-southwesterly course till it discharges itself into the Bay of the Colorodo, at lat. 32° 15′ north, long. 114° 27′ west.

Its whole length is about eight hundred miles, for most of which distance navigation is impracticable, with the exception of some forty miles or more at its mouth.

These two rivers are said to afford immense quantities of fish, especially near their confluence with the Gulf of California.

The Gulf also contains a large variety and exhaustless supplies of the finny tribe, together with several species of the crustaceous and testaceous order. Among the last named are lobsters, crabs, clams, and oysters.

Oysters are very numerous and of an excellent quality, including in variety the genuine *mother pearl*. A small trade in the shells of the pearl oyster is carried on with the Arapahos, Chyennes, and Sioux, by the Spaniards, which yields a very large profit,—a single shell frequently bringing from six to eight robes. These Indians make use of them for ear-ornaments, and exhibit no little taste in their shape and finish.

The eastern section of Upper California is accessible by land as well as sea from several feasible passes through the mountain ranges forming its eastern boundary.

The best land routes for waggons from the United States is through the South Pass,—thence, to the Great Salt Lake by Bear river valley,—thence the emigrant can direct his course to any part of the country, as interest or inclination may suggest.

Another pass is afforded by way of the Santa Fe trail near lat. 37° north; this, however, is a very difficult one for waggons, and should only be travelled on horseback.

There are said to be one or two other passes further south, in reference to which I cannot speak with certainty, but am inclined to accredit their reported existence.

## CHAPTER XXIII.

Minerals.—Western California.—The Sacramento and contiguous regions.—Principal rivers.—Fish.—Commercial advantages.—Bay of San Francisco.—Other Bays and Harbors.—Description of the country; territory northwest of the Sacramento; Tlamath mountains; California range and its vicinity; Southern parts; timber; river-bottoms; Valleys of Sacramento, del Plumas, and Tulare; their extent, fertility, timber and fruit; wild grain and clover, spontaneous; wonderful fecundity of soil, and its products; the productions, climate, rains and dews; geological and mineralogical character; face of the country; its water; its healthiness; game; superabundance of cattle, horses, and sheep, their prices, &c.; beasts of prey; the inhabitants, who; Indians, their character and condition; Capital of the Province, with other towns; advantages of San Francisco; inland settlements; foreigners and Mexicans; Government; its full military strength.—Remarks.

In the preceding chapter the reader must have acquired some tangible idea of the true condition of Eastern California, with all its varied beauties and deformities; its Edens and wastes of desolation; its enchantments, and scenes of awe and terrific grandeur.

To have treated the subject more *in extenso*, would have trespassed upon prescribed brevity; yet, doubtless, many will regret my having said so little relative to the mineralogical character and resources of that country. The truth is, comparatively little is known upon this important matter. Were I to give ear to common report, I would say there are both gold and silver, with copper, lead, and iron. But such stories are not always to be credited unless they come in a credible shape.

However, it is very probable these metals do exist in various parts; and certain it is that immense beds of coal and rock-salt are afforded, with large quantities of gypsum, the truth of which is placed beyond doubt by an accumulation of testimony. With these few remarks I turn from the subject, and bring before the reader another and more interesting topic.

Following the only practicable waggon route from the U. S. to Western California, *via* South Pass,—thence, after bearing northwest some forty miles, by a long sweep southward around the Sierra Nevada to the Rio Sacrimento,—the emigrant is taken through a succession of mountains, hills, plains, and valleys, furrowed by frequent affluents from the north;— now, sterile wastes of intervening sand; now, pleasant spreads of arable prairies; now, rugged superfices of naked rock; then, beautiful valleys arrayed in all the loveliness of perennial verdure, and profuse in vegetation of extraordinary growth, intermixed with wild-flowers of unrivalled hues and lavish fragrance, till he finally reaches his destination.

The Sacramento and its tributaries water the greater part of Western California.

This river is formed by the confluence of two large streams which rise in the Cascade Mountains, properly termed the North and South Forks the former heading near lat. 41° 43' north, long. 114° 51' west. (The South Fork is the stream defining the waggon route from the U. States, *via* South Pass.)

The Sacramento, measured by its windings, is about eight hundred and fifty miles in length. It receives many important auxiliaries above the junction of its two forks, which greatly increase the volume and depth of its waters. From its mouth it is said to afford a good stage of navigation for crafts of tolerable burthen, as high up as three hundred miles,—tide water setting back for one hundred and fifty miles.

Three other rivers, flowing from the southeast, have their discharge in the Bay of San Francisco. These streams are severally called the Rio del Plumas, American Fork, and Tulare.

The former derives its name from the great abundance of water-fowls which congregate upon it at all seasons of the year, so numerous and tame that the natives not unfrequently kill large quantities of them with clubs or stones as they fly through the air.

The del Plumas is said to be navigable, for boats of a light draught, till within a hundred miles of its head,—its whole length is about two hundred and fifty miles. The American Fork, or the Rio de los Americanos, is a clear and beautiful stream about one hundred and fifty miles long, emptying into the Sacramento Bay below the del Plumas, and between it and the Tulare. Owing to frequent rapids, however, its navigation is destroyed.

The Tulare is said to be four hundred miles long, and navigable for one half that distance. It is represented as watering one of the most interesting sections of Western California, and hence is considered next in importance to the Sacramento. This stream affords some of the finest localities for settlements found in the whole country.

Below the Bay of San Francisco several other small streams find their way into the Pacific, but none of them are navigable to any great extent. The principal of these empty as follows: into the Bay of Monterey, into the Ocean near Point del Esteros, Point Arguello, St. Barbara Channel, San Pedro Bay, and opposite the island of St. Clement.

Above the Bay of San Francisco, Russian river is discharged into Bodega Bay; further on, Smith's river empties into Trinidad Bay; and two other small streams find their discharge near Point St. George, a few miles below the boundary line between Oregon and California.

Smith's river is the largest stream either above or below the Bay of San Francisco, and is about two hundred miles in length, though unnavigable.

All these various rivers and their affluents are stored with innumerable supplies of delicious fish, the principal of which are salmon and salmon-trout. The Ocean too affords an exhaustless quantity of the piscatorial

## SOIL, CLIMATE, ETC.

family, including whales, cod, and haddock, with oysters, clams, lobsters, &c.

So great is the abundance of fish at certain seasons, that, with a rude seine, the natives frequently take fifteen or twenty barrels full at a single draught; fish constituting their principal subsistence.

There are few, if any, countries in the world possessed of superior commercial advantages to the western section of Upper California.

True, its inland navigation is limited; yet, with an extent of nearly eight hundred miles of sea-coast, accessible at almost any point, it includes some of the finest bays and harbors ever known. Of these, for commodiousness and safety at all times, the Bay of San Francisco stands pre-eminently conspicuous.

This bay is an arm of the sea extending some forty miles or more inland, shut in, for the most part, upon each side by precipitous banks of basalt and trap, that skirt a very broken and hilly country contiguous to it. The entrance from the ocean is by an opening, a mile or more in width, through rock-formed walls, between one and two hundred feet high. A recent traveller,* in describing this bay, says:—

"From the points forming the entrance, the sea gradually expands to some eight or ten miles in extent, from north to south, and twelve from east to west. At the extreme eastern part of the vast basin thus formed, its shores again close in abruptly, contracting so as to leave a pass of about two miles in width, which forms the entrance to a second bay of still larger dimensions. From this gorge their high rocky banks again diverge for some ten miles, when they still again contract to the narrow space of one mile, and form the passage to a third. The latter is more spacious than either before mentioned, and, formed in like manner, extends twelve miles from east to west and fifteen from north to south, affording the safest and most commodious anchorage."

There is ample water at all times for the entrance of ships of the largest class, and it is asserted confidently, that these three united bays would afford perfect safety, secure anchorage, and ample room for the fleets and navies of all nations.

Several other bays and harbors are situated along the coast, all of which, to a greater or less extent, are favorably spoken of for general safety and good anchorage.

Among the above are mentioned the Bay of Monterey, San Pedro, St. Diego, Bodega, and Trinidad. Bodega, however, is represented as being, at times, very unsafe and even dangerous.

With such extraordinary facilities for commerce, it needs no prophetic eye to forsee the position Western California is destined to assume, before many years have passed, and, from her position and natural resources, will be enabled successfully to maintain among the foremost nations of the earth—provided, always, that some other people more enterprising and enlightened than the present inert, ignorant, stupid, and mongrel race infesting it with their presence, take possession of the country, develop its energies and bring to light the full beauty of its natural lovliness.

We are now led to speak of the peculiarities of soil, landscape, scenery

* Hastings.

climate, productions, and mineral resources of this interesting country, and in so doing, I would first draw a succinct view of the territory lying between the Rio Sacramento and Oregon.

Here we find the most forbidding aspect, with one exception, of any in Western California. The soil is generally very dry and barren, and the face of the country broken and hilly. The streams of water (as in the Eastern Division) frequently sink and become lost in the sand, or force themselves into the Ocean and parent streams by percolation or subterranean passages.

In many places is presented a surface of white sun-baked clay, entirely destitute of vegetation; and in others, wide spreads of sand, alike denuded; and yet again iron-bound superfices of igneous rock.

Now and then groves of pines or firs spread their broad branches as it were to cover the nakedness of nature; while here and there a valley of greater or less extent smiles amid the surrounding desolation.

All the various streams are skirted with bottoms of arable soil, ofttimes not only large but very fertile, though perhaps unadapted to cultivation, on account of their dryness, without a resort to irrigation.

Smith's river pursues its way, for forty or fifty miles, through a wide bottom of rich soil, most admirably suited for agricultural purposes were it not for its innate aridity;—however, during the summer season, it is, to a limited extent, watered from nightly dews, which enable it to sustain a luxuriant vegetation.

Not one fourth part of the northwestern portion of this section is fit for tillage. That part contiguous to the sea-coast is sandy and far less broken than those sections less interior.

The Tlameth Mountains, pursuing a west-southwest course from Oregon, strike the coast near lat. 41° north. This range has several lofty peaks covered with perpetual snow, and shoots its collateral eminences far into the adjacent prairies.

There is one feasible pass through this chain a few miles inland from the coast, that serves well for the purpose of intercommunication with Oregon.

The less elevated parts of these mountains are frequently covered with groves of small timber and openings of grass suitable for pasturage, while intermingled with them are occasional valleys and *prairillons* of diminutive space, favorable to the growth of grain and vegetables. The same may be said in reference to the California chain for its whole extent, especially in the vicinity of the prairie.

Following the course of this latter ridge from north to south, we find upon both sides a reach of very broken and highly tumulous landscape, some twenty or thirty miles broad.

Near the head-waters of the Sacramento, these lands are well watered and possess a general character for fertility, producing a variety of grass, with shrubs and a few scattering trees. Below, however, they are more sterile, owing to the deficiency of water; but yet they afford numerous inviting spots.

A considerable extent of country, south of the South Fork of the river above named, is arid and sterile, and has but few streams of water. It sustains, however, among its hills and in its valleys, a sparse vegetation that might be turned to a favorable account for grazing purposes. Only about one fourth of this country is adapted to other uses than stock-raising.

Further south from the head-waters of the Tulare and del Plumas, ranging between the coast and the high rolling lands skirting the base of the California Mountains to the boundary of the Lower Province, a section of gently undulating prairie, now and then varied with high hills and sometimes mountains, affords a rich soil, generally consisting of dark, sandy loam, between the hills and in the valleys; the highlands present a superfice of clay and gravel, fertilized by decomposed vegetable matter, well adapted to grazing, and about one half of it susceptible of cultivation.

Timber is rather scarce, except at intervals along the watercourses and occasional groves among the hills; but along the coast dense forests are frequently found claiming trees of an enormous size.

But, one grand defect exists in its general aridity, which renders necessary a resort to frequent irrigation in the raising of other than grain products. In some parts, the abundance of small streams would cause this task to become comparatively an easy one; and the profuseness of dews in sections contiguous to the rivers in some measure answers as a substitute for rain.

The bottoms are broad and extensive, yielding not only the most extraordinary crops of clover and other grasses, but incalculable quantities of wild oats and flax of spontaneous growth, with all the wild fruits natural to the climate.

In returning to the Sacramento and the rivers which find their discharges in the Bay of San Francisco, we have before us the most interesting and lovely part of Upper California.

The largest valley in the whole country is that skirting the Sacramento and lateral streams. This beautiful expanse leads inland from the Bay of San Francisco for nearly four hundred miles, almost to the base of the California Mountains, and averages between sixty and sixty-five miles in width.

The valleys of the del Plumas and American Fork are also very large, and that of the Tulare gives an area of two hundred and fifty miles long by thirty-five broad.

These valleys are comparatively well timbered with several varieties of wood, consisting principally of white-oak, live-oak, ash, cottonwood, cherry, and willow, while the adjacent hills afford occasional forests of pine, cedar, fir, pinion, and spruce.

The soil as well as the climate is well adapted to the cultivation of all kinds of grain and vegetables produced in the United States, and many of the varied fruits of the torrid and temperate zones can be successfully reared in one and the same latitude.

Among the grains, grasses, and fruits indigenous to the country are wheat, rye, oats, flax, and clover, (white and red,) with a great variety of grapes, all of which are said to grow spontaneously.

Wild oats frequently cover immense spreads of bottom and prairie land, sometimes to an extent of several thousand acres, which resemble in appearance the species common to the United States. They usually grow to a height of between two and three feet, though they often reach a height of seven feet.

The wild clover of these valleys is much like the common red, and, in some places, is afforded in great abundance. It attains a usual height of two feet and a half, though it often measures twice that height—standing as thick as it can well grow.

Forty bushels per acre is said to be the average wheat crop, but sixty and even one hundred bushels have been grown upon a like spot of ground. This grain generally reaches its maturity in three or four months from the time of sowing.

Corn yields well, and affords an average of from fifty to sixty bushels per acre, without farther attention from the time of planting till picking. Potatoes, onions, beets, carrots, &c., may be produced in any quantity with very little trouble. Tobacco has also been raised by some of the inhabitants with most flattering success.

Perhaps, no country in the world is possessed of a richer or more fruitful soil, or one capable of yielding a greater variety of productions, than the valleys of the Sacramento and its tributaries.

The articles previously noticed are more or less common to the bottoms and valleys of other sections. Grapes abound in the vicinity of most of the creeks, which afford generous wines and delicious raisins in immense quantities.

The climate is so mild that fires are needed at no season of the year for other than cooking purposes. By aid of irrigation, many kinds of vegetables are fresh-grown at any time, while two crops of some species of grain may be produced annually.

Flowers are not unfrequently in full bloom in mid winter, and all nature bears a like smiling aspect. In this, however, we of course refer only to the low-lands and valleys.

The traveller at any season of the year may visit at his option the frosts and snows of eternal winter, or feast his eyes upon the verdure and beauty of perennial spring, or glut his taste amid the luxuriant abundance and rich maturity of unending summer, or indulge his changeful fancy in the enjoyment of a magnificent variety of scenery as well as of climate, soil, and productions.

The only rains incident to this country fall during the months of December, January, February, and March, which constitute the winter; at other times rain is very rarely known to fall. Perhaps, for one third of the four months before named, the clouds pour down their torrents without intermission; the remaining two thirds afford clear and delightful weather.

During the wet season the ground in many parts becomes so thoroughly saturated with moisture, particularly in the valley of the Sacramento, that, by the aid of copious dews to which the country is subject, crops may be raised without the trouble of irrigation; though its general aridity constitutes the greatest objection to California.

Of its geological and mineralogical character little is yet known. The prevailing rock is said to be sandstone, mica slate, granite, trap, basalt, puddingstone, and limestone, with occasional beds of gypsum. Among its minerals as commonly reported, are found gold, silver, iron, coal, and a variety of salts. The mineral resources of the country have not been as yet fully investigated to any great extent, but the mountains, in different parts, are supposed to be rich in hidden stores.

To speak of Western California as a whole, it may be pronounced hilly, if not mountainous, and about two thirds of it is probably fit for agricultural purposes.

The creeks are frequently immured by precipitous walls of several hundred feet in altitude, that, expanding here and there, give place to beautiful valleys of variable width, while most of the low-lands upon their banks are skirted by continuous and abrupt acclivities leading to the high prairies, table lands, and mountains contiguous to them. Their currents are generally clear and rapid, flowing over beds of sand, pebbles, and rock, and afford wholesome and delicious water.

The air is almost invariably pure and free from the noxious exhalations common to many countries, which contributes greatly to render the climate uniformly healthy—a character which it has hitherto sustained by common report.

Some travellers, however, speak of large Indian villages in different parts, deserted and in ruins, whose sites are bestrown with human bones and sculls, as if the entire population had been swept off by the frightful ravages of deadly pestilence, and so suddenly that not a soul was left to bury their dead; and hence they suppose the country occasionally subject to devastating sicknesses. The above, however, may with equal propriety be charged to the account of war.

Game is quite plentiful in the Western Division of Upper California, and in many places extremely abundant, especially in the mountains near the head-waters of the Tulare and Sacramento rivers.

Among the different varieties are enumerated deer, (black-tailed and white-tailed,) elk, antelope, goats, bear, (black, red, and grizzly,) beaver, geese, brants, ducks, and grouse, with wild horses and cattle;—buffalo are unknown to the Province.

Never was a country better adapted to stock-raising than is this, and perhaps none, according to the number of its inhabitants, so abundantly supplied with horses, cattle, and sheep. The former of these abound in countless numbers, whenever a white man or a Spanio-Mexican makes it his residence. A single individual frequently owns from eight to ten thousand head of horses and mules; and, not rarely, even as high as fifteen or twenty thousand.

These animals are very hardy and trim-built, and only a trifle smaller than those common to the United States. I have seen many of them equally as large as the American breed, and, as a general thing, they are more durable under fatigue and hardship.

The choicest animals from a band of several thousand may be purchased for ten dollars, and the ordinary price for prime selections ranges from three to five dollars, while mares may be procured for two dollars per head.

Cattle are equally plenty, at prices varying from two to four dollars per head.

Stock is raised without trouble, as the abundance of grass affords pasturage the entire season, nor is necessary a resort to either hay or house. In fact, both cattle and horses not only thrive best but are fattest in the winter season, owing to the absence of flies and insects, as well as the partial freshness of vegetation.

The common method of stock-raising is by turning them loose into the bottoms and prairies, accompanied by a herdsman, or two, or more, *a la Mexican*, (according to the size of the band,) where they are left to increase, and no further care is bestowed upon them.

Sheep too are raised in vast numbers after the above manner. They increase with astonishing rapidity, and usually produce their young twice a year. Their wool, however, is much coarser than that grown in the United States. This latter fact is accounted for by their inferiority of breed, though their flesh is sweeter and better than the American mutton.

Wolves are said to be numerous and troublesome, and not unfrequently prove a source of great annoyance to the inhabitants by destroying their sheep, calves, colts, and even full-grown cattle and horses.

Among them are included the black, gray, and prairie wolf. The black wolf is the largest and most ferocious, equalling the size of our common cur-dog.

Foxes are also said to be numerous, but are of a diminutive size. The above are the only beasts of prey worth naming.

The foregoing summary leads us to notice the present state of the country, its inhabitants, government, and military strength.

Upper California at the present time is in the united possession of the Indians, Mexicans, English, and French; not as rulers, but as land-holders and inhabitants.

The Indians are supposed to number some thirty or forty thousand souls, and are scattered over the entire Province. Excepting the Diggers, the Utahs, the Snakes, and those residing in the vicinity of the Sierra Nevada and the Tlameth Mountains, they are quite similar in character and condition to those noticed as being residents of the Gila and adjacent regions.

They are mild and timorous, and incapable of opposing any very serious impediment to the progress of settlements. Fifteen Americans, armed with good rifles, are equal to one or two hundred of such enemies in ordinary cases.

The Catholics have twenty or more missions among them, the effect of which has been not so much to advance their civilization, or convert them to the truths of Christianity, as to render them the *slaves* of a corrupt and vicious priesthood.

Monterey is the present capital of Upper California. It is beautifully situated upon a gently undulating plain, in full view of the Ocean and harbor, and contains about one thousand inhabitants. Its houses are constructed of *adobies*, after the Mexican fashion.

South of this town are several other places of considerable importance along the coast, viz: San Diego, San Gabriel, and San Barbara; all of which are well located for commercial purposes.

A town called the Pueblo is situated upon a small river that debouches between San Diego and San Gabriel. This town is a few miles removed from the coast, and is said to be the largest one in California. It contains a population of about fifteen hundred, and is the grand centripot of overland intercourse with New Mexico.

Above Monterey are two other towns, bearing the names of Sonoma and San Francisco.

MEXICAN INDIANS. — *Page 246.*

The latter is situated upon the bay of that name, and, from its superior commercial advantages, is destined to become one of the largest and most important business cities upon the western coast of the American continent. Possessed of one of the finest and most commodious harbors in the world, (emphatically the harbor of harbors,) and located at the mouth of a large navigable river, that waters a vast expanse of country unsurpassed in fertility, what should hinder it from assuming that commanding position designed for it by nature?

It is built after the English manner, and its inhabitants, numbering about two hundred, are principally American, English, and French, with a few Mexicans and Indians.

There are also several settlements upon the Sacramento and other rivers, consisting mostly of foreigners.

The Catholic missions are generally the *nucleus* of small Mexican and Indian villages, and derive their support from agricultural pursuits.

Aside from these, the country is entirely devoid of population other than wild beasts and uncultivated savages. The white inhabitants are computed at one thousand or more, and are generally Americans; while between ten and twelve thousand Mexicans curse the country with their presence, and disgrace the Edens they possess.

The government of California has been, like all Mexican governments, very lax and inefficient. It was but little other than a despotism, or, rather, *a complicated machine for the oppression of the people and the perversion of justice!* and infinitely worse than none.

Whether the late revolution has produced a better order of things remains to be determined; but, one fact is worthy of notice—no *permanent* reformation can be effected so long as Mexicans exercise any controlling influence in the administration of the laws; and, to speak plainly, not until the government is placed in other and better hands.

The Mexicans occupy eight military stations at different points along the coast, garrisoned by about three hundred and fifty soldiers, and mounting some fifty pieces of artillery. The largest of these fortifications is at Monterey. This post is garrisoned by two hundred soldiers, and twelve pieces of canon—while the fort at New Helvetia, *held by the Americans*, mounts an equal number.

In case of an emergency, it is supposed the whole Mexican force might possibly amount to between ten and eleven hundred men—in efficiency nearly equal to a party of one hundred and fifty well-armed Americans.

It will be seen at a mere glance, that Mexico *cannot* maintain her hold upon California for many years to come. Emigrants from the United States and other countries, attracted by its fertile soil and healthful climate, will continue to pour into it with increased ratio, until, by outnumbering the degraded race that at present bears sway, this delightful portion of the globe shall of necessity become either the dependency of some foreign power or assume a separate and distinct existence as an independent nation.

## CHAPTER XXIV.

Visitors at Uintah.—Adventures of a trapping party.—The Munchies, or white Indians; some account of them.—Amusements at rendezvous.—Mysterious city, and attempts at its exploration,—speculation relative to its inhabitants.—Leave for Fort Hall.—Camp at Bear river.—Boundary between the U. States and Mexico.—Green valleys, &c.—Country en route.—Brown's-hole.—Geological observations.—Soda, Beer, and Steamboat springs; their peculiarities.—Minerals.—Valley of Bear river; its fertility, timber, and abundance of wild fruit.—Buffalo berries—Superior advantages of this section.—Mineral tar.

Our stay at the Uintah was prolonged for some ten days. The gentleman in charge at this post spared no pains to render my visit agreeable, and, in answer to enquiries, cheerfully imparted all the information in his possession relative to the localities, geography, and condition of the surrounding country.

A trapping party from the Gila came in soon after our arrival, bringing with them a rich quantity of beaver, which they had caught during the preceding winter, spring, and summer upon the affluents of that river and the adjacent mountain streams. They had made a successful hunt, and gave a glowing description of the country visited, and the general friendliness of its inhabitants.

The natives, in some parts of their range, had never before seen a white man, and, after the first surprise had subsided, treated them with great deference and respect. These simple and hospitable people supplied them with corn, beans, and melons, and seemed at all times well disposed.

The only difficulty encountered with them took place upon one of the northern tributaries of the Gila. Two or three butcher-knives and other little articles being missing from camp, the trappers at once accused the Indians of stealing, and demanded their prompt restoration. The latter they were either unable or unwilling to do, and thereupon a volley of riflery was discharged among the promiscuous throng, with fatal effect. Several were killed and others wounded, and the whole troop of timorous savages immediately took to their heels, nor dared to return again.

In narrating the events of their long excursion, an account was given of visiting the Munchies, a tribe of *white Indians*.

What added much to the interest I felt in this part of their story, was the recollection of an article which went the newspaper rounds several years since, stating the existence of such a tribe. I had disbelieved it at the time; but this, and subsequent corroborative evidence, has effectually removed from my mind all doubts upon the subject.

Our trappers had remained with the Munchies for four weeks, and spoke of them in high terms.

In reference to their color they were represented as being of a much fairer complexion than Europeans generally, a thing easily explained if we remember this one fact, i. e., my informants must have spoken comparatively, taking themselves as the true representatives of that race, when in reality their own color, by constant exposure to the weather, had acquired a much darker hue than ordinary; then drawing their conclusions from a false standard, they were led to pronounce the fair natives much fairer, as a body, than the whites.

By information derived from various sources, I am enabled to present the following statement relative to this interesting people:

The Munchies are a nation of *white aborigines*, actually existing in a valley among the Sierra de los Mimbros chain, upon one of the affluents of the Gila, in the extreme northwestern part of the Province of Sonora.

They number about eight hundred in all. Their country is surrounded by lofty mountains at nearly every point, and is well watered and very fertile, though of limited extent. Their dwellings are spacious apartments nicely excavated in the hill-sides, and are frequently cut in the solid rock.

They subsist by agriculture, and raise cattle, horses, and sheep. Their features correspond with those of Europeans, though with a complexion, perhaps, somewhat fairer, and a form equally if not more graceful.

Among them are many of the arts and comforts of civilized life. They spin and weave, and manufacture butter and cheese, with many of the luxuries known to more enlightened nations.

Their political economy, though much after the patriarchal order, is purely republican in its character. The old men exercise the supreme control in the enactment and execution of laws. These laws are usually of the most simple form, and tend to promote the general welfare of the community. They are made by a concurrent majority of the seniors in council,—each male individual, over a specified age, being allowed a voice and a vote.

Questions of right and wrong are heard and adjudged by a committee selected from the council of seniors, who are likewise empowered to redress the injured and pass sentence upon the criminal.

In morals they are represented as honest and virtuous. In religion they differ but little from other Indians.

They are strictly men of peace, and never go to war, nor even, as a common thing, oppose resistance to the hostile incursions of surrounding nations. On the appearance of an enemy, they immediately retreat, with their cattle, horses, sheep, and other valuables, to mountain caverns, fitted at all times for their reception,—where, by barricading the entrances, they are at once secure without a resort to arms.

In regard to their origin they have lost all knowledge or even tradition, (a thing not likely to have happened had they been the progeny of Europeans at any late period,—that is, since the time of Columbus;) neither do their characters, manners, customs, arts, or government savor of modern Europe.

Could a colony or party of Europeans in the short period of three centuries and a half lose all trace of their origin, religion, habits, arts, civilization, and government? Who, for a moment, would entertain an idea so estranged to probability?

And yet the Munchies cannot be real Indians,—they must be of European descent, though circumstances other than complexion afford no evidence of identity with either race. Where, then, shall we place them?—from whence is there origin?

We are forced to admit the weight of circumstantial testimony as to their having settled upon this continent prior to its discovery by Columbus. Here we are led to inquire, are they not the remote descendants of some colony of ancient Romans?

That such colonies did here exist in former ages, there is good reason for believing. The great lapse of time and other operative causes combined, may have transformed the Munchies from the habits, customs, character, religion, arts, civilization, and language of the Romans, to the condition in which they are at present found.

Among the visitors at the Fort were several old trappers who had passed fifteen or twenty years in the Rocky Mountains and neighboring countries. They were what might, with propriety, be termed "hard cases."

The interval of their stay was occupied in gambling, horse-racing, and other like amusements.

Bets were freely made upon everything involving the least doubt,—sometimes to the amount of five hundred or a thousand dollars—the stakes consisting of beaver, horses, traps, &c.

Not unfrequently the proceeds of months of toil, suffering, deprivation, and danger, were dissipated in a few hours, and the unfortunate gamester left without beaver, horse, trap, or even a gun. In such cases they bore their reverses without grumbling, and relinquished all to the winner, as unconcernedly as though these were affairs of every-day occurrence.

These veterans of the mountains were very communicative, and fond of relating their adventures, many of which were so vested with the marvelous as to involve in doubt their credibility.

Were it not for extending the limits of this work too far, I should be tempted to transcribe the choicest of them for the reader's amusement; but, as it is, I cannot refuse place to one (here for the first time related in my hearing, which has subsequently reached me from other sources) relative to a subject deeply interesting to the curious.

Stevens, in his "Incidents of Travel in Yucatan," admits it to be quite possible that cities like those in ruins at Uxmal and Palenque, may yet exist in the unexplored parts of the Mexican Republic, and be inhabited by a people in all respects similar to that once occupying the before named.

Those acquainted with the nature of the country embraced in the mountainous portions of Mexico, must admit the possibility of such a thing. With this premise I give, the story as I heard it.

Five or six years since, a party of trappers, in search for beaver, penetrated into an unfrequented part of the mountains forming the eastern boundary of Sonora.

During their excursion they ascended a lofty peak that overlooked an extensive valley, apparently enclosed upon all sides by impassable mountains. At a long distance down the valley, by aid of a spy-glass, they could plainly distinguish houses and people, with every indication of a populous city.

At the point from whence this discovery was made, the mountain-side facing the valley was a precipitous wall of vertical rock, several hundred feet to its base, rendering a descent impossible.

After trying at other places, with like ill-success, they were at length compelled to relinquish the design of further investigation for the time being.

Subsequently, on visiting Arispie, a town of Sonora, several foreigners were induced to join them in a return expedition, and a company of some twenty or twenty-five repaired to the place for the purpose of prosecuting a research so interesting.

On arriving at the mountain from whence the object of their curiosity had been first seen, there lay before them the valley and city with its domes and palaces, amid which a swarming population was distinctly observed, apparently engaged in the prosecution of their various avocations. There could be no doubt of its reality, but how to reach it was the next question.

A number of days were occupied in vain search for a pass into the valley. The creek upon which it lay was found to emerge from the vast enclosure, through the mountain, by a frightful chasm formed of vertical rocks upon each side, for hundreds and even thousands of feet in altitude. The current was rapid, and interrupted by frequent falls that precluded the possibility of a passage up its bed. They crossed it, and, finding a convenient slope, again ascended the mountain.

On reaching the summit, a counterscarp was observed, where, by dint of great exertion, a descent could be effected; but not with horses.

Arrangements were made accordingly, and one half of the party remained with the animals and baggage, while the others, continuing the exploration, finally succeeded in entering the valley.

Meanwhile, the movements of the advancing party were viewed with great anxiety by those in reserve. In the course of the succeeding day they were seen to enter the city and mingle among its inhabitants; but, after that, they were never again seen or heard of.

Three weeks elapsed and no sign of them appeared. At length their companions were forced by hunger to leave the spot and abandon them to their fate.

Another attempt to explore this mysterious locality is reported to have been made by a company of Spaniards, some of whom penetrated the valley, but never returned.

The site of this city, if the story of its existence be true, is undoubtedly the bed of an ancient lake, whose waters have become gradually drained by a forced passage through the mountain, thus forming the chasm and creek above noticed.

The people inhabiting it are probably from the stock of original Mexicans,[*] who sought this as a secure retreat from the terror of Spanish oppression

---

[*] Baron Humboldt and some other travellers speak of quite extensive ruins in the vicinity of the Gila, which are attributed to a different race of people from those now inhabiting that country, or even the ancient Mexicans. Some of them are represented as being in a tolerable state of preservation, particularly one, which is known as the "cassa grand." No reasonable conjecture as to their origin has yet been adduced. If they are not the ruined fabrics of ancient Mexican grandeur, to whom are we to look for their parentage?

The diversity of character between them and those of Uxmal, Palenque, and other

in the time of Cortez; since which their posterity have lived here unknown to the rest of the world.

Taught by the bitter experience of past ages to hate and distrust the white man, and still cherishing their traditionary animosity, they permit none of that race to return who visit them, and, from the peculiarity of their position and jealous caution, have successfully maintained an uninterrupted *in cog.*

Several trappers rendezvoused at the Uintah being about to leave for Fort Hall, on the head waters of the Columbia river, I improved the opportunity of bearing them company.

My necessary arrangements were completed simply by exchanging horses; and, on the morning of Oct. 29th, I bade farewell to my new acquaintances at the Fort, and joined the party *en route,* which, including myself and *compagnons de voyage* from Fort Lancaster, numbered eleven in all, well mounted and armed.

The weather proved delightful considering the lateness of the season, and our journey was rapid and uninterrupted.

On leaving the Uintah we continued northward, over a rough country, for some twenty-five miles, and passed the night at Ashley's Fork,* with a small village of Snake Indians.

Resuming our course through a mountainous region, diversified by beautiful little valleys, late in the afternoon of the third day we camped in the vicinity of Brown's-hole.

Bearing from thence a southwesterly course, two days afterwards we arrived at Bear river, and obtained, from an adjoining eminence, a distant view of the Great Salt Lake.

Continuing down the river a few miles, we struck camp, and remained some three days for the purpose of hunting.

Being unwilling to leave the vicinity without a more perfect observation of this vast inland sea, I improved the interval for that purpose, and, in a few hours' ride, came to a point which overlooked its briny waters and spread out before me an object of so much interest to all beholders.

Its whilom waves now lay slumbering upon its bosom, for not a breath of air stirred to awake them from their transient repose, save that caused

---

ruined cities of Central America, puzzles us still more; and, as the feeble ray of conjecture is the only source from whence light may be thrown upon this mysterious subject, we would prefer the suggestion, that the progenitors of the Munchies, or white Indians, might have been their builders; or, if the reported existence of the city of the mountains as stated in the text be true, might not the ancestors of the people now inhabiting it have had some hand in their original construction? But, if the latter be the case, and these relics are not the product of Mexican civilization, the question yet remains unanswered, viz: who are the residents of that city and whence is their origin?

* This stream is named in memory of Gen. Ashley, of Mo., who, while engaged in the fur trade, attempted to descend the Colorado in boats, thinking thus to reach St. Louis by a direct water communication! However, he was compelled to relinquish his strange enterprise at the mouth of this creek, on account of the difficulty and danger attendant upon a further progress.

by the flutterings of countless water-fowls which beskimmed the crystal blue or rode upon its surface.

No sound disturbed the stillness of its solitude, save that of my own footsteps commingling with the incessant chatter of aquatic birds. In solemn grandeur it lay before the eye a desert of waters, bounded upon three sides by the curving horizon, while from the fourth a beautiful expanse of verdancy smiled upon its solitude.

The island with its lone mountain, of which I have spoken in a former chapter, arose in full view, apparently a short distance to the southwest. It was a grand and imposing spectacle, and I much regretted the impossibility of reaching it. Its giant piles of naked rock and sun-baked clay, seemed scanning the surrounding waves, to smile upon their soft blandishments or frown at their rudeness.

But the Island, the Lake, and the country contiguous, have been fully described in former pages, which of right precludes a further notice at this time.

On resuming our course we continued up Bear river to the famous mineral springs,—thence bearing a northwesterly direction, we arrived at Fort Hall late in the afternoon of Nov. 9th.

The route from Uintah to this point presents many interesting localities some of which call for more than a mere passing notice. That situate upon Green river, known as Brown's-hole,* coming first in order, seems to assert a merited precedence.

Descending by a steep, difficult pass from the west, fifty miles north of Ashley's Fork, the traveller is ushered into a beautiful valley, some fifteen miles long by ten broad, shut in upon all sides by impassable mountains

---

* This locality has received the soubriquet of Brown's-hole from the following circumstance :

Some six or seven years since, a trapper, by the name of Brown, came to it in the fall season for the purpose of hunting in its vicinity. During his stay a fall of snow closed the passes so effectually, he was forced to remain till the succeeding spring before he could escape from his lonely prison.

It was formerly a favorite resort for the Snake Indians, on account of its exhaustless stores of game and wild fruits, as well as its security from the approach of enemies.

NOTE.—Taking latitude 42° north as the northern boundary between Oregon and California, these interesting regions of country are embraced within the limits of the latter; but taking the head-waters of the Arkansas as the true point, and thence, by a line running due west to the Pacific, nearly the whole of it will be found within the United States.

The treaty with Spain in 1819, defining this boundary, which was subsequently confirmed by Mexico, after noting Red river as the northern boundary of its eastern provinces, to longitude 100° west from Greenwich, and thence north to the Arkansas, uses the following words:

" Thence, following the course of the south bank of the Arkansas TO ITS SOURCE, in latitude 42° north, thence by that parallel of latitude to the South Sea."

If the source of the Arkansas, by its south bank, is in lat. 42° north, then the matter of boundary admits of no question; but if it is not in that parallel of latitude, should the latter be regarded as the true boundary, when it is evident, from the words of the treaty that the source of the Arkansas by its south bank, was the intended

that guard it from the world without. The only feasible entrance is upon the east side through a remarkable cañon sixty yards wide, formed by craggy rocks six or eight hundred feet in altitude, succeeded by a still narrower and more precipitous one, towering to a height of twelve or fifteen hundred feet.

This valley is intersected by Green river, which, emerging from the lofty ridges above, and tracing its way through the narrow and frightful cañons below, here presents a broad, smooth stream, fifty or sixty yards wide, with sloping banks, and passably well timbered.

Here all the various wild fruits indigenous to the country are found in great abundance, with countless multitudes of deer, elk, and sheep.

The soil is of a dark loam, very fertile and admirably adapted to cultivation. Vegetation attains a rank growth and continues green the entire year.

Spring wedded to summer seems to have chosen this sequestered spot for her fixed habitation, where, when dying autumn woos the sere frost and snow, of winter she may withdraw to her flower-garnished retreat and smile and bloom forever.

The surrounding mountains are from fifteen hundred to two thousand feet high, and present several peaks where snow claims an unyielding dominion year after year, in awful contrast with the beauty and loveliness that lies below.

Few localities in the mountains are equal to this, in point of beautiful and romantic scenery. Every thing embraced in its confines tends to inspire the beholder with commingled feelings of awe and admiration.

Its long, narrow gate-way, walled in by huge impending rocks, for hundreds of feet in altitude,—the lofty peaks that surround it, clothed in eternal snow,—the bold stream traversing it, whose heaving bosom pours sweet music into the ears of listening solitude,—the verdant lawn, spreading far and wide, garnished with blushing wild-flowers and arrayed in the habiliments of perennial spring,—all, all combine to invest it with an enchantment as soul-expanding in its sublimity as it is fascinating in its loveliness.

The country contiguous to Bear river, back from the valleys, is generally rugged and sterile. Sometimes the surface for a considerable extent is entirely destitute of vegetation, and presents a dreary waste of rocks, or clay hardened to a stone-like consistency by the sun's rays. Now and then a few dwarfish pines and cedars meet the eye amid the surrounding desolation, and occasional clusters of coarse grass intervene at favoring depressions among the rocks.

FARTHEST northern extremity of Mexico, where the line between the two countries shall commence, and thence run due west to the Pacific?

But, instead of being in lat. 42° north, the source of the Arkansas is in lat. 39° north, as indisputably ascertained from recent explorations, and thus an interval of three degrees occurs between the two points named in the above treaty!

If the United States are obligated by this treaty to receive the 42d degree as their southern boundary, Mexico is equally obligated to receive the parallel from the source of the Arkansas due west to the Pacific, as her true northern limits; thus, a territory of eleven hundred and twenty-five miles from east to west, and nearly one hundred and forty from north to south, is left unowned by either party!

The landscape, as a whole, possesses a savage wildness peculiar to itself, and bears strong indications of volcanic action. The mountains are not so high as those of other parts, but are far more forbidding in their aspect. The prevailing rock is lava, scoriated basalt, trap, bituminous limestone, and calcareous tufa.

The valley of Bear river affords a number of springs strongly impregnated with various mineral properties, which cannot fail to excite the curiosity and interest of the traveller. They are found upon the left bank of the stream, a short distance below a small affluent from the north.

Two of them are situated in a small grove of cedars, within a short distance of each other.

In passing their vicinity the attention of the traveller is at once arrested by the hissing noise they emit; and on approaching to ascertain the cause, he finds two circular-shaped openings in the surface, several feet in diameter, and filled with transparent fluid in a state of incessant effervescence, caused by the action of subterranean gases.

The water of the one he finds on tasting to be excellent *natural soda*, and that of the other, slightly acid and beer-like;—the draught will prove delicious and somewhat stimulating, but, if repeated too freely, it is said to produce a kind of giddiness like intoxication. These singular natural curiosities are known among the trappers as the Beer and Soda springs, names not altogether inappropriate.

A few hundred yards below these, is another remarkable curiosity, called the Steamboat spring. This discharges a column of mineral water from a rock-formed orifice, accompanied with subterraneous sounds like those produced by a high-pressure steamboat.

Besides the above-described, there are a number of others in this vicinity of equally mineral character, as well as several hot springs, varying in temperature from blood to that of extreme boiling heat.

Bear river valley contains many wide spreads of most excellent land, susceptible of a high state of cultivation. In fertility it is unsurpassed, and varies in width from one and a half to three miles.

The stream is not heavily timbered, but the scattering groves of pine and cedar among the adjoining mountains partially atone for any apparent deficiency.

Towards its head, the hills upon either side are less rugged and barren, and present more frequent intervals of verdancy.

I noticed a large number of fruit-bearing shrubs and bushes, including cherry, service, goose, and buffalo-berries, (two kinds,) with currants.

The bushes of the buffalo-berry were not as yet entirely divested of their delicious burthen, and afforded a new variety of that fruit hitherto not having come under my observation.

This berry is about the size of and similar in shape to the common currant. There are three kinds,—the white, yellow, and red, (*shepherdia argentia*.)

The red is of a slightly tartish taste, but not unpleasant; the yellow is somewhat less acid, but otherwise similar to the red; the white, however, is most excellent tasted, and possesses a delicious sweetness which causes it to be highly relished.

This fruit has several small seeds in it, like those of the whortleberry, and grows upon a bush in shape and size quite like the common shrub-oak.

It produces in such immense quantities, that the parent bush is not unfrequently flattened with its superincumbent weight.

The grizzly bear delights to revel among the thickets of this his favorite berry, and is almost certain to make from it his last autumn meal ere he retires to winter quarters and commences the long fast that follows.

The valley of Bear river presents to emigrants many advantages. Possessed not only of a rich soil, well adapted to cultivation, and vast mineral resources, with natural curiosities that must ever make it a central point of attraction, but situated in the immediate vicinity of the prospective population of the Great Salt Lake and upon the the direct line of over-land intercourse between the United States, California, and Oregon, it must command for its future inhabitants a sure source of prosperity and wealth.

There is little doubt of its eventually becoming the most important section of Southeastern Oregon.

In descanting upon the natural curiosities of this valley, the trappers accompanying me spoke of a spring further to the northward, which constantly emits a small stream of mineral tar, from the mountain-side, in no respect inferior to the manufactured article. However, I am not certain in regard to the locality of this interesting phenomenon.

## CHAPTER XXV.

Fort Hall; its history, and locality.—Information relative to Oregon.—Boundaries and extent of the territory.—Its rivers and lakes, with a concise description of them severally.—Abundance and variety of fish and water-fowl.—Harbors and islands.—Oregon as a whole; its mountains and geographical divisions.—Eastern Division; its wild scenery, valleys, soil, and timber; volcanic ravages; country between Clarke's river and the Columbia.—North of the Columbia; its general character.—Middle Division; its valleys, prairies, highlands, and forests.—Western Division; a beautiful country; extensive valleys of extraordinary fertility; productive plains; abundance of timber, its astonishing size and variety.—A brief summary of facts.

Our journey from the Uintah to Fort Hall occupied twelve days, and took us a distance of about two hundred miles. Most of this time the weather continued mild and pleasant; the only interval of inclemency was a single bleak and cloudy day, succeeded by a slight fall of snow during the night, which the bright sunshine of the ensuing morning dissipated in a few moments.

Along the entire route we found an abundance of green grass at sheltered places in the valleys, and also large quantities of game, especially black-tailed deer, bear, and elk. Bear are more numerous in this section than in any other I am acquainted with.

Fort Hall is located upon the left bank of Snake river, or Lewis' Fork of the Columbia, in a rich bottom near the *delta* formed by the confluence of the Portneuf with that stream, in lat. 43° 10′ 30″ north, long. 112° 20′ 54 west.

In general structure it corresponds with most of the other trading establishments in the country. It was built by Capt. Wythe of Boston, in 1832, for the purpose of furnishing trappers with their needful supplies in exchange for beaver and other peltries, and also to command the trade with the Snakes. Subsequently it was transferred to the Hudson Bay Company in whose possession it has since remained.

Mr. Grant, a gentleman distinguished for his kindness and urbanity, is at present in charge, and has some sixty Canadians and half-breeds in his employ.

This post is in the immediate vicinity of the old war-ground between the Blackfoot, Snake, and Crow Indians, and was formerly considered a very dangerous locality on that account. Its early occupants were subject to frequent losses from the hostile incursions of the former of these tribes, and on two or three occasions came very near being burnt out * by their unsparing enemies.

The country in the neighborhood of Fort Hall affords several extensive valleys upon the Snake river and its tributaries, which are rich, well timtimbered, and admirably adapted to the growth of grain and vegetables.

The adjoining prairies also, to some extent, possess a tolerable soil, and abound in a choice variety of grasses. Back from the valleys and plains, the landscape is extremely rugged and mountainous, poorly timbered, and bears the character of general sterility.

My stay at the Fort brought me in contact with gentlemen from various parts of Oregon, who kindly imparted to me all the information in their possession relative to the nature and true condition of this interesting and highly important section of our national domain. With the data thus obtained, assisted by subsequent personal observation and intelligence derived from other sources, I am enabled to arrange the following brief outlines of its geography, geology, climate, and soil, including a description of its productions, inhabitants, natural advantages, inducements to emigrants, &c., which the reader may rely upon as strictly correct in every essential particular.

With the northern extremity of Bear river valley, the traveller enters the southeastern limits of Oregon Territory. By referring to the map it will be seen that this country is bounded upon the north † by the British and Russian possessions, east by the Rocky Mountains, south by Upper California, and west by the Pacific. It is not my present purpose to argue, or endeavor to sustain, the claims of our Government to the whole area embraced in the above; but conceiving the matter now settled, I shall proceed to the task in in hand without further preliminary.

Oregon, like California, is possessed of many important rivers and har-

---

* A portion of the Fort was formerly constructed of wood;—it is now built of "adobies" like other trading establishments of the country.

† The treaty now in process of negotiation with Great Britain, relinquishes to that government all above the 49th deg., and consequently admits its claims to the entire northern boundary, to wit: from 49° to the Russian possessions.

bors, that, considering their intimate relation to the general interest of commerce, seem to demand our first attention.

The Columbia and its branches water almost the entire territory, and open a highway from the ocean to the lofty mountain ranges which form its eastern boundary. This river heads in lat. 52° north, long. 119° west from Greenwich, and, after pursuing a serpentine course for fifteen hundred or two thousand miles, finds its discharge in the Pacific, at lat. 46° north.

One hundred and twenty miles of this distance are navigable for ships of the largest class, but the remainder of its course is interrupted by occasional rapids and falls, that render frequent portages necessary.

The upper and lower "dalls" and "cascades," present the most serious impediments to navigation. The former of these, situated above Clarke's Fork, are caused by the passage of the Columbia through immense ledges, that leave huge vertical walls of basaltic rock upon either side, and compress its waters to a narrow, chasm-like channel. There, dashing and foaming in wild fury, the torrent rushes past its lateral dikes with frightful velocity.

The distance between these two "dalls" is some thirty miles.

The "cascades" lie at the base of a mountain range of the same name, one hundred and fifty miles from the Ocean. Near this place the whole stream is plunged over a precipice of fifty feet descent, forming a sublime and magnificent spectacle.

Between the dalls and cascades, a reach of high-lands, formed almost entirely of naked basalt, presents another barrier, through which the river forces itself by a tunnel-like pass for ten or fifteen miles, leaving vast mural piles upon the right and left, that attain an altitude of three hundred and fifty or four hundred feet.

A few miles above the junction of the southern and middle forks of the Columbia, two considerable lakes have been formed by the compressure of its waters among the adjoining mountains.

The first of these is about twenty miles long and six broad, shut in by high, towering hills, covered with stately pine forests.

Emerging from this, the river urges its way through lofty embankments of volcanic rock for some five miles or more, when a second lake is formed in a similar manner, which is about twenty-five miles in length and six in width.

NOTE.—Capt. Fremont, in speaking of the Columbia, makes use of the following just observations:

"The Columbia is the only river which traverses the whole breadth of the country, breaking through all the ranges, and entering into the sea. Drawing its waters from a section of ten degrees of latitude in the Rocky Mountains, which are collected into one stream by three main forks (Lewis', Clarke's, and the North Fork) near the centre of the Oregon valley, this great river thence proceeds by a single channel into the sea, while its three forks lead each to a pass in the mountains, which opens the way into the interior of the continent.

"This fact, in reference to the rivers of this region, gives an immense value to the Columbia. Its mouth is the only inlet and outlet to and from the sea; its three forks lead to passes in the mountains; it is, therefore, the only line of communication between the Pacific and the interior of North America; and all operations of war or commerce, of national or social intercourse, must be conducted upon it."

## OTHER RIVERS OF THE TERRITORY. 261

There are also several other lakes, of greater or less extent, at different points along its course.

Perhaps no river in the world, of the same length, affords such varied and picturesque scenery as does the Columbia.

Its lakes, tunnels, cascades, falls, mountains, rocky embankments, prairies, plains, bottoms, meadows, and islands, disclose an agreeable medley of wild romance, solemn grandeur, and pleasing beauty, far surpassing that of any other country.

During its course it receives numerous tributaries, the most important of which are the Clarke, Flat-bow, Spokan, Okanagan, Snake, Yakama, Piscous, Entyatecoom, Umatilla, Quisnel, John Day, D'Chute, Cathlatates, Wallawalla, Wallammette, and Cawlitz.

The Clarke, Snake, and Wallammette rivers, seem to call for more than a bare allusion.

The former of these rises in the Rocky Mountains, near lat. 46° north, and following its windings, is about five hundred and fifty miles in length. A lake, some thirty miles long and eight broad, is also formed in its course, about one hundred miles above its mouth. During its windings it receives a large number of affluents, which unite to swell the volume of its waters to the full size of its parent stream.

The Snake, or Lewis' Fork, is equally important. It rises in lat. 42° north, and, pursuing a northwesterly direction for five hundred miles, is discharged into the Columbia, at lat. 46° north. This river also receives several tributaries, the largest of which are the Kooskooskie and Salmon.

The Wallamette heads in the Cascade Mountains, in Upper California, near lat. 41° north, and bears a northerly course for nearly three hundred and fifty miles. One hundred and twenty-five miles of this distance are navigable for boats of a light draught.

Several tributaries, both from the east and west, unite to increase its magnitude and enhance its importance.

The Umpqua, which is the next river worthy of notice below the Columbia, has its source in the Cascade Mountains, near lat. 43° north, and running westerly for almost three hundred miles, is finally discharged into the Pacific. Some forty or fifty miles of this distance are said to be navigable.

South of the Umpqua a stream of nearly equal size empties into the Pacific, called Rogue's river. This also rises in the Cascade Mountains, at lat. 42° north, and is said to be navigable for boats of a light draught, some seventy miles or more.

The Chilkeelis is the first river north of the Columbia, and rises in the mountains, near lat. 48° north. Pursuing a westerly course, it discharges itself into the Pacific at Gray's Harbor, after flowing a distance of about two hundred and fifty miles.

Fraser's river is the extreme northern one of Oregon. It heads in the Rocky Mountains, near lat 54° north, and empties into the Gulf of Georgia, at lat 49° north. In its course it receives several large tributaries, and pursues its way for a distance of about four hundred miles, eighty of which are navigable.

Besides those above named, there are several other streams, of less magnitude, emptying into the Pacific at various points along its coast, all of which, as the country becomes settled, will contribute to the facilities of commerce and manufactures.

The rivers of Oregon, in the abundance and quality of their fish, are unparalleled. At certain seasons of the year, their waters are completely alive with the countless myriads that swarm them to their very sources.

Even the small streams are not exempt from this thronging population. So great is their number they are frequently taken by the hand; and, with the aid of a net, several barrels may be caught at a single haul. It requires but little effort to obtain them, and large quantities are annually shipped to the Sandwich Islands and various other points.

Fish are undoubtedly destined to furnish an important item in the future commerce of Oregon. At the present time they supply the principal food of its inhabitants, both Indians and whites. Among the different varieties abounding in these streams, salmon and salmon trout claim the precedence, both in numbers and qualities.

These delicious fish attain a size seldom surpassed, and are found in every accessible river and creek. The bays, harbors, and mouths of rivers are also thronged with cod, herring, sturgeon, and occasionally whales, while vast quantities of oysters, clams, lobsters, &c., may be obtained along the coast.

Next to fish, in connection with the rivers, the extraordinary number of aquatic birds arrests the attention. These consist of geese, brants, ducks (of three or four varieties,) swans, pelicans, and gulls.

At certain seasons, they throng the rivers, creeks, lakes, and ponds, at different parts, in innumerable multitudes, and not only keep the waters in constant turmoil from their nautic exercises and sports, but fill the air with the wild clamor of their incessant quackings. An expert sportsman may kill hundreds of them in a few hours.

So abundant are they that their feathers may be obtained of the Indians in any requisite quantity, for a trifling consideration—in all respects equal, for bedding, to those procured from domesticated geese and ducks.

In regard to harbors, the natural advantages of Oregon are not equal to those of California; though, as the country becomes settled, the ingenuity of man will speedily atone for these apparent deficiencies; and if she has not the matchless basin of the Bay of San Francisco, she has other localities upon her sea-board that, with a small expenditure of money and effort, may be made secure and adapted to all her commercial requirements.

It is much to be regretted, however, that the Columbia affords not an easy and secure entrance for ships from the Ocean, as this will undoubtedly become the most important point of the whole coast.

At present, the mouth of this river, between Points Adams and Hancock, is partially blocked up by large sand-bars, deposited by the current, and maintained in their places through the repulsive action of the sea-waves.

How far these impediments may operate to the future detriment of commerce, remains to be seen. Unless some remedy should be adopted, the harbor of this great embryo depot of Western trade will continue to oppose a difficult entrance.

The estuaries of the Umpqua and Rogue rivers are more difficult of access than the Columbia. It is even said, that there is not a good harbor on the coast of Oregon below lat. 46° north. Above this parallel there are several, not only easy of access but secure of anchorage; the principal of which are those of the Straits of Juan de Fuca and the Gulf of Georgia. The islands of Vancouvre and Queen Charlotte* also possess a number of excellent harbors.

These islands are large, well timbered, and generally fertile. Though, like the mainland, quite broken and hilly, they embrace many beautiful plains and lovely valleys, abounding with game, and coursed by ample streams of fresh water. Vancouvre's Island is two hundred and sixty miles long by fifty in width, and Queen Charlotte's one hundred and forty by twenty-eight. In addition to the above named, there are a number of smaller islands near the Straits of Juan de Fuca—more important on account of their fisheries than the quality of their soil.

The whole extent of the sea-coast, connected with the territory, (i. e.. from California to the Russian possessions,) is about one thousand miles, besides that of its various islands. Reckoning from the above data, the area included within its limits is not far from nine hundred and two thousand, two hundred and fifty square miles.

To speak of this vast country *in toto*, we could give no general character either in regard to its climate, soil, or productions, possessed, as it is, of every diversity, from the piercing frosts of perpetual winter, to the smiling verdancy of unfading spring—from the dwarfish herbage of the arctic regions, to the generous fruits of warmer zones—and from the barren sterility of a Lybian desert, to the exuberant fecundity of earth's choicest garden-spots.

However, from the numerous peaks that rear their cloud-capped heads in almost every direction, and the continuous ridges intersecting it from side to side and from end to end, we might with safety pronounde it mountainous.

The Rocky Mountains, forming its eastern boundary, branch off westerly and northwesterly at various points, and, in connection with other ridges, beline the whole country. It is my present purpose merely to classify some the more extensive of these ranges, and note their locality, as auxiliary to a more accurate and comprehensive disposal of the leading subject before the reader.

The Blue Mountain chain commences not far from 45° 30' north latitude, and bears a southerly course, till it passes into California and unites with the intersecting ridges of that province. It runs nearly parallel with the Rocky Mountains, at an interval varying from one hundred to one hundred and fifty miles, forming the Eastern Division of Oregon.

The Cascade chain (before noticed, in connection with California) commences in the Russian possessions, and pursues a southerly course through both countries, till it finally becomes lost in the sea-girt isthmus of the Lower Province. It runs parallel with the coast, at a distance varying from one hundred to one hundred and fifty miles, and defines the Western and Middle Divisions of Oregon.

* By the terms of the proposed treaty, the islands of Vancouvre and Queen Charlotte are transferred to Great Britain, leaving only a few diminutive and comparatively valueless ports in the Straits of Juan de Fuca and in islets south of Vancouvre, within the limits of the U. S. territory.

The country north of the Columbia is also traversed by numerous branches and spurs of the Rocky and Cascade Mountains, many of them presenting lofty peaks, covered with never-melting snow and ice.

The mountain ranges before described, have many summits towering far above the snow-line. They are generally less sterile than the main chain of the Rocky Mountains, and, amid their snow-clad tops and denuded eminences, present alternate spreads of high table land and rolling prairie, clothed with vegetation, and dense forests of pine, cedar, fir, and oak, or opening valleys arrayed in all the enchantment of vernal loveliness.

The Eastern, or Southeasterly Division of Oregon, partakes of a greater variety of wild and savage scenery, intermixed with beauty and desolation, than any other section in the whole territory.

The valleys of Bear river and those parts contiguous to Fort Hall, have already been described on a preceding page, and all their varied attractions fully descanted upon. Besides these, there are other valleys in the neighborhood of the South Pass, upon Little and Big Sandy, and the New Forks of Green river, that claim a passing notice.

The valleys last referred to are of variable width and possess a fertile soil, adapted to either grazing or agricultural purposes, and assume an additional importance from their situation in reference to the grand routes from the United States to Oregon and California. They are capable of sustaining a small population with peculiar advantage, were it not for the troubles that might be anticipated from the hostile incursions of the Blackfeet and Sioux.

Below Fort Hall, the valleys of Snake, or Lewis' river, are somewhat limited, but very fertile, though enclosed for the most part by denuded and sterile mountains. In the vicinity of Fort Boisé, on the bank of Lewis' Fork, are several rich and extensive plains and valleys, more or less adapted to cultivation.

The Kooskooskie and Salmon rivers, also, present some fine bottoms. Another beautiful valley is situated upon Powder river, a considerable creek, about forty miles below Fort Boisé. It is large and very fertile, but lacks a sufficiency of timber without a resort to the dense pine forests of the neighboring hills.

The next section that attracts the traveller's attention as he proceeds towards the Columbia, is a favored spot known as *le Grand Rond*, bounded on all sides by mountains, in the vicinity of the Blue range. This locality is nearly circular, and about one hundred and fifty miles in circumference, well watered and possesses a soil of matchless fertility.*

---

* The following analysis of the soil of this valley, as furnished by Col. Fremont, will attest its superior quality:

| | |
|---|---|
| Silicia | 70, 81 |
| Alumnia | 10, 97 |
| Lime and magnesia | 1, 38 |
| Oxade of iron | 2, 21 |
| Vegetable matter partly decomposed | 8, 16 |
| Water and loos | 5, 46 |
| Phosphate of lime | 1, 01 |
| | 100, 00 |

Timber of the best kind may be procured, in any quantity, from the adjoining mountains, and, to a limited extent, from the valley.

Trappers speak of the *Grand Rond* with an enthusiasm which is cordially responded to by all who have hitherto visited it. So far as soil and climate are concerned, a better section of country than this is rarely found.

Southeast from the place last described, sixty miles or more, lies a long stretch of desolate country which bears a strikingly volcanic appearance.

This region is thickly paved with vast piles of lava and igneous rock, strown about in confused fragments, as if the mountains had been rent asunder and dashed in horrid medley upon the adjoining plains, and earth, itself, had undergone all the indescribable contorsions of more than agony,—now opening in frightful chasms,—now vibrating with unheard-of violence, oversetting hills and rooting them from their foundations by the impetuosity of its motion, or elevating half vertically, the immense layers of subterranean rock forming the valves of distorted fissures, and depressing the opposing ones in frightful contrast,—in haste to complete the picture of destruction by an imposing array of wild and savage scenery.

Numerous boiling springs are also found among these wide-spread heaps of ruined nature whose waters are frequently so hot that meat may be cooked in a very few minutes by submersion in them.

Several streams trace their way through this region, affording occasional bottoms of fertile soil and luxuriant vegetation, that smile with bewitching enchantment upon the relentless havoc surrounding them.

Upon Clarke's river and its tributaries, as well as the numerous lakes adjacent to them, there are large quantities of excellent land, well adapted to agricultural and grazing purposes. The hills, too, are generally studded with dense forests of pine and fir, some of them of gigantic growth, while the intervning plateaux and high prairies present frequent intervals of lusty grasses.

The same may be said, though in a more restricted sense, of most of the country lying between Clarke's river and the Columbia.

The streams of water and lakes are most of them skirted with bottoms and valleys of greater or less extent, tolerably well timbered, while the neighboring hills afford frequent groves of heavy pines, diversified with openings of grass-clad prairies or of denuded barrenness.

Many interesting localities lie along the Columbia, above the confluence of Clarke's river, as well as upon the several tributaries finding their way into it. A tract of country circumjacent to the Lower Lake possesses a rich soil, with other advantages, which in due time will command the attention of emigrants.

The section lying still north of this is but little better than a barren waste of frost and snow, with now and then choice spots of rank vegetation and rich floral beauty, shut up in their stern recesses, in wonderful contrast with the savage sublimity and wild disorder of the masses of naked rock that surround them.

Frasier's river has an extensive valley of excellent and well timbered land, skirting it in variable width, from mouth to source. The same may be said of many of its tributaries. The Chilkeelis, also, possesses many choice spots.

But, as a general thing, that portion of country north of the Columbia is the most worthless part of Oregon.

A vast share of it is mere naked rock or deserts of ice and snow, with now and then dense forests of pine, cedar, and fir. There are, comparatively, few arable prairies; and not more than one half of the whole extent can be turned to any useful purpose. Perhaps one sixth of it is susceptible of cultivation. In fact, the only localities worthy of mention are the valleys scattered among the Claset and Cascade Mountains, and along the different rivers and creeks.

The cause of this general sterility is more to be attributed to the severity of the climate, consequent upon a high northern latitude, combined with the broken and mountainous character of the country, than to any great natural deficiency of soil. Of course it can never become thickly populated.

Its timber, fisheries, and facilities for manufactures, stock-raising, and the growth of wool, embrace its greatest inducements to emigrants; though, in a commercial point of view, its extensive fur trade and commodious harbors, with other kindred advantages, should not be overlooked.

We now come to the Middle Division, or that section south of the Columbia, between the Blue and Cascade Mountains.

In this division of Oregon the face of the country is very much diversified. As a whole, it presents a continued series of conical hills, huge masses of rock, and undulating prairies, intermixed with lofty, cloud-capped peaks, shooting transversely from the ridges that form its eastern and western boundaries. These mountains are usually clothed with rank vegetation, and frequently present stately forests of valuable timber, particularly the Blue range.

It also contains many extensive valleys of great fertility, situated among its mountains and upon the John Day, Quisnell, Umatilla, D'Chute, and Wallawalla rivers, and their numerous affluents.

The southern extremity likewise affords many fertile and extensive valleys, but it is rather sparsely timbered. In the immediate vicinity of the Columbia, the land is sandy and barren, though back from the river, the hills are tolerably rich and coated with heavy pine forests.

Nearly the whole of this section may be considered available for agriculture and stock-raising.

The Western Division next commands our attention. Below the Cascades, the country contiguous to the Columbia presents a vast extent of thickly timbered and extremely fertile bottom land, one hundred and twenty miles wide, interspersed with frequent openings of lusty vegetation.

The forests of this section afford some of the largest and most beautiful pine and fir trees in the world. Its valleys, plains, and hills are likewise possessed of a most excellent soil, adapted to every practicable use.

Above this, and bordering upon the Straits of Juan de Fuca are also large tracts of fine land, well watered, timbered, and fertile.

Southward, towards the confines of California, the Umpqua and Rogue rivers claim several very extensive and fertile valleys and bottom lands. Upon the former of these are said to be two, one of which is forty miles in length by ten in width, and the other seventy by fifteen;—upon the latter, is one eighty miles long, and varying from fifteen to fifty in width.

Besides the above mentioned, there are numerous other valleys, all of which are well timbered and of unparalleled fertility.

No country in the world affords a better soil, or a more romantic scenery. The mountains bounding them rise in stately grandeur, oftentimes far above the clouds, to converse with the relentless snows of successive ages,—now presenting their nude sides, paved with dark masses of frowning rocks, or proud forests of evergreen, verdant lawns, flowery dales, and sterile wastes, to overlook the perennial beauty and matchless fecundity at their feet,—while the lesser eminences with their deep ravines, o'erhanging cliffs, and shadowy recesses, tell the place where the storm-winds recruit their forces and the zephyrs creep in to die.

There are also large valleys, of equally fertile soil, upon the head waters of the Tlameth river, near the southern boundary, well worth the attention of emigrants.

The most interesting portion of the Western Division, however, is that bordering upon the Wallammette and its affluents. The valley of this river is one hundred and fifty miles long by thirty-five broad. The soil is a deep alluvion, of extraordinary fertility.

It is not only well watered, but well timbered, and produces all the vegetables, fruits, and grasses indigenous to the country, with astonishing profuseness. No region was ever better adapted to agricultural or grazing purposes.

The Fualitine Plains, adjoining this beautiful expanse of fertility upon the left, towards the Columbia, embrace an area of forty-five miles in length by fifteen in breadth, well watered and amply timbered, with a soil in all respects equal.

The Klackamus, Putin, Fualitine, Yamhill, and other rivers, are all of them skirted by beautiful and fertile valleys of greater or less extent, while the adjacent hills and prairies afford not only frequent forests of excellent timber, but generally a very good soil.

The landscape of this vicinity, though not, strictly speaking, hilly, is highly indulating, but quite productive in grass and herbage.

The Cawlitz river, which empties into the Columbia a short distance below the Wallammette, has several rich bottoms, and waters a large extent of country, admirably adapted to stock-raising and agriculture.

At the mouth of the Wallammette river is an island some fifteen miles in length by nearly the same distance in breadth, called Wappato; it is of a deep alluvial soil, formed from sedimentary deposites and decayed vegetable substances, and is very rich and densely timbered.

The country at the mouth of the Columbia and for some ten or fifteen miles interior, is sandy and sterile,—a fact much to be regretted, as from its peculiar locality this point must necessarily become the site of a vastly important commercial emporium, vieing in population, splendor, and opulence, the time-grown cities of more eastern climes.

The stately forests of pine and fir, in the Western Division of Oregon, have for a long time challenged the admiration of the world, and it is strongly doubted whether the chosen veterans of foreign woods can produce a rival to some few specimens of the proud giants of its soil.

These not unfrequently tower to a height of two hundred feet, and even more,—leaving from one hundred and fifty to one hundred and seventy-five feet clear of limb, with scarcely a curve in the entire length.

One of them, standing near Fort George on the Columbia river, is said to measure forty-seven feet in circumference, three hundred and fifty feet in altitude, and two hundred and sixty-five feet clear of limb; another, upon the Umpqua river, is reported even larger, and yet another, in the same vicinity, very nearly equals it in size.

Timber of this kind affords the choicest article for lumber, which bears a very high price at the Sandwich Islands and in various parts of Mexico, and will no doubt become a staple commodity in the commerce of Oregon; while the immense forests of pine, fir, and oak, rearing their stately heads in thick array, must prove a sure source of wealth to its future inhabitants.

The principal kinds of wood indigenous to the country are white-oak, live-oak, maple, ash, pine, fir, cedar, hemlock, spruce, cottonwood, aspen, and cherry.

Live-oak is found chiefly in the southern part, and, in quality, stands foremost among the denizens of the forest for ship-building. Several other species of oak are more or less abundant in various parts.

In review of the subjects occupying the preceding pages, we may present the following summary:

Nearly one-fifth of the entire territory is timbered; three-eighths of it may be successfully cultivated, (embracing the richest lands in the Federal Domain,) and two-thirds of it may afford pasturage for cattle, horses, and sheep.

It is generally better watered and much better timbered than California; and, though its harbors are inferior in regard to safety and ease of access, Oregon possesses other advantages, aside from soil and climate, compensating, in some measure, for these obvious deficiencies, and which combine to render it a most eligible point of emigration.

## CHAPTER XXVI.

Climate of Oregon; its variableness; its rains; a southern climate in a northern latitude.—Productiveness; grain, fruits, and flowers, wild and cultivated.—Geological characteristics.—Soils and prevailing rock.—Minerals, &c.—Variety of game.—Wolves.—Horses, and other domestic animals.—Population, white and natives; Indian tribes, their character and condition.—Missionary stations, and their improvements.—Present trade of Oregon.—Posts of the Hudson Bay Company.—Settlements.—Oregon City, its situation and advantages; about Linnton; about Wallammette valley, Fualitine Plains, and Umpqua river; Vancouvre, and its superior advantages.—Kindness of Hudson Bay Company to settlers.

The next which seems to demand our notice, in due order, is the climate of this interesting country.

We need only bear in mind the geographical position and diversified character of Oregon, to satisfy ourselves of the true merits of the subject now before us. A mountainous country like this must necessarily embrace every variety of climate, from that of the ice-bound coasts and even scathing frosts of the polar regions, to the burning heat of the equator,— from the mild atmosphere of Italian skies, to the genial temperature which paints the wild-flowers in their primeval beauty, while month succeeding month doles out the year, nor feels nor knows the chill-breath of winter.

A short jaunt at any time translates the traveller, at his own option, to regions of winter, spring, summer, or fall, and spreads before him all the varied beauties and deformities of either.

As a general thing, however, the winters of Oregon are much more temperate than those of countries in the same latitude bordering upon the Atlantic—a fact which may be attributed to the usual prevalence of westerly winds at that season.

These winds, on passing the mountains and traversing the vast extent of snowy prairie and open land in their course, become vested with a chilling severity unknown to its incipiency, when, from the warm bosom of the broad Pacific, they first waft themselves o'er the blooming valleys, smiling plains, grass-clad hills, and mountains garbed in stately forests, commingled with stern desolation, to lavish upon all these varied scenes the soft blandishments of the Indies, and engender the interesting phenomenon of a southern climate in a high northern latitude.

The country contiguous to Frasier's river, and even below it for some distance, is usually visited with long and severe winters, and enjoys comparatively but a short interval of genial weather during the spring and summer months.

The valleys, however, not unfrequently afford exceptions to this remark, when favorably located in regard to the wind and sun. In this section it seldom rains, a circumstance causing an unproductive and arid soil.

## CLIMATE OF OREGON.

The Eastern Division is, perhaps, more variable in regard to temperature than any other portion of Oregon. Its valleys are usually possessed of a mild and delightful climate, so much so that stock will subsist the entire winter without being fed or housed.

The plains and high prairies present a longer interval of inclement weather, and the snow continues on the ground for a much greater length of time, than in the low-lands.

Some particular localities are subject to very sudden changes, and not unfrequently experience the warm breath of summer with the chill blasts of fresh-born winter during the short lapse of a single day and night.

In reference to the high mountains, it is sufficient to remark, that with them winter is a season too congenial not to be felt in all its rigors, to the entire extent of its duration. The diversity of temperature in these parts depends mostly upon the altitude. The lower benches experiencing a mild atmosphere even in the severest weather, permit the snow to remain only for a short interval succeeding its fall, and woo the willing spring; while the higher ones treasure up each descending flake to nourish the scathing blasts that leap from the mountain-tops, fresh-cradled in the lap of winter.

Notwithstanding these apparent disadvantages, the Eastern Division may be regarded as universally healthy. The purity of the atmosphere, and its absence from noxious exhalations and disease-engendering effluvia, undoubtedly contribute the prime cause in producing a result so favorable.

Rains are not usual to this part in the summer months, nor even in the winter and spring are they common to any great extent. The snows of winter, together with the rains of that season and autumn, and the occasional dews of summer, in most cases, afford a sufficient moisture to the low-lands for agricultural purposes.

That section situated between the Blue and Cascade Mountains, known as the Middle Division, is said to possess, comparatively, a much milder and less variable climate.

The winters are usually open and of short duration, snow lying upon the ground, in the valleys, rarely exceeding four days in succession, and vegetation, in some instances, remains green the entire season. The prairies, too, are generally covered only for a short time.

The heat of summer lacks that oppressiveness so common to most countries. In regard to the health of this section, we may correctly apply the observations made relative to the Eastern Division. A country situated like the one now forming the subject of our remarks, cannot be otherwise than healthy, as a general thing.

The snow of winter and the rains of spring and autumn, coupled with the light dews of summer, furnish all the moisture usual to the soil, which the moderate heat of the latter season renders sufficient for the growth of vegetation and the production of grain and other crops.

The Western Division possesses not only a soil but a climate more favorable to vegetation than any other portion of Oregon. In the southern part it seldom snows, and the weather is so mild, that the grass continues green and flourishing the entire year. Water never freezes, unless it be in some elevated pool or lake.

The absence of sufficient rains and dews, however, during the summer months at some points, renders an occasional resort to irrigation necessary for the production of corn, potatoes, and articles of a like nature.

Two crops of some kinds of produce may be raised with success in a single year.

In the vicinity of the Wallammette, the winters are only a trifle colder. Running water seldom freezes. Snow never falls to exceed the depth of a few inches, and disappears in a very short time succeeding.

Vegetation in the valleys, and even upon the plains, to some extent, remains green year in and year out. Of course no better climate could be selected for stock-raising.

These remarks may be applied with equal propriety to the other portions of the Western Division south of the Columbia and in its immediate vicinity. The country further north, for a considerable distance, possesses a climate almost as favorable. The snows of winter, however, are usually more frequent and less transitory in their continuance.

The cold season is confined almost exclusively to the three winter months. The heat of summer is moderate and agreeable, generally ranging at 62° Fahrenheit, above zero, in its mean temperature.

The wet season of the Western Division usually occurs from October to March of each year, inclusive; at other times rain seldom falls. During this season it descends in gentle showers, or in the shape of mist, at intervals, for about one half of the time. The moisture received into the earth meanwhile, together with the nightly dews and other favorable agencies during the summer months, renders the soil adapted to cultivation.

Back from the valleys and bottoms, the atmosphere is quite wholesome and salubrious. Fevers are seldom known, and pulmonary complaints are equally rare.

In the vicinity of the Columbia, intermittent fevers are not uncommon, though by no means as bad as in some parts of our frontier States.

Next in the order before us come the various productions which may be, and are, successfully cultivated in the different sections of this part of our national domain.

The soil and climate of the Eastern Division have been sufficiently tested to know their capacity for producing nearly, if not quite, all the various grains, vegetables, and fruits usually grown in our Northern and Middle States. A great variety of wild fruits and vegetables grow spontaneously, in different parts, and in great abundance.

The soil and climate, as a whole, seem better adapted to the culture of fruits and grains, than vegetables; and perhaps we might add, for the raising of cattle, horses, and sheep, than agriculture; though the latter observation is not to be so construed as to affirm that farming may not be successfully and profitably prosecuted in many parts.

The Northern Division, or that portion of Oregon lying on the headwaters of the Columbia, in the vicinity and south of Frasier's river, and upon the Chilkeelis, being much colder and more sterile, must necessarily be regarded in a less favorable light than the country referred to in the preceding paragraph. But, little is known as to its products or the capacities of its soil and climate; yet, it is said that some particular kinds of fruit are indigenous to this region, and it is generally supposed that wheat, barley, oats, buckwheat, flax, and other articles of like nature, might be raised within it. Of course, these remarks apply only to the valleys.

The Middle Division affords a finer soil and a more favorable climate than the Eastern; but, in regard to productions, it is much the same. All the northern fruits, grains, and vegetables, may be produced in great abundance, with the exception of corn—the land being generally too dry and too much subject to unseasonable frosts; corn, however, has been successfully cultivated on the Wallawalla.

There are several varieties of wild fruits found here, among which are included cherries, with larb, buffal, gooee, and service berries, and currants, plums, and grapes, together with several other species not recollected, as well as vegetables and roots.

The Western Division not only maintains its pre-eminence in relation to soil and climate, but stands equally conspicuous in the variety and abundance of its productions. It is thought, and not without reason, that cotton, sugar-cane, and various other productions of a warm and even tropical climate might here be raised without difficulty.

When the ground is in a suitable condition, the avarage crop of wheat is from twenty to twenty-five bushels to the acre. Vast quantities of it are annually produced by settlers in different parts of the country. A surplus of one hundred thousand bushels is reported to have been grown, in the region adjoining the Wallammette, during the summer of 1844.

The Hudson Bay Company, at Fort Vancouvre, have several very extensive farms under improvement, upon which they raise nearly every variety of grain and vegetables, with flattering success.

In the garden of McLaughlin, the chief factor of this company, are found almost every species of fruits and flowers indigenous to this country and to foreign soils of the same latitude, with several varieties produced only in warm climates.

We barely allude to the above facts, in order to prove the adaptation of Western Oregon to agricultural pursuits. The data relative to its extraordinary facilities for rearing countless herds of cattle, horses, and sheep, have already been placed before the reader, and need not here a repetition.

The components of the soils of Oregon are equally varied in character, according to their situation. The bottoms are usually of a deep, sandy alluvion, intermixed with vegetable and organic matter. The valleys are of a heavy loam, enriched by the debris and other fertilizing properties borne from the high grounds by the annual rains, together with the constant accumulation of decayed herbage and grass so lavishly bestrown at each returning season.

The prairies are possessed of either a light sandy superfice, or a mixture of gravel and stiff clay. The superstratum of the hills and mountains varies from wastes of naked sand, sun-baked clay, and spreads of denuded rock, to a thin vegetable mould, and a light marly loam of greater or less fecundity.

The rock of this territory also presents many different specimens; the prominent classifications, however, are volcanic, viz: basalt, (columnar and scoriated,) trap, lava, pumicestone, limestone (fossiliferous, bituminous, and earthy,) and mica slate, with sandstone, puddingstone, granular quartz, calcareous tufa, and agglomerated boulders of various kinds, particularly in the Eastern Division. The varieties of some parts present strong characteristics of the oolite formation. The hills contain many excellent quarries for the structure of buildings or other useful purposes.

Hitherto but little investigation has been had relative to the mineral resources of Oregon; though sufficient is known to warrant the statement, that copper, lead, iron, coal, salt, soda, sulphur, nitre, and alum, are abundant in some parts; and, from the nature of the country, we may safely infer that yet more valuable metals are waiting to reward with their hidden treasures the researches of man.

Game, in the Eastern and Middle Divisions, is not generally plentiful; yet, in places, there are an abundance of deer, elk, antelope, bear, wolves, and foxes;—buffalo are also found occasionally in the vicinity of the Rocky Mountains. In the Northern Division, moose, deer, elk, bear, foxes, and wolves, are the varieties most common. Game is more abundant in the Western than in the other Divisions, and is nearly of the same kind.

Ducks, geese, brants, pheasants, partridges, &c., are common throughout the whole territory.

Wolves are very numerous in the neighborhood of the settlements, and prove a great source of annoyance to the inhabitants by preying upon their cattle and other stock. These wolves consist of three kinds,—the black, gray, and prairie wolf, *b.* which, as in California, the black wolf is the largest and most ferocious.

As a grazing country, the available lands of the three divisions of Oregon, south of the Columbia and the one immediately north of that river, are little inferior, if, indeed, not fully equal, to the far-famed meadows and lawns of California.

Horses are reared in vast numbers by the Indians, among whom it is not uncommon to find a single individual owning three or four hundred head. Select horses may be bought at prices ranging from twelve to twenty dollars each.

These animals are generally stout and hardy, capable of enduring a vast amount of fatigue, and are but little inferior in point of size to our American nags.

Large herds of horses are also raised by the settlers, and at the Hudson Bay Company's establishments.

Latterly, cattle, hogs, and sheep, are beginning to receive the attention of the farming community, and, without doubt, soon will become immensely numerous. It needs only the operation of time to render Oregon as famous for its countless herds, as for the abundance and variety of its productions.

The entire population of the territory at this time, may be estimated at thirty-five thousand, of which about seven thousand are whites and halfbreeds, and the balance Indians.

The Indians principally consist of the following tribes: the Snakes, Blackfeet, Flatheads, Nesperces, Bonarks, Cyuses, Wallawallas, Chinooks, Shatchets, Chalams, Killamucs, Squamishes, Clasets, Tohandos, Klackamus, Clatsup, Umpquas, Klackatats, Kallapuyas, Tlamaths, and Chilkeelis.

The Blackfeet, though included among the Oregon tribes, properly belong to that portion of the Rocky Mountains contiguous to the head waters of the Missouri. They make occasional irruptions into the country occupied by the Flatheads, Snakes, and Nesperces, and for this reason are included in the above list.

The Tlameths and two or three other inferior tribes in the neighborhood of California and north of the Columbia river may be considered troublesome and rather ill-disposed; but not dangerous, unless it be in cases where they have a very decided advantage.

The Indians of this country are less warlike than those east of the Rocky Mountains, and far less dangerous, even as enemies. They may be considered, on the whole, as friendly to the whites, and quite susceptible of civilization. They are tolerably industrious, and ready at all times to work for the settlers at a trifling compensation.

Many of them cultivate the ground and raise corn, potatoes, beans, and melons,—but fish, horses, and game, as a general thing, furnish their principal food. As an evidence of their quiet disposition, they rarely go to war, and are usually found at or near the several places claimed and occupied by them individually.

The Nesperces are, perhaps, farther advanced in civilization than any other tribe. Many of them (and some of other tribes) are beginning to live after the manner of the whites, and the philanthropic efforts of Christian missionaries in their behalf have been attended with great success.

There are eight of more missionary stations in Oregon, belonging as follows: to the Presbyterians, the Methodists, and the Roman Catholics.

Four of these are situated between the Blue and Cascade Mountains, viz: one near the Dalls one at Waiilatpu on the Wallawalla, one at Tshimakain, and one at Clear Water.

The mission at Waiilatpu is under the direction of Dr. Whitman, and has a flouring mill and a very considerable farm connected with it, upon which large quantities of grain and vegetables are annually raised, and also numerous herds of cattle and horses. The station near the Dalls, with the exception of a mill, is said to be but little behind that of Waiilatpu in point of prosperity.

The remaining four are in the Western Division.

The most important of these are situated as follows: one at the Wallammette Falls, about twenty-five miles below the Columbia, and the other in the Wallammette valley, some forty or fifty miles farther south.

Both of the above belong to the Methodists, and may be considered rich.

There are two large farms and a store connected with the station in the Wallammette valley, and also large herds of cattle, horses, and hogs;—it is said to drive quite a profitable trade with the Indians and settlers in the line of dry goods and groceries.

The station at the Wallammette Falls has also a store, and carries on a small business by way of merchandize.

The two other stations are south and west of the last named, but have, as yet, no very extensive improvements in connection with them.

The Methodists have a press at one of their stations in Oregon, which is employed in printing religious books for the benefit of the Indians.

In addition to the different stations above alluded to, the Catholics have several agents and teachers in this territory, who labor with great zeal and earnestness to make proselytes to their own peculiar notions. The number and locality of these agents I have not the necessary information to state. They were, not long since, under the superintendance of one Father De Smit, a Jesuit priest, and have exerted considerable influence among the Indian tribes.

Nearly the entire trade of Oregon, at the present time, is in the hands of the Hudson Bay Company, from whom dry goods and groceries may be obtained by the settlers at less than the common price in the United States; this, as a necessary consequence, precludes all opposition. The principal exports (raised at the stations or received by way of barter) are flour, fish, butter, cheese, lumber, masts, spars, furs, and skins.

The Forts, or trading establishments, are eighteen in all, and have a large number of hands employed about them, in conducting the fur trade and laboring upon the farms and in the workshops and mills.

Each of these posts presents a miniature town by itself, whose busy populace pursue most of the varied avocations incident to the more densely inhabited localities of civilized countries.

We will not occupy the reader's time in an extended description of them severally, but rest content by simply giving their names. The first post belonging to this company, upon the route to the mouth of the Columbia, is Fort Hall; the next, Fort Wallawalla; then, Fort Vancouvre, and Fort George.

The others are situated at different points, and are known as follows: Colville, Okanagan, Alexandria, Barbine, Klamloops, St. James, Chilcothin, Simpson, McLaughlin, Langley, Nisqually, Cawlitz, and Umpqua; of which eight are located in or above lat. 49° north.

The principal settlements, disconnected from the trading establishments and different missionary stations, at present, are upon the Umpqua and Wallammette rivers, on the Fualitine Plains, and near Fort Vancouvre. These settlements are represented as being in a very flourishing condition, and rapidly increasing in population and wealth.

At the Wallammette Falls, a town has been regularly laid out called Oregon City, which, in the year 1844, numbered a hundred or more houses; among them was a church, with several stores and mills.

At this place the temporary legislature, already instituted by the settlers for mutual benefit in the absence of all other legitimate jurisdiction, holds its regular sessions. A mayor was elected in the spring of 1845; and recently a printing press and materials have been procured from New York for the purpose of publishing the territorial laws, with such other documents and papers as the interests of the community may require.

This embryo city, situated as it is in a place so admirable in regard to agriculture, commerce, and manufactures, possesses many superior advantages in point of locality.

The falls of the Wallammette are thirty feet perpendicular, and afford abundant water privileges for mills and factories,—two important rivers, the Klackamus and Fualitine, find their discharge near it, while below is presented an uninterrupted navigation to the Ocean, and above it boats may ascend for a distance of one hundred miles or more. The country contiguous is unsurpassed in fertility, and will undoubtedly soon acquire a dense population.

Another town, called Linnton, has recently been commenced upon the south bank of the Columbia, near the mouth of the Wallammette river, and bids fair to become of some importance.

The settlements in the valley above, and at the Fualitine Plains, are scattered like those of the farming sections of our Western States;—the same observation may also be applied in reference to those upon the Umpqua river.

The settlement at Vancouvre is more compact, and assumes the air of a flourishing village. It is near the falls of the Columbia, at the head of ship navigation, and is made the great commercial depot of the Hudson Bay Company for the articles required in their trade.

Connected with the Fort is an extensive flouring mill, and also a saw mill, which is said to do a very active and lucrative business.

The number of buildings at Vancouvre is not far from sixty. The site is a most admirable one for some future emporium of trade and manufactures. Its water privileges are almost without limits, while its other advantages are equally inviting.

The geographical condition of the country is such that, as it becomes settled, an enormous amount of commercial interest must necessarily concentrate here; and, doubtless, a more favorable locality for a city could not be selected upon the Columbia. It is destined to command almost the entire trade of Eastern and Middle Oregon.

The agents of the Hudson Bay Company at present are of great advantage to emigrants. They extend to them every reasonable assistance by selling goods and necessaries on credit at very low prices, and receiving their various products in payment upon most favorable terms. They furnish seed-corn, wheat, potatoes, and other articles of like nature, to the settlers, to be returned in kind at the end of the year, with a small additional amount by way of interest.

This company is equally accommodating in other respects. It affords employment to numbers at a fair compensation, and supplies them with cattle, hogs, horses, and implements of agriculture for their farms. Its agents and factors seem much disposed to encourage the influx of emigrants, and are never backward in evincing a friendly disposition by their acts.

## CHAPTER XXVII.

The manufacturing facilities of Oregon.—Commercial and agricultural advantages reviewed.—Rail Road to the Pacific.—Route, mode of travelling, and requisite equipments for emigrants.—Importance of Oregon to the United States.—Incident in the early history of Fort Hall.—Why the Blackfeet are hostile, and bright spots in their character.—Mild weather.—Leave for the Platte.—Journey to the Yampah, and sketch of the intermediate country.—New Park.—Head of Grand river.—The landscape.—Different routes to Fort Lancaster.—Old Park.

PERHAPS no country is possessed of greater manufacturing facilities than Oregon. Its numberless watercourses, with their frequent falls and rapids, upon every side, point out the sites for mills and factories, while the adjoining forests and hills produce the timber for their construction, and the metal for their machinery; and the plains and valleys, the food for their operatives, and raw materials for their fabrics. The ships of all nations await as their carriers, and render accessible the best markets of the world.

A large portion of the sterile and otherwise valueless lands of the territory might be turned to good account in the growth of wool, and the valleys and bottoms would easily yield exhaustless supplies of flax and hemp. The southwest displays her cotton fields, and the plains and hills hold out their rich stores of timber and minerals; the busy operatives and thrice effective machinery of the flourishing establishments, as yet scarcely hidden from view by the thin veil of futurity, would achieve the transformation of these varied products into broadcloths, linens, calicoes, and other auxiliaries of comfort and utility; while California, with the other provinces of Mexico, the western Republics of South America, the islands of the Pacific, the Northwestern Coast, and the numerous Indian tribes of the interior, impatient to gaze upon the evidences of creative skill, even now stand their willing purchasers.

With such advantages before her, who might not augur well for the future pre-eminence of Oregon.

But, in other respects, the prospect is still more flattering. Her extensive plains, valleys, and bottoms, need no long lapse of time to transform them into smiling fields; her prairies and hills will then become thronged with countless herds of cattle and flocks of sheep, and the beef, pork, and wool of the stock-grower, the butter and cheese of the dairyman, with all the surplus of the farmer, will find an inviting market at the populous manufacturing towns and commercial cities that will have sprung up close around him, nor need he look elsewhere for a more lucrative disposal.

An interchange of commodities with China, Japan, South America, the East Indies, and the Polynesian and Australian islands, will pour the wealth of nations into her lap, and swell the opulence of her citizens.

A continuous rail-road, from the Mississippi and the great lakes across the Rocky Mountains to the falls of the Columbia, (a project quite practicable, and even now seriously contemplated,) will open a new channel for commerce, and then our merchantmen and whalers, instead of performing a dangerous homeward-bound voyage of twelve thousand miles, by doubling the southern extremity of Africa, or that of the American continent, will discharge their cargoes at the ports of Oregon for a re-shipment to every part of the Union, and thus unite their aid in the magic work of up-building the Great West.

It is then that the mighty resources of our national confederacy will begin more fully to develop themselves, and exhibit to an admiring world the giant strides of civilization and improvement, when liberty is their birthright, and freemen are their nursing fathers. It needs no prophetic eye to foresee all *this*, nor the effort of centuries to transform this rough sketch of fancy into a more than sober reality.

The over-land route, from Independence, Mo., to Fort Hall, affords a good waggon-road; but that from Fort Hall to Vancouvre is generally considered impassable for other than pack-animals. It is said, however, that a new route has recently been discovered, by which waggons may be taken, without much difficulty, the entire distance. Should this report prove true, the emigrant may convey everything needed for his comfort during the long journey before him.

Emigrants should never go in companies exceeding one hundred and fifty or two hundred persons. The reason for this is obvious,—they will proceed more harmoniously; there will be less difficulty in obtaining food for their animals; less delays *en route*; a better opportunity for the procurement of provisions by hunting, and the number is amply sufficient for mutual defence.

From my own experience and observation, I would advise the use of pack-mules or horses altogether, instead of waggons. One pack-horse, suitably laden, would convey an ample supply of provisions and other necessaries for two individuals, if recruited by occasional levies upon the game that, in many cases, throng their course.

A company thus equiped, can travel with far greater expedition and even more comfortably.

In case of sickness, a litter might easily be constructed for the conveyance of the invalid by affixing to a horse two light poles, some twelve or fifteen feet in length, like the shafts of a wagon, the smaller extremities being fastened to the saddle and the larger ones left to drag upon the ground, while two short pieces placed transversely upon them, astern the horse, present the framework for a bed in which the sufferer may repose or lie at his ease, with as much quiet as the tender object of a mother's care in its infantile cradle.

A company acting upon the above suggestions (numbering say two hundred) should employ an efficient pilot, with a commandant and sixteen skilful hunters.

Strict regulations for its government must also be adopted and enforced. Each individual should be furnished with a good riding horse or a mule, a good percussion rifle, (bore thirty or thirty-five balls per lb.,) ammunition sufficient for five hundred rounds, and a butcher-knife, with pistols and the requisites for procuring fire.

The company should be divided into messes of six each, and one hunter and his assistant should be assigned to every two messes. Each mess should be provided with three pack-mules, exclusively for the transportation of its baggage and provision, and at least one loose animal for extra service.

It should be further furnished with two camp-kettles, a tomahawk, a large tin mess-pan, and a tin-cup and plate for each of its number.

A light tent might also be taken if deemed necessary; though such an article is of little use. A robe and a blanket for bedding, four shirts and a single change of clothes are as much baggage as any individual should think of taking for his own use. By these means his movements will be free and unincumbered, while the whole company pursues its way with ease and rapidity.

On reaching his destination the emigrant may procure everything in the line of dry goods, groceries, and the implements of husbandry, at less prices than in the States; hence the folly of burthening himself with extra baggage for a long and tiresome journey.

The immense importance of Oregon to the United States is doubtless apparent to every one. The facts upon which this inference is based, may be briefly presented as follows:

*First.* By the occupation of this country we shall secure to our own citizens the best trade of the whole world.

*Second.* We shall preclude the dangerous supremacy of foreign powers upon our western frontier, and place our relations with the intermediate Indian tribes upon a safer and more permanent footing.

*Third.* We shall retain to the Union a vast territory, unexcelled in climate, rich in soil, and exhaustless in its various resources; and thus lay open for the general welfare new channels for commerce and fresh fields for enterprise.

*Fourth.* We shall (in the event of the proposed rail road) greatly enhance the prosperity and wealth of the Western States.

*Fifth.* We shall prevent the annual sacrifice of an immense amount of life and property in the navigation of a dangerous sea, for a distance of some twelve thousand miles.

*Sixth.* We shall afford to our whalemen and ships engaged in the China and East India trade ports for supplies and repairs, and thus save to ourselves the yearly amounts now paid to foreign nations.

*Seventh.* We stand in actual need of some point upon the coast of the Pacific as a rendezvous for our navy.

There are many other weighty reasons that might be adduced in support of this inference, but why should we further review the subject? A candid perusal of the preceding pages will have suggested them to the reader's mind without greater amplification on our part.

In conclusion we need only to add, *time will usher forth the embryo greatness and glory of Oregon;* but whether that greatness shall increase the strength, or that glory commingle with the glowing lustre of our Federal Union, while she figures as one in the proud family of States, or whether they, discarded by the fostering hand of maternal care, shall assume the energy of a giant's power and shine with the brightness of innate effulgence as a *distinct nation*, depends much upon the prompt and judicious action of our government upon this momentous subject.

During our stay at Fort Hall an incident connected with its early history was narrated to me, which, as it tends much to illustrate the bold daring and spirit of inbred republicanism possessed by the mass of trapping parties frequenting the mountains, I am tempted to transcribe.

Soon after this post came into the possession of its present owners, several squads, on returning from their regular hunts, rendezvoused in its vicinity. According to the custom of the Hudson Bay Company on such occasions, the British flag was hoisted in honor of the event. Thereupon the proud mountaineers took umbrage, and forthwith sent a deputation to solicit of the commandant its removal; and, in case he should prove unwilling to comply, politely requesting that, at least, the American flag might be permitted a place by its side. Both of which propositions were peremptorily refused.

Another deputation was then sent announcing that, unless the British flag should be taken down and the *stars and stripes* raised in its place within two hours, they would take it down by force, if necessary. To this was returned an answer of surly defiance.

At the expiration of the time named the resolute trappers, mustering *en masse*, appeared before the Fort, under arms, and demanded its immediate surrender.

The gates had already been closed, and the summons was answered by a shot from the bastion. Several shots were forthwith exchanged, but without much damage upon either side; the trappers directing their aim principally at the British flag, while the garrison, feeling ill-disposed to shoot down their own friends in honor of a few yards of parti-colored bunting, elevated their pieces and discharged them into the air.

The result was that the assailants soon forced an entrance, took down and tore in pieces the hated flag, and mounted that of their own country in its stead, amid deafening huzzas and successive rounds of riflery.

The commandant and his sub-cronies, retreating to a room, barricaded the entrance, when the trappers promptly demanded their surrender upon the following terms:

1st. The American flag shall occupy its proper place hereafter.

2d. The commandant shall treat his captors to the best liquors in his possession.

3d. Unless the offenders comply with these conditions, the captors will consider Fort Hall and its contents as lawful plunder and act accordingly.

After a short parley the besieged agreed to a capitulation. In compliance with the second article of the terms, a barrel of whiskey, with sugar to match, was rolled into the yard, where the head was knocked out, and the short but bloodless campaign ended in wild frolicking, as toast after toast was drunk in fancied honor of the American flag, and round after round of responsive cheers told who were they that stood ever ready to proudly hail it and rally beneath its broad folds.

BLACKFEET AND FLATHEAD INDIANS. — *Page 283.*

At the time of our visit, there were some sixty men connected with this establishment. These consisted principally of half-breeds and Canadian French, among whom were several who had seen service in the unrelenting war between the whites and Blackfeet that had been so long prosecuted. Many a thrilling story was narrated in connection with the history of this war, none of which more interested me than the following explanation of its origin:

The Blackfeet at first were friendly to the whites, and a very considerable trade in guns and ammunition was carried on with them by the latter. Like most savages, they became great admirers of the potency and use of gunpowder, and were quite curious to ascertain the process by which it could be had independent of the whites. In answer to inquiries, they were informed it was the seed of a species of grain, and might be multiplied in like manner to any extent by cultivation.

Accrediting the story and captivated with the idea of raising their own powder, a large quantity was purchased for that purpose, which was carefully planted, in full expectation of an abundant harvest.

Their disappointment at the result will be readily supposed. Denouncing the whites as liars and cheats, they were not slow to avow their meditated revenge.

It needed, however, yet another act of perfidy to work the more perfect transformation of friends into foes. This soon after was consummated as follows:

The Blackfeet and Flatheads met, at an appointed place, for the purpose of trade and the maintenance of friendly relations, as was their annual custom.

During this conference, the head chiefs of the two nations commenced descanting upon the merits and fleetness of their respective horses, which resulted in a banter, a bet, and a race.

The Flatheads, producing two of their fastest chargers, were backed by the Blackfeet in a like number; and, upon the success of the particular favorites, not only the honor of the two nations was staked, but a large amount of other valuables. The race was run, and, the result proving close, both parties claimed the wager.

Upon this a dispute ensued, and finally the whole matter was referred to three white men, by whose decision they agreed to abide. The arbitrators, through mere personal predilection, instead of pronouncing it a tie, as they should have done, awarded the palm to the Flatheads.

The Blackfeet gave in to the decision and relinquished the stakes, but from that day forth avowed themselves the eternal enemies of both whites and Flatheads. This occurrence dated the commencement of an unrelenting war of extermination on their part, nor have they permitted any suitable opportunity of wreaking their vengence upon the offenders to pass unimproved.

Notwithstanding the bad character generally ascribed to the Blackfeet, they possess traits worthy of admiration. As enemies, they make no disguise of their hostile designs; and though they have been known to meet with parties of whites without coming in colission, and even to smoke with them; yet, on such occasions, they have uniformly declared the armistice a temporary one, and in force only for the time being.

Instances have been known of trappers penetrating into their villages unawares, who received the treatment of guests during their stay, and were allowed to depart unmolested upon expressing their wishes to that effect.

The bright spots in the character of these Indians are more fully developed in the following example:

Several years ago, two trappers, in their excursions for beaver, discovered a Blackfoot engaged in butchering. Thinking the present a favorable opportunity to reduce the number of their enemies, they cautiously approached the unsuspecting operator with the design of affording him a speedy transition to the Spirit Land.

Having advanced within gun-shot, they were almost in the very act of firing, when a casual glance revealed the dusky forms of savages who surrounded them at no great distance, and in such a manner as to preclude all possibility of escape; but as yet, however, the intended victim was ignorant of their presence.

On observing the danger of their situation, they rushed up to him, and, seizing his hands, claimed his protection. The excitement of the moment having subsided, he replied:—

"Your lives belong to me,—you might have taken mine; it must not be said that the Blackfoot is ungrateful. Come with me and you are safe."

Upon this he led the way to the village near by, and made them the guests of his own family.

Everything that generous hospitality could devise for comfort and pleasure, was placed at their disposal. The villagers seemed to vie with each other in their attestation of friendship and good will, and repeatedly solicited them to remain and join the tribe.

However, on expressing a wish to leave, they were escorted for some distance *en route*, and left to choose their own course of travel, with the parting monition: "We are now friends.—When next we meet it will be as enemies!"*

---

* The Blackfeet are generally accounted brave, though instances have been known of three or four whites defeating a large party of them. On one occasion, three trappers fell into an ambuscade of these Indians, and two of them were instantly shot from their horses, but the third was left untouched, and spurring his animal to the height of its speed, broke through the whole throng and was soon out of reach.

Four mounted Indians immediately started in pursuit, and gained rapidly upon him till they came within shooting distance, when the lone trapper turned upon them, and with his double-barreled rifle picked off two of their number, and again fled.

Confident of securing their intended victim, now that they supposed his fire-arms were uncharged, the remaining two hurried after him, and in a few moments were within range of pistol-shot. The trapper then again halted, and the discharge of a pistol brought the third to the ground.

Drawing forth a second from his belt, the work of slaughter would have been complete, had not the terrified savage, in his turn, fled with the utmost precipitancy. The trapper pursued, but was far in the rear when the Blackfoot regained his comrades, and hurriedly exclaimed:

"Haste, ye! flee! It was the Big Medicine we pursued, and at his word three of our warriors breathe not, and of four I only have escaped! His single medicine-

*Nov. 20th.* Yielding to the solicitations of my comrades demontés, I am again journeying for the Platte. During the brief period of our stay at Fort Hall, we enjoyed mild and agreeable weather, as a general thing; only one inconsiderable fall of snow having occurred meanwhile, and the grass, even yet, in many places, is green and fresh.

Notwithstanding the lateness of the season, we anticipate but little difficulty in crossing the mountains, *via* New Park and Grand river pass, as the journey has been performed on several occasions in the dead of winter. But, a further stimulant to our hopes is the possession of good mules and horses, which are every way competent to the task before them; my two companions are, also, intimately acquainted with the mountains, and well know how to shape our course to advantage.

For the first few days our progress was rapid and uninterrupted. Following the regular trail by way of Bear river, on the 24th we struck Black's fork, a considerable tributary of Green river, and one of several in its neighborhood, down which we continued to its confluence with the main stream; thence, crossing to the east bank, we kept its general course, sometimes by its valley, then again by long *detours* among the hills, owing to the rugged nature of the country, and in three days subsequent, reached the Yampah, or Little Snake, an affluent from the left.

The intermediate country from Fort Hall to the Yampah has been partially noticed in connection with Oregon and California, and for that reason it will not be expected of me to waste time in repetition.

I need only add, that among the hills we noticed much nude sterility, intermingled with frequent clusters of *absinthe, aretmisia* (or greasewood, as it is familliarly called,) and bunch-grass, with occasional groves of pine, cedar, and balsam.

In the valleys the grass was yet green, and indicated the presence of winter only by its withered tops. Snow was seen only upon the hills and mountains, and even there in no great quantity. Game appeared plentiful for most of the distance, particularly black-tailed deer and sheep.

The section of country hereabouts is inhabited by the Snake Indians, from whom the river above referred to derives its name.

This stream heads in the New Park Mountains, and pursues a southwest course for about one hundred miles, recieving in that distance several large tributaries from the east, when it finally discharges itself into Green river, near lat. 41° North.

Crossing the Yampah, we soon struck the Elk Head, or Little Bear, a principal affluent from the right, and continuing our course up its valley. After passing a small ridge, on the 30th Nov. we found ourselves upon the head waters of the Platte.

iron twice spoke the death-word, and at the same time; then with his pipe-stem he bade a third one go to the Spirit Land; and, as he drew forth his butcher-knife to shoot me, I had fled beyond reach, that I might tell you how to escape! Haste, ye! flee! It is the Big Medicine that comes from yon! Flee, lest he kill us all!"

Following his advice, the astonished savages immediately fled with the greatest consternation, fully persuaded it was their only mode of escaping from certain destruction at the hands of the BIG MEDICINE!

Proceeding by the valley of a creek tributary to the above river, the day following we came to a considerable branch from the south, and camped near its mouth, for the purpose of killing buffalo, of which vast numbers thronged the vicinity.

The valleys of the Yampah and Little Bear were broad, in places, with a deep soil of dark, sandy loam, and tolerably well timbered.

The country contiguous to them was rugged and generally sterile; the soil, with the exception of the creek bottoms, being shallow and sandy, and infested with extensive fields of *absinthe*.

By the way we passed a fort, formerly occupied by a company of trappers under the command of Frapp, near which himself and four other whites were killed in an engagement with the Sioux some two years since. The Indians lost fifteen or twenty of their warriors in killed and wounded, but succeeded in driving off eighty head of horses as their booty.

Among the rocks of the hills I noticed frequent clusters of larb, richly laden with its deep red berry,* both tempting to the eye and pleasing to the taste.

On reaching the Platte we were ushered into a large and beautiful circular valley, known as the New Park.

This valley is thirty-five miles in width by thirty in breadth, and is shut in upon all sides by lofty mountains, whose summits tower far above the snow-line and sport their white-caps through each returning year. It is well watered by numerous streams that trace their course from the neighboring heights to commingle with the Platte.

The river makes its exit from this place by a forced passage through narrow defiles, between the Medicine Bow and New Park Mountains, forming a cañon several miles in length, defined by precipitous walls, varying in height from fifty to six hundred feet.

The New Park valley affords considerable timber of various kinds, and a fertile soil, well adapted to cultivation. The superfice is usually a thick mould, compounded of clay, sand, and gravel, with decomposed vegetable matter; while the bottoms disclose a rich alluvion of two or three feet depth.

The entire country was crowded with game, in countless numbers, both of buffalo, elk, and deer. It seemed as though a general ingathering from mountain, hill, and plain, had taken place to winter in this chosen spot.

It is said the great abundance of game first suggested the christening of the locality as the *New Park*.

We remained in our encampment till the 5th of December, and improved the interval in procuring a choice supply of meat, and feasting upon those delicious viands which mountaineers so well know how to acquire and dispose of.

The day preceding our departure, a fall of snow covered the ground for

---

* The larb-berry is of a deep red color, and somewhat larger than the common currant. It is of a sweet spicy taste, and very pleasant. It grows upon a small ground-vine of evergreen, with a leaf assimilating the winter-clover in shape, and is found only in mountainous regions.

several inches, but the lapse of a few hours served to disclose the bare vegetation of the valleys, and denuded spots upon the mountain sides.

Again *en route*, we continued up a large stream from the south and struck into a broad trail, which led through large openings and forests of aspen across the main mountain chain, to the waters of Grand river, into a beautiful valley known as the Old Park, where we remained encamped the two days subsequent.

Our nearest route to Fort Lancaster would have been by Cáche a la Poudre, or Long's Peak; but, accumulating snows admonished us to abandon the Atlantic side of the mountains for a more southern latitude.

The country in the vicinity of the Old Park is highly interesting. It embraces a large tract of fertile territory, well watered and timbered, but more or less undulating, and is hemmed in by high mountains, which are clothed with lateral forests of pine, cedar, and aspen.

This valley ranges from east to west; and, heading at the base of Long's Peak, finds its opposite extremity at the cañon by which Grand river emerges through the opposing barriers of mountain spurs.

The Old Park also, like the New, receives its appellation from the great abundance of game for which it is celebrated.

## CHAPTER XXVIII.

From Grand river to Bayou Saláde.—Observations by the way.—Description of the Bayou.—Voracity of magpies.—Journey to Cherry creek.—Country en route.—Crystal creek.—Abundance of game.—Antelope hunting.—Remarkable sagacity of wolves.—Snow storms and amusement.—Ravens.—Move camp.—Comfortable winter quarters.—Animal food conducive to general health and longevity.—A laughable instance of sound sleeping.—Astonishing wolfine rapacity.—Beaver lodges and all about beaver.—Hunting excursion.—Vasque's creek, its valleys, table lands, mountains, and prairies.—Camp.—Left alone.—Sensations, and care to avoid danger.—A nocturnal visitor.—Thrilling adventure and narrow escape.—A lofty specimen of " gettin down stairs."—Geological statistics.

WHILE camped at the Old Park, I improved the opportunity for ranging among the adjacent mountains, whose stern recesses disclosed many smiling beauty-spots. The weather continued pleasant, though somewhat colder than usual; and, notwithstanding the snow in places lay quite deep, it had acquired great solidity and compactness.

On the 10th of December we were again under way.

Crossing Grand river and continuing up a southern tributary, through a a narrow defile of mountains, to a large valley formed at the junction of three principal branches, known as La Bonte's-hole, and choosing the middle one, we proceeded to its head,—thence, passing the dividing ridge by a well-beaten buffalo trail, to the right of Long's Peak, on the 16th we reached Bayou Salâde, another extensive valley at the head of the South Fork of the Platte. Here, selecting a good camping place in a beautiful grove of aspen, we remained till the 19th inst.

This last stage of our journey proved difficult and tedious. Although the passing throngs of buffalo had afforded a well-marked trail, our horses frequently became so mired in snow we were compelled to extricate them by main strength,—two or three storms, in the mean time, having increased the quantity to an average depth of twelve or fourteen inches.

The valleys and sunny hill-sides, however, were generally bare, and afforded some agreeable respites to the toil of travelling.

The prevailing rock appeared to be granite, mica slate, and sandstone. The soil of the valleys gave evidence of fertility, as did occasional spots upon the hill-sides.

The streams were most of them skirted with cottonwood, aspen, and box-elder, while the hills and mountains presented frequent groves of pine and cedar.

Game, in all the different varieties common to the country, was seen in great abundance the entire route.

Bayou Salâde is a valley some thirty-five miles long by fifteen wide, bounded upon all sides by lofty mountain chains, with the exception of the south, where a broad stretch of high, rugged hills and rolling prairies separates it from the Arkansas.

The Platte, on emerging from this place, makes its final entrance into the grand prairie by a narrow gorge in the mountain chain that extends to a distance of several miles. Upon the southeast, the frowning summits of Pike's Peak tower to a height of 12,500 feet above the level of the Gulf of Mexico, and upon the west the continuous chain of the Green Mountains, clothed in eternal snow, point skyward in solemn grandeur.

The numerous streams that find their sources in the neighborhood are well timbered, and present many interesting bottoms of rich alluvial soil.

The valley is densely thronged with buffalo, while vast quantities of deer, elk, and antelope unite to increase the number and variety of its game.

The weather at this time proved uncomfortably cold. Snow lying upon the ground to the depth of several inches, we were necessitated to feed our horses upon cottonwood bark during the interim.

Bayou Salâde bears the name of being subject to severe winters, but whether correctly or not, I am unable to say. It is undoubtedly well adapted to stock-raising, and, were it not for unseasonable frosts, might be turned to good account for agricultural purposes.

The magpies were more troublesome and audacious in their depredations hereabouts, than in any place we had yet visited. Two mules, whose backs had become sore from continued service under the saddle, were severely annoyed by these relentless pesecutors, which, despite opposing effort, would pierce the skinless flesh with their beaks and feast upon their agonizing victims.

To save the poor sufferers from being devoured alive, we were compelled to envelope them with thick coverings of buffalo robes, and even then the rapacious cormorants could scarcely be prevented from renewing their cruel repast.

*Dec. 19th.* Again resuming our journey, we continued in a southeast direction, over a low ridge of hills, and found ourselves in a very rough country, interspersed with frequent valleys which head several well timbered affluents of the Arkansas;—thence, passing around the southern extremity of a lofty mountain range, we struck *Fontaine qui Bouit* a few miles below the Soda spring.

Crossing this stream, we travelled north by west, following the mountain ridge at its base for some forty miles, which brought us to the Platte; —thence, keeping the river bottom, on the 28th we made camp at Cherry creek, a short distance above its mouth.

The interesting and romantic country in the vicinity of Pike's Peak and *Fontaine qui Bouit* has already been described in full, and needs but one passing remark in attestation of the mildness of its climate, viz: the ground was free from snow, and afforded occasional spots of green grass.

Near this place we encountered a small hunting party of Arapaho Indians, and obtained from them a choice supply of fresh meat.

The interval from the Soda spring to the Platte, after passing the high, towering and isolated walls of red granitic sandstone to the northward, betrays a mixed character of wildness and beauty. The vast forests of stately pines, surmounting the long rolling hills to the right, which are relieved as the traveller advances by high table lands and quadrangular-shaped eminences that disclose their bare sides, ever and anon graced with lateral cedars and dwarf oaks; and then the heaven-scaling summits that, in continuous chain, oppose an impregnable wall upon the left, unite to define a broad-spread of undulating prairie, some eight or ten miles wide, well watered and possessed of a good soil.

The prevailing rock of this section appeared to be sandstone and limestone, intermixed with conglomerates of various kinds.

I noticed two or three small ridges, several miles long, running parallel with the mountains at regular distances, in an uninterrupted course, presenting continued lines of thin strata planted vertically in their sharp crests, and reaching to an elevation of thirty or forty feet, that, with broken fragments encumbering their sides, looked like the half-fallen walls of some ancient fortification.

Among several affluents of the Platte from the right, we crossed Crystal creek, a stream which derives its name from the existence af crystal in its sandy bed. This creek is tolerably well timbered and possesses a rich bottom of variable width, producing at the proper season a luxuriant growth of vegetation.

Our horses being quite enfeebled from the fatigue of travel, we gladly availed ourselves of the presence of buffalo to prolong our stay at Cherry creek some ten days, and meanwhile found no difficulty in procuring a continued feast of good things from the dense herds that thronged the country upon every side.

The severe weather and frequent snows of the past two months, had driven these animals from the open prairie into the creek bottoms and mountains, whose vicinities were completely blackened with their countless thousands.

The antelope, too, seemed to have congregated from all parts, and covered the country in one almost unbroken band. Their numbers exceeded any thing of the kind I ever witnessed before or since. We amused ourselves at times in shooting them merely for their skins, the latter being superior to those of deer or even sheep in its nicity of texture and silky softness.

One day, as was my custom, I left camp for the above purpose, and had proceeded but a short distance, when, happening upon a large band of antelope, a discharge from my piece brought down one of its number.

Before reaching it, however, my supposed victim had rejoined his companions, and the whole throng were lost to view almost with the speed of thought.

The profuseness of blood that marked its trail through the snow, induced me to follow it in expectation of soon obtaining the object of my pursuit; but in vain.

At length, after travelling four or five miles, I began to despair of success, and, feeling weary, sat down upon the point of a small hill that commanded a view of the surrounding prairie. While here an unusual stir among the wolves attracted my attention, and I amused myself by watching their movements.

Upon a neighboring eminence some fifty or a hundred of these insatiate marauders were congregated, as if for consultation. Adjoining this, two parallel lines of low hills led out from the river bottom into the prairie, for five or six miles, defining a narrow valley, at the extremity of which a large band of antelope were quietly grazing.

The chief topic of the wolfine conference seemed to have particular reference to this circumstance; for, in a very short time, the council dispersed, and its members betook to the hills skirting the valley before described, and, stationing themselves upon both lines at regular intervals, two of them commenced the attack by leisurely approaching their destined prey from opposite directions, in such a manner as to drive the whole band between the defile of hungry expectants. This done, the chase began without further preliminary.

Each wolf performed his part by pursuing the terrified antelope till relieved by his next companion, and he by the succeeding one; and so on, alternately; taking care to reverse their course at either extremity of the defile—again and again to run the death-race, until, exhausted by the incessant effort and crazed with terror, the agile animals, that were wont to bid defiance to the swiftest steed, and rival the storm-wind in fleetness, fell easy victims to the sagacity of their enemies.

I watched the operation until several of them yielded their lifeless carcases to appease the appetite of their rapacious pursuers, when I returned to camp with far more exalted ideas of the instinctive intelligence of wolves (savoring so strongly of reason and calculation) than I had previously entertained.

Two or three severe snow-storms occurred shortly after our arrival; but having constructed commodious shantees in regular mountain style, with large fires in front, we were both dry and comfortable.

These occasions, too, afforded their own amusement. Snugly stowed away in bed, with our rifles at hand, whenever a straggling wolf ventured within gun-shot, in fond hopes of a deserted camp, he was almost sure to fall a victim to his own temerity.

Bands of five or ten would frequently approach almost to the camp-fire, totally unsuspicious of danger till the sharp crack of a rifle told the fall of some one of their number.

A swarm of ravens, allured by the carcases of these animals, peopled the grove near by. Having devoured the timely feast, still the poor birds remained, making the day dismal with their tireless croakings, as if in importunate supplication for a further boon.

Three of them soon became quite domesticated, and would approach fearlessly to the very verge of the camp-fire in quest of the offals of our culinary department.

One, however, by far exceeded his two companions in boldness, and would venture within a few feet of us at any time.

So audacious was his conduct, and so insatiate his appetite, his comrades took occasion to bestow upon him frequent chastisements; but all to no purpose. At length, abandoning all hope of effecting the desired reformation, they set upon the offending bird, nor relinquished their purpose till the life of the luckless gormandizer had expiated the crime of his unravenlike conduct, and his executioners were left to enjoy their daily repasts without the annoyance of his presence.

*Jan. 16th*, 1843. Having received an accession of three men to our number, from Fort Lancaster, we removed some six or eight miles further down the Platte, and camped in a large grove of cottonwood upon the right bank.

At this place it was our daily practice to fell two or three small trees for our horses, as we now considered ourselves fully established in winter quarters. Game was plenty, and wood abundant; nothing, therefore, remained for us to do but to recruit our horses, eat of the best the prairie afforded, drink of the crystal waters that rolled by our side, and enjoy life in true mountain style; nor did we neglect the opportunity of so doing. In fact, had the world been searched over, it would have been hard to find a jollier set of fellows than we.

The effort of a few hours was sufficient to procure a month's supply of the choicest delicacies, nor is it marvellous that, to use a cant phrase of the country, we soon became "*fat, ragged, and saucy.*"

Perhaps nothing is more conducive to good health than animal food. In proof of this I need only to refer to the uniform good health of those subsisting entirely upon it.

Sickness of any kind is rarely known to the various Indian tribes confined exclusively to its use. These people almost invariably live to an extraordinary age, unless cut off by the ravages of war or some unforeseen event. Consumption, dyspepsy, colds, and fevers, are alike strangers to them.

The same observation holds good in regard to the whites who reside in this country and subsist in a similar manner.

I have known confirmed cases both of consumption and dyspepsy cured by visiting these regions and submitting exclusively to this mode of living.

For my own part, I felt not the least indisposed during the entir period of my stay, nor did I even hear of an instance of death from natural causes in the mean time, and but rarely of a case of sickness, however slight. The same also has been repeatedly remarked in my hearing by persons who have resided here for ten or twelve years, and whose united experience corroborates my own.

A further fact, relative to the teeth, is worthy of note in connection with this subject. These never suffer by decay or aches, when employed only in the mastication of flesh; or, at least, I have never seen or heard of an instance of the kind.

I am, therefore, led to conclude from the foregoing facts, that animal food is in every respect the most wholesome and innocent diet which can be adopted.

A person in the enjoyment of good health and a quiet mind, generally sleeps sound. In proof that such was the case with our party, I need only advert to a circumstance which here occurred.

Having awoke one moonshiny night, and observing an unusual number of wolves in the vicinity of camp, I seized my rifle and shot one of them; soon after I improved the opportunity to lay another prostrate, and in a few minutes subsequent a third fell in like manner; all at three several shots.

A continuation of the sport seemed likely to detract too much from the hours of sleep, and so, placing the victims in front of the camp-fire, I addressed myself to repose.

A light snow fell in the interval, and sunrise found us all in bed, patiently waiting to see who would have the courage to rise first. At length, one man jumped up and turned to renew the fire. On noticing the wolves before it he wheeled for his rifle, in his eagerness to secure which he fell sprawling at full length.

"Hello!" says one; "what's the matter, my boy. Is that are a sample of the *ups* and *downs* of life?"

"Matter?" exclaimed our hero, gathering himself up in double-quick time, and rushing for his gun; "matter enough! The cursed wolves have grown so bold and saucy, that they come to the fire to warm themselves! Only look! A dozen or more of 'em are there now, in broad day-light! Get up, quick! and let's kill 'em!"

Aroused by this extraordinary announcement, the whole *posse* were instantly on their feet to repel the audacious invaders; when, lo! the cause of alarm proved three dead carcasses.

But, where did they come from? When were they killed? Who placed them there? These were questions none were able to solve, and in regard to which all were profoundly ignorant. Finally, the circumstance occa-

A BEAVER.—Page 295.

sioned quite an animated discussion, which was soon merged into angry dispute; and, after amusing myself awhile at their expense, I unravelled the mystery, to the surprise of all.

"Can it be possible!" was the general exclamation,—" can it be possible that we should have slept so sound as not to hear the report of a rifle fired three times in succession, and under our very ears, at that!"

"This reminds me," said one, "of dreaming that somebody fired during the night. But it seemed so much like other dreams I had forgotten it till now."

"Well," retorted a second, "we are a pretty set of customers to live in a dangerous country! Why, a single Indian might have come into camp and killed the whole of us, one after another, with all the ease imaginable!"

The above incident induced the narration of a circumstance, happening to an individual of my acquaintance two or three weeks previous.

He had been into the mountains after deer, and was on his return to the Fort for a fresh supply of ammunition, and, having occasion to camp out at night, like a genuine mountaineer, he took his saddle for a pillow. This, being covered with raw hide, excited the cupidity of a marauding wolf.

The hungry beast felt ill-disposed to let slip an opportunity thus favorable for appeasing his appetite with a dry morsel, and so, gently drawing it from beneath the head of the unconscious sleeper, he bore off his prize to devour it at his leisure.

In the morning our hero awoke minus saddle, and nothing save a number of wolf-tracks at his head furnished clue to the mystery of its disappearance; and, after spending several hours in fruitless search, neither hide or hair of it could be found.

In the river bank near camp were two lodges of beaver, whose sagacious occupants gave frequent indications of their industrious habits by the magnitude of their performances. Several trees, ten or twelve inches in diameter, had been freshly felled by them to furnish their families with food.

In such operations they exhibit an instinctive intelligence well-nigh approaching to reason. They uniformerly select trees that stand above their lodges, in order to avail themselves of the current in conveying their timber to the destined place of deposit.

When a tree is thus chosen, the cautious little animal first carefully notices the point towards which its top inclines, and then sets himself to work at the opposite side. As his task approaches its completion, he frequently retires a short distance to observe the direction in which the tree is likely to fall, by watching its motions, and renews his labors with great caution. Upon the first indication of the *finale*, like an experienced woodsman, he instantly withdraws beyond the reach of danger, and leaves the tottering forest-monarch to announce his fallen greatness in the awful crash by which he is bespread upon the ground.

The process of chopping is then performed by severing the trunk into blocks, some three feet in length, suitable for transportation, which are severally taken to the "slide" and rolled into the stream, by the cunning animal—using his tail as a substitute for hands. As they fall one after another, he plunges in and guides them to their destination, where they are safely moored for future use.

The beaver possesses great strength in his tail, which is twelve or fifteen inches long, four broad, and a half inch thick. This part of the animal is highly esteemed by trappers, and assimilates a fish in taste, though it is far superior to any of the finny tribe.

His teeth are very sharp, (incisors,) two inches or more in length, perfectly round and of a uniform size, with the exception of the cutting extremities, which are gouge-like, about the eighth of an inch in diameter, and nearly in the shape of a semicircle.

Beaver lodges are commonly constructed in holes carefully excavated in the banks of streams, in such a manner that the entrances are entirely covered by water. It is very rarely they build in any other manner, notwithstanding most writers upon this subject assert the contrary.

The female usually produces two, and sometimes three, at a birth, but seldom rears more than one;—first destroying the least likely, she bestows much attention upon her favorite offspring, and nurses it with great tenderness.

The character and habits of this curious animal, in other respects, have probably met the reader's eye through other sources, so that a more extended notice under this head would be unnecessary.

Having procured a fresh supply of ammunition from Fort Lancaster, some two weeks succeeding our arrival at this place I visited the mountains on a hunting excursion, in company with a single *voyageur*.

Our course lead up Vasque's creek for fifteen or twenty miles, to a ridge of high table land, through which we passed, by a circuitous route, and were ushered into a broad and beautiful valley, bounded upon the east by the ridge before named, and on the west by a lofty mountain chain.

Vasque's creek is well timbered, and has a rich bottom, averaging one mile in breadth, and is skirted by a slightly undulating prairie, quite productive in various kinds of grasses.

This creek is from eight to ten yards wide, and affords a body of water more than a foot in depth. It heads in the main chain of the mountains, where it claims a valley of considerable extent, enclosed upon al sides by lofty ridges that preclude the possibility of approach, except a two points marking an Indian pass to the waters of Grand river.

From thence it winds its way between long defiles of mountains, tha close in abruptly upon its very water's edge, till it finally intersects the valley first spoken of, and forces itself through the high ridge of table land into the open prairie.

Finding an abundance of deer in the vicinity, we struck camp and made it our hunting-ground for the time being. Our efforts were very successful, and seldom a favorable day passed without giving us the skins and choice parts of two or more deer.

Nothing occurred to mar our enjoyment for the first two or three weeks, at which time my comrade, having unfortunately broken his gun-lock, was compelled to return to the Fort for repairs. I resolved, however, to remain *solo*, despite his entreaties to the contrary.

This was the first trial I ever made of hermit-life, and I must confess, that after the first sensations of repulsive loneliness had been overcome, I felt much attached to it, as subsequent pages will prove.

Yet there was something so forbidding in the idea of my real situation, I seldom reverted to it without experiencing feelings of gloomy apprehension. Nor need it be wondered at, removed as I was far away from friendly aid, and in a dangerous country, with a thousand terrific scenes awaiting me at every step.

Still, in a little time I learned to forget all this, and roamed as freely by day, and slept as soundly by night, as though surrounded by friends and guarded by hosts of armed men.

But the reader must not infer from these remarks that I had settled down in a state of careless security, for I took especial care a all times to avoid surprise, by close attention to certain indications which my own observation had taught me to regard as the general precursors of danger from a savage foe, in order, by a timely movement, to escape a contact so fraught with peril.

For several nights I had a constant visitor in the shape of a prairie-fox,— a creature about twice the size of a large red squirrel. He came to appease his hunger from the small scraps of esculents that lay scattered about camp,—devouring them while seated composedly by the fire.

My stock of provisions was usually secured, at night, by substituting it for a pillow; but Mr. Reynard soon became so emboldened that he repeatedly took occasion to help himself, even at the risk of sundry cuffs it was my wont to bestow upon him whenever his eagerness led him to deal too roughly with my hair.

Two incidents of perilous adventure occurred during this interval, which are perhaps not unworthy of narration.

One day, having proceeded farther from camp than was my custom without finding game, towards night I came to the broad escarp of a mountain, covered with scattering pines, and ascended to its summit in hopes of encountering deer or sheep, as the place gave indications of both. Here I stood at the very verge of a vast precipice, some four or five hundred feet high, overlooking a narrow valley, counter-scarped by a rough mountain chain, where a large band of elk were quietly grazing. The sight appeared so tempting I was unwilling to forego the opportunity of giving them a passing shot.

But how to get at them was the question. To go around the hill would require a *detour* of some six miles, and consume too much time, as the day was fast closing. Unless some means could be found enabling me to descend the wall, it was evident I must abandon my design.

Accordingly, after a short search, having found a ravine-like pass, worn by the rains and falling rock, that apparently led to the valley below, I attempted a descent.

The breakage was steep and narrow, and the loose fragments and *det-*

*ritus* from the crags above, rendered a foot-hold quite insecure. Yet I progressed without much difficulty, and began to congratulate myself on an anticipated speedy exit from seeming danger, when, coming suddenly to an abrupt precipice, of sixty or seventy feet perpendicular descent, and paved far around its base with sharp rocks presenting their keen edges like so many hatchets set on end, I was thrown all aback at the appalling spectacle.

In va n I tried to retrace my steps. The sides refused to sustain my weight, and the yielding surface, to which I clung with a death-like tenacity, threatened every moment to plunge me headlong from the frightful steep, to be dashed in pieces among the rocks below.

That moment was an awful one! Retreat was impossible,—advance was certain death,—the time for reflection was fast waning, for every instant brought me nearer and still nearer to the fatal verge!

It was then I bestowed a fleeting thought upon loved and absent friends, —one fleeting thought upon a far distant home and all the cherished endearments of childhood,—and, commending my soul to the Great Author of its existence in a brief prayer, I turned to gaze calmly upon the yawning jaws of fate that awaited my speedy destruction.

But here a ray of hope burst from the thick cloud which till now seemed just ready to merge the sun of existence into the density of its own darkness.

A tall pine grew at the base of the precipice, some fifty yards distant,— two narrow shelves of protruding rock, six or seven feet apart, led towards the tree, affording a sufficient hold for hands and feet to a person standing at full length.

My decision was instantly formed. Carefully dropping my rifle from the steep, by dint of great exertion I gained the shelves, that seemed as if made expressly for an occasion like the present;—then, by moving laterally, inch by inch, along the dizzy side, in a short time I had progressed to the tree, whose topmost branch lay just within my reach. Grasping this firmly in one hand, and disengaging the other to be used as the emergency might require, I threw myself backward among the surrounding boughs, and, lodging in safety, was left to descend at leisure the remaining distance.

Once more upon a sure footing, the occurrences of the day had proved a sufficient gorge to present ambition; so, seizing my rifle, (which had luckily fallen uninjured,) I bade farewell to the unconscious elk and returned to camp. There, with early night I found myself transported to the land of dreams in the drowsy car of sleep.

But, instead of wild beasts and prowling savages thirsting for blood, such as the danger of my lonely situation would naturally inspire, my mind was filled with visions of deep chasms, frightful precipices, and yawning steeps, that seemed to meet me at every turn, affording no possible way of escape; and thrice glad was I when wakeful morning chased these horrid phantoms far away, and revealed to me the welcome reality of conscious safety.

Soon after the adventure above related, another transpired of a somewhat similar nature

## GEOLOGICAL REMARKS.

The rugged mountain chain forming the western boundary of the valley, afforded numerous black-tailed deer and sheep. The skins of these animals being much larger than those of the common deer and antelope, I was induced to scour the vicinity, occasionally, in pursuit of them.

One day, having gone to a considerable distance on this errand, I was passing along upon the crest of a sharp peak, of great height and steep sides.

The ridge ranged from northwest to southeast, leaving upon its right side a vast spread of smooth snow, encrusting it from summit to base, and upon its left, a lateral *vallon*, entirely bare and graced with frequent spots of grass, as yet green and flourishing.

One of these niches was occupied by a band of wild sheep, which were so situated they could not be successfully approached, unless from the opposite side of the peak. Attempting this, I was proceeding slowly along, by means of steps implanted in the thick crust with the breech of my rifle, and had almost attained the point designed, when, losing foot-hold, I fell prostrate, and, after gliding the distance of a full mile, almost with the speed of thought, found myself immersed in a huge bank of loose snow, at the foot of the mountain.

It is all nonsense to talk of steam-boats and rail-road cars, in comparison with the velocity of such a lofty specimen of "gettin down stairs!" Few mortals, I may venture to say, ever got along in the world half so fast as did myself in this grand avalanche from the mountain-top.

The country contiguous to this valley is generally possessed of a very good soil, both in the prairies, table lands, and mountains. Bordering upon the watercourses, the surface discloses a deep mould of sand and gravel, exceedingly fertile, reposed upon a substratum of granite and micaceous sandstone; the prairies presented a mixed superfice of sand, clay, and gravel, rather thin and light, and strongly impregnated with various salts, —and the table lands, a compound of stiff clay, stone, and gravel, partially enriched by the fertilizing properties of vegetable and animal matter and the genial auxiliaries of disintegrated rock, with now and then a diminutive spot destitute of grass or herb and whitened by a thin coating of saline efflorescence.

The prevailing rock is sandstone, granite, gneiss, limestone, and large boulders of the primitive formation.

The only indication of minerals, so far as my observation extended, was that of iron, though doubtless due research would bring to light a rich supply of other valuable ores.

## CHAPTER XXIX.

Return to the Fort.—Texan recruiting officer.—New plans.—Volunteer.—The Chance Shot, or Special Providence.—Texan camp.—Country contiguous to the Arkansas, from Fountaine qui Bouit to the Rio de las Animas.—Things at rendezvous.—A glance at the company.—Disposal of force.—March up the de las Animas.—The country; Timpa valley, and its adjoining hills, to the de las Animas.—The latter stream; its cañon, valley and enchanting scenery.—Tedious egress.—Unparalleled suffering from hunger, toil, and cold.—Wolf flesh and buffalo hide.—Painful consequences of eating cacti.—A feast of mule meat after seven days' starvation.—Camp at the Taos trail.—The adjacent country.—Strict guard.—A chase.—The meet reward for Treason.

On the 16th of Feb., my stock of ammunition having failed, I proceeded to Fort Lancaster for a fresh supply, where I encountered a Texan recruiting officer, sporting a Colonel's commission, that bore the signature of "Sam Houston," President of the Republic.

The object of this personage was to raise a company of volunteer riflemen, to act in conjunction with a large force said to be then on its way for the invasion of Santa Fe. The main design of the expedition was to annoy the Mexican frontier, intercept their trade, and force them, if possible, to some terms by which a peace might be secured between the two countries.

The proposed rifle company was to be vested with discretionary powers, and perform the duties of a scouting party to the main army. Each of its members was to be regularly enlisted for the term of nine months,—armed with a good rifle and pistols, and mounted upon a stout, serviceable horse.

Great inducements, by way of promises, were also held out, to secure a prompt and ready enlistment; and, in fact, the whole affair was represented in a light so favorable, few possessed of the necessary means for equipping themselves refused to enter their names upon the muster-roll, and rally beneath the banner of the Lone Star.

One thing, however, served to awaken in the bosom of each the genuine martial spirit, more than all the eloquence of the fluent Colonel;—this was the unfurlment of the identical flag, bullet-pierced and tattered, that had stood as the genius of victory at the sanguinary battle of Corpus Christi, in the early days of the Texan revolution.

Who could refuse to respond favorably to a call backed by arguments so potent ?—not I.

Soon after Colonel Warfield, for such was the officer's name, set out on his return to the scene of intended operations, accompanied by some twelve or fifteen men, having named for his rendezvous a point within the Mexican territory, near the confluence of the Rio de las Animas and the waters of the Arkansas. Circumstances were such at the time it was inconvenient for me to leave, and eight or ten days intervened before my departure to join the expedition.

Meanwhile, it stormed almost incessantly, and the prairies presented naught save one vast expanse of gloomy desolation covered with deep and trackless snow.

The distance to be travelled was not far from two hundred miles, through a country inhabited only by wild beasts and strolling savages. Yet, nothing daunted by the cheerless aspect of affairs, having completed my arrangements, I improved the first fair day to launch forth upon the drear waste.

Relying upon the great abundance of game usually encountered *en route*, I took but a small supply of provisions, as, fully equipped, with rifle, pistols, butcher-knife, and other requisites, I mounted my horse, and, solitary and alone, commenced the long journey before me.

Hurrying on as fast as the nature of the case would admit, in the afternoon of the second day, an object, several miles in advance, arrested my attention. Suspicious of danger, but anxious to know its character and extent, I cautiously approached and was gratified to find it, instead of the lurking savage my imagination had depicted, a white man, hastening with eagerness to greet me.

He was on foot, and looked way-worn and weary to a deplorable extent. His story was soon told. He was the bearer of despatches from the Arkansas to Colonel Warfield,—and being compelled to abandon his mule by the way, on account of the depth of snow, had proceeded thus far on foot, and, for the last three days had been without eating, in the tedious performance of the duty committed to his trust.

Hearing this, I invited him to a creek near by, where I immediately struck camp, and laid before him my small stock of eatables, with the assurance it was at his disposal.

The speedy disappearance of the scanty supply, attested the keenness of his appetite, and left us both in a state of utter want.

On learning that Colonel W. had left for the Arkansas several days since, and now most probably had reached his destination, my new acquaintance concluded to retrace his steps and bear me company.

The next morning we arose breakfastless and resumed our journey, trusting to a kind Providence and our rifles to meet the demands of nature. But the snow became deeper the farther we advanced, and prospects more and more gloomy at every step.

Not a living creature presented itself to view, nor even the least vestige of any thing possessing the breath of life. Before and around lay a vast spread of winter-bleached desolation, bounded upon our right by the distant mountains, whose towering summits pierced the blue heavens and laughed at the clouds and storms below, while in front, and rear, and on our left, the curving horizon alone gave limit to vision.

Still hope bade us advance, although difficulties continued to multiply in threefold ratio. The second and third day our progress did not exceed twelve miles, and yet we had gone so far retreat or advance seemed alike hopeless.

Starvation stared us in the face, and continued travel through snow, ofttimes waist deep, reduced our strength and wasted our spirits.

On the fourth day, however, the weather having become more favorable, we were enabled to make further headway than the preceding one. We also saw a few ravens, but they, as if conscious of our desperate condition, cautiously avoided coming within gun-shot;—a big rabbit likewise showed itself in the distance, but, being at the top of its speed, disappeared almost as soon as seen;—thus we were again doomed to go supperless to bed and feast upon the well-furnished tables of dreams, which, though they please the fancy during their continuance, serve only to increase the appetite and stimulate its cravings.

On the morning of the fifth day, as we arose to continue our journey, determined to hold out as long as possible, the haggard looks of my comrade excited my compassion, and wishing to cheer him, I observed,

"Well, what would you think were I to predict for us a good supper tonight?"

"Really," said he, "I don't know. But there's a poor show for its fulfilment, any how."

"We shall have one, I know it."

"God send we may. But, pray, where is it to come from."

"I am quite confident we shall find game. If so, as my rifle bears the name of Old Straightener, and it has never been known to fail in a case of emergency, I know she will maintain her ancient honor."

"What if we don't find game? Then how."

"Why, here's my horse. It will be of no service to me if I am to die from starvation. In case we find nothing, its carcase shall save our lives."

"Horse meat or any thing else wouldn't go bad, just at this time."

Thus resolved, we continued our way, plodding along in gloomy silence, brooding over the sad realities of our deplorable situation,—ever and anon, scanning the vacant expanse, in the fast-waning hope of looked-for relief, —but as yet looked for in vain.

The day was fast verging to a close, and I was summoning a sufficiency of fortitude to submit to the sacrifice of my favorite beast, and ruminating upon the many difficulties and inconveniences that must result from such a step, volving and revolving all the pros and cons the case admitted of, when I was roused from my reverie by the shrill voice of my comrade, who joyfully exclaimed,

"Look!—look! A buffalo!"—at the same time pointing in the direction it appeared.

I looked, and sure enough a venerable old bull presented himself a few hundred yards to the right.

"Aye, aye, my hearty! There's a chance for Old Straightener!" said I, as, lowering my rifle, I started towards the intended victim.

"Don't forget," cried my comrade, "that all my hopes of salvation are centred in your rifle-ball."

The animal was feeding quietly, and I was enabled to approach within some sixty yards of him, when levelling, I pulled trigger,—but the cap, being damp, burst without a discharge. The noise caught the quick ear of the buffalo, and caused him to look round;—however, seeing nothing to excite his alarm, he soon resumed an employment more agreeable to his *taste* than needless vigilance.

Having put fresh powder into the tube, and supplied it with another cap, I was again raising to take aim, and had brought my piece nearly half, shoulderward, when it unceremoniously discharged itself, burying its ball in the *lights* of the buffalo—the very spot I should have selected had it been optional with myself. The old fellow staggered a few steps and *fell dead!*

My companion coming up, we soon completed the process of butchering, and, after furnishing ourselves with an ample supply of choice beef, proceeded to a neighboring creek, where, finding a few sticks of drift-wood, a fire was quickly kindled, and we ended our *fast of five successive days and nights* with feasting and glad hearts.

I have always regarded this event as a *special* Providence, and ever revert to it with no ordinary feelings of gratitude. Had the ball, thus accidentally discharged, missed the animal, or had it only wounded him, in all human probability, becoming alarmed at the presence of danger, and prompted by the instinct common to the species, he would soon have been beyond the reach of pursuit, leaving me to the dernier resort of slaughtering my horse or perishing among the snows and chill blasts of the prairie.

Enfeebled as we were from continued toil and suffering, we could have scarcely held out a day longer, and even the partial relief afforded by a poor supply of horse flesh, left, as we would have been, to travel on foot and carry our beds, guns, and provisions, must have served only to prolong our miseries a brief space, finally to meet the inevitable fate that threatened us! as this solitary buffalo was the only living creature that met our view during the entire journey.

I have never consented to dispose of the rough-looking piece long previously christened "Old Straightener," and, when asked the reason, have uniformly replied, "It is the only gun I ever saw or heard of that has killed game *of its own accord!*

The second day succeeding this occurrence, my companion left me to obtain his mule, and I completed the remainder of my journey alone,—arriving the appointed rendezvous late in the afternoon of the 20th of March.

The country travelled over, from the Platte to the Arkansas, near the mouth of Fontaine qui Bouit, has been fully described in former pages.

My route, from the mouth of this stream, followed the Arkansas for some forty miles. The landscape, back from the river-bottoms, was quite undulating, presenting upon the left a superfice of gravel, clay, and sand, mixed with vegetable matter; and, upon the right, a light, sandy soil, somewhat sterile and unproductive.

Many rich spots of a deep bluish loam meet the eye of the traveller, interspersed with spreads of naked sand, or clay whitened by exuding salts, or clothed in dwarfish grass; among which numerous clusters of *absinthe*, frequently five or six feet high, are seen in almost every direction.

The country, as a general thing, is evidently ill-adapted to other than grazing purposes.

Two broad beds of sand-creeks are passed upon the left, a few miles below Fontaine qui Bouit, one of which is Black Squirrel creek, and the other is known as the Wolf's Den. Upon the right, the Rio San Carlos, Cornua Virda, Apache, and Huaquetorie, after tracing their serpentine courses from the Taos Mountains, commingle with the Arkansas.

Some six miles below the mouth of Fontaine qui Bouit are the ruins of an old fort, occupied several years since by one Capt. Grant as a trading post.

The last of my course, being upon the side of the river, was much impeded by mud; and, although the surface was generally bare, travelling was even more tedious than it had been at any time hitherto.

After a series of suffering and deprivation so continued and severe, right gladly did I hail the Lone Star banner upon the opposite shore, as their point of present termination.

Fording the Arkansas about a mile above the Texan encampment, I found it nearly swimming deep, with a swift and muddy current over a bed of quicksand and gravel.

My appearance created no little surprise among all present, as they had several days since numbered me with those who had volunteered with great readiness, so far as *promises* were concerned; but, when PERFORMANCES were required, "*came up missing.*"

I must confess, however, to great disappointment in the diminutive force that here met my view, which consisted of only twenty-four men, including officers—all told. But several accessions were expected, sufficient to swell the number to fifty-five or sixty. A party of eighty volunteers from the States were to meet us at the "Crossing" of the Arkansas, on the Santa Fe trail, together with a detachment of two hundred and fifty from Texas; and, with these reinforcements, it was confidently asserted we would be equal to the combined force of all New Mexico.

I immediately reported myself to the commanding officer, and was kindly welcomed, with the remark,

"Well, sir, you are just in time. Another day and you would have been too late. We move camp to-morrow morning."

(A pity it was I had not been too late!)

Withdrawing from the conference, the lapse of a few moments gave me an opportunity to look around and see among whom I had fallen.

It would have been hard to *scare up* a more motley group of humanity in any place this side of Mexico. Each individual presented a uniform as varied as the imagination could depict, though tallying well with the general appearance of the whole company—it was a *uniform of rags!*

Still from beneath the dusky visages, half obscured by beards to which the kindly operations of their razors had been for weeks and even months a stranger, I detected the frank expression indicating the generous-hearted mountaineer, and began to feel at home, notwithstanding the fast-rising feelings of regret that fortune had thrown me in their way.

Early in the morning of the following day we were drawn up in line and divided into two detachments,—one consisting of ten, and the other of fourteen men. The first of these, under the command of Colonel Warfield, were to proceed to the Crossing of the Arkansas, and await the arrival of the main army, or otherwise act as circumstances suggested, while the second, headed by a lieutenant, marched up the Rio de las Animas to the Toas trail, to perform the duties of a corps of observation until further orders.

It was my lot to accompany the latter, and we promptly commenced movement.

## DESCRIPTION OF THE DE LAS ANIMAS.

After riding a few miles we struck the Timpa, a small affluent of the Arkansas, up which we travelled till the next day about noon, when, coming to an Indian trail leading south-southwest to the de las Animas, we followed it and reached the latter stream on the 27th of March; continuing up the de las Animas, three days subsequently we arrived at our destination.

The country passed over at the commencement of our journey, for fifteen or twenty miles, was a slightly undulating prairie, of a sandy soil, with few indications of productiveness.

The Timpa is entirely destitute of timber, and its valley, though plentiful in *absinthe*, is scarcely superior to the surrounding prairie. Several miles previous to leaving it, our course lay between two ridges of forbidding and sterile hills, nearly destitute of vegetation, and affording only now and then a few scraggy cedars and shrubs. Indeed, but very little good land is found in this vicinity.

On diverging from the Timpa the trail crossed a high, arid prairie, which was furrowed by deep ravines, and ridged by long rolling hills, that were occasionally surmounted by cedars and pinions, until it struck the de las Animas.

The watercourses through this section are rare, and sparsely timbered, being for the most part shut in by high banks of earth or lofty walls of precipitous rock, varying in altitude, and presenting vast chasms, passable only at certain points. Their valleys are narrow, but possess a fertile soil which is to some extent susceptible of cultivation, while many parts of the adjacent prairies might answer for grazing purposes.

The prevailing rock, so far as my observation extended, was coarse-grained granite and limestone. I noticed at places along the creek valleys occasional spots of calcareous earth; and, in fact, their soils generally indicated the presence of calcium in their compound, to no inconsiderable extent.

The valley of the Rio de las Animas was by far the most interesting and romantic section of country we had as yet entered upon in the Mexican, or, as it is now claimed, *Texan* territory. This stream, in English, bears the name of *Purgatory creek;* in French, it is known as the *Piquer l'eau,* or Water of Suffering; in Indian, it is called the Wild River, and in Spanish, it is christened by the term above used, which means the River of Souls.

It rises in the Taos Mountains by two separate heads, a little south of the Spanish Peaks, and emerges from its rugged birth-place into the plains, where the two branches trace their way for some fifty miles and then unite to form one stream. These forks are passably well timbered, and are skirted at intervals with rich bottoms; but the circumjacent country is dry, rolling, and generally barren.

A short distance below their confluence the river cuts its way through an expanse of high, barren table lands, for sixty or sixty-five miles, leaving abrupt walls of rock and earth on both sides, piled to a varied height of from fifty to three or four hundred feet, surmounted by groves of cedar and pinion, interspersed with broad pavements of naked rock, nude wastes of stiff sun-baked clay, and occasional clusters of coarse grass.

These walls are often perpendicular, though they generally accline somewhat, and are ornamented with scattering shrubs and cedars, which in vain seek to hide the forbidding deformity of nature.

They frequently intrude to the very water's edge, and pile at their feet and in the foaming current huge masses of rock, strown about in all the wild disorder of savage scenery; then, expanding at brief intervals, they picture many sweet, enchanting spots, that smile and bloom in unfading loveliness, where angels might recline, and, listening to the chime of their own voices, echoed from rock to rock and reverberated with unheard-of melody, might fancy themselves in heaven; then again closing, to open in like manner at some favored point, till they finally give place to a broad and beautiful valley, from one to three miles in width, of unsurpassed fertility, and abounding at the proper season in every variety of fruit and flower known to the country, which, mingling amid the the scattering cottonwoods, (free from under-brush and mimicing in their arrangement the regularity of art,) seem to portray the fabled fields of Elysian bliss.

This valley extends from the mouth of the cañon to the junction of the de las Animas with the Arkansas—a distance of twenty-five or thirty miles; for ten or fifteen of which it is skirted with receding hills, that maintain their stern sublimity till they at length become swallowed up in the far-spreading prairie.

This is a favorite resort for deer, antelope, and turkey, which are found in great numbers, gambolling amid its varied beauties, or winding along its narrow defiles and forbidden recesses.

We entered the cañon through a narrow and steep declivity, formed by a small stream, which was shut in by continuous cliffs, that increased in height as they approached their lofty counterparts immuring the angry river.

After winding a day and a half among the crags and confused masses, which constantly intervened to impede our way, in vain searching for an egress, we found it impossible to proceed further, and were forced to climb the almost vertical bank, at an ascent of five or six hundred feet,—frequently lifting our horses over the rocks by means of ropes attached to their bodies and drawn from the impending summit;—this tedious process occupied nearly a day in its completion, and left us upon the lateral table land exhausted in strength and worn down with fatigue.

We were eleven days *en route*, during which time we suffered greatly from the severity of the weather, hunger, toil, and watching.

The air was bleak, the winds cold and piercing, and the sky almost continually over-cast with clouds, while two or three snow storms contributed their mite to swell the catalogue of comfortless hours.

Our horses, too, had become so exhausted from hard fare and previous service, we were necessitated to travel on foot for most of the distance. But the grand climax of miseries was experienced through lack of food.

A scanty supply of buffalo meat, taken with us at the outset, was consumed at the next meal, and we were left without one morsel to appease the gnawings of appetite for the two days and three nights succeeding.

A straggling wolf that chance threw in our way, at the expiration of this time, most luckily furnished us with a breakfast, though nothing further entered our mouths till the morning of the third day from this, when, coming to the site of a recent Indian encampment, we succeeded in gathering a few pieces of dry buffalo hide, that lay scattered about—so hard and tough the wolves had tried in vain to gnaw them; these, after being boiled some twelve or fourteen hours, afforded us a paltry substitute for something better, but of so glutinous a nature it almost cemented the teeth employed in its mastication.

The two days following we were again doomed to go hungry and began to talk seriously of the imminent danger of starving to death.

This interval had brought us into the cañon of de las Aminas, where, having struck camp, several of the men sought a temporary respite from the torments of hunger by eating roasted *cacti;*—the article at first tasted well, and from the recommendation of the essayists, several were induced to partake of it quite heartily.

But the lapse of a brief hour or two brought with it the "tug of war," when the inherent properties of the *cacti* began to have their effect upon the enervated systems of the participants.

The painful consequences of this strange diet at first were a weakness in the joints, succeeded by a severe trembling and a desire to vomit, accompanied with an almost insufferable pain in the stomach and bowels.

Three or four of the unfortunate sufferers were in such extreme pain they rolled upon the ground for agony, with countenances writhing in every imaginable shape of frightful distortion.

Hereupon it was decided to sacrifice one of our animals as a last resort, which was promptly done, and we ended our fast of nearly seven days' continuance with a feast of mule meat.

I had heretofore cherished a decided repugnance to this kind of food, but am in justice bound to say, it proved both sweet and tender, and scarcely inferior to beef. The supply thus obtained lasted till we came among buffalo, when ample amends were made for previous abstinence.

The only game encountered during the march was an occasional band of antelope or wild horses, whose extreme vigilance and caution set at defiance all attempts to approach them, and sported at the phrensy of our desperate efforts.

Our camp, at the termination of this arduous and eventful journey, was in a small grove of cottonwood, about eight hundred yards below the point at which the trail, from Bent's Fort to Taos, crosses the right hand fork of the de las Animas.

It was faced on the north by a broad sandy prairie, gently undulating, that, at intervals, disclosed a good soil, and led to a distant ridge of pine-clad hills; while from the west, at a distance of some twenty or thirty miles, the proud and isolated summits of the Spanish Peaks, or Huaquetories, arose to view, and from the southwest, the lofty and noble *tierras templadas* that skirt the heads of the Cimarone and Colorado, whose broad tops showed themselves in beautiful contrast with the sharp, snow-clad mountain forming the eastern boundary to the valley of Taos; then, upon the south and east, a steep bank, twenty-five or thirty feet high, shut us from the contiguous plain.

While here, we kept strict and constant guard, in view of anticipated movements of the enemy, as, from certain information previously obtained, we knew him to be quartered in full force at the nearest settlements.

Our daily and hourly expectation was to meet a detachment of the Mexican army, then out for the purpose of reconnoitering; and, weak as we were in point of numbers, we felt quite equal to a hundred such soldiers, and were anxious for a trial of arms.

Our stay was prolonged for three or four weeks, and the abundance of choice buffalo meat that continued to grace our larder, with the rank growth of fresh grass for the sustenance of our animals, imparted an air of cheerfulness and thrift both to man and beast.

Nothing occurred worthy of note during the interval, save the following incident. One day, late in the afternoon, our sentinels announced the appearance of a small party of Mexicans at the crossing, and immediate preparations were made for an attack. Before these could be completed, however, our expected enemy was reported as having raised camp and being likely to escape by a precipitate retreat towards the Arkansas. Six men, mounted upon fleet horses, were immediately detached in pursuit,—of whom I was one.

The chase continued for several miles, and terminated in our overhauling three persons,—but, instead of Mexicans, two of them were Americans, and the other an Englishman, on their way to the United States with two pack mules heavily laden with gold and silver.

On receiving from them information, of the disposition and probable whereabouts of the Mexican forces, they were permitted to depart unmolested,—a circumstance not likely to have happened had we been the gang of "*lawless desperadoes,*" so hideously depicted in several of the public prints of the day, as I have since learned.

An item of the intelligence received through them, gave us mingled sensations of pain and pleasure.

An European Spaniard,—who had made one of the Texan army in its unfortunate expedition against Santa Fe, in the fall of 1842, and had been retained a prisoner of war for a number of months subsequent, having effected his escape to the Indian country,—on hearing of the recent movements of the Texans under Col. Warfield, had come and reported himself ready again to enlist.

On the strength of this assurance he was partially admitted to *confidence*, —a thing rarely to be reposed in any one of Spanish extraction. The result was, that, after gleaning all the information circumstances would admit of, he proceeded, post haste to *Santa Fe*, and laid the whole affair before Gen. Armijo, the Mexican Governor, in hopes of a handsome reward.

The old Governor, however, had received more exact intelligence, with the *names* and *number* of volunteers composing the party under Col. W., (furnished him through the medium of certain *Americans*, base enough in principle and sordid enough in motive, to act as his *spies*, for a paltry bribe in the shape of stipulated remissions of tariff duties on imported goods, etc.,) and treated the traitor to his cause quite cavalierly,—not hesitating to tell him he lied, and even accuse him of being a Texan spy—threatening to try and execute him as such!

Were this ever the *reward of treason*, how few would be TRAITORS!

## CHAPTER XXX.

March down the Cimarone.—Junction of the two divisions.—Country between the de las Animas and the Cimarone.—Perilous descent.—Cañon of the Cimarone.—Soil and prevailing rock.—A fort.—Grandeur and sublimity of scenery.—Beauty of rocks.—Cimarone of the plain.—Fruits and game.—Wide-spread desolation.—A dreary country.—Summer on the Desert.--Remarks.—Encounter with Indians.—Nature's nobleman.—Wild horses and different modes of catching them.—Failure of expected reinforcements.—March into the enemy's country.—Ancient engravings upon a rock.—Boy in the wolf's den.—A man lost.—Forced march.—Torment of thirst.—Remarks.—The lost found.—Expulsion for cowardice,—its effect.

Soon after the incident related at the close of the preceding chapter, an express arrived from the Col. commandant, with dispatches ordering our division to join him at a small creek near the Pilot Buttes, or "Rabbit Ears," two noted landmarks situated some forty miles above the Santa Fe trail, and nearly equidistant between the Arkansas and Cimarone.

We accordingly took up our line of march and proceeded nearly due south for two days and a half, to the Cimarone; thence, down the valley of the latter, five days' travel to the Santa Fe trail, and thence, west-northwest, one day and a half to the place of rendezvous, which we found without difficulty after a journey of one hundred and seventy miles.

Between the de las Animas and Cimarone, we crossed a long reach of arid prairie, slightly undulating and generally barren, with the exception of small fertile spots among the hills, here and there, clothed with rank grasses.

In some parts, the *cacti* so completely covered the ground that it was impossible to step, for miles in succession, without treading upon their sharp thorns; in others, the thick clusters of *absinthe* monopolized the vicinity of creeks, nearly to the exclusion of all dissimilar vegetation; and yet in others, though of more brief space, naked sterility refused foot t aught save gravel and stiff clay, or saline efflorescences.

The water of most of the streams was so highly impregnated with mineral salts, it was often unfit to drink. The creeks afforded very little timber, and frequently none at all.

The section immediately at the base of the high table lands to the right, exposed some beautiful spreads of fertile prairie, well watered and suitably timbered. The soil, as a whole, presented all the prominent characteristics of like portions of country previously described.

The prevailing rock was limestone and sandstone, with various conglomerates, and extensive beds of gypsum. I noticed some very large specimens of mica, of great beauty and transparency,—one, in particular, was nearly a foot square, and two inches thick.

The only indication of minerals coming under my notice, was iron and salts; though gold has been found in the immediate vicinity of the Husquetories, and silver in the neighborhood of the de las Animas,—some very rich specimens of the latter ore, said to have been procured in this region having met my observation.

Near the Cimarone the country is very rugged and mountainous. Upon the right a lofty expanse of table land, some eight hundred or a thousand feet high, leads far off till it becomes lost in the distance; while, upon the left, the more elevated *tierras templadas* of the Colorado, gently curving from south to east, mark the division between the Cimarone and the latter stream.

Every watercourse is immured by cañons of craggy rocks that often preclude all access to it for many successive miles. The side-hills and prairie ridges, to some extent, are clothed with pines, pinion, and cedars; and the creeks, whenever the narrow space of their prison-walls will permit it, afford beautiful groves of cottonwood and thick clusters of fruit-bearing shrubs and underbrush.

Our course for a number of miles, previous to descending to the valley of the Cimarone, lay at the base of the table mountain on the right.

The entrance to this valley was by a narrow buffalo trail, leading down a perpendicular wall of clay and rock, sidelong in a shelf-like path, barely wide enough for a single horse or man to advance carefully, as the least misstep might plunge him down the abyss to be dashed in pieces upon the sharp fragments detached from the overhanging cliffs.

The wall thus descended was from eight hundred to a thousand feet in altitude, and faced by another of equal height at a distance of twenty-five or thirty yards.

The spectacle was grand and awful beyond description. A rock, that broke loose about midway as we descended the pass, fell thundering down the frightful steep with a tremendous crash, and made the welkin ring as it reverberated along the vast enclosure with almost deafening clamor. I have witnessed many romantic and picturesque scenes, but never one so magnificently grand, so awe-inspiring in its sublimity, as that faintly delineated in the preceding sketch.

Entering the cañon at this point, after wandering a short distance among the huge masses of broken rock thrown from its towering sides, the traveller is ushered into a valley nearly a mile broad, shut in by mural mountains that rise to a varied height of from eight to fifteen hundred or two thousand feet, gradually expanding as he proceeds till it attains a width of from two to four miles.

This valley generally possesses a very rich soil, sometimes of a deep, gravelly mould, and almost of vermilion-like color, assimilating the famous *redlands* of Texas, and, in appearance, equally fertile,—then, a dark brown loam obtrudes to view, sustaining a dense vegetation of lusty growth,—and, yet again, a light sandy superstratum, affording but small indications of productiveness; or dimniutive spreads of stiff clay, frowning in their own nudity; or barren wastes, of less extent, that, in deep penitence for their utter worthlessness, exude their briny tears in unremitting succession, which, as the solar rays strike on them with kind intent to wipe away, spread o'er their parent surfaces bleached shrouds of shining salt.

The latter part of this description, so far as my observation has extended, will apply to nearly the entire valley of the Cimarone after it emerges from the cañon.

The place at which this romantic valley first attains its full width, is the confluence of a small tributary to the main creek, near an isolated summit, that protrudes far out from the mountain range and commands the approaches from either direction.

This peak is five or eight hundred feet high, and inaccessible, except from the back ground by a gradual acclivity scarcely wide enough for two persons to ascend abreast. The top presents a small area of level surface, securely defended by an enclosing wall of rock, five or six feet in height, raised at its brow evidently by the hand of art. A better position, in a military point of view, for a fortification, is rarely found. Fifty men, suitably provisioned and equipped, might successfully defend it against an army of thousands.

The rocks of this vicinity exhibit a more striking variety of color than any I ever before witnessed. Their predominant classification enumerates granite, sandstone (generally ferruginous,) limestone, and slate. These were disclosed in abrupt escarpments of several hundred feet altitude, or in isolated, quadrangular masses with vertical sides, assuming the appearance of gigantic fortifications, temples and palaces;—or in a more multiform aspect, now portraying vast walls with narrow basements, that, diverging from the mountains, intersect the valley at intervals from side to side, except, perchance, at a well-formed gateway,—now, towering monuments, spires, and pyramids, and again sculptured statues of men and beasts.

All these magnificent representations are gorgeously decked with particolored strata lying tier above tier, in regular order, some white, others black, blue, brown, green, gray, yellow, red, purple, or orange, and so strangely intermingled that they cannot fail to excite the admiration of every beholder.

The Cimarone rises in the range of table lands thirty-five or forty miles east-southeast of Taos, and, after following a serpentine course for nearly six hundred miles, empties into the Arkansas some distance above Fort Gibson. As it emerges from the mountains, (where it is a stream of coniderable depth and a rapid current, confined to a narrow space between high clayey banks, with a bed of rock and pebbles,) it expands to a great width, and, in a short distance, its waters become brackish and unfit for use, till they finally disappear among the quicksands, and leave a dreary waste of worse than emptiness, to mark the course of the transient volumes produced by the melting snows of spring and the annual rains of autumn.

During its course through the Great American Desert, not a tree or shrub graces its banks. Its mountain valley, however, is ornamented with numerous and beautiful groves of cottonwood, that present among their underbrush a profuse abundance of plum, cherry, gooseberry, and currant bushes, with grape vines; while the adjoining hills afford oak, pine, pinion, and cedar.

Here also game abounds in great quantities, including, buffalo, wild horses, deer, antelope, elk, and turkeys.

We frequently encountered four or five hundred head of wild horses in a single band, and turkeys showed themselves in every direction.

The pleasant moonlight nights, that favored our journey through this delightful valley, were the source of great success in turkey-hunting, and afforded us no small sport. Nearly every large cottonwood tree was occupied as a roost, and the season as yet had not far enough advanced to hide its tenants amid the growing foliage. Each night, as the moon reached a suitable position, my practice was to seek out these perching-trees, from which I rarely failed to return heavily laden.

One night myself and companion killed ten of these fowls—some of them having an inch thickness of pure fat upon the back. It is unnecessary to say that with such abudance, strown so lavishly on every side, the fare upon our march adown this thrice-enchanting valley was one continued scene of sumptuous entertainment.

But, loveliness gives place to arid sterility, and verdure to dreary desolation, as the traveller makes his exit from the mountains.

Almost the entire expanse, from the Arkansas nearly to the Gulf of Mexico, an interval ranging south-southeast, from fifty to two hundred miles in width, between longitudes 100° and 104° west from Greenwich, is said to be little else than a vast desert of barrenness, destitute of tree or shrub, or spire of grass relieve the aching eye, nor favoring stream with kindly flow to quench the fevered thirst.

The whole country is subject to high winds, that sweep over it at brief intervals in maddened fury, bearing in their course immense clouds of dust, and engendering amid the waste landscape a scene of frequent change. To-day the wayfarer may find his progress impeded by no inconsiderable hills of loose sand, and to-morrow he may pass in the same direction and find a level prairie,—a fact not unaptly expressed in the words of the Psalmist, "the *mountains* skipped like rams, and the *little hills* like lambs!"

Between the Cimarone and the Arkansas, back from the watercourses, the prospect is but little better.

In the vicinity of the former are numerous spreads of rolling sand-prairie, if not entirely naked, but scantly clothed with coarse, scattering grass, growing upon a surface so loose that a horse or mule will sink to his fetlocks at every step in passing over it; then come broad reaches of slightly undulating plains, mantled with sickly, dwarf vegetation, and sustained by a thin clayey soil, so baked and indurated by the sun as to become almost impervious to water.

The snows of spring and the rains of autumn, as before hinted, afford the only moisture ever known to these arid regions. Here dews, alike with transient showers, are entire strangers to the summer months, and save the scorching heat of a vertical sun to snatch the fading beauties of spring and turn their loveliness into stubble.

The following lines, written upon the spot, as our little party were about to withdraw from this dreary solitude, but poorly portray some of the dismal realities then presented:

## SUMMER ON THE GREAT AMERICAN DESERT.

Ye dreary plains, that round me lie,
　So parch'd with summer's heat,
No more ye please my wand'ring eye,
　Or woo my weary feet.

Why hath the spring your beauty borne
　Into his hiding place,
And left the widow'd winds to mourn
　The charms they would embrace?

Why should those flowers, whose honey'd breath
　With incense filled the breeze,
Drooping and wither'd, lie in death,
　And now no longer please?

That grassy carpet, green and wide,
　Why turn'd to stubble now?
Save 'chance along some streamlet's side,
　Where less'ning waters flow!

And why those gently murm'ring rills,
　Whose soft melodious strains
Were wont to echo 'mong the hills,
　No longer reach the plains?

The lark no longer meets the morn,—
　Nor linnet pours his throat,—
Nor feather'd warbler hails the dawn
　With his sweet, mellow note;—

Nor even insect cheers the scene,
　Where Solitude alone,
In wither'd garb, as Desert Queen,
　Rears her eternal throne!

These thirsty plains, with open mouth,
　Implore the gentle shower;
But vainly plead, while summer's drouth
　In schorching heat doth pour!

Nor grateful shade, of spreading tree,
　Invites my feet to rest;
Nor cooling stream, in melody,
　Attempts my quicken'd zest.

So dismal all! why should I stay
　And sicken by their view?
Thrice gladly will I turn away,
　And bid these scenes adieu!

The only inhabitants of this vast region are strolling bands of buffalo and wild horses, with wolves, prairie dogs, and a few scattering antelope. The only human beings that visit it are Mexican traders and occasional war-parties of Pawnee, Apache, Kuyawa, Cumanche, and Arapaho Indians, and they only for the brief interval required in its hurried passage.

Who, then, so wild as to suppose for a moment that *such* a country can ever become inhabited by civilized man?—unless the time should *literally* be ushered in, when, to use the language of Scripture, "the *desert* shall bud and blossom as the rose!"

Late in the afternoon, towards the close of our journey, a little below the point at which the Santa Fe trail crosses the Cimarone, we came upon two horses that appeared to have recently strayed from some travelling party. According to the custom of the country anything encountered in this manner is good and lawful prize to the finder, and we forthwith set about taking possession.

One of them, however, a two-year-old colt, proved so unmanageable we were obliged to kill it in order to secure the other. Being rather scantily supplied with provisions, the fresh-slaughtered animal (fine and fat as it was) presented an opportunity too tempting not to be improved in replenishing our stock, which induced us to encamp for that purpose.

Soon after a large party of horsemen made their appearance from over the neighboring hills, and, having devoted a few minutes to reconnoitering, advanced upon us at full charge. In an instant our little force was drawn up in readiness to repel the expected attack. But, instead of enemies, the objects of our apprehension proved a squad of Arapahos, and they were accordingly allowed to come into camp.

One of our visitors happened to be the owner of the two horses we had found, which, as he stated, (having described them minutely,) had strayed from his village, some six miles distant; he then enquired of us if we had seen them. Here was a dilemma; should we deny the fact, and run the risk of being caught in a falsehood? or should we confess and abide the consequences? Our commandant decided upon the latter course; but, in so doing, had resort to an artful duplicity to bear upon the finer feelings of the Indian, and replied:

"My warriors had suffered long for lack of food. Three suns had sunk behind the mountain, and not one morsel had entered their mouths to give them strength for travel. In their distress they enquired of the Great Spirit, and He showed them the lost animals of my brother.

"My warriors were not slow to receive the welcome gift. The flesh of the younger one hath caused us to bless the Good Spirit; the other is with our own medicine-dogs, that my brother may search for it no longer."

The owner, on hearing this, looked very sorrwful. The colt had been a favorite of his squaw and children. In a moment, however, he arose, and, extending his hand to the commandant, exclaimed:

"My heart is good. My white brother did well to receive the gift of the Good Spirit, that his warriors might eat."

*Commandant.* But the young medicine-dog of my brother was the beloved of his wife and little ones. What will he that I give him so they sorrow not?

*Indian.* Now, my heart blesses the pale face. If he would bestow his gifts, what better could I receive at his hand than a small present of tobacco, that my pipe may be filled to the undying friendship of him and his people.

A few pieces of tobacco were accordingly given, and the good-hearted Indian, after shaking hands with each one of our party, took his horse and departed to his village.

Where, let me ask, do we find, in civilized countries an instance of noble generosity equal to that of the poor savage?

The Arapaho village, as we learned from our visitors, had been camped in the vicinity several days, for the twofold purpose of awaiting the Cumanches and catching wild horses. This, by the way, reminds me of not having as yet described the manner of performing the latter feat.

In taking wild horses, two methods are resorted to, alike displaying considerable tact and ingenuity. Of these the following is the most common:

A large party of Indians, mounted on their fleetest chargers, having discovered a band of these animals, carefully approach from the leeward, scattering themselves to a distance of eight or ten miles along the course their intended captives are expected to run. This done, the chase is started at a given signal, by the nearest Indian, who is relieved by the next in succession, and he by the next, and so on (taking their cue from the strategy of wolves in their capture of the antelope) until these proud rangers of the prairie, exhausted by their long-continued and vain efforts to escape, cease to assert their native liberty, and fall easy prey to the *lasso* of their pursuers.

Another plan frequently adopted is, to erect a stout fence from side to side, between two impassable walls of rock. The unsuspicious band are then so started as necessarily to be driven within the enclosure, when their ready pursuers, closing in upon the rear, take them without the trouble of a long chase.

Great numbers of wild horses are annually captured by these means, which become domesticated in a very short time. But, as a general thing, they are less adapted to hard service than those reared in the ordinary way, and are far more disposed to re-assert their birthright of freedom at the first opportunity that occurs.

Our visitors communicated the important intelligence that a detachment of four hundred Mexicans had passed their village only two days previous, on its way to Arkansas; which statement was further corroborated by certain indications noticed in the trail. The enemy was evidently in pursuit of us, and, weak as we were numerically, none expressed any other feeling than that of a willingness to meet him.

From this camp, our course bore west-northwest for thirty or forty miles, during which distance we found no water, and suffered greatly from the agonizing effects of thirst. One of our pack-horses, also, took the "*stampede*," and ran off with his entire load, consisting principally of ammunition, and all our efforts to retake him proved abortive.

About noon the succeeding day, we reached our destination, where a junction was formed, not with the *army* we had hoped to find, but with the mere handful who had parted from us a few weeks since at the Arkansas.

Discouragement and discontent were depicted upon the countenance of every one, as the lateness of the season admonished us of the extreme uncertainty of the arrival of expected reinforcements. The dreaded approach of the Cumanches, those unsparing enemies of the Texans, of whom we had received reliable intelligence, far more than the proximity of four hundred Mexican troops, gave us just cause for apprehension. A council was held forthwith, to decide upon the course proper to be pursued. Prudence seemed to dictate an abandonment of our present position,—while the enemy were looking for us in another quarter, we might steal a march upon him in his own country.

These suggestions gave tone to subsequent movements, and early in the morning of the day following we were under way. For ten or fifteen miles, our course continued up the dry sand-creek that had marked our place of rendezvous, and the night following was passed with a few lodges of Arapahos, who were encamped at a small pool of water near a bluff bank of sandstone.

This rock exhibited many rude engravings upon its smooth side, representing men, women, and children, dogs, snakes, and lizards, with various other devices,—evidently the work of ancient artists in commemoration of some remarkable occurrence connected with the former history of the country.

I examined the sketch with deep interest, and felt as if glancing at the obscure records of the greatness and glory of some extinct nation, written in a language, like itself, now no longer known.

Our hunters, having accompanied the Indians to the chase, soon after returned with a choice supply of fresh meat, and four wolf pups. The .atter had been taken by an Indian boy, three or four years old, who fearlessly entered the den, during the absence of the dam, and bore away her defenceless family in triumph.

The next day saw us again *en route*. One of our men, having obtained permission of the commanding officer, proceeded a short distance in advance of the main party for the purpose of hunting. Not paying strict attention to the course proposed, he mistook his way, and, despite our continued efforts to set him aright, could no longer be seen or heard of, and we were at length reluctantly forced to give him up.

Continuing up the creek some two days, we found it very difficult to procure water, and were often compelled to dig for it in the sand to a depth of three or four feet.

From this point, we bore south-southwest, and after more than a day and night's hard travelling, over an arid sand-prairie, favored by neither tree, shrub, nor watercourse, we arrived at the head of a small affluent of the Cimarone, inducting us to the bewitching scenery of the thrice lovely valley that lay immured within its giant walls.

The fatigue of a forced march, combined with the sweltering heat of an almost torrid sun by day and scorching winds by night, in addition to the indescribable torments of burning thirst for nearly thirty hours, had rendered us almost frantic with agony.

What tongue can tell the sweetness of the draught that first greeted our parched lips, at the termination of this painful interval? What mind can conceive the inestimable value of water, until destitution unfolds its real merits?

Hunger, one may forget in the sweet unconsciousness of sleep, or glut his appetite, meanwhile, upon the tasteless feasts of fancy,—but thirst, withering thirst, can never be forgotten while it continues,—it will burn as if to scorch the vitals and dry up the heart's blood!

Before leaving the sand-creek above alluded to, we passed several diminutive bottoms and *vallons* that assumed an air of fertility. In these, I noticed an abundance of the bread-root, and in the creek banks, two or three places gave indication of coal. The prevailing rock was sandstone and limestone. The country adjacent, with the exception of its being more tumulous, is much like the *llanos* peculiar to this region.

On striking the Cimarone we contiued our march up its valley for some three days, and camped for a short time, to make a câche of our surplus baggage for the purpose of travelling with greater expedition.

The day preceding, however, afforded two incidents worthy of note. One was the re-appearance of our lost man, who, having found his way to this point, and knowing we must necessarily make it in our line of march, had been awaiting us for the past two days. He was hailed as one risen from the dead, and welcomed back to our midst.

But the expulsion of three for cowardice almost immediately followed the re-accession of one. Considerable dissatisfaction had existed for some time, in reference to our plan of operations. Several of the company had openly talked of desertion, and were using their earnest endeavors to persuade others to this course. As we approached the enemy's country, the spirit of insubordination showed itself with increased violence. The time and place, even, were pitched upon for raising the standard of rebellion against all orders and those who gave them. Affairs at length reached a crisis that loudly demanded a resort to some prompt measures to restore them to their proper equilibrium—an example must be had.

Accordingly the company was drawn up in line, when the articles subscribed to by each of its members were read. This done, the commanding officer addressed the malecontents in a few brief words, demanding which of those articles he had violated,—if neither, they were equally binding as at first;—then, alluding to the rumors that had reached his ears from various sources, he stated his readiness to release any one requesting it from further obligation,—but the discharge should be a dishonorable one,—a discharge for *cowardice!*

"Yes," said he, "COWARDICE! We are on the eve of entering the enemy's country, and the hearts of *some* doubtless begin to fail them. Texas wants no *cowards* to fight her battles! None but brave men and true, are worthy of that honor! Now, I repeat it, if any timorous spirit,—any pusillanimous heart,—any *despicable poltroon*, wishes his discharge, I stand ready to give it; let him step one pace in advance from the ranks and ac knowledge himself a *coward!* His name shall be erased from the muster-roll."

At this announcement, three men stepped forward, and their names were severally repeated, as they received their discharge, accompanied by the cutting words,—" reason—*cowardice!*"

After this the commanding officer again addressed them: " You are now dishonorably discharged, and, as sentenced, before high heaven, I pronounce you *cowards.* If either of you considers this sentence unjust, let him shoulder his rifle and choose his own distance. I stand ready to give him any satisfaction he may demand in reparation of his wounded honor. But, you *shall* pocket the disgrace. To-night you may stay with us.—to-morrow you must and shall leave.

" And you, my brave comrades, who have chosen to abide by that flag which has graced the triumphs of by-gone days, may you never desert it in the hour of danger. Look up with hope, and as you gaze upon its bright star of lonely grandeur, consider it the harbinger of success,—the genius of victory."

The next morning, the three faint-hearted volunteers accordingly left camp, reducing our little number to twenty-one ;—a lean force, truly, for an expedition so hazardous. Yet none flinched at the thick array of anticipated dangers. All were ready and anxious for the encounter.

The above summary proceeding completely effected its designed object, at least for the present, and reduced the turbulent spirits to the wholesome restraints of discipline.

## CHAPTER XXXI.

Mexican camp.—Pursuit.—Advance upon Mora.—Enemy discovered.—Country between the Rio de las Animas and Mora; its picturesque beauty.—Admirable point of observation.—Fortified position.—Battle of the pass; order of attack, passage of the river, storming the enemy's camp, and number of killed, wounded and prisoners.—Council of war.—Prisoners released.—Message to Amijo.—Return march.—Mexican army.—Attacked, and results of action.—Mexican bravery.—Retreat.—Cross the Table Mountain.—New species of wild onions.—March down the de las Animas.—Discouragements accumulate.—Disband.—Sketch of factions.—Texan prisoners.—Arrival of reinforcements.—Battle of the Arroyo : killed, wounded, and prisoners.—Retreat of Amijo.—" Stampede."—Frightful encounter with the Camanches and Kuyawas.—Discharge of troops.—Affair with Capt. Cook.—Surrender to U. S. Dragoons, and failure of expedition.—Return to Texas.—Journey to the Platte.—Country between the Arkansas and Beaver creek.—Feasting at camp.—Crows' eggs.—Lateness of season.—Snow-storm in June.—An Indian fort.—Serio comico adventure with a wolf.—Indians.—Song of the night-bird.

From Cáche Camp we resumed our march, and, on the fourth day subsequent, struck the Taos trail at the crossing of the de las Animas;— thence, continuing up the river about forty miles, we came to a place recently occupied by a detachment of Mexicans. After a careful examina-

## FORTIFIED POSITION. 319

tion, we became satisfied that it had been some sixty cavalry, who were then doubtless awaiting our advance at no great distance; and, from appearances, not more than three days had elapsed since its evacuation. Feeling ill-disposed to try the patience of our enemy by keeping him in too long a suspense, we immediately started in pursuit.

The route led by a rough pass over a spur of the Toas Mountains which heads the *tierras templadas* southwest of the Cimarone, into a prairie ranging from east to west, forty-five or fifty miles long and thirty or more broad, and skirting the three principal streams that unite to form the Colorado. From this point it continued over another spur of the mountain chain into a valley some ten miles broad, ranging from north to south and intersected by the trail from Taos to the Santa Fe road, striking the latter near the Waggon Mound,*—thence, for about twenty-five miles, across a spread of high prairie, (quite rough and undulating, with frequent hills assuming a mountainous character,) to a considerable creek, four or five miles southeast of the town of Mora.

At this point our scouts reported the enemy as occupying a fortified camp, which commanded the only feasible pass leading to the adjoining settlements. Upon the reception of this intelligence we withdrew to a deserted *ranche* and encamped for the night, in order to obtain, if possible, more certain information relative to his position and force.

The country between the de las Animas and this place, as a general thing, gave indications of a good soil, but was quite arid, particularly the prairie skirting the head branches of the Colorado. The hills and mountains were less sterile than those farther east. They also afforded an abundance of timber, consisting of pine, oak, cedar, and pinion. The creek bottoms embraced considerable quantities of excellent land, though but sparsely timbered.

The mountains to the right towered majestically to an altitude of ten or twelve thousand feet, opposing their snowy crests in stern defiance to the heat of a summer's sun.

Toward the close of our march, the landscape disclosed a scene of romantic beauty and grandeur. Mingled among the pleasing diversity of mountain, hill, dale, and lawn, *vegas* and *llanos*, forests and prairies, here and there a small lake mirrored forth its bright waters, swarming with innumerable water-fowl, decorated by broad flowery banks, and shut in by rugged highlands and rocky cliffs, that seemed like some fairy's home, where enchantment held Nature's self in spell-bound admiration. The creeks and valleys of this section were also enclosed by abrupt banks, that sometimes protruded their precipitous walls to the very water's edge, and then again expanded to give place to the grass, fruits, and flowers of mimic Edens.

The prevailing rock appeared to be gray granite, ferruginous sandstone, and limestone. Game was rather scarce, and consisted principally of buffalo, deer, and bear.

As a whole, this entire region may be considered as admirably adapted

* This mound is a singular natural elevation in the form of a covered waggon, near the road from the United States to Santa Fe,—about fifty miles south of Taos.

to grazing purposes, and, were it not for its aridity, might be cultivated to a considerable extent.

The men sent to reconnoitre returned about midnight, but had succeeded in obtaining no satisfactory information of the enemy's position, owing to the darkness and their ignorance of the topography of the country. However, they reported having discovered a point overlooking his camp, from which our whole force might watch his movements, screened from his observation by a dense thicket of pines, and recommended it for our occupancy the ensuing day. Accordingly, in the morning orders were given to that effect; and, after a march of four or five miles, covered by an unbroken forest of pine and cedar, we arrived at the place designated, and encamped almost within speaking distance of the enemy.

No point could be more admirably situated for our purpose. The gradual acclivity by which we had advanced, studded with pine, hemlock, and pinion, led to the summit of a high ridge, bounding a broad valley upon its opposite side with vast piles of perpendicular rock, several hundred feet in altitude. Through this valley a large creek traced its way, graced by occasional groves of cottonwood and willow. In one of these, appeared the Mexican encampment.

So matchless was our position, by aid of a spy-glass we could observe his every movement without incurring the risk of being ourselves discovered.

A mere glance revealed the true state of affairs. The hostile force, consisting of some sixty strong, completely commanded the only entrance into the valley from the east, and was otherwise so advantageously posted as to render an immediate attack extremely hazardous. We accordingly awaited the cover of night for further operations, and contented ourselves meanwhile with watching the unsuspecting foe.

Our plan was to storm the Mexican camp and force a passage into the adjoining town, where we expected to encounter another detachment, and, after defeating it, make good our retreat before a sufficient reinforcement could be rallied to oppose us.

Soon after sundown, arrangements being completed, we commenced our march. A *detour* of four or five miles led us to the head of a narrow and circuitous defile, marking the entrance to the valley; winding our way through which silently, in a few moments we were in the immediate vicinity of the enemy.

Here dismounting, the company was drawn into line, and the plan of attack communicated to each, as follows: three men, mounted upon fleet horses, were to dispose of themselves, if possible, in such a manner as to prevent an escape, while the remainder, in two divisions, (the one headed by the Col. commandant and the other by the first lieutenant,) commenced a sumultaneous attack at different points. Orders were given to scale the enemy's breastwork, seize his arms, and demand his surrender,—but not to fire a shot, unless in case of resistance or an attempt to escape; and, even then, to avoid all unnecessary effusion of blood.

Thus disposed, we advanced to the charge;—but a new difficulty here arose. The creek which, from our high point of observation during the day, had appeared only a diminutive stream, now presented its broad surface, with a current of swift and deep water, while a steep bank upon the other side showed the enemy at its very verge. Nothing daunted we plunged in, and, almost as soon, gained the opposite shore. Ascending the bank we attracted the notice of the sentinels, and received the challenge:

"Quienes veniren?"—who comes?

"Que dijo?"—what do you say?

"Quienes veniren, carraho?"

At this a rush was made upon the challengers, who were almost instantly disarmed, and our whole party, leaping into camp, gave to the enemy the first intimation of its presence.

"Munchos Tajanos!"—exclaimed one, as the astonished Mexicans snatched their arms.

"Si, munchos Tajanos.—Quieron los scoupetas!"—was the reply, as we sprang to prevent them.

Here a smart struggle ensued, which resulted in the defeat of the enemy with a loss of five killed, four wounded, and eighteen prisoners,—the remainder having escaped despite our efforts to prevent it,—but all the camp equipage fell into our hands, with seventy-two head of horses and mules. Among the arms taken were two or three pieces that had belonged to the Texan Santa Fe expedition of the fall of '41.

A council was now held to decide upon the expediency of proceeding immediately to the neighboring town. A majority at first were favorable to the proposition;—but some objected, and urged the imprudence of weakening our force by a division, as we should either be necessitated to do, in that event, or relinquish the advantages already gained,—and, further, the enemy, being aware of our approach, was doubtless prepared to oppose a dangerous resistance, such as would be attended with great risk of life on our part, without securing any possible benefit in its result. The latter reasons influenced the decision, and orders were accordingly given to withdraw from the scene of action.

In the interim the wounded had been carefully attended to, and, as we were about to leave, the prisoners were all set at liberty, with these words:

"You are now free. Bury your dead, and remember in future how vain it is to resist the arms of Texas. Tell Amijo, your General, the Texans are men, and not wild beasts. They never kill an unresisting enemy,—they never kill a prisoner of war. He has done both,—but let him beware how he does it again, for the lives of ten Mexicans shall be the forfeit for each offence."

All things being arranged for a retrograde movement, we were promptly under way upon our return march to the Cimarone. The route led within ten or twelve miles of the Waggon Mound, at which point a large number of dark-looking objects appeared, but so indistinctly we were unable to determine their nature;—these, as we subsequently learned, were a body of Mexican troops, numbering seven hundred and fifty men.

Continuing our course, about noon we made camp at a gap in the mountain ridge, facing from the west the head branches of the Colorado.

The sentinels were cautiously posted, two upon the summit in the rear, and two with the horses in front, and express orders given to them not to leave their stations until relieved, and to give immediate notice of the appearance of any suspicious object. The remainder of the party were soon busily occupied, some in preparations for dinner, and others in making amends for a night of wakefulness.

In fact, each one conducted himself apparently with as little concern as though it were impossible that a Mexican could be found this side of the halls of Montezuma. Participating in this general feeling of security, and anxious to enjoy the relaxations of camp, in a brief intervel the sentinels deserted their posts and mingled among the loungers.

This remissness was first noticed by a private, who hurriedly enquired, "Where is the guard?" Scarcely were the words spoken, when another exclaimed, "There go our horses!"

The latter announcement aroused all hands—but only in time to witness our whole *cavallard* under full headway before a small party of Mexican cavalry, while at the same instant a brisk fire was opened upon us from the rear, and the dusky forms of the enemy appeared both right and left; thus we had the mortification to find our little band surrounded by a superior force.

Orders were given to dislodge the foe, and occupy his position in the rear. At the word "*charge*," our dauntless partizans, with a shout, rushed up the steep hill-side and drove the panic-stricken Mexicans before them, who fled with the utmost precipitancy in all directions, throwing away their blankets, robes, arms, and even clothes, to aid them in their hurried escape. So great was their consternation, in less than fifteen minutes not one remained in sight, either far or near.

On examining the premises, we found fifteen or twenty saddles, with a mule, which they had likewise abandoned,—but only two half-jaded animals told the remnants of the noble *cavallard* of more than eighty head that had grazed around us scarcely thirty minutes before; a thing of itself equivalent of a defeat.

What could twenty-one footmen do in an open prairie opposed by hundreds of cavalry, able at any time to choose their own place and mode of attack? The issue was quite apparent,—we must retreat. In an advantageous position, surrounded by game, and acquainted with the topography of the country, we might hold out against a force of thousands; but it would be presumption to think of either maintaining our present ground or advancing upon the foe.

Preparations were therefore immediately commenced for acting upon the only prudent alternative now left. Each man selected for himself a blanket, or robe, which, with such other necessaries as he could conveniently carry, was bound in the form of a knapsack and strapped to his shoulders; our animals were then heavily laden with provisions, and the remaining luggage (consisting of arms taken from the enemy, saddles, robes, blankets, knives, &c.,) committed to the flames; the value of property thus destroyed, amounted to several thousand dollars. It was a melancholy thing to witness this wanton waste; yet such is the custom of war under like circumstances.

Toward sundown we took up our line of march, each one on foot with his shouldered pack, in every appearance illustrating the soldier's return "from the war!"

In the above manner we trudged along, bearing a course due east, till the evening of the third day, which brought us to the base of the table moun-

STAMPEDE.—Page 332.

tain at the head of the Cimarone,—having discovered the enemy's scouts hovering in the distance on two or three occasions during the interval. The day following we crossed the mountain, upon whose summit was a beautiful plateau, some ten miles in width and of unknown length.

The soil gave every evidence of fertility, and was well watered. I noticed a number of strawberry vines—the first I had seen in the country, as well as a profuse array of floral loveliness. A considerable lake also appeared, whose banks were of perpendicular rock measuring a descent of fifteen or twenty feet; while on its shady side a pile of snow bade defiance to the heat of summer, and looked pleasingly strange amid the surrounding verdure.

After a lengthy search, we finally found a place of descent upon the opposite side of the mountain, which led us into the valley of the extreme left hand fork of the Rio de las Animas.

The bottom of this stream, as it emerged from the mountains, disclosed a soil of extraordinary fertility. Among its indigenous productions I noticed a spread of fifty acres or more, so densely covered with onions that hundreds of bushels might be gathered in a short time. This plant was of a different kind from any I ever before saw. Its color was white, size about equal to a pigeon's egg, and appearance much like that of the common onion; but it had flag-shaped stalks, and was much less offensive in taste and smell than is natural to this species of roots.

Continuing down the valley of this creek, we struck the de las Animas on the third day subsequent, and on the seventh, arrived at the egress of that stream from its frightful cañon, nearly opposite Bent's Fort on the Arkansas. From this place an express was sent to the latter point to obtain, if possible, some information relative to the expected reinforcement from Texas, and, also, in regard to the movements of the enemy.

The next day, however, the messenger returned with a report so far from encouraging, that it served still more to depress our fast-sinking hopes. A general despondency seemed to weigh like an incubus upon the minds of both officers and men. Our inability to hold out under existing circumstances was too apparent, as the sphere of operations embraced a circuit of five hundred miles or more, over deserts and mountains, that would waste us away with fatigue, watchings, hunger and thirst, by long and dreary marches to be performed on foot, through a country swarming with savage and half-civilized foes. A council was accordingly held, which resulted in the almost unanimous decision to *disband*.

Discharges previously made out, bearing date May 24th, were now presented to each one, absolving him from all further connection with the Texan army, and, on the morning of the 29th inst., our little band separated in three parties; one of these, consisting of four men, left for the cañon of the Cimarone; another, headed by Col. Warfield, started for Texas; and the remainder commenced their return journey toward the Platte river.

The story of the former of these fractions, so far as relates to the difficulties between Mexico and Texas, is briefly told. Our adventurers bearing for the Cimarone reached their hoped-for Elysium; but, soon after, having fallen into an ambuscade of one hundred and thirty Mexican troops, were taken prisoners, and, in a few days subsequent, found themselves in irons and snugly stowed away in the *calaboose* at Santa Fe; while there, one of them died from bad treatment, and the others would have been shot had not the dread of Texan vengeance prevented the deed. Succeeding events, however, effected their liberation.

The party accompanying Col. W. fell in with the expected reinforcements from Texas, near the Crossing of the Arkansas, and again submitted itself to the fortune of war. This force consisted of one hundred and eighty volunteers, under the command of Col. Snively, an old veteran of the Texas revolution.

Soon after, a detachment of forty Texans, headed by Col. Warfield, encountered the advance guard of the enemy, numbering one hundred picked men. The approach of the latter had been observed from an eminence, when the Texans were drawn up under cover of a small sand-bank, near a creek, (arroyo,) awaiting to intercept him. Ignorant of the presence of danger, the Mexicans were pressing on at a rapid rate, till brought to a sudden halt by an opposing force within half rifle-shot.

"Quienes?" demanded the Texan officer.

"Mexicanas. Quienes sons uste?" replied the commandante.

"Tajanos," returned the Texan, through his interpreter. "We have come to fight, and shall fight unless you surrender. But, that you may know with whom you have to deal, we give you thirty minutes to decide whether to fight or surrender. If you choose the former, a signal from your sword will announce the answer."

A brief discussion ensued among them upon this summons. The Mexicans were disposed to surrender, but the Pueblo Indians, of whom fifty or more were included in the party, scornfully refused to accede to any such proposition, declaring that they had come to *fight*, and not to surrender like women upon the first appearance of an inferior enemy. At length, a chief ended the dispute by advancing to the front line and giving the prescribed signal.

The onset of the Texans was terrific beyond description. The enemy's line was instantly broken, and the cry of "misericordia!" (mercy) sounded upon all sides. The conflict lasted scarcely five minutes; but, though short, it was decisive and bloody.

Twenty-two of the enemy were killed, thirty wounded, and the remainder taken prisoners, with the exception of one who succeeded in affecting his escape. Not a Texan was hurt.

General Amijo, who at this time lay encamped at the Cimarone, forty or fifty miles distant, with an army of seven hundred Mexicans, on receiving intelligence of the defeat of the flower of his *invincibles*, like other examples equally illustrious, felt his courage "ooze out at his fingers' ends," and, not being disposed to encounter such dangerous enemies, ordered an immediate retreat and fell back on Santa Fe.

Col. Snively was on the point of marching in pursuit, when an incident occurred which altered the whole aspect of affairs, and finally frustrated all the purposes of the expedition. This was effected by a war-party of eighty Kuyawa and Cumanche Indians, who succeeded in *stampeding* a large band of the army horses.

They were followed by eleven men under the command of Col. Warfield, and, after a running fight of two or three miles, an action was brought about. As they halted, Col. W. ordered his men to dismount and form a breastwork with their horses, which was promptly done;—meanwhile the Indians, numbering sixty or more, had closed around, with whoops and yells, and other demonstrations of their expected triumph.

A discharge from the Texans brought four of their warriors to the ground, and wounded six more. This broadside was returned through a shower of arrows, and repeated by the intrepid eleven in a pistol-round, when three more of the assailants fell, and twice that number felt the effects of an unerring aim. Hereupon the Indians hastily retreated with their wounded, leaving seven of their number to grace the scene of action. Not one of the Texans was injured, and only one of their horses killed and three wounded. Further pursuit, however, was abandoned, and the captive horses were left to honor the service of their new masters.

A loss so inopportune caused the postponement of further operations for the present, and, in connection with other difficulties, created so much discontent in the minds of some, that one entire company declared its intention of returning to Texas, and requested its immediate discharge. An emergency of this kind, not having been provided for in the terms of enlistment, left the commanding officer no other alternative than to accede to a measure he had no power to prevent, and the demands of the disaffected were accordingly complied with.

The army was thus reduced to eighty effective men, which made it necessary to release the prisoners as yet retained in custody. These during their detention had been treated with great kindness, and their wounded carefully attended to by the company's surgeon; on their release twelve horses were allowed for their conveyance, while the other prisoners were furnished with four rifles and a quantity of ammunition, two running horses, and enough provisions to serve for several days. Thus provided, they were set at liberty with the pithy message: "Bid your countrymen learn, from this example, how to treat prisoners of war!"

Soon after the events above related, the army took up a position on the Arkansas river, a few miles below the Santa Fe road, for the purpose of procuring a supply of provisions from the vast quantities of buffalo afforded by that vicinity. While encamped here, hunting parties were allowed to cross into the United States territory in quest of game,—not in a national capacity, but as mere private individuals.

On one of these occasions the hunters were discovered and pursued by two companies of United States Dragoons, under Capt. Cook, on their way to escort the Santa Fe traders as far as the Crossing of the Arkansas. The chase was continued to the river bank opposite the Texan camp, when a conference was requested, and the commanding officers of both armies met, as was supposed, for an interchange of mutual civilities; but such proved not to be the case.

Captain Cook, on the part of the Americans, contended that the Texans had invaded the United States territory, and that they even now occupied a position within its limits;—his duty was plain. He must demand, and, if necessary, enforce their immediate surrender. Thirty minutes only would be allowed for a decision.

Cols. Snively and Warfield urged many arguments to prove the injustice of his demand and the fallacy of the premises upon which it was based, but all to no purpose. The Captain was inflexible.

Meanwhile, the American troops had crossed the river, and were drawn up in front of the Texans ready for action. It was vain for a force of eighty men to attempt holding out against one hundred and sixty United States Dragoons, backed by two field-pieces. Retreat, too, was impracticable, and they accordingly surrendered their arms, upon Texan territory, in compliance with the unjust demands of the American commander.

Forty of the prisoners were escorted to Fort Leavenworth, and the remainder set at liberty, and left with only twelve rifles to fight their way back to Texas, through the heart of the Cumanche country. They had, however, previously managed to secrete a quantity of arms and ammunition, and, in a few minutes subsequent to their release, were fully equipped and ready to meet a Mexican force of eight times their number.

Col. Warfield was elected commander of the newly organized company, who immediately set out in quest of the enemy.

But here a new obstacle presented itself;—the whole country was swarming with Cumanche and Kuyawa Indians; so much so that a further prosecution of the campaign must inevitably prove most disastrous. This circumstance led to the abandonment of the purposes of the expedition, and the scanty remnants of the army engaged in it took up their line of march for Texas, where they arrived during the month of July following, wasted by toil and suffering, as well as by repeated conflicts with a relentless savage foe.

Thus ended the second attempt to subjugate the province of Santa Fe to the government of the new-born Republic of Texas.

A few days preceding this grand *finale*, a small party, including myself, commenced its journey to the mountains adjoining the head waters of the Platte river. We were all on foot, and suffered greatly from fatigue and thirst during our dreary march over the plains of burning sand and withered stubble that impeded our progress for some distance.

Crossing the Arkansas at a point several miles below Bent's Fort, we proceeded up one of the numerous dry creeks finding their discharge into that stream from the north, and, on the fifth day subsequent, arrived at a grove of cottonwood, upon a watercourse near the eastern extremity of the "Divide," and in the immediate vicinity of several tributaries of both the Platte and Kansas rivers. Here the abundance of buffalo induced four of us to remain for a short time, while the others continued their course.

The intermediate country from the Arkansas to this place, presents an uninviting aspect, and, though not naturally sterile, is rendered repulsive from its extreme aridity. The creeks are most of them mere beds of sand, entirely destitute of water, except at brief intervals when their percolated currents are shown in brackish pools, soon again to inhume themselves in the willing earth.

There is rarely a tree in the whole distance, which circumstance adds much to the cheerlessness of its solitude. A general scarcity of rock also prevails, and the only specimens I noticed were exhibited in the banks of watercourses, and consisted of slate and fossiliferous limestone (formed of an extinct species of shell-fish, principally *bivalves*.) The soil in many places might be called fertile, and, were it not for lack of moisture, could be turned to good account for agricultural purposes.

The landscape is generally undulating, disclosing at the north and northeast broken ridges of hills, which were now and then surmounted by scattering pines.

The buffalo having left the vicinity soon after our arrival, we again moved camp eight or ten miles, to Beaver creek, an affluent of the Platte, where we remained for fifteen or twenty days.

Our stay at this place was one continued series of feasting, as we lacked nothing of all the varied delicacies procurable in a country abounding with game. But one item in our entertainment was indeed a novelty,—viz. crows' eggs. Almost every tree and bush, skirting the creek at intervals for miles above and below, had been appropriated to the use of the countless swarms of crows that populated the surrounding prairie. Sometimes four or five nests of these birds might be seen upon a single tree. On two or three occasions I obtained from six to ten dozen of eggs in the course of an hour. These, whether boiled, roasted, or fried, were found quite an acceptable addition to our bill of daily fare.

The climate of this region is evidently less mild, and its warm season much shorter, than is common to other places in the same latitude.

It was now the middle of June, and yet the wild fruits, currants, cherries, and plums, were only in blossom, and all other kinds of vegetation assumed the appearance of recent spring. Indeed, the day succeeding our arrival, snow fell to a depth of three or four inches, and remained upon the ground for several hours. Whether such occurrences are common, I have not the necessary information to decide.

In our excursions after game, the remains of an Indian fort had been discovered in a small grove, a short distance below camp, which received the honor of our subsequent occupancy. A few hours devoted to repairs rendered it a complete shelter from either wind or rain; and, still farther to enhance its conveniences, we succeeded in digging a small well adjoining the entrance, thus securing a most welcome supply of cool water. Here revelling in the midst of plenty, with nothing to think of or care for but our own personal comforts, we had no mind to exchange our situation for the fatigues of war and the drudgery of camp-duty.

Several incidents also occurred in the interim to enliven the scene and relieve its otherwise dull monotony. On one occasion a strolling wolf, venturing too near camp, received the contents of my rifle and instantly fell. Supposing the shot to be a fatal one, I advanced and seized him by the tail with the design of taking his skin.

But the creature, having been only stunned by a neck wound, now revived in full strength, and, enraged at his rough treatment, called into exercise the utmost tension of his energies to afford a bitter sample of the fierceness of wolfine vengeance. Here was a quandary—to relinquish the hold would have been to invite a doubtful collision—to allow him an instant's time for turning upon me, must have proved equally perilous;—the only resource was to retain my grasp with twofold energy, and run backwards as fast as possible, which I did, pulling the struggling beast after me,—now twisting this way, now that way, in vain effort to attack, —and growling and snapping his teeth with all the ferocity of his savage nature.

What would have been the result of this strange adventure, it is hard to tell, were it not that one of my camp-mates hastened to the rescue, and with a club despatched his wolfship At any rate I had no curiosity to submit the question to a further test.

With us the practice of early rising was remembered only as the whim of visionary theorists, and this important item in the routine of daily duties, was often postponed to an unreasonable hour. Once we came very near paying dearly for the indulgence. The sun had told more than two hours of his daily round, and only one of our number had doffed the drowsiness of sleep and betaken himself to an eminence to scan the surrounding solitude. Here the first object that met his gaze was a war-party of mounted savages, advancing upon him at full charge.

He had scarcely time to reach camp and give the alarm, when the whole troop came pouring in upon all sides with the rapidity of a torrent, making the air resound with their terrific yells. Seizing my arms I was the first to meet the assailants, and, levelling at them, made signs that an advance would be at their peril. Upon this they recoiled, and shouted at the top of their voices, "*Amigos! Arapahos!*" accompanied with the signs of friendship and their nation.

Satisfied of the truth of these declarations, we permitted them to come up, and, in a few minutes, all were quietly seated, and the "pipe" performing its tireless rounds.

Our boldness in daring to offer a resistance greatly excited their surprise, and the more so, as we had only four rifles, while they had many arrows, and were more than ten times our number. An old chief, after listening to their remarks, replied :

"My people must not deceive themselves. The pale faces are brave and kill their enemies a long way off. Those " said he, pointing to a brace of pistols, " would have laid many of my warriors low, after the medicine-irons had spoken their death-words. The Great Spirit has taught the pale-face how to fight."

Our visitors had at first supposed us a war-party of Pawnees, and came with the full design of securing a scalp-dance. Had they caught us napping, without doubt our own lives would have been substituted for those of their enemies.

In a few hours the motley crew again resumed their course, and left us to the undisturbed enjoyment of our sequestered retreat, thankful indeed to be free from their presence.

In addition to the howling of wild beasts and the hooting of prairie-owls by night, the locality afforded other music to sooth the hours of slumber. A bird of unknown species had built her nest in the boughs of a cottonwood that expanded directly over our heads, and devoted her maternal care to the sustenance of her fledgelings. But her unwearied industry by day less commanded our admiration than the sweet melody of her nocturnal warblings.

Soon as the "pointers" told the "noon of night," her song commenced in all its variations, like the soft breathings of an angel's lute, nor ceased till the gray of morning broke from the empurpled east. Often have I listened half dreamingly to the bewitching notes that mingled with the harsh discord of the wilderness around me, and fancied myself guarded by celestial spirits against the assaults of harm.

With such kindly thoughts, who might not mount in his slumbers on the wings of imagination, and step from star, as 'mid the changeless realms of bliss.

## CHAPTER XXXII.

Lost.—Night on the Prairie.—Head of the Kansas river.—Minerals.—Country.—Gold.—Wonderful incident relative to a wounded bull.—Indians.—Join the Arapahos.—Moving village.—Country between Beaver creek and the Platte.—Cañon.—Reach Fort Lancaster.—Fortune bettered.—News from the States.—Murder.—Extraordinary instances of human tenacity to life.—Arrival of Indians.—Theft.—Chyenne outrage.—Return of Oregon emigrants.—" Old Bob," and his adventures.—A " Protracted Meeting," or Indian Medicine-making.—Indian oath.—Jaunt to the mountains.—Mountain scenery.—Camp on Thompson's creek.—Wild fruits.—Concentration of valleys.—Romantic view.—A gem in the mountains.—Grand river pass.—Salt lakes.—Astonishing scope of vision.—The black-tailed deer.—Peculiarity in horses.—Remarkable natural fortification.—Return.—Travelling by guess.

ONE day, on leaving camp in quest of game, I carelessly travelled till near sundown, without success. The hills, hollows, and ravines which intersected my way and continually changed its bearings, so completely bewildered me, that, as night shut down upon the cheerless expanse, I found myself far away from any suitable camping-place, and alone amid the realms of loneliness. Thus conditioned, I was forced to submit to circumstances, and accordingly accepted of such lodgings as nature afforded.

My lonely and dangerous situation, with the thrilling sensations experienced during the interval, gave birth to the following lines, which, by aid of a rude pencil formed from a bullet, were next morning traced upon a small scrap of paper. I submit them to the reader, not that they possess any intrinsic merit, but because they will enable him to derive some faint idea of the terrific wildness and beauty of the surrounding scenes.

## NIGHT ON THE PRAIRIE.

### I.

The sable garb of darkness clothes the land,
  And twilight's sickly hue bids day farewell;
The prairie's vast expanse on either hand
  Marks solitude's domain. O'er hill and dell,
And wide-extended plain, I cast my eyes,
  To view, perchance, some grove or fav'ring stream,
And hie me thitherward while yet the gleam
Of day's fast-failing light bepaints the skies
  With tints scarce seen,—for there I'd seek repose,—
But for them look in vain; so here, alone,
  Wearied and worn, I sit me down and close
My tiresome wanderings,—nor bate to own
  The chilling thrill of terror o'er me creeps,
  And from my mind all thoughts of slumber keeps!

### II.

Oh, Solitude! First-born of Night! 'Tis here
  Thy reign is undisputed! Here no noise
Of human feet doth greet thy list'ning ear,—
  Save chance as mine, or savage want enjoys
His arms at chase or rage at bloody war!—
  Here haunts the beast of prey. The starved wolf's howl
  In ceaseless concert swells! The midnight owl
Joins in his dolesome lay;—the raven's caw
  Loud mingles with the panther's yell,—and then
The hoarse-toned bison grunts his bass, and makes
  Thy dismal realm more drear to lonely men.
Æolus here his fresh-form'd wind awakes,
  And marks its speed unchecked; whose whistling moan
  O'er thy domain makes loneliness more lone!

### III.

My thoughts, now kindred to the scene, arise
  In hurried flight, whose hideous aspects wake,
Full quick, imagination's sleepless eyes,
  That conjure up such frightful forms as shake
The boldest hearts with dread. In every herb
  Of prouder growth,—whose prongs the sweeping blast
  Hath taught to move,—some foe of savage cast
Appears and threatens ill, as if to curb
  The onward progress of the god of sleep:—
(For here man sees his fellow man, unknown,
  As foe; and, arm'd for fight, he minds to keep
The strictest watch, lest, from advantage shown,
  He tempt unlucky war.) So hurriedly
  I snatch my arms to fight each form I see!

### IV.

But, why thus fear? Give place, ye visions dread!
  Ye thoughts of boding danger, drearisome,
Cease to oppress! Is not the path I tread
  So by Omniscience mark'd, that perils come
Not near, to even hurt a single hair,
  Without His wise permit? Are not my days
  Securely meted out, and all my ways
So guarded, too, that thronging dangers share
  No part in harm's advance or death's progress
Till all are told? And can my vigilance,
  Father'd by childish fear, make more or less
The given sum? Cheerly, draw courage thence,
  My cowering heart; feel safety here. Give room
To other thoughts, and chase these clouds of gloom!

### V.

Thus, banished fear, at reason's bid, I cast
  My willing gaze toward heaven. In every star
That forms the sparkling crown of night, though fast
  In regions of unbounded space, so far
As scarcely seen by mortal ken,—appears
  Some guardian angel, robed in light, to keep
  His ceaseless vigils o'er my couch of sleep,
Lest in my slumbering moments danger near
  To cut the thread of life, and thus undo
The purposes of God. The silver moon
  Sheds forth her radiance unconfined, and through
The desert wild to flower and herb gives boon,
  And decks each blade with dewy pearls, and pours
  Them on the earth, to cheer my waking hours.

### VI.

Nature's vast caravansera, above,
  Below, around, on either side, begirt
With midnight's varied splendors, scenes I love,
  Becomes enchantment's self, while zephyrs sport
The fragrance of the wild-flowers multiform,
  And greet my nostrils with their rich perfume,
  To please my senses. Thus my thoughts resume
Their wonted course, and hush the passing storm
  Of fear. Alone! Not lonely I. For here
E'en loneliness companion proves to me,
  And solitude is company. My ear
Drinks music from these savage sounds; I see
  Amusements in these forms; my heart's as strong,
  And easy beats, as 'mid a city's throng!

## VII.

To me thrice welcome then, ye prairies wild !
  Midnight, and gloom, and solitude, ye please
My restless fancy !  Welcome then your child !—
  For here's my home. And so, with mind at ease,
I will embrace my mother earth, and court
  The soothing power of sleep. The clear blue sky
My canopy, the ground my bed, I lie
Encurtain'd by the pale moon-beams, which sport
  Beside my lowly couch, and light the dew
With mimic diamonds' glow—while flowers around
  My pillow'd head their willing incense strew,
And the sweet dreaming bird anon doth sound
  Some isolated note of melody !—
  Thus chamber'd here, may not kings envy me ?

My return to camp the next day served to quiet the apprehensions that had been experienced on my account during the interim.

This excursion took me some fifteen miles eastward, to the head waters of the Kansas river. The country in that neighborhood wore a barren aspect, and was generally sandy and undulating.

I noticed a kind of mineral substance, of a jetty lustrous appearance, which I took to be black-lead. I also remarked certain indications of gold, but whether this metal actually exists here I am unable to say; yet true it is, the surface affords large quantities of "gold blossom," and it is said also, that gold has been found in these parts.

The region lying upon the head branches of the Kansas river is considered very dangerous,—it being the war-ground of the Pawnees, Caws, Chyennes, Sioux, and Arapahos,—and hence comparatively little is known of its character and resources. It is represented as quite sandy and sterile back from the watercourses, and in many other places but little better than a desert waste. The gold story alluded to in the preceding paragraph came to me from various sources, in the following shape:

Some twenty years since, while the Arapahos were at hostilities with the whites, a war-party of that tribe advanced against the Pawnees, led on by a noted chief, called "Whirlwind." Three only of them had guns, and they soon expended their stock of bullets in shooting small game, there being no buffalo upon the route. Finally, left without any thing to eat, they became discouraged, and a council was held to discuss the expediency of relinquishing the expedition.

Having seated themselves upon a small eminence, the question of return was debated with great earnestness,—a majority being in the affirmative. But the head chief, "Whirlwind," bringing all his eloquence to bear upon the opposite side, at last obtained their consent to proceed.

During the conference, several small pieces of a glittering yellow substance were discovered upon the surface, which proved soft and easily worked into any shape. From these a supply of bullets was procured, and, resuming their course, they soon after met the Pawnees, with whom

WHIRLWIND.— Page 334.

they fought, and were victorious,—every bullet discharged killing an enemy.

This victory was so signal and complete, that the superstitious warriors attributed it solely to the *medicine-doings* of the yellow balls,—three or four of which were finally buried with the chief at his death. The only white man permitted to see them, describes them as having been precisely the color of brass,—very soft and heavy. Admitting that the story is true, * there are doubtless very rich mines of gold in this vicinity, that being the only metal assimilating brass in color.

Previous to our leaving Beaver creek, an incident occurred showing the remarkable tenacity of life peculiar to buffalo.

An old bull appeared in the distance, travelling at a rapid rate almost directly towards camp. Being in want of a re-supply of fresh meat, I seized my rifle and advanced to intercept him. Owing to the unfavorable state of the wind, I was forced to make so long a shot that the ball fell some two feet below the mark, and struck near the knee-joint of the fore leg, shivering it to pieces.

Still, however, the animal kept on, with scarcely diminished speed, and held me a chase of three miles or more before I could overtake him to finish the work. At length he was dispatched; but, on butchering him, I was surprised to find a third bullet-wound, apparently three or four days old. The ball was full one-half the size of my own, and, incredible as it may seem, had penetrated the butt of the *buffalo's heart.*

I could scarcely believe my own eyes,—yet such was the fact. The creature had survived a heart-shot for days, and then, with a broken leg, had held me a chase of three miles.

Our final adventure at this camp, was with a party of Indians. Having discovered the latter, early one morning, and supposing them Pawnees, we prepared for an encounter. The objects of our apprehension, mistaking us for the same, continued manœuvring upon the adjoining hills the entire day, in such a manner as to lead us to conclude the whole country was filled with Indians.

Toward sundown, after vainly endeavoring to procure an attendant, I armed myself and proceeded alone to the spot where they had been last seen, determined to discover, if possible, the nature and extent of the danger that awaited us. Here, a single warrior advanced to meet me,—giving signs of friendship and of his nation. In answer to the inquiry, why his party had acted so strangely, he said they had thought us enemies, and were afraid.

He accompanied me to camp, and, soon after his companions came up; but, instead of the powerful war-party of Pawnees awaiting to slaughter us by night, as our imaginations had depicted, and their cunning movements led us to infer, they proved but three Arapaho warriors, three squaws,

---

* The country adjacent to the head branches of the Kansas river is but little known to the whites, who seldom visit it on account of its dangerous nature. That valuable minerals are contained in its soil is quite probable, and no doubt they will be brought to light upon due research.

and two children. Our surprise at this laughable *denouement* was only equalled by their own.

They announced themselves in search of the Arapaho village, and expressed much pleasure at meeting with the whites. Our visitors having passed the night with us, the next morning we yielded to their solicitations, and set out with them to the village, some eighteen miles distant, in a northwest direction.

About noon we arrived at the place, and found six or seven hundred lodges of Arapahos, Chyennes, and Sioux, encamped in a large valley skirting a small affluent of Beaver creek.

The village, being prepared to move, in a few moments succeeding our arrival, was *en route* for the Platte river. The spectacle was novel and imposing. Lodge followed lodge in successive order,—forming vast processions for miles in length. Squaws, children, horses, and dogs, mingling in promiscuous throng, covered the landscape in every direction, and gave it the aspect of one dense mass of life and animation.

Here a troop of gorgeously dressed and gaily painted damsels, all radiant with smiles and flaunting in conscious beauty, bestriding richly caparisoned horses, excited the admiration and commanded the homage of gallantry; there a cavalcade of young warriors, bedaubed with fantastic colors—black, red, white, blue, or yellow, in strict accordance with savage taste—habited in their nicest attire, swept proudly along, chanting their war-deeds in measured accents to the deep-toned drum; and then another band of pompous horsemen scoured the spreading plain, in eager race to test the speed of their foaming chargers; and, yet again, a vast army of mounted squaws, armed with the implements for root-digging, spread far and wide in search of the varied products of the prairie; then, among the moving mass, passed slowly along the travées, conveying the aged, infirm, and helpless, screened from the heat of a summer's sun by awnings of skins, that beshaded their cradled occupants,—while immense trains of pack-animals, heavily laden with provisions and camp equipage, as they crowded amid the jogging multitudes, united to complete the picture of a travelling Indian village.

Yielding to the request of our new friends, we proceeded with them ten or twelve miles further and passed the night in their lodge.

Our route from Beaver creek led over a tumulous country, interspersed with valleys of a rich soil, and prolific in rank vegetation. The side-hills afforded large quantities of *pomme blanc*, and the prairies and bottoms a splendid array of choice floral beauties.

The creeks disclosed wide, sandy beds, often dry and skirted by broad valleys which were passably well timbered. The principal ridges were not high, but surmounted by dense pine forests, with pleasant openings, smiling in all the loveliness of spring.

Notwithstanding the scanty volumes of the streams, the country presents to the traveller the appearance of being well watered by frequent rains, while ever and anon a gurgling fountain strikes upon his ear with its soft music.

Stratified rock is usually rare; the only species noticed were limestone and sandstone. I remarked a great abundance of silex and hornblend, with some curious specimens of ligneous petrifactions. The only indication of minerals observable, was that of iron and coal.

The entire section from Beaver to Cherry creek possesses nearly the same geological and mineralogical character. Its indigenous productions are such as are common to the mountain prairies, and are found in equal abundance;—a remark which will also apply to its game.

As a whole, perhaps two-thirds of it might be cultivated, to some extent, were it not for unseasonable frosts; and all of it might be turned to good account for stock-raising.

The next day we bade farewell to our Indian friends, (leaving behind us one of our number, who chose to accompany them to the Fort,) and again launched forth upon the broad expanse. Bearing a course west-northwest, about noon of the second day we struck Cherry creek, some thirty-five or forty miles above its mouth;—thence, crossing the lofty plateaux, on the west, with two or three intervening creeks, toward evening of the third day we reached the Platte river at its exit from the mountains.

Our intention was to enter the mountains and spend a few weeks in deer-hunting; but, the river proving impassable, on account of high water, we were compelled to forego that purpose for the present, and accordingly started for Fort Lancaster to procure a re-supply of ammunition.

Continuing down the Platte, on the third day we reached our destination, and were kindly received, though humorously rallied upon our way-worn and forlorn appearance. Nor were we backward to join the laugh, occasionally retorting, when the jocose current set too strong against us, "Well, what do you know about *war?*—You've never been to Texas!"

The 6th of July dated our arrival,—the glorious fourth having been spent in plodding over a broad prairie, on foot, with rifles upon our shoulders and packs upon our backs. By comparison, I concluded my fortune had slightly improved since July 4th of the preceding year, which found me in a cheerless prairie, on foot, packing my bed, almost naked, without knife or gun, or having had a mouthfull to eat for two days previous.

Capt. Fremont, elsewhere spoken of, had just arrived from the States on an expedition to Oregon, ordered by the United States Government, and brought intelligence of an existing *armistice* between Mexico and Texas. Accompanying his party was one whom I recognized as an old acquaintance of other lands, the first and only one I had the pleasure of meeting with during my long sojourn in the country.

*July* 11*th,* witnessed the death of an old mountaineer at Fort Lancaster, who came to his end from the effects of a pistol wound received in a drunken frolic on the 4th. The ball entered the back about two inches below the heart, severely fracturing the vertebræ and nearly severing the spinal marrow.

He lived just one week succeeding the occurrence, but meanwhile suffered more than the agonies of death. His body below the wound was entirely devoid of feeling or use from the first, and, as death preyed upon him by piecemeal, he would often implore us with most piteous and heart-melting appeals kindly to ease his miseries by hastening his end. The *murderer* was left at large, and in two or three weeks subsequent accompanied Capt. Fremont to Oregon.

The above is the most remarkable exhibition of human tenacity to life that ever came under my personal observation; I have, however, heard of instances far more extraordinary. The case of Ex-Governor Boggs, of Mo., in '41, who recovered from the effects of a wound, that not only fractured his scull, but actually emitted particles of the brain, is doubtless well known; yet another of like nature, still more wonderful in its details, occurred to an old French trapper, named Augustine Clermont, with whom I am well acquainted.

Clermont, in an affray with a Spaniard, had been prostrated by a blow that fractured his scull in the occiput. His antagonist then fell upon him and thrust the point of a knife into the brain repeatedly, and finally left him for dead.

Soon after, he was found by his friends in this deplorable situation, who, on perceiving he yet breathed, kindly dressed his wounds, and bestowed upon him the attention his situation demanded, and in a short time he became perfectly sound and hearty.

*July 13th.* The Indian village before spoken of, on its way in quest of buffalo, visited the Fort, and, as is customary on such occasions, the squaws and children made themselves busy in appropriating to their own use such little articles as came within their reach. I was minus a blanket through their artfulness, and several other individuals suffered equally with myself.

Some six weeks afterward they returned, and again called at the Fort, when, recognizing my stolen blanket in the possession of a young warrior, I immediately took it from him. At first he stoutly resisted, and the more so as several hundred of his tribe were present,—but, all to no purpose; and he at length yielded, as he saw me on the point of enforcing my claims to it in a more *feeling* way, such as would doubtless have endangered his own personal safety.

I remained at Fort Lancaster for two months or more; and the several incidents which occurred in the interim may be thus briefly summed up:

The first in order was an outrage of the Chyennes, in cruelly murdering the young man with whom I had passed a portion of the preceding winter upon Vasques' creek.

The next was the appearance of a small party of emigrants, on their return to the States,—having become displeased with the management of the company then *en route* for Oregon.

A third was the arrival of one of the four men who had left for the Cimarone at the first disbanding of the Texan volunteers, and were subsequently taken prisoners by the Mexicans.

After being incarcerated at Santa Fe for two or three weeks, they were finally liberated, with the exception of one, who had died in the interval. Toward the last of their imprisonment, they were treated kindly, owing to the exemplary conduct of the Texans, as spoken of elsewhere.

The fellow thus introduced, responding to the name of "Old Bob," made himself quite conspicuous by his subsequent conduct. The gentleman in charge at Fort Lancaster, pitying his deplorable condition, kindly afforded him employment at a liberal compensation, and Old Bob set to work faithfully. In the course of twelve or fifteen days, however, he improved the opportunity of stealing a rifle and ammunition, with which he absconded and set his face for the mountains.

All that he now lacked to complete his equipment was a good horse, which deficiency seemed luckily made up by the discovery of one recently strayed from the Indians. "I must have him," said Bob. So, carelessly dropping his rifle and pack, he commenced a fruitless effort to capture the erratic steed.

For a while his success seemed almost certain; but, after a tedious trial for several hours, he was finally obliged to relinquish the attempt, and turned to recover his rifle and pack. Alas, for Old Bob! here an unlooked-for calamity presented itself—they were not to be found!

Vainly it was that he searched diligently for four successive days, enduring in the mean time all the pangs of hunger and the goadings of a guilty conscience—his scrutiny gave not the slightest indication of their whereabouts. "Truly, 'the way of transgressors is hard!'" thought Bob, as with reluctance he abandoned all,* and despairingly set his face to go—ne knew not whither!—half-starved and half-naked, with neither pistol, gun, nor butcher-knife, for his defence in a dangerous country; nor one morsel to renew his strength by day, nor even a solitary rag to screen him from the chill air of night!

The next place at which Old Bob showed himself was at an Indian lodge, thither driven by the impulse of hunger—having starved for more than five successive days. Here he procured a temporary supply from the compassionate inmates, who also kindly gave him a robe.

Nothing further was heard of him for eight or ten days, and the generally conceded opinion was, that he had either starved to death or had been killed by savages, when an express from the Arkansas brought intelligence of having encountered him by the way.

The luckless wight, after being without eating for five or six more days, had been robbed by the Apache Indians of everything about him except a pair of ragged pantaloons, and barely escaped from them with his life! The express furnished him with a quantity of provisions, a pistol, robe, and ammunition, when, bidding him farewell, the two resumed their respective courses.

From this date, his story is briefly told. Pursuing his way toward the Arkansas, he soon after met a small party of Mexican traders, and, creeping upon their encampment at night, helped himself to a couple of horses. "It's a straight road that has no turns," muttered Old Bob, as he mounted one of them and returned to the Platte, where he bartered the other for a rifle and ammunition.

For a brief interval he seemed to prosper in his iniquity, but erelong the tables were again turned upon him, and he experienced the literal fulfilment of that other declaration of holy writ which says, "The wicked shall not go *unpunished*."

Elated by his recent success, he again started for the Arkansas, with

* Two weeks subsequently, while on a hunting excursion, the person to whom the stolen rifle belonged found it, with all the property of the thief;—a most remarkable circumstance, as the country had been filled with strolling Indians during the interval.

the intent of renewing his depredations, accompanied by two other adventurers whom he had pursuaded to become the partners of his criminal enterprise; but, before proceeding far, he fell in with the same company of Mexican traders from whom he had stolen the horses. They immediately recognized him and the animal he rode, and took possession of the latter. As for Old Bob, notwithstanding his protestations of innocence and stout resistance, they stripped him of gun, pistol, and ammunition—gave him a severe *flogging*, and again turned him adrift upon the prairie, destitute of everything except the baseness of his own heart!

"Well, Bob," said one of his comrades; "this business appears not so *profitable*, after all; though you, doubtless, have become quite *warmed* in its pursuit. For my own part I shall quit it before I begin, and return to the States."

"And I, too;" chimed in the other.

"The fact is," replied Bob, "this country is getting rather too *hot* for me, and I'll bear you company! What d'ye say to that?"

"Just as you like," responded his two companions; "that is, provided you wont attempt the *grab* game on us."

"Come, boys; now that's too bad! Oh, you may rest assured I will never repay a kindness with ingratitude, neither will I abuse the confidence of friends."

Thus arranged, the three started on their way. Coming upon a camp of hunters, a few miles below Bent's Fort, they concluded to remain a short time in order to procure a supply of meat for their journey. Here our slippery customer borrowed a horse and rifle of his comrade, pretendedly for a buffalo hunt, and under a most solemn pledge of returning them; however, on finding himself again armed and mounted, he was not slow to improve the opportunity of bidding an abrupt farewell to the unsuspecting dupe, and resumed his course toward the States.

How he eventually succeeded through this last shift, I am unable to say; yet, the brief story of his adventures thus far is sufficient to prove, that iniquity sometimes, even in this life, receives a *severe* reward.

Toward the last of August the Arapahos and Chyennes held a grand convocation, in the vicinity of Fort Lancaster, for the porpose of *medicinemaking;* or, in other words, paying their united devotions to the Great Spirit. The gathering might with propriety have been termed a "*Protracted Meeting*," as it continued for three successive days and nights, exclusive of the time occupied in preliminary arrangements.

Besides the two tribes above named, a large number of Sioux, Cumanches, Blackfeet, and Riccarees, were present, swelling the concourse to nearly a thousand lodges.

The regular participants in the ceremonies of the occasion had previously prepared themselves by a fast of three days, attended with frequent washings and purifications. A large lodge had been erected in the form of an amphitheatre, as described upon a former page, with a pole in its centre pointing to the zenith, near the top of which was affixed the head of a buffalo. Here the throng assembled, with up-turned eyes, encircling it around in solemn dance, accompanied by a low musical chant, as they addressed the "*Big Medicine*." This strange worship was maintained day and night, without intermission,—the devotees meanwhile neither eating nor drinking. So exhausted were they, that at times, they fell from effects of weakness and fatigue.

Some of their performances savored much of Hindoo origin. Those wishing to be thought particularly good, attested their piety by cutting themselves in various places,—and, yet others, by drawing after them the heads of buffalo fastened upon hooks inserted in their own flesh. As the exercises were about to close, an offering of blankets, robes, beads, tobacco, &c., was made to the Good Spirit, after which the crowd dispersed.

Their object appeared to be a threefold one, viz: to do penance for sin, to thank the Author of Good for past favors, and to implore a continuance of His beneficence for the future.

The head around which they danced was evidently not the object of their veneration, but was placed there simply to remind them that, as the buffalo constituted their principal sustenance, the Good Being should be more especially adored on its account.

A number of articles having disappeared from the Fort rather mysteriously, suspicion was fastened upon an Indian for appropriating them in the usual way. He was accordingly charged with the theft, but strongly affirmed his innocence, and, to place the matter beyond doubt, took an oath in attestation of his words. The ceremony observed was as follows:

Taking his bow, he selected the stoutest of his arrows, and, holding it in his right hand, pointed successively to the sky, the ground, and his own heart; then, kissing the bow, he again protested his innocence. This being considered satisfactory, he was honorably acquitted of the charge.

An Indian is rarely known either to violate his oath or to swear falsely, as in such a case he would be looked upon as being irrecoverably exposed to the immediate wrath of heaven and the vengeance of man. The import of this ceremony may be expressed in these words: "Thou who dwellest in the air and earth, receive from me this arrow, and with this bow plunge it to my heart, if I do not speak the truth!" I leave the reader to judge in regard to the binding nature of its obligations.

*Sept. 25th.* Having purchased a horse for the purpose, I proceeded to the mountains on a hunting excursion, where, unattended by any one, I had a further opportunity of testing the varied sweets of solitude.

My course lay directly west some eight miles to Soublet's creek, a considerable affluent of the Platte, heading at the base of Long's Peak,—thence, continuing up its right hand branch, I penetrated into the mountains, on the second day, a distance of several miles and camped. One of the passes to Grand river, which is generally thought much the nearest route, leads up this branch.

The interval from the 27th to the 30th was devoted to exploration, and I ascended the main chain of the mountains left of Long's Peak. The usual height of this ridge is about ten thousand feet, upon which the stern chambers of deathless winter are repeatedly exposed to the eye.

The mountains and creeks were well timbered,—the former with pine, cedar, and balsam, and the latter with cottonwood, aspen, and box-elder.

Along the wartercourses and intermingled with the rude array of hills and rocks, were many beautiful valleys, *prairillons*, and plateaux, all clothed with rank vegetation; and, indeed, the soil of the entire section appeared tolerably fertile.

The prevailing rock of this region is feldspathic granite, gneiss, micaceous sandstone, and slate. These different classifications (here strown about in confused piles, and there again towering in massive walls of immense altitude) presented an impressively grand appearance, and united to render the scenery one of varied sublimity and magnificence.

*Sept. 30th.* In the afternoon I raised camp and proceeded for ten or twelve miles, through a broad opening between two mountain ridges, bearing a northwesterly direction, to a large valley skirting a tributary of Thompson's creek, where, finding an abundance of deer, I passed the interval till my return to the Fort.

Upon all the principal streams were large quantities of cherries and plums, which proved quite acceptable. The cherry (*cerasus virginiana*) indigenous to this country is quite similar in appearance to our common wild cherry, though it is generally larger and more pleasantly tasted. It grows upon a small bush, and yields in lavish profusion.

Three different varieties of plums are common to these parts, but are so similar in most respects to the wild species of that fruit found in our Southern and Western States, that I shall not take the trouble to describe them.

The locality of my encampment presented numerous and varied attractions. It seemed, indeed, like a concentration of beautiful lateral valleys, intersected by meandering watercourses, ridged by lofty ledges of precipitous rock, and hemmed in upon the west by vast piles of mountains climbing beyond the clouds, and upon the north, south, and east, by sharp lines of hills that skirted the prairie; while occasional openings, like gateways, pointed to the far-spreading domains of silence and loneliness.

Easterly a wall of red sandstone and slate extended for miles northward and southward, whose counterscarp spread to view a broad and gentle declivity, decked with pines and luxuriant herbage, at the foot of which a lake of several miles in circumference occupies the centre of a basin-like valley, bounded in every direction by verdant hills, that smile upon the bright gem embosomed among them.

This valley is five or six miles in diameter, and possesses a soil well adapted to cultivation. It also affords every variety of game, while the lake is completely crowded with geese, brants, ducks, and gulls, to an extent seldom witnessed. What a charming retreat for some one of the world-hating *literati!* He might here hold daily converse with himself, Nature, and his God, far removed from the annoyance of man.

Four miles further north the traveller is brought to one of the main branches of Thompson's creek, up which is another pass to the waters of Grand river.

This stream traces its way through a fertile valley, two or three miles oroad, stretching from the prairie almost to the base of Long's Peak,—a distance of nearly thirty miles. The valley is well timbered and admirably adapted to stock-raising.

The hills and mountains, enclosing it upon each side are also studded

## NATURAL FORTIFICATION.

with forests of pine and cedar, while the entire section is stored with all of the usual varieties of game known to contiguous regions, in addition to its rich treasures of fruits, flowers and grasses.

In surveying, from a commanding summit, the vast prairie skirting the muntain range upon the east, several small lakes are discernible at different points. The water of these is usually brackish, and their shores, whitened by constant saline efflorescence, glisten in the sun's rays, and present a striking contrast with the surrounding verdure.

The mind is perfectly astounded at the immense expanse thus brought within the scope of vision. In a clear day, objects favorably situated no larger than an ox or a horse, may be seen at a distance of twenty miles, and the timber of creeks even for sixty or seventy miles. Here the beholder may scale beyond the clouds far heavenward, and gaze upon a world at his feet!

My hunting was confined principally to black-tailed deer. These animals are much larger than others of the *genus cervi*, and their flesh is of a superior flavor. Their habits are similar to those of the wild sheep,—leading them constantly to seek the regions of spring; in the winter, descending to the valleys, and in the summer, keeping pace with the melting snows upon the mountain-sides.

The extremity of their vertebræ is shorter than that of other species of the deer family, and has upon it a small cluster of coarse, jetty hair, from which the animal derives its name. Their hair is usually of a dark brown color, coarse and brittle, with the exception of a strip of dirty white upon the hams. Their ears are very large and long,—quite similar to those of a mule; in other respects, however, they conform to the peculiarities of the common deer.

I was quite successful with my rifle, and, by degrees, became much attached to the versatile life of lordly independence consociate with the loneliness of my situation. My horse, too, seemed to have forgotten all the allurements of former scenes, and presumed at no time to wander many yards from camp,—a peculiarity in this noble animal I have frequently had occasion to remark. When thus alone, a horse will substitute the society of man for that of his own species, and, as if conscious of surrounding danger, will seldom leave the vicinity of a camp for a long distance.

*Oct.* 29*th*, I started for the Fort. It had been my intention to visit a remarkable natural fortification upon one of the affluents of Crow creek, but, ammunition failing, I was reluctantly compelled to abandon it.

This fortress is said to be complete in nearly all its parts, and capable of garrisoning a thousand men, yet even one or two hundred might defend it from the repeated assaults of vast armies, and, with a small amount of labor, might render it impregnable.

Its walls are huge masses of solid rock, one or two hundred feet in height,—apparently strata planted on end,—enclosing an area of several acres, unenterable except at limited openings. According to the glowing descriptions of it given by hunters, it must be an object well worthy the attention of the curious.

At night, I encamped at the base of the mountains, upon the right hand fork of Soublet's creek, and the next day reached the Fort.

The last ten or twelve miles of the route (leading over an unbroken prairie) were travelled during a heavy fall of snow, which rendered the air so dark it was impossible to see a dozen yards in advance. But what added still more to the uncertainty of my course was the frequent variance of the wind, changing the position of the grass, and otherwise increasing the constant liability to misjudge. Notwithstanding these accumulated difficulties, I struck the Platte river only half a mile below the intended point.

## CHAPTER XXXIII.

Newspapers.—False reports.—Singular grasses.—Sale of skins at Fort Lancaster.—An excursion.—An incident.—Camp.—Huge horns.—Leopard.—Panther.—Slaughter of eagles.—Dressing skins.—The hunter's camp.—Vasques' creek.—The weather.—Return of comrades to Fort.—Sweets of solitude.—Exposure in a snow-storm.—The cañon of S. Fork Platte.—A ridge.—A valley.—Beautiful locality.—Choice site for a settlement.—Flowers in February.—A hunting incident.—Fate of the premature flowers.—Adventure with a sheep.—Discovered by Indians.—A pleasant meeting.—Camp at Crystal creek.—Thoughts of home.—Resolve on going.—Commence journey.—The caravan.—"Big Timber."—Country to the "Crossing."—Big Salt Bottom.—Flowers.—A stranger of other lands.—Difficulty with Indians. —"Friday."—Tedious travelling.—No timber.—Detention.—Country.—Pawnee Fork.—Mountain and Spanish companies.—Spy Buck, the Sawnee war chief.—Pawnee Fork.—Cure for a rattlesnake's bite.—Further detention.—Sketch of adjacent country.—Pawnee Rocks.—En route with Friday.—Musquitoes.—Observations.—Friday as a hunter.

THE different trading companies had just arrived from the States, bringing their winter stock of goods, and, what was still more acceptable to me, a bundle of newspapers. Every item of intelligence contained in the latter was greedily devoured, but what afforded me no little amusement was the palpable falsity and ignorance their editors exhibited in relation to matters of this country.

For instance, in giving the particulars of the murder of *Charvis*, a Mexican trader, which occurred in March, 1843, the crime was represented as having been committed near the Little Arkansas, by a party of Texans on their way to join Col. Warfield, who was then encamped in *that vicinity* with *forty men!* whereas, at that time Col. Warfield had only *nine* men with him, and was at least *three hundred miles* from the Little Arkansas; and further, the murderers of Charvis *were not* Texans!

Subsequently, an article in another paper came under my observation referring to a statement made to the National Institute, by an officer of the

United States Dragoons, purporting to give a description of the the *buffalo grass* common to the grand prairie. This grass was represented as growing six or eight inches high, and as being abundant n the mountains, particularly of New Mexico, where (if I rightly remember) it was said it remained green the entire winter. The truth of the matter is, *buffalo grass* very rarely exceeds *two* and never attains *four inches* in height,—is *not* found in the mountains *at all*, so far as my observation has extended, and is green only about *one month* in the year!

By the way, speaking of grass reminds me of a remarkable characteristic in some varieties indigenous to this country, and which will afford matter of speculation to the inquiring mind. The blade, killed by the frost of winter, is resuscitated in the spring and gradually becomes green from the root up, without casting its stubble or emitting new shoots!

The skins obtained during my hunt found a ready sale, at prices ranging from one to three dollars each, according their to quality and condition. These articles were in great demand for the manufacture of clothing among the Fort hands, and are considered far preferable to cloth.

*Nov. 10th.* I again returned to the mountains, heading a small party that insisted upon bearing me company. Late in the afternoon of the second day we made camp in a valley, behind the first ridge of hills, upon the right hand fork of Soublet's creek.

An incident *en route* afforded some little amusement at the time. We had left the Fort without provisions, and I accordingly proceeded a short distance in advance for the purpose of killing antelope. Riding slowly on, I noticed a badger not far ahead, and dismounted to shoot him. But the creature becoming alarmed sprang for his hole, and I hastened to stop him. This I effected by tightly grasping his tail as he was in the very act of entering his burrow. In the chase my rifle had accidentally discharged itself, and here commenced a struggle between me and the badger, —I to retain my hold while I unbelted my pistol to dispatch him, and he to enforce his liberty. At length I succeeded, and a choice supper was made from his carcase, which, to all intents, was the fattest thing I ever saw.

We remained encamped at the place above named for some six weeks, and devoted the interval principally to hunting sheep, of which there were vast numbers in the neighborhood. In attestation of the monstrous horns borne by some of them, I need only mention the simple fact of my having killed three sheep while here whose horns measured nineteen inches in circumference, and nearly three feet in length.

One of our party encountered a strange looking animal in his excursions, which, from his description, must have been of the leopard family. This circumstance is the more remarkable, as leopards are rarely found except in southern latitudes. However, they are not unfrequently met with in some parts of the Cumanche country, and their skins furnish to the natives a favorite material for arrow-cases.

The only beast of prey other than wolves, encountered during the entire winter, was a solitary panther, whose extreme shyness defied all attempts to approach within shooting distance.

My more lengthy rambles brought me to a large valley immured by lateral hills, that had been occupied a short time previous by a party of Indians, for the purpose of eagle-catching. As proof of their success, I counted the bodies of thirty-six eagles, lying in piles at their recent camp. These consisted of the only two varieties found in the mountains, viz: the American and bald eagle. The wing-feathers of these birds command a ready sale among the Indians, by whom they are highly prized for the empluming of arrows.

The usual mode of dressing skins, prevalent in this country among both Indians and whites, is very simple in its details and is easily practised. It consists in removing all the fleshy particles from the pelt, and divesting it of a thin viscid substance upon the exterior, known as the "grain;" then, after permitting it to dry, it is thoroughly soaked in a liquid decoction formed from the brains of the animal and water, when it is stoutly rubbed with the hands in order to open its pores and admit the mollient properties of the fluid,—this done, the task is completed by alternate rubbings and distensions until it is completely dry and soft.

In this manner a skin may be dressed in a very short time, and, on application of smoke, will not become hardened from any subsequent contact with water.

The winter-camp of a hunter of the Rocky Mountains would doubtless prove an object of interest to the unsophisticated. It is usually located in some spot sheltered by hills or rocks, for the double purpose of securing the full warmth of the sun's rays, and screening it from the notice of strolling Indians that may happen in its vicinity. Within a convenient proximity to it stands some grove, from which an abundance of dry fuel is procurable when needed; and equally close the ripplings of a watercourse salute the ear with their music.

His shantee faces a huge fire, and is formed of skins carefully extended over an arched frame-work of slender poles, which are bent in the form of a semicircle and kept to their places by inserting their extremities in the ground. Near this is his "graining block," planted aslope, for the ease of the operative in preparing his skins for the finishing process in the art of dressing; and not far removed is a stout frame, contrived from four pieces of timber, so tied together as to leave a square of sufficent dimensions for the required purpose, in which, perchance, a skin is stretched to its fullest extension, and the hardy mountaineer is busily engaged in rubbing it with a rough stone or "scraper," to fit it for the manufacture of clothing.

Facing his shantee upon the opposite side of the fire, a pole is reared upon crotches five or six feet high, across which reposes a choice selection of the dainties of his range, to wit: the "side ribs," shoulders, heads, and "rump-cuts" of deer and sheep, or the "dèpouille" and "fleeces" of buffalo. The camp-fire finds busy employ in fitting for the demands of appetite such dainty bits of hissing roasts as *en appolas* may grace its sides, while, at brief intervals, the hearty attendant, enchaired upon the head of a mountain sheep, (whose huge horns furnish legs and arms for the convenience of sitting,) partakes of his tempting lunch.

Carefully hung in some fitting place, are seen his "riding" and "pack saddles," with his halters, " cavraces," " larrietts," " apishamores," and all the needful *materiel* for camp and travelling service; and, adjoining him at no great distance, his animals are allowed to graze, or, if suitable nourishment of other kind be lacking, are fed from the bark of cottonwood trees levelled for that propose; and, leaning close at hand, his rifle awaits his use, and by it his powder-horn, bullet-pouch, and tomahawk.

Thus conditioned are these lordly rangers in their mountain home, nor own that any creature of human kind can possibly enjoy life better than they.

The events of each day varied so little in their nature, that a minute notice of them would prove uninteresting to the general reader. Suffice it to say, we remained here till Jan. 1st, 1844, and then removed to Vasques' creek, some thirty-five miles further south, where we encamped in the valley that formed my hunting ground of the previous winter.

The weather continued cold, and several falls of snow had occurred, covering the prairies to the depth of six or seven inches, and the mountains to the depth of many feet, though it rarely remained in the warm valleys and upon the sunny side-hills to exceed three successive hours.

Our camp, as a general thing, was quite favorably situated in regard to temperature; the day time frequently affording a spring-like warmth, though the nights were usually cold.

A peculiar species of grass among the hills retained its verdancy the entire season, as did also another variety in the valleys. Our horses and mules continued to thrive and even fatten upon the nourishing herbage thus afforded by these secret chambers of spring.

Soon after our removal to Vasques' creek, three Indians, from a neighboring village, paid us a visit, who brought vague information of the approximity of the Sioux, which so excited the apprehension of my campmates relative to their own safety and that of their animals, that they were not satisfied to remain here any longer, and accordingly left for the Fort. Wishing to ascertain the true situation and locality of such suspicious neighbors, I proceeded to the Indian village for that purpose. The report proved unfounded; but yet my extra-prudential comrades were unwilling to compromise their own safety by a further hunt, and argued stoutly to persuade me to accompany them beyond the reach of danger.

In the morning, however, as all were ready to resume their journey, I mounted my horse, and, bidding them adieu, with my lead pack-animal returned to the mountains, resolved on a further test of the sweets of loneliness.

Remaining at our former camp for a week or more, I enjoying full scope for my trusty rifle among the vast quantities of deer which showed themselves in every direction; and, in one of my many excursions, penetrated to the head valley of Vasques' creek;—being belated on my return by killing a very fat deer, I was forced to pass the night among the mountains, without even a robe or a blanket to screen me from the severities of a pitiless snow-storm that fell in the mean time. Strange as it may seem, I experienced not the slightest ill effect in consequence.

On removing from my old hunting grounds, I halted at two or three different points still further south, upon small affluents of the Platte, and in the course of twenty-five days encamped a few miles below the exit of the main stream from the mountains, in an opening made by the forced passage of a large creek into the prairie through a sharp line of hills.

The scenery in the vicinity of this camp was romantic, wild, and beautiful. The ridge thus bisected was about four hundred feet in heighth, and opposed to the creek vast mural cliffs of limestone and sandstone that formed a gateway nearly three hundred yards wide. It ranged parallel with the mountains, two miles or more removed from them, presenting to the prairie a gentle escarpment ornamented with scattering pines and clothed at intervals with rank grasses of the preceding year's growth.

On ascending to its summit you stand at the verge of a steep precipice, two hundred or more feet in descent,—as if the earth, opened by internal convulsions, had forced the right valve of its fissure to an unnatural position, and thus formed the elevation beneath you.

This ridge extends for many miles, and overlooks a beautiful valley of remarkable fertility, fifteen miles in length by three in breadth, and intersected by numerous streams, more or less timbered, that find their way from the mountain side. The valley is divided by a continuous ridge that runs parallel with its length, which is much the same in character with, though more diminutive in size than the one previously described.

The huge masses of red granitic sandstone that tower to a surprising altitude, isolated and in almost every conceivable form and shape, add vastly to the wildness of the place. The rock is quite friable and constantly yielding to the action of the weather, while the soil of the valley is of a ruddy color and gravelly nature as will be readily inferred from the above fact.

This superfice is fertilized, not only from the debris of its rocks, but by the immense bods of *gypsum* contained in its hill-sides, which are incessantly decomposing to enhance the general fecundity. Vegetation, of course, must attain a rank growth in such a soil, and, in favored spots, it remains green the entire year.

All the different varieties of wild fruits and game indigenous to the mountains are found here in great abundance. Among the timber of the creek bottom, I noticed hazel-bushes, old acquaintances of the States, which looked like messengers from a far off country, and reminded me of other scenes.

There are few localities in the vicinity of the mountains better situated for a small settlement, or possessed of greater agricultural advantages than this.

The prairie at the base of the first range of hills is quite saline in its character; and several small lakes of brackish water, and well stocked with almost numberless water-fowl, are seen at different points, the incrustations upon whose shores assume a snowy whiteness. Notwithstanding this, it possesses a good soil and is admirably adapted to the growth of stock.

*Feb. 26th.* The fresh grass upon the hill-sides has assumed a thrifty appearance. Insects have begun to quit their winter retreats, and, commingling their shrill notes with the music of birds, hail the approaching spring. I was delighted to find in my rambles a cluster of wild-flowers in full bloom, shedding their fragrance to the breeze from a sweet, sunny spot among the hills, and I sat for a time to admire its new-born loveliness.

One of my horses, having been for some time wasting under the effects of a disease peculiar to those animals, died this afternoon,—a loss which subjects me to no little inconvenience. It was a noble beast, and cost me sixty dollars only four months since.

*Feb. 28th.* A light snow which fell yesterday night prevented me from leaving camp, but having shouldered my rifle early this morning, I ranged along the valley. The snow had entirely disappeared. Three buffalo bulls, alarmed at my approach, rushed down a steep hill-side, quartering towards me, at the height of their speed. Running to intercept them, I shot as they passed, prostrating one at the instant. So great was the impetuosity of his headway, the carcase was thrown to the very base of the descent, a distance of about three hundred yards!

The interest awakened by the picture of loveliness that greeted me two days previous, led again to the sweet spot among the rough hill-sides,—but, how changed! The cruel frost had done his death-work—the "flowers had withered and the beauty thereof had fallen away." A tear to their memory, despite my efforts to restrain it, stole its way to the ground. Such was the fate of the first flower of spring! What a prolific theme for a melancholy fancy to brood upon, and, in its musings, catch the inspirations of poesy!

*March 4th.* The dull monotony of four days past has afforded nothing worthy of note. Spring is making rapid advances. To-day, however, an incident occurred, which, with suitable forethought, might have been turned to good account. Soon after leaving camp I encountered a band of sheep, and, despairing of a near approach, shot one of its number at a distance of nearly three hundred and fifty yards. The animal immediately fell, having been stunned by a neck wound, ("*creased*,") but recovered as I reached it, barely affording me time to grasp one of its legs.

Here commenced a struggle,—the sheep to get free, and I to retain my hold. In the energy of its efforts I was dragged over the rocks for some two hundred yards, when, having caught its fore-leg, I succeeded in throwing it, and unthinkingly despatched it with my butcher-knife. I might have preserved it alive, as a rare and valuable addition to some zoological collection. My not having done so, I regretted the more, as it was a female and would have soon produced another of its species.

*March 7th.* Having discovered a large band of deer in the prairie towards the Platte, early this morning I started to approach them. Being within the required distance, I was preparing to shoot, when, on glancing to the left, a party of horsemen met my view, advancing at full gallop. Their bare heads and fluttering robes at once announced them Indians.

Here was a dilemma! My first thought was to retire to the creek and there await them, under cover of the trees,—but this would convey an im pression of cowardice, a thing which uniformly receives ill treatment at the hands of Indians, while bravey commands their respect. I therefore resolved to stand my ground and fight it out, if necessary, let the consequences be what they would. So, after examining the condition of my firearms and making the suitable arrangements for an expected rencounter, I calmly awaited their approach. My design was to shoot the foremost when within proper distance, (first forbidding their advance,) then, having discharged my pistols at the two next, if not previously killed, to close in with the remainder, butcher-knife in hand. From hostile savages I expected no quarter, and was therefore determined to sell my life as dearly as possible.

A nearer approach, however, changed my gloomy apprehensions into a transport of pleasure, as I recognized two old hunters from Fort Lancaster at their head,—the first of human beings, white or Indian, that I had seen for two months. Their gratification scarcely surpassed my own, they having long since supposed me murdered by prowling savages.

Having camped the day previous about three miles distant with the party accompanying them, they were now in quest of buffalo. However, as it threatened to be unpleasant weather, an invitation to my camp was gladly accepted, where the choice stores my larder afforded, were discussed with epicurean gusto.

Yielding to their persuasions, in the afternoon I bid adieu to my lovely retreat and proceeded with them to their encampment upon the opposite side of the Platte, near the mouth of Crystal creek.

Here a small party of whites from the Fort were occupied in building a boat, with which to descend the river. A Mexican woman, from Taos, the wife of an engagé, honored the scene with her presence, as did also three squaws and two Indians. Commodious shantees had been erected for the accommodation of the men, which, together with a huge fire and a proportionate pile of meat, imparted an air of comfort to everything.

Remaining here for a week or two, I then proceeded to the Fort, a distance of about forty miles. The different trading companies were already *en route* for the States, having left several days previous. The thoughts of other lands, and more congenial associations, were now revived in all their vividness. They filled my mind by day, and crowded my dreams by night. Eight years had already intervened since the view of a distant home and much-loved childhood scenes had last greeted me, nearly three of which had been passed amid the dangers and vicissitudes of prairie and mountain life. Yet, I was at a loss to decide what to do. The object of my excursion had not been satisfactorily accomplished. I wished to visit the Pacific and familiarize myself more perfectly with several parts of Oregon and California; this would yet require a year, or even more.

However, the subject now uppermost in my thoughts influenced the decision, and, bidding a present adieu to other plans, I made prompt arrangements for returning to the States. These were soon completed, and on the 17th of March I commenced my journey.

With the intermediate country from the Platte to Bent's Fort on the Arkansas the reader is already familiar; and, as few incidents worthy of note occurred between these two points, I shall content myself with a mere passing notice and hasten with becoming brevity to a conclusion of the task in hand.

The fourth day succeeding my departure I overtook a division of the caravan of mountain traders, numbering ten men and three waggons, with which I proceeded to the Big Timber of the Arkansas, distant about two hundred miles southeast from Fort Lancaster.

The country at this place, in the immediate vicinity of the river, is fertile and well timbered, but the prairies are slightly undulating, arid, and generally unproductive. The prevailing rock is exhibited in abrupt cliffs and bold escarpments from the hill-sides and banks of watercourses, and consists of various conglomerates, with limestone and sandstone; the latter being very fine-grained and admirably suited to the preparing of edgetools. I noticed indications of coal in some parts, and the usual quantity of saline efflorescences, particularly upon the south side of the river.

On the 10th of April, the caravan being augmented by an accession of three other waggons and several men, we again resumed our journey, and, on the 28th inst., struck the Santa Fe trail near the Crossing of the Arkansas, one hundred and ten miles below the Big Timber.

The geological character of the prairie and the river bottoms is much the same as that previously described, with the exception of a general scarcity of rock; though to the southward it is very sterile in appearance, and a continuous chain of hills, that in some places are mere knobs of naked sand entirely destitute of every semblance of vegetation, plainly points out the cheerless *llanos* of the Great American Desert.

Below the Big Timber the rank growths of *absinthe*, which have been heretofore so prevalent, almost entirely disappear.

The river gradually expands to the width of nearly two miles, forming several small islands, and scatters its waters in numerous channels, over beds of quicksand, so shallow and variable as to preclude the possibility of successful navigation.

Timber becomes very scarce,—so much so, that in many places it is difficult to obtain a sufficiency even for the camp-fires of travellers. The bottoms are usually broad and fertile, but possess a highly saline character.

One of the above, known as the Big Salt Bottom, is some forty miles in length and four or five miles broad. It contains frequent streams and pools of brackish water, with spots in which vegetation entirely gives place to thick coatings of mineral salts.

Among the prairie hills I occasionally noticed extensive spreads completely covered with a singular species of blue flower in full bloom. which imparted to the otherwise forbidding prospect an air of loveliness and beauty; but, in glancing over the far-reaching landscape, I looked in vain for the floral attractions peculiar to mountain regions.

A few miles above the Crossing, an incident occurred which renewedly aroused my recollection of other lands. This was the appearance of a fine-looking *coon*, the first I had seen since leaving the States. These animals are strangers to the mountains, and were never before known to penetrate thus far westward.

30 *

In passing a village of Arapahos, near the Salt Bottom, we had considerable difficulty with them on account of ten or fifteen domesticated buffalo connected with the caravan. The Indians were highly exasperated, and accused the whites of *stealing* their buffalo. They even armed themselves to fight us, and were deterred from their purpose only by a large present of tobacco, but still threatened vengeance in case of a renewal of the offence.

Soon after this we were joined by a young Arapaho Indian, named Friday, who was desirous of visiting the States. He had formerly lived in St. Louis, where he had acquired a knowledge of the English language, and still maintains a reputation for honesty, intelligence, and sobriety. Hereafter I will have occasion to speak of him more particularly, in connection with his previous history.

Resuming our course, we bore leftward from the river and struck into the high prairie. Late rains had rendered the ground muddy, and travelling consequently became slow and tedious.

The weather continued wet and disagreeable, in addition to which the unprecedented size and velocity of the streams caused us frequent detention.

The trail, for four or five days, led over a number of timberless watercourses, known as "the coon creeks," which subjected us to great inconvenience in the item of fuel, as neither tree nor stick could be procured for cooking purposes, and *bois de bache*, the substitue of buffalo countries, had become so thoroughly saturated with water it was almost impossible to ignite it.

On the 23d of April, having arrived at Pawnee Fork, we were obliged to remain some four weeks before a ford could be effected,—but the dense bands of buffalo that thronged the vicinity abated somewhat the annoyance of delay.

The country, between the "Crossing" and Pawnee Fork, varies but little in its general character from that previously described, and exhibits a favorable contrast to the forbidding wastes of naked sand upon the opposite side of the Arkansas. Although not absolutely sterile, it is not rich, and suffers more from lack of moisture than any actual defect of soil. Its entire destitution of timber will prevent it from ever becoming inhabited to any great extent.

Rock of all kinds is very scarce, and almost the only specimens prevalent are found in the pebbles and diminutive fragments which lie scattered over the prairie.

During our stay we were joined by Messrs. Bent and St. Vrain, and three or four Spanish companies, which increased our caravan to fifty or more waggons and nearly one hundred men.

With the former of the companies was a Chyenne chief, (Slim Face,) on his way to Washington to solicit the U. S. Government to adopt some effectual means for the suppression of the sale of ardent spirits among his people. (A very laudable object, indeed.)

Three or four Mexican ladies and several children (being the family of one of the Spanish traders, from Chihuahua) were also included with the new accession ; but the most noted personage among the whole was Old Spy Buck, the famous Shawnee war-chief, who had distinguished himself as the leader of a small band of his countrymen in connection with Kirker and the Americans employed by the governments of Santa Fe and Chihuahua to fight the Apache and Navijo Indians.

The old chieftain was on his return home, venerable in age and covered with scars, which gave indubitable evidence of the place he had occupied in the hour of danger. The history of his exploits would fill a volume far more interesting in its details than those of the proudest heroes of fiction.

Pawnee Fork afforded an inexhaustible supply of cat-fish, which were caught in great numbers by our party. I know of no other stream near, upon the Atlantic side of the mountains, where fish are found in any quantity or size worth naming.

This creek heads at the eastern extremity of the "Divide," in the vicinity of the Smoky Hill branch of the Kansas, and by pursuing a southern course for about one hundred and fifty miles, finds its discharge in the Arkansas. It is heavily timbered, and is known among the Indians as Otter creek, on account of the great number of those animals found upon it. The valley which skirts it is several miles broad, and very fertile, presenting a large extent of excellent land, well adapted to cultivation.

While here, I became acquainted with the salutary properties of gunpowder in an interesting case. My horse, having been bitten by a rattlesnake, was cured by the following simple process: The wound being slightly creased immediately above and below, a small portion of powder was burnt upon it for four or five times in succession, which completely destroyed the effects of the poison. I am informed by those who have repeatedly tried this remedy, that it has never been known to fail when promptly applied.

On the 21st of May, we finally effected a crossing, and by the 24th had reached Walnut creek, twenty miles distant, where high water again opposed a present barrier to further progress. The bottoms were so completely flooded that we were forced to occupy an adjoining eminence for a camp.

This stream is heavily timbered, and derives its name from the abundance of black walnut found along its banks. Its valley is very similar to that of Pawnee Fork as regards size and fertility, while the country between the two is evidently possessed of a good soil.

About twelve miles below Walnut creek, near the trail, is a huge and isolated mass of coarse sandstone, known as the Pawnee Rocks. This is a noted landmark, and, like Independence Rock elsewhere spoken of, is covered with the names of passers by, *en route* to and from the mountains and Mexican States.

Here was a confused medley of cognomens,—English, French, Spanish, German, Irish, and Scotch,—all entered upon the register of fancied immortality; and here, too, as I glanced over the strange catalogue, a number of our company were busily engaged in carving their own; but remembering a former resolution, I declined the honor of imitating their example.

*June* 16*th.* More than three weeks have intervened since our arrival at Walnut creek, and still there is no present possibility of proceeding with the waggons. This continued delay is becoming extremely irksome, notwithstanding the countless thousands of buffalo which afford us an inexhaustible feast of "fat things." Time is precious and I must go on; and there are several who would do likewise, but hesitate,—while frightful visions of Pawnees and Osages disturb their midnight dreams and fluster their waking thoughts. Friday, the Arapaho, asks to accompany me;— our arrangements are completed, and to-morrow we leave.

*June* 17*th.* About noon, bidding adieu to vexatious hindrances, we started, and, after a short ride, forded the Arkansas above the mouth of Walnut creek,—thence, following the course of that river upon its opposite bank, we halted for the night in a broad sandy bottom, four or five miles below.

The musquetoes here proved so troublesome to ourselves and animals, we were compelled to defend the former by means of a dense smoke and protect the latter with a close envelope of robes. The next morning we recrossed the Arkansas, and, striking the waggon road soon after near Plum Butte, continued our way to Cow creek.

A few miles above this point the regular trail leaves the Arkansas upon the right, and, following a northwesterly course for about three hundred and fifty miles, strikes the States at Independence, Mo.

The interval between Walnut and Cow creeks is generally sandy and somewhat tumulous, but is different in many respects from any other section previously noticed. The hills, adjacent to the river and near the trail, are coniform and not unfrequently naked piles of dry sand, while the hollows and depressions among them afford a humid soil, coated with rank vegetation.

Cow creek is a small stream with very steep, clayey banks, and is sparsely timbered. Its bottom is about four miles broad and of variable fertility,—doubtless susceptible of cultivation.

On resuming our course we leave the buffalo region, a transition for which we are now fully prepared. Aware that this must shortly occur, I had sent Friday in advance with my rifle, who very soon prostrated three fine bulls, affording us a stock of most excellent beef from which to make our selections.

Few Indians or whites can compete with Friday as a buffalo-hunter, either in the use of the bow or rifle. I have seen him kill five of these animals at a single chase, and am informed that he has not unfrequently exceeded that number. Conscious skill, in this respect, is the occasion of some little pride to its possessor.

But it is not in hunting exploits alone that he excels; his deeds of war equally command the respect and admiration of his tribe, among whom he is known as the "Arapaho American." A brief sketch of his early life I have reserved for the succeeding chapter, which the reader may rely upon as strictly true.

## CHAPTER XXXIV.

The Arapaho American, a sketch of real life.—Tenets of the mountain Indians in reference to a future state of rewards and punishments.—The "water bull."—Country between Cow creek and Council Grove. Inviting locality for settlement.—Sudden rise of water.—Separate routes.—Dangerous travelling.—Osage village.—Osages, and all about them.—Arrival at Van Buren, Arkansas.—Concluding remarks.

EARLY in the year 1828, ere peace had been established between the whites and the Arapahos, a large village of that tribe made its temporary encampment upon the waters of the Cimarone, in the vicinity of the Santa Fe trail.

An opportunity so favorable for amusement was not suffered long to pass unimproved by the younger ones, and group after group of merry boys and girls were soon bescattered over the adjoining prairie, engaged in their innocent sports,—for of play all children possess an intuitive fondness, be they white, red, or black.

Each successive day yielded its tribute to the routine of pleasure, as, true to the teachings of childish philosophy, they seized the enjoyments of the present, nor thought or cared for the future,—and thus far, it may be said, some men are but overgrown boys.

Impelled by the restless spirit of their years, on an occasion, several frolicksome lads had wandered to an unusual distance from camp, and passed most of the day in a fruitless effort to catch prairie-dogs.

At length, wearied with a bootless task, they set their faces homeward. Scarcely had they started, however, when the village made its appearance, bearing directly towards them; whereupon the happy band, seating themselves at the point of an eminence, awaited its approach, and soon mingled with their relatives, one after another, as they were disclosed by the passing throng.

In a short time a little boy, some six years old, alone remained—watching with eager impatience the appearance of his father's lodge; but still it came not. The crowd had passed and a solitary old man brought up the rear. On seeing the lone stripling, he enquired the cause of his delay.

"My parents come not, and I await them," said the little fellow.

"Haste you," replied the man; "they have gone towards the sun-rising for a day's travel. Run quick, that you may join them."

The lad promptly followed the old man's direction, and set off in pursuit. His route led over a long reach of dry sand-prairie, eastward of the Cimarone, which was entirely destitute of water, and soon after crossing the creek a heavy wind obscured the trail,-in addition to which the thick clouds of dust, with fast-closing night and insufferable thirst, compelled him to turn again to the Cimarone.

Another attempt to reach the village the day following was unsuccessful, and each repeated effort proved equally unavailing.

At length, weakened by hunger and suffering, he laid himself down to die, in a grass plat by the creek side.

Seven days of continued fasting which followed, left him so debilitated he could scarcely stand. His mind began to wander; he thought himself a dweller of the Spirit Land and a ranger of the hunting ground of happy souls.

His bewildered vision pictured the joyous chase, bounding along the celestial plains. Strange voices greeted his ear, and sounds broke upon the stillness of solitude. He gazes around, and sights still stranger close in upon him,—not visionary, but real.

"It must be so," said he. "Here are the horses for me to ride, and there is the game for me to chase. But, what singular buffalo! How long their horns, and how white!—What strange colors, too!—white, red, black, and mixed! And, who are they?—Ah! the pale-faces! They approach! What do they here?—I cannot escape them!" Thereupon he found himself in the firm grasp of two white men, who cut short his soliloquy by bearing him to their camp.

His fancy, though illusive in its inception, had ended in sober reality. The strange voices greeting his ear were those of his captors, who had just encamped near him; the horses and singular buffalo exciting his wonder, were the horses and cattle of a caravan of Santa Fe traders; and the pale-faces were two of the company, by the names of Fitzpatrick and Soublet, by whom he was taken.

They were on their return to the States, and, noticing a strange object in the vicinity of camp soon after their noon halt, approached to learn its character and found the little sufferer as above related.

He had never before seen the whites, and, knowing them only from the representations of his people, they were associated in his boyish fancy with all that was hateful and wicked. But, instead of the cruel death he had supposed would be his certain allotment at their hands, they administered to his wants and plied him with kindnesses. Everything about him was so strange, he could scarcely be convinced it was not a picture of the imagination—that he was not yet dreaming of the happy country, or actually initiated into its delightful mysteries.

From the date of this event he was ushered into a new state of existence, and soon acquired the language and habits of the whites. Taken to St. Louis, he remained there for some five years, and received a partial education during the interval. So complete was the transformation, he even forgot the name and language of his nation, and became an adept in the customs of civilized life.

About the year 1832, Capt. Grant succeeded in effecting a treaty with the Arapahos, and pending its negotiation mention was made of a boy, said to have been lost upon the Cimarone several years previous, who was supposed to have fallen into the hands of a trading company, and for whose ransom a large number of horses was offered.

It is needless to say our hero was the subject of this request, and, in order to conciliate their good will and place the new-formed treaty upon a permanent basis, word was forwarded to his benefactor, Fitzpatrick, informing him of the circumstance.

Friday, for this was the name by which the Indian youth had now become known, on hearing the proposal of his relatives, steadily refused compliance, declaring the whites to be his only relatives, and that with them he would live and die.

Subsequently, however, he was persuaded to accompany his guardian to the mountains, expecting shortly to revisit the States. Here his father and mother came forward to claim him as their long-lost son.

But the lapse of seven years had served to efface all the recollections of early childhood. Parents and friends were alike strangers to him; he refused to own them, and recoiled from their advances. Their language grated upon his ear in a confused jargon of unknown sounds. His mother wept from mingled emotions of grief and joy, while his father and brothers pressed their mouths in unfeigned astonishment. Still his obstinacy was unyielding, and the united entreaties of relatives failed to exert upon him the least influence.

At length, the arguments and advice of the fur traders induced him to visit the Arapahos village, where he was received with distinguished honor by his relatives and nation. Every one hastened to pay him respect,—while feast succeeded feast, and council succeeded council, to welcome his return, and the little boy, who, seven years before—lost amid the cheerless sands of the American Desert, and weakened by hunger and suffering—had lain down to die upon the bank of the Cimarone, now found himself suddenly made famous as the " Little Chief " of his tribe,—the " Arapaho American."

Honor, whose potent spell exerts its influence upon older heads and more enlightened minds, gradually reconciled him to the rude mode of life his destiny seemed to mark out, and he again became identified with the associations of former years.

Still, however, he retains an undiminished attachment to the whites, and continues to merit and command their esteem. His character, for honesty, integrity, and sobriety, has as yet stood unimpeached. A chief by birth, he might assert a more prominent station among his people; but he declines it, with the noble resolve :—" Until by my own achievements I have earned that honor, I shall never consent to become a *chief;* for certainly, then my people will listen to me!"

The hero of the above sketch is now on his way to visit his friends in St. Louis for the second time, and is at present my only travelling companion. As such I find him agreeable and interesting. I am indebted to him for much valuable information relative to the habits and peculiarities of his own and various other Indian tribes, while his vast fund of ready anecdotes and amusing stories serves to beguile the weariness of camp hours.

The religious peculiarities of the mountain tribes furnished us a theme for frequent conversation, inasmuch as their sentiments with regard to a future existence are strangely interesting in detail. Most of them are firm believers in the immortality of the soul, as well as the condition of rewards and punishments after death—though some accredit the Hindoo notions of metamorphosis or metempsychosis, while yet a very few look for annihilation.

The majority, however, aver that the good, at death, after a long and tedious journey, reach a happy country, abundant in everything the heart can desire, or thought conceive of; where, free from pain and sickness, and removed from every ill, they shall bask forever in the sunshine of perfect beatitude.

To aid in this long journey, horses are occasionally sacrificed for the feeble and decrepit, (more generally squaws and aged warriors,) that, by mounting their disembodied chargers, the spirits of the deceased may gain a speedy entrance within its confines and taste the joys of their eternal home.

Of those adhering to different opinions, some believe in the transmission of souls from body to body through successive ages; and others, that they become the spirits of either men or animals, according to the virtues or demerits of the departed.

With regard to the final allotment of the wicked, their general theology consigns them to an interminable wandering over a desert waste, without purpose or rest, or even one moment's respite from their miseries, and subject to all the bitter pangs of hunger, thirst, and nakedness; and tormented with the sudden and intolerable extremities of heat and cold. The Scripturian here will not fail to recognize an obscure delineation of the world of woe, as portrayed in the sacred writings.

The ideas of some few, on the other hand, transform these condemned spirits into wild beasts or reptiles, but more frequently into prairie-dogs, that, by penance and suffering through a long succession of years, they may atone for previous misdeeds.

Many incidents of adventure related by Friday would doubtless interest the general reader, but space precludes their insertion. However, I cannot refuse place to the following, as affording to the curious a more special matter of speculation.

"On my return from an expedition against the Utahs," said he, "in crossing the mountain chain south of Long's Peak, I went in advance of the main party.

"My course led over one of the highest points of the range, whose summit disclosed a level surface of considerable extent. While passing leisurely along, the crowing of a mountain fowl, a short distance to the right, caught my ear. (There are fowls in some parts of the mountains similar to those raised by the whites,—but they are very wild and shy.) Following the sound, I was led to the verge of a small lake, with steep banks of rock, and sat down by it, in hopes of discovering the object of my curiosity.

"While here, my attention was directed to a strange movement in the lake-waters, accompanied by a loud noise and turmoil; soon after which a large creature arose from the middle and swam to the shore, where he stood upon a rock in full view. His looks frightened me. In size he was equal to the largest buffalo, and much like one of those animals in form; he was black, with a singularly shaped head, and had tusks instead of horns, which curved downward.

"He looked so terrible I hurried away as quick as possible, and related my adventure on rejoining the party. The old men laughed at my expressions of wonder—asserting that they had before seen such creatures in the high mountain-lakes, and called them '*water bulls.*'"

Resuming our course, we travelled by easy stages for five succeeding days, which brought us to Council Grove, a noted place of rendezvous for Santa Fe companies.

The intervening country from Cow creek exhibits an entire change in its geological character. The landscape is gently undulating, and furrowed by frequent watercourses. Timber is becoming more abundant. The soil appears humid, and presents an air of general fertility. The grasses also differ in their species and assume a lusty growth.

The sand-hills which had before skirted the Arkansas, as the traveller advances, lose their naked deformity amid dense groves of timber, and finally disappear in the distance.

There is throughout a marked scarcity of game common to the grand prairies, and everything denotes an approach to the frontiers of civilization.

Council Grove is a stream of considerable magnitude, tributary to the Osage river, and, by the Santa Fe trail, is one hundred and forty-four miles west of Independence. Its bottoms are broad, fertile, and well timbered with heavy forests of oak, walnut, maple, and most other varieties of wood indigenous to the States.

The country in its vicinity is highly interesting to the agriculturist, and presents a soil remarkable for its fertility, inviting the hand of industry to a rich reward.

Here, too, all the varied products of the farmer might find a ready cash market, from the numerous mountain and Spanish companies that constantly pass and repass, and, doubtlessly, at commanding prices. This locality, in fact, being situated upon the very verge of the grand prairie, affords a most eligible point for a settlement, and will doubtless soon acquire a merited importance as the place of general out-fit and supply for the western and southwestern trade.

Through the agency of Friday I became acquainted with the existence of a vegetable found in these parts, which is known as the prairie-potato. This attains a size almost equalling our common potato. It is of a rough, knotty appearance, somewhat oviform, and when cooked is dry and sweet tasted. It is found generally in the banks of watercourses, and produces a low ground-vine, not dissimilar to a species of that vegetable usual to warm climates.

We were detained here for five or six days, by a continuous rain which raised the creek to an extraordinary height,—overflowing its banks and completely flooding its extensive bottoms. So sudden was the rise that we were compelled to move camp three times in the course of an hour, and were finally driven to an adjoining hill.

Improving the first interval of fair weather presenting itself, I bade adieu to my Indian companion and renewed my journey alone, as our routes led in different directions, his for Independence, Mo., and mine for Van Buren, Ark. Following the course of the creek by its right bank for some twenty miles, I then struck over to the Neosho, and, continuing on, the fourth day subsequent I reached the Osage village.

The country passed in travelling this distance, presented much excellent land. The creek valleys were broad and heavily timbered, and the adjoining prairies undulating and clothed with luxuriant vegetation. The streams were so swollen I was forced to swim most of them, which rendered my progress one continued scene of toilsome and perilous adventure.

My stay at the Osage village was prolonged for two days, during which time I was kindly entertained by a chief who served as my host.

The Osages number between four and five thousand souls, and inhabit the section of country bordering upon the Neosho river. Their territory is well timbered, abundantly watered, and remarkably fertile.

In dress and appearance these Indians assimilate the Pawnees and Caws; but their dwellings are neater and more spacious, being constructed of water-flags fastened to frame-works of poles, so ingeniously thatched and tightly interwoven as to prevent the ingress of either wind or rain.

This tribe are beginning to make advances in civilization, and devote some little attention to agriculture. A farmer and blacksmith are furnished them by the U. S. Government, while the philanthropic efforts of the American Board of Missions are directed to their amelioration with considerable success.

On resuming my course, a branch of the Neosho which intercepted it proved unfordable, and its passage was otherwise rendered particularly dangerous on account of the swiftness of its current. However, my landlord, on seeing my determination to cross at all hazards, procured two large pieces of raw hide, which were firmly sewn together in boat shape and held to their proper position by slender boughs; these he conveyed to the stream, and desired me to put my baggage into them, remarking that there was "plenty room" for myself, too. Following his directions, the frail bark was soon launched and towed to the opposite shore by a son of the old man, who swam across for that purpose, while his brother, leading my mule after him, plunged into the current, and in a few moments everything was safely landed.

To reward this generous act I presented the old chief with a blanket, and bade him remember that "Good acts pay a sure tribute to a good heart, for they nourish its possessor with happy thoughts; very often, too, they yield a twofold return by the gratitude of the one upon whom such acts are bestowed; and then, again, sometimes the practiser is more than blessed by the acceptance of such presents as the grateful one may chance to offer. So, let my brother always do good, and the Good Spirit will own him as a subject well worthy of his special blessing."

Bidding the friendly natives adieu, I mounted my mule and hurried onward. My course led through the territory occupied by a division of the Shawnees, and that settled by the Quapaws and Cherokees. These tribes are partially civilized; but the Cherokees are farther advanced in refinement than any other Indian nation I am acquainted with. In fact, they are better educated, better livers, and a better people than their immediate white neighbors upon the frontiers of Arkansas and Missouri.

Late in the afternoon of July 4th I reached Van Buren, my point of destination, happy again to mingle amid scenes and associations from which I had been so long separated; and here I would take leave of the reader, provided I have been so honored as to command his interest and attention thus far. If the preceding pages have added aught to his stock of useful information, or served to while away a leisure hour agreeably, the object which primarily influenced their publication will have been accomplished,—if contrariwise, it remains for me to beg pardon for the trespass I have undesignedly committed upon his time and patience.

CPSIA information can be obtained at www.ICGtesting.com
Printed in the USA
LVOW06*0236200214

374350LV00006B/352/P